American Management
and British Labor

American Management and British Labor

A Comparative Study of the Cotton Spinning Industry

Isaac Cohen

Contributions in Economics and Economic History, Number 109

Greenwood Press
New York • Westport, Connecticut • London

Library of Congress Cataloging-in-Publication Data

Cohen, Isaac, 1946-
   American management and British labor : a comparative study of the
cotton spinning industry / Isaac Cohen.
      p.   cm. — (Contributions in economics and economic history,
ISSN 0084-9235 ; no. 109)
   Includes bibliographical references.
   ISBN 0-313-26780-4 (lib. bdg. : alk. paper)
      1. Cotton textile industry—United States—History.   2. Cotton
textile industry—Great Britain—History.   I. Title.   II. Series.
HD9875.C63   1990
338.4'76772122'0973—dc20   90-2753

British Library Cataloguing in Publication Data is available.

Library of Congress Catalog Card Number: 90-2753
ISBN: 0-313-26780-4
ISSN: 0084-9235

First published in 1990

Greenwood Press, 88 Post Road West, Westport, CT 06881
An imprint of Greenwood Publishing Group, Inc.

Printed in the United States of America

The paper used in this book complies with the
Permanent Paper Standard issued by the National
Information Standards Organization (Z39.48-1984).

10 9 8 7 6 5 4 3 2 1

Contents

List of Tables

Acknowledgments

I incurred substantial debts in writing this manuscript. My debt to David Brody is great. He read selected chapters as well as the entire manuscript, suggested valuable revisions, and spent long hours discussing different aspects of the study with me. I also benefited from the incisive comments of William Lazonick, who read the entire manuscript and provided advice which helped me clarify both my arguments and my perspective. The San Jose State University School of Business supported this study by granting me a partial released time from teaching during 1985-89.

Parts of this study have originally appeared in articles published in *Labor History*, *Comparative Study in Society and History*, and *Political Power and Social Theory*. I am grateful to the editors of these publications for the permission to use materials from these articles.

A brief note on sources. Although I have used many primary sources, I have relied more heavily on secondary sources than what is customary in a standard historical study. Given the abundance of historical research on the cotton industry, I have used manuscript sources only when the printed evidence was inadequate. This book, it should be noted, never intended to be based primarily on manuscript sources. It is a study in historical and comparative industrial relations, not a monograph in economic history or labor history.

American Management
and British Labor

Introduction

This is a study of the early American cotton industry seen from British perspectives. It is a comparative work that explains why American industrialists acted differently than British millowners, why American factory workers responded to industrialization in a different manner than British operatives. It contrasts workers' control in England with management control in the United States; the triumph of craft production in Britain with the victory of mass production in the United States. It shows how labor-management cooperation in Britain encouraged the use of craft technologies, how the struggle over control in the American cotton industry encouraged the shift towards mass production techniques.

This book covers a period of roughly one hundred years from the 1780s to 1880. It concerns mainly Lancashire County and New England, though references to Scotland on the one hand and Pennsylvania and New York on the other are abundant. I have concentrated on the spinning and not the weaving branch of the cotton industry because the first offers a considerably broader range of comparisons between different types of technologies, workers, markets, and goods than the second. Technological change in cotton spinning, for instance, was far more drastic than any improvement in cotton weaving during the nineteenth century. Similarly, while power-loom weaving was uniformly a machine-tending job, factory spinning gave employment to two kinds of workers: machine tenders and artisans.

The question of whether we need another book on the cotton industry—an industry that has already been studied extensively—deserves immediate consideration. There are two sorts of justification for the present study. First, while studies of the Lancashire and New England cotton industries in the nineteenth century are numerous, there are but a few comparative ones. One purpose of this book is to shed more light on the American development by constantly referring to the earlier British example, comparing and contrasting the evolution of the two industries from their origins to the close of the century, point by point, phase after phase.

Second and more important, the American cotton industry has not been examined as thoroughly as had previously been thought. Significantly, the study of mule spinning in the United States has been neglected. Apart from a few insightful articles by William Lazonick and other economic historians (Lars Sandberg, Gary Saxonhouse, Gavin Wright) and a brief treatment of the topic in Anthony Wallace's *Rockdale*, there is virtually no systematic study of American mule spinning. Yet mule spinning was an important industry: nearly half of all cotton spindles in use in the United States from the mid 1830s until after the Civil War were mounted on mule machines. Why the topic has been neglected is not hard to guess given the disproportionally greater focus of historical research on Lowell and Lowell-type corporations. Mule spinning was not used in Lowell until about 1840 and at no time during the remainder of the century did it occupy such a prominent position in Lowell as it did in many of the smaller mills in southern New England, New York, and Pennsylvania. More recently, however, there has been a growing interest in the smaller mills. References to mule spinners who were employed in the cotton factories of southern Massachusetts, Rhode Island, and Philadelphia may now be found in the writings of Jonathan Prude, Barbara Tucker, Gary Kulik, Philip Scranton, and Cynthia Shelton.[1]

Three interrelated themes define the theoretical subject matter of this study: mass production versus craft production; technology and organization; and craft control. Each was present at the beginning as well as the end of the century, in Britain as well as the United States. Hence the book has three goals: 1) to examine the role played by the dual system of craft and mass production in Britain and the United States over a period of nearly a century; 2) to explore the relations between technology and factory organization in the two countries at different points in time during the nineteenth century; and 3) to analyze the concept of craft control and utilize it to interpret strikes. Each theme will be discussed briefly in order.

CRAFT PRODUCTION VERSUS MASS PRODUCTION

"Throughout the nineteenth century, two forms of technological development were in collision," Michael Piore and Charles Sabel write in the opening chapters of *The Second Industrial Divide*. "One was craft production. Its foundation was the idea that machines and processes could augment the craftsman's skill, allowing the worker to embody his or her knowledge in ever more varied products."[2] The more flexible the machine, the more diverse is the product, the more skilled the operative, and the higher are labor costs.

The spinning mule is a perfect example of a machine that complemented the craftsman's skill. The mule was a multi-purpose machine that specialized in manufacturing luxury goods, namely, fine, high-quality cotton threads. The mule was also a flexible machine that was designed to turn out a large and changing variety of goods for large and constantly shifting markets. Because everything in the original design of the mule was aimed at achieving greater flexibility, it is hardly surprising that all nineteenth century attempts to make the mule truly "self-acting" failed. Notwithstanding the steady erosion of the skilled elements of the job, never did the mule become completely automated, never did two mule spinners produce cotton yarn of an entirely identical quality.

The other form of technological development in the nineteenth century, according to Piore and Sabel, was mass production. A more rigid manufacturing technology, mass production was based on direct substitution of skill by machinery. Its aim was the ever-increased division of labor and specialization. "The more specialized the machine—the faster it worked and the less specialized its operator needed to be—the greater its contribution to cutting production costs."[3]

Specialized machines for cotton yarn production were called spinning throstles. They were single-purpose machines designed to spin a very narrow range of coarse cotton yarns cheaply in bulk. The throstle suited manufacturers who supplied stable, unchanging markets (throstle-spun yarn was used for the manufacture of staple cloths). From the outset, throstle spinning was an automated production process; operatives were required only to watch the machinery, correct its failures, and feed it.

The two systems—mule and throstle spinning—craft and mass production—were used simultaneously in Britain and the United States during the nineteenth century. Their relative importance in each country, however, varied enormously. One question this study addresses is why the British cotton-spinning industry in the nineteenth century was overwhelmingly dependent on craft production while mass production machinery always accounted for at least half of all cotton spindles in operation in the United States. How, in other words, does one explain the choice of technology in Lancashire and New England? Why, furthermore, did mule spinning in America decline steadily after the Civil War as manufacturers were replacing mules with improved ring-throstles while British millowners clung tenaciously to the mule? In short, what caused the victory of mass production in the American cotton-spinning industry? To answer these questions I have considered a number of factors: the supply and cost of labor, the nature of market demand, the quality and cost of raw cotton, productivity and the cost of power, and the role played by unions and strikes in encouraging or discouraging the use of a given technology.

TECHNOLOGY AND ORGANIZATION

The distinction between craft and mass production raises at once an additional set of questions. What are the relations between certain types of factory technologies and the form of control they are associated with? Why did the introduction of different technologies of cotton spinning in the early nineteenth century give rise to distinctly different methods of labor management? Why, furthermore, did British and American employers who share a given technology also utilize the same means of management?

Two alternative methods of management were used in the early cotton mills. The first is associated with what Richard Edwards calls "simple" control, the second with "technical" control.[4] Subcontracting was the principle means of supervision used in craft production (mule spinning); in mass production (throstle spinning) it was foremanship. During the first round of industrialization, each technology was managed the same way in Lancashire and New England. Craft production was organized in autonomous work teams, craft-oriented machinery ran intermittently, and the craftsman himself controlled the pace of work. Under mass production, on the other hand, the speed of the machinery was set by managers, the machinery operated continuously, and control flowed from top to bottom through many layers. Both British and American manufacturers, accordingly, delegated the mule-spinning craftsmen the authority to hire and fire helpers, granted them autonomy at work, and paid them in proportion to output. Similarly, employers in both countries subjected throstle machine tenders to close supervision by foremen and paid them daily wages independent of their output. What such a resemblance in management practices between Britain and the United States clearly implies is this: during the early factory age technology played a critical role in the organization of factory production.

What it does not imply, however, is any sort of technological determinism. On the contrary, the developments in mill management that took place during the second half of the nineteenth century reveal the limits of technology's explanatory power. The very same technological change—the introduction of the improved self-acting mule around mid-century—led to a transition from subcontracting to foremanship in the United States but not in Britain. American mule spinners became subject to the absolute rule of foremen. British mule spinners, by contrast, retained intact their autonomous status despite the introduction of advanced machinery.

The case of the self-acting mule is significant as it represents one of the classic examples of technological change aimed at deskilling craftsmen. Karl Marx, to take a notable example, insisted that the self-acting mule was invented "for the sole purpose of supplying capital with weapons against the revolts of the working class." Andrew Ure, the "philosopher of manufacture" whom Marx cites repeatedly in volume 1 of *Capital*, believed that the self actor was built "in order to emancipate the trade from galling slavery and impending ruin" caused by the unions' control. Samuel Smiles thought that the new invention would "render [manufacturers]...independent of the more refractory class of their workmen," and Factory Commissioner Edward Tufnell was convinced that the self-acting mule would "give a death blow to the Spinners' Union."[5] Yet they were all wrong, overestimating the omnipotence of technology. The improved machine did not put an end to the craft status of British mule spinners. What Ure, Tufnell, Smiles, and ironically Marx underestimated, was the sheer power of British trade unions, the power to prevent capitalists from undermining the craftsmen's control.

CRAFT CONTROL

The issue of craft control and technological change has been of a continual concern for two decades. In *Labor and Monopoly Capital* Harry Braverman demonstrated how the introduction of improved machinery diluted the craft status of skilled workers. In *Workers' Control in America* David Montgomery covers a topic much neglected by Braverman, the craft unions' resistance to technological change. Workers' control, according to Montgomery, "was not a condition or state of affairs which existed at any point in time, but a struggle, a chronic battle in industrial life which assumed a variety of forms." These forms can be understood in terms of three successive "levels of development": 1) the functional autonomy of the craftsman, 2) the union work rules which codified the autonomy, and 3) the mutual support of different trades in rule enforcement and sympathetic strikes. The three levels of control struggles emerged among British mule spinners very early, some fifty years before the arrival of the self actor. Among American mule spinners, by contrast, control struggles began to appear only after mid-century.[6]

The decisive battle over control in the American mule spinning industry was fought in Fall River, Massachusetts, during the 1870s. Contemporaries saw it as a wage-related struggle, yet unmistakably it was a battle over craft control. It involved primarily British immigrant mule spinners who sought to defend their craft status. Significantly, the Fall River struggle was typical not only of the mule spinning industry but of other American trades and industries with a large proportion of British immigrants.

Contemporary writers as well as present-day historians have all emphasized the role British immigrant workers played in organizing unions and strikes in industrial America. On the one hand, British industrial immigrants were experienced trade unionists; on the other, many came from the ranks of blacklisted militants who could not find jobs in Britain, who received union funds for immigration across the Atlantic, and who consequently became the frontline carriers of the British tradition of union militancy.

But union tradition was only one factor. Another element in the growth of militancy among British immigrants—a factor largely ignored by historians— was the attitude of the American employer. In the United States, by contrast to Britain, control was firmly in the hands of management. Moving from Lancashire to New England, from Preston and Blackburn to Fall River and New Bedford, British immigrant spinners experienced a substantial loss of control. The transformation of the mule spinner from an autonomous craftsman in England to a subordinate machine tender in Fall River led to a bitter struggle over control. The Fall River strikes of the 1870s, it follows, were essentially collective efforts of British craft workers to retrieve their customary rights.

The Fall River strikes were defeated. So powerful were the Fall River employers that they managed to crush every important strike throughout the 1870s. The cotton firms of Fall River, like those of Lowell, Lawrence, and other

New England factory towns, were closely connected through a dense web of corporate interlocks. Unified, Fall River employers cooperated closely to suppress competition, oppose unionization, blacklist union agitators, and enforce general lockouts in which time after time the spinners were defeated.

The struggle of the 1870s was a turning point in the history of mule spinning in America. Mule spinning in the United States survived for another fifty years and spinners continued to wage strikes, but the industry was in a perpetual, irreversible decline. One far-reaching consequence of the militancy of the 1870s was the encouragement it gave cotton manufacturers to replace mules with ring-throstles. The mule spinners' struggle over control, I conclude, contributed something to the victory of mass production over craft production as the dominant form of technology in the American cotton-spinning industry.

Chapter 1
Pre-Factory Production

Q. Are no jealousies entertained by the American workmen towards their masters?
A. In America we never hear the word master; they usually speak of the manufacturer by name, or as their employer, and view him rather as a tradesman to whom they dispose of their labour, than as a person having a hostile interest. There are no jealousies between American master and workman of the nature of those which appear to prevail between the English workmen and their employers.

James Kempton of Connecticut
First Report of the Factory Inquiry Commission,
Parliamentary Papers, 1833, XX, E., p. 21.

Factory production in Britain evolved from a highly developed system of domestic industry. The "making" of the British working class was not a spontaneous generation of the factory system. Industrial capitalism in Britain preceded the coming of the factory; the changing productive relations of the Industrial Revolution were not imposed upon some "undifferentiated raw material of humanity," as E.P. Thompson put it, but upon an already formed and highly organized class of wage-earning artisans with well entrenched craft traditions.

Pre-industrial America had no organized class of proletarian outworkers. Industrial capitalism was little developed in colonial United States, and production was organized primarily on a household basis. The small number of American artisans in the eighteenth century did not produce for the mass market as in Britain, but were employed, above all, as independent producers on a custom basis. The weakness of craft traditions in the United States underlay the transition to factory production.

The purpose of this chapter is to describe these essential differences between the United States and Britain and their relation to the rise of the early cotton factory industry.

BRITAIN

The Domestic System

Of all forms of industrial production that preceded the factory, the domestic system was organizationally the closest. The original basis of the system was a small-scale manufacture linked to a large-scale mass market. Distant markets for English woolen goods reach back to the fourteenth century when the wool-exporting counties of northern England began producing cloth. By the middle of the fifteenth century more wool was exported from England in the form of cloth than in raw material.

Between the 1450s and the 1550s, according to one economic historian, the total English exports of woolen cloth increased about threefold, and between 1485 and 1714 the money value of English textile exports multiplied fifteen-fold. In 1700 as in 1500, the making of woolen cloths was England's largest manufacturing industry, still responsible for over 70% of the country's total value of export.[1] Gross estimates based on contemporary accounts suggest that from 1688 to 1695 the foreign market took nearly 40% of the output of the woolen industry. By 1740 exports took just over half the output, and in 1770-71 slightly under a half. Between 1695 and 1741 the money value of the total English output of woolen goods remained unchanged, but during the next three decades it doubled from five to over ten million sterling.[2]

Such a great industry, noted a witness before the House of Commons in 1726, gave employment to 700,000 people. A writer in the *Gentleman's Magazine* in 1739 believed the figure to be much higher: 1,500,000 people in England were engaged fully or partly in the manufacture of woolens of one sort or another.[3] Two other accounts in 1741 and 1747, each written separately by a knowledgeable and careful commentator, concluded that the total number of people engaged in the woolen industry of the United Kingdom might have been just under 1,000,000; the probable figure for England alone was estimated at 800,000[4]. Given the small population of England at the time—6.3 million in 1750[5]—even the more conservative estimate is impressive enough; significantly, England in 1750 was by no means a "pre-industrial" society.

The enormous expansion of both the home and foreign markets for woolen goods gave rise to the domestic system of production. When it was first used in England in the 1806 Report of the Select Committee on the Woollen Manufacture, the term *domestic system* applied to Yorkshire alone, where the independent producer and the small employer were far more characteristic of the industry than the large-scale capitalist. Soon, however, the term was commonly used to describe any form of manufacture of goods for sale carried out in the rural districts; the "domestic system" in this respect was sharply distinct from the household manufacture for home consumption, on the one hand, and from the town's guild system of handicraft production, on the other. In England, more than anywhere else, guild restriction on the supply of labor, the nature of the product, the technique of manufacture, and the size of enterprise, drove the center of production from the towns to the countryside and as a result "in no economy was the countryside so closely integrated into the commercial circuit; nowhere were the local pockets of self sufficiency so broken down."[6]

The organization of the domestic woolen manufacture, to be sure, was diverse. E.P. Thompson, for example, distinguishes four kinds of wool weavers in eighteenth century England: the customer weaver, the self-employed weaver working for a choice of masters, the journeyman weaver working for a single master, and the yeoman or small holder weaver. While the size of the first group—weavers making up orders for customers—was steadily shrinking, and while the small holders were divided among self-employed and dependent weavers, two distinct groups emerged in England in the eighteenth century: the self-employed artisan of Yorkshire, and the proletarian outworker of East Anglia and the West of England.[7]

How typical was the self-employed weaver in the Yorkshire woolen industry? In Yorkshire, apparently, the "little clothiers," or wool manufacturers, were "carrying on business with their own capital."[8] In strictly limited parts of the West Riding such as the parish of Saddleworth, nearly all the woolen cloth woven in the eighteenth century was produced by small clothiers who rarely employed any workers apart from their own family members.[9] But in the Yorkshire domestic industry as a whole, the 1806 Select Committee concluded: "The manufacture is conducted by a multitude of master manufacturers... assisted by their wives and children, and *from two or three to six or seven journeymen.*"[10] Testimonies given by clothiers before the Committee make it quite clear that in the Yorkshire domestic industry at the end of the eighteenth century most weavers were journeymen working for a single employer;[11] in all likelihood, therefore, only a minority of journeymen would have ever attained the status of independent clothiers.

The growing dependency of the Yorkshire weavers on wage earning was partly a result of the rise in the 1720s of the worsted branch of the industry, worsteds being cloths made from combed long-staples wools. Centered in the Bradford district, the worsted trade was organized from the start in large units of production and by the middle of the eighteenth century most weavers were already wage earners employed by master manufacturers who closely resembled the wealthy clothiers of the West of England. "The worsted master," wrote the historian of Yorkshire, "carried on his trade with real division of labour; he employed his wool-combers, spinners, and weavers, each a well-defined class in itself. He utilized a considerable quantity of capital, and thus stood in a position high above that of the people he employed."[12] In 1806 one employer estimated that 3,500 broadcloth manufacturers in the West Riding of Yorkshire gave employment to between 50,000 and 60,000 workers.[13]

In the West of England and in East Anglia the small independent clothier rarely existed; rarely would a journeyman weaver become a clothier.[14] In one small village in Wiltshire, for example, as early as 1597, 100 households out of 170 were forced to supplement their income from agriculture by weaving and spinning for clothiers. In the 1620s a maker of white cloth claimed to have employed nearly 1,000 people, two brothers gave the number of their employees as 400, and another clothier kept about 280 people busy. The three manufacturers, all from the West of England, employed a larger number of workers than the typical clothier. The more usual size of enterprise, according to Julia Mann, was that of a clothier who had an annual income in 1639 of close to 300 sterling and employed nearly 100 outworkers.[15] All the same, the contrast between the West of England and Yorkshire is telling: the entire trade of the west county of Gloucestershire was dominated by less than 400 clothiers, versus the 3,500 or more broadcloth manufacturers in the West Riding.[16] Yet, "the general impression that one gets," wrote Wadsworth and Mann in their classic study of the early cotton industry, "is that until the end of the seventeenth century there was not the same accumulation of large capital [in the woolen industry] as in the fustian manufacture."[17]

Fustian was the leading branch of British cotton manufacture from the early seventeenth century until the transformation of the industry by modern machinery. It was a mixture of linen warp—the hard yarn running lengthwise in a piece of a woven cloth, and cotton weft—the soft yarn interlaced at right angles to the warp. The spinning wheel was incapable of producing cotton warp in large quantities and therefore scarcely any English goods were made entirely of cotton until after the introduction of the Arkwright technique of spinning by rollers. Fustian nevertheless was commonly referred to by contemporaries as "cotton." It was most probably sold mainly in the home market, for it could hardly compete with the rival, better-quality products of the continent. Still, by 1699 English fustians had already been exported to four markets: Ireland, continental Europe, America and the West Indies, and Africa; and until 1759 the American market took the largest share.[18]

Towards the end of the sixteenth century fustian reached Lancashire and soon ousted the woolen industry from the country areas between Blackburn, Bolton, and Oldham.[19] Originally, fustian was spun and woven in Lancashire and then sent to London for bleaching, printing, and marketing. The fustian production process in the seventeenth and eighteenth centuries was organized on what is known as the putting out system:

> The entrepreneur was a merchant resident of Manchester, Bolton or Blackburn, and having trade connections with London. He distributed raw cotton and linen to a disperse army of domestic spinners and weavers through local agents (or middlemen) called fustian manufacturers. The domestic workers were wage earners, but they might own their own wheels and looms, and some drew support from farming activities.[20]

Although the smaller employers no doubt performed the putting out function themselves, the frequent advertisements for "putters out" found in the Manchester newspapers in the second part of the eighteenth century lend support to the above description.[21] A map drawn by George Daniels from data compiled from the Manchester Directory in 1772 shows how extensive was the use of local country agents or "manufacturers" in organizing the domestic system of cotton goods' production. The residences of seventy-seven country fustian manufacturers with warehouses in Manchester are marked on the map. They form an outer northward semicircle around Manchester that runs from Oldham in the east across Bolton westbound to Leigh. The three towns were all within a day's walking distance from Manchester. The location of twenty-six country manufacturers of check—another fabric of cotton and linen mixture—forms an inner circle, while seventy-eight bleachers are distributed in another circle right around Manchester.[22]

The number of workers employed by putting out merchants through these middlemen was large by any standards, and very much larger than that employed by early millowners. In 1736 a Lancashire fustian manufacturing firm owned by two brothers gave employment to about 3,000 people in the Blackburn district (they used 600 looms for weaving fustian, with each weaver requiring, on average, four spinners to supply him with yarn). In 1749 a Warrington sailcloth manufacturer was reported to have employed as many as 5,000 people, and a Reading employer in the same year had 500 families made up of 2,000 individual workers on his books. In 1758 a small group of Manchester checkmakers controlled much of the Lancashire trade; one manufacturer employed 500 people in weaving checks.[23]

Large-scale enterprises on the eve of the industrial revolution were not limited to cotton or wool but were found in other British industries as well. The hosier, the shoe manufacturer, the nail ironmonger, and the producer of silks each, "like a spider at the center of a vast web," gave out material, collected the goods, and paid wages to hundreds of outworkers.[24] In the middle of the eighteenth century there were over fifty "putters out" in the hosiery business of Nottingham alone. Research based on contemporary accounts suggests that before 1790 a typical Nottingham hosier would employ 800 domestic workers, men, women, and children, on 200 frames.[25] In 1769 a Warrington shoemaking firm employed 400 to 500 men, and a Glasgow firm gave employment to 500 shoemakers in 1773.[26] In the Midland the nailmakers were nearly always wage earners paid by the piece; a wealthy ironmonger might have employed several hundred nailers in the eighteenth century.[27] One nail manufacturer, for example, insisted that before 1810 he regularly put out work to some 1,200 or 1,500 men, women, and children.[28] A silk manufacturer, to take another example, stated that before 1762 he employed 1,500 people at a time—500 in London, 200 in Gloucestershire, 400 in Dorsetshire, and 400 in Cheshire—and although some of his employees no doubt worked in centralized silk throwing mills, a far greater number worked in silk winding and doubling at home.[29]

The vast majority of all these workers lived in the rural districts outside the principal towns. A distinctive feature of the English economy in the seventeenth and eighteenth centuries, so much in contrast with the American experience, was the industrialization of the countryside. In the woolen districts, "most of the Weavers lived in Cottages erected on the waste Lands in the *villages* and *Hamlets* near the Clothing Towns," one contemporary writer noted in 1737.[30] In the nailmaking country area along the road from West Bromwich, near Dudley, to Birmingham, Arthur Young saw in 1776 "one continued village of nailers."[31] In Lancashire cotton districts since the early years of the seventeenth century, opportunities for industrial employment increased and led to the transformation of the countryside in two different fashions. First, a large number of small holders supplemented their income from agriculture by spinning and weaving, and second, a growing class of rural wage earners emerged which was almost completely dependent on industry.

Precise figures for the seventeenth century are hard to find but data for later years are abundant. According to a 1713 petition presented to the House of Commons, 60,000 people in Lancashire were engaged in the manufacture of linen alone, and they were found "in almost every part of the country."[32] In 1725, 76% of the fathers recorded in baptismal registers in Saddleworth—an area of some forty square miles between Oldham on the eastern edge of Lancashire and Huddersfield within the West Riding of Yorkshire—were dependent on the textile industry. In 1750, 85% were engaged in the manufacture of textiles, and by 1770 nearly 90%.[33] The Oldham Parish Register shows a similar trend . In Oldham, admittedly, "the number of fustian weavers who were cottagers working for manufacturers, without holding land, were few,"[34] yet nearly 51% of the parents recorded in 1725 whose occupation was stated were employed in some branch of the textile industry and over 63% of those recorded in 1765 were so employed. The second largest occupational group in Oldham was that of the ordinary village handicrafts: for example, masons, carpenters and joiners, tailors and shoemakers, butchers and breadbakers, millwrights, smiths, and tanners and saddlers.[35] In Mellor near Stockport, William Radcliffe recalled that in 1770 only six or seven farmers out of fifty or sixty were completely dependent on agriculture; the rest derived part of their income from spinning and weaving wool, linen, and cotton.[36] Similarly, in the area of Manchester it was estimated that in 1774 some 30,000 people were employed in the domestic cotton manufacture.[37]

In those Lancashire districts that supplied factory recruits for Manchester and its surrounding towns the domestic industry had become the predominant form of employment and most migrants had former industrial experience. Unfortunately, British government census figures do not yield information on previous occupations of migrants to the new factory towns. Occupational background can nevertheless be inferred from the household schedules of the census which show whether the migrant came from an industrial or an agricultural village. Such research was conducted by Michael Anderson in Preston and Bryan Roberts in Oldham, and both concluded that most migrants came from the surrounding *industrialized* rural areas of these towns. In Preston, for example, only 13% of all residents in 1851 who were migrants came from villages in which most adult males were engaged in agriculture. In Oldham, too, just a small minority of all adult males who migrated from the countryside had formerly been agricultural laborers. "The predominant impression one gets," Roberts summarizes his research, "is that most adult migrants to the Manchester urban areas had prior experience in industrial work[38].

This conclusion falls in line with the little we know about early factory mule spinners. In Britain, the major inventions in cotton spinning had been introduced a generation before parallel changes in weaving took place, and the typical firm in the last quarter of the eighteenth century, and perhaps during the 1800s and 1810s as well, combined factory spinning and hand-loom weaving, thus employing simultaneously "in" and "out" workers. How many of the early mule spinners were former hand weavers, how many came from the ranks of other trades, what was the proportion of small holders and agricultural laborers among the spinners, and what actually was the occupational background of early British mule spinners—all these questions cannot be fully answered. We have only scattered contemporary references to the issue and informed inferences from these references made by later historians. Sidney Chapman, T.S. Ashton, and H.A. Turner each assures us that many of the first spinners were former hand-loom weavers; the examples of James Hargreaves, the inventor of the spinning jenny (the forerunner of the mule), and Samuel Crompton, the inventor of the spinning mule, are the most famous.[39] Factory mule spinning initially required a great deal of mechanical skill, and experienced weavers who ordinarily built and repaired their own looms were attracted by the high wages paid for mule spinning. Artisans from other trades such as shoemakers, hatmakers, and joiners were also leaving their previous occupations and joining the ranks of mule spinners, as noted by John Kennedy, one of the largest millowners in Manchester between 1795 and 1826.[40] In Oldham—an important center of hand-loom weaving and the hatting trade—journeymen weavers and hatters were almost certainly among the early mule spinners in town.[41]

Yet to say that the spinners were recruited among the weavers is not to deny that hand-loom weavers refused to enter the early factories in large numbers. After all, such highly skilled and well paid artisans as mule spinners rarely made up more than one-tenth of the work force employed in a typical mill (and that, in a specialized mule-spinning establishment) whereas the vast majority of all cotton factory workers held low paid, machine tending jobs. Whether a hand-loom weaver would take a factory job was not, of course, just a simple matter of earnings. After 1820 and certainly after 1825 the piece rates of hand weavers sunk so low that they fell below the rates of throstle spinners and power-loom weavers[42]—two of the principal categories of unskilled or semiskilled operatives employed in the cotton industry. By 1833, for example, the weekly wages of all cotton hand-loom weavers averaged six shillings while throstle spinners earned eight shillings and power-loom weavers received eleven shillings a week.[43] Still, relatively few hand loom weavers, who ordinarily were adult males, entered the mills. The overwhelming majority of Britain's cotton factory population in 1835 was made up of women and children.[44]

We may gain a better understanding of the motives that kept the hand-loom weavers in the cottage for decades by shifting the focus from factory earnings to factory discipline, from economic benefits to social control. Such a change in perspective will also explain why from the standpoint of the domestic artisan—either a hand-loom weaver, a hatter, or a shoemaker—factory spinning was an attractive alternative occupation. Spinning cotton yarn on mule machines in the early factories was a skilled job that guaranteed almost full protection from the harsh factory discipline. It provided nearly the same degree of autonomy as was enjoyed by handworkers under the domestic system of production. The social organization of factory mule spinning, in other words, resembled so closely the organization of work under the putting out system that it posed no real threat to the craftsman's autonomy at work. Like the domestic craftsman, the mule spinner was in complete control of production, independent from management supervision. He hired, fired and disciplined his own helpers and apprentices, was paid in proportion to output, regulated entry into the trade, and bargained with the employer on prices (all these points are discussed later in detail). On the other hand, unskilled machine tenders, like the operatives employed in early Arkwright-type mills, had none of these prerogatives. To tend a continuously moving machine under close supervision by foremen—whether the Arkwright water-frame, the throstle, or later the power loom—was a task so radically different from anything hitherto known under the domestic system of manufacture that it required first the destruction of old labor traditions and customs, and then the cultivation of new work habits, the inculcation of a new factory discipline. The reluctance of the hand-loom weavers to enter the mills as machine tenders may thus be explained in terms of their efforts to defend customary notions of work, to protect an entire way of life.

Yet they entered the mills as mule spinners. Here not only traditional work habits survived into the early factories but the industry itself originated in the cottage as a pure handicraft manufacture. British mule spinning was actually a domestic industry during the first two or three decades of its existence; and again, the contrast with the American cotton manufacture in this respect is truly far-reaching.

"Before the year 1790," John Kennedy observed, the British "mules were turned by hand, and were confined chiefly to the garrets of cottages."[45] In the 1780s, noted another commentator, mules "were erected in garrets or lofts, and many a dilapidated barn and cow-shed was patched up in the walls, repaired in the roof, and provided with windows, to serve as lodging room for the new muslin wheels" (i.e., mules).[46] In the same decade spinners gathered to work hand mules in sheds or workshops which were mostly converted corn mills,[47] and only later, in 1790, was the first mule yoked to power initiating the rapid transformation of the mule spinning into a factory trade. Testimonies given in 1816 before the select committee on children employment show that domestic mule spinning had still been widespread around Manchester and in Glasgow between 1795 and 1801,[48] and moreover, it survived until after 1815.[49]

Once it is established that cotton mule spinning in Britain began as a putting out industry in the cottage, that the mule machine was not dependent on mechanical power from the start but was rather "a domestic implement" turned by hand, then it becomes all the more plausible that former handicraftsmen predominated among the early mule spinners. Just as the hand-loom weavers often built, maintained, and owned their own looms, so did many of the first spinners become "proprietors of a single mule."[50] And just like any skilled artisan in the eighteenth century, domestic mule spinners were above all "mechanics"—the contemporary term for handicraftsmen.

The Emergence of Trade Unions

Like any other group of hand workers in pre-factory Britain, the Lancashire mule spinners organized in opposition to employers: they combined in friendly societies of journeymen. The earliest known records of the Stockport (1785) and Oldham (1796) mule spinners' societies clearly demonstrate that these could not have been other than pure handicraft associations for the plain reason that both antedated the first mule-spinning mill in town. Other spinners' organizations active during the first two decades of the mule—the 1780s and 1790s — were probably composed largely or partly of domestic spinners but we do not know. Nevertheless, one thing is clear: by 1799 "nearly every town in Lancashire [had a] local combination" of mule spinners.[51]

The entry of handworkers into mule spinning facilitated, no doubt, the rise of factory trade unionism. Domestic artisans in every important trade and industry in eighteenth century Britain were organized in local societies and when they first entered the cotton mills they reproduced their older association in a more sophisticated and complex form of a trade union. In the West of England and in Norwich, weavers and wool combers' associations reach back at least to the beginning of the eighteenth century, while in Lancashire the first recorded organizations of domestic workers appeared around mid-century. In Manchester in 1760, at the coronation of George III, eight different trades were represented in a procession throughout the city's streets: the tailors, wool combers, worsted weavers, shoemakers, dyers, joiners, silk weavers, and hatters. The absence of the cotton weavers among these artisans is noteworthy; it was asserted, however, that "not being at that time a body sufficiently numerous to form a shew of themselves," they probably marched together with either the worsted or silk weavers.[52] There is a good deal of evidence, however, that at least one group of cotton workers—the check weavers—had already formed a "combination" in 1757.

Looking at it from a different angle, the history of the Combination Laws in eighteenth century Britain is the history of early British trade unionism. Whenever and wherever labor organization appeared, prohibition followed closely. Parliament outlawed combinations in the woolen industry as early as 1726. The prohibition was later extended to the silk, linen, cotton, fustian, felt, hat, leather, and iron industries in 1749. In 1799 the British Parliament passed a universal law against combinations of workers.[53]

Notwithstanding these prohibitions trade unions flourished under the cover of "boxes", "box clubs", "charity boxes", "charity stocks", and above all "friendly societies." In 1793, with the first legal recognition of Friendly Societies, total British membership reached 648,000.[54] By 1800-1801 Lancashire alone had 820 registered friendly societies—some 200 more than any other county. Nearly all these societies were local, self-governing bodies, and they combined mutual aid and trade union functions. The Oldham weavers' society, to give an early example, was a typical mixed club: "If the weavers sign to withdraw their subscriptions from the boxes they will at the same time withdraw their charity from one another," says a 1758 resolution of the Oldham weavers.[55]

It has long been customary to emphasize the continuity between the friendly society and the older craft guild (hence to challenge the Webbs well known view on the issue).[56] It is worth pausing, however, to identify which elements of the guilds survived in early British trade unions. A pamphlet written in 1741 by "a lover of his country" provides us with an extraordinarily detailed description of such an early union among the wool combers, the aristocracy of labor in the British worsted trade:

> Our combers have for a number of years past, erected themselves into a sort of corporation (tho' without a charter), their first pretence was to take care of their poor brethren that should fall sick, or be out of work; and this was done by meeting once or twice a week, and each of them contributing two-pence or three-pence towards the box to make a bank, and when they became a little formidable, they gave laws to their masters, as also to themselves, viz:—that no man should comb wool under two shillings per dozen; that no master should employ any comber that was not of their club, if he did, they agreed one and for all not to work for him; and if he had employed twenty, they all of them turned-out, and often times were not satisfied with that, but would abuse the honest man that would labour, and in a riotous manner beat him, break his comb-pots, and destroy his working tools; they further support one another, insomuch that they become one society throughout the kingdom.[57]

The wool combers, of course, sought to insure themselves against sickness and unemployment. But far more important were two other goals of the combers' society, goals that were the characteristic features of the medieval guild: first, the regulation of prices, and second, the restriction of entry into the occupation. Ideally, the town guild was composed of masters and journeymen, enjoyed the legal status of a closed corporation, monopolized skill, and controlled prices and wages. The wool combers, on the other hand, were wage-earning artisans who organized in opposition to their employers. Yet their unchartered "corporation" attempted to achieve the very same goals as the guild by different means: through collective bargaining by strikes and riots. A typical dispute over prices thus led in 1752 to a "formidable turn-out" of 300 Norwich journeymen wool combers against their employers.[58]

In principle, the same was true of other early trade unions. It is one of the arguments of this book that craft control in the nineteenth century rested on the ability of workers to regulate recruitment, to fix piece rates, and to direct production. The first two elements can be found in the rules of the London guilds from the thirteenth century onward.[59] Control over production, however, had not become a major preoccupation of craft unions until after their members moved into workshops and factories, as the experience of British mule spinners clearly suggests. Friendly societies among domestic mule spinners thus closely resembled the wool combers' club. Entry control and wage regulation, we shall see as we proceed, survived in the union rules of British mule spinners well into the twentieth century.

In one respect, however, the Combers' Combination was rather exceptional. The wool combers' local societies developed such close links of dependency that they practically formed a national association. Most organizations of hand-workers in eighteenth century Britain, by contrast, were strictly local; it is only in the following century that artisans attempted to form national federations. The hand-loom weavers' experience is a case in point. Although the weavers imitated the combers, they did not form "one society throughout the kingdom" but were "confined to the places where they work[ed]," as noted in 1741.[60]

The earliest weavers' combination in Lancashire for which dated record survived was the Manchester worsted smallware weavers' society, whose first regulations were drawn up in 1747. Within the next ten years the Manchester check and silk weavers formed similar organizations. The smallware and check weavers issued not only rules and regulations but also "Apologies" for their existence which throw a good deal of light on the nature of these associations.

George Daniels examined the 1756 Apology of the smallware weavers in the manchester library. "The articles show," he concluded, "that there were two main classes engaged in the trade: first, the manufacturers, who were the real employers; second, the undertakers, journeymen and apprentices." The "undertakers" were the fully apprenticed weavers who, on the one hand, employed a few journeymen and apprentices as helpers, and on the other, were themselves employed as wage earners by the large manufacturers. As subcontractors they undertook work from "masters," and from their own wages they paid their assistants. An apprentice who completed seven years of service received a "blank" from the society and was free to work either as a journeyman or an undertaker. Both undertakers and journeymen were enrolled in the society, and according to a 1754 rule, undertakers were prohibited from employing journeymen without a blank. Furthermore, according to two additional articles drawn up in 1747 and 1753, no undertaker was permitted to take more than three apprentices, each serving a minimum of seven years.[61]

The primary goal of this early union, it seems clear from the above, was to restrict entry into the craft. An additional union goal, however, was the regulation of wages, as shown in the 1758 Apology of the Manchester check weavers. The check weavers, like the smallware weavers, demanded that their employers exclude "unfair weavers," yet at the same time they also insisted upon a fixed price for a standard length of a piece of woven cloth. A cut in the piece rates was among the causes that led the check weavers to stage a massive strike soon after they issued their Apology. The strike lasted four months, involved thousands of weavers, and spread throughout the entire Lancashire check region from Ashton and Oldham in the east, to Eccles and Clifton westward to Manchester.[62] The smallware weavers struck in 1781 over the same issue. They sent an ultimatum to their employers:

> It is unanimously agreed by the whole of the Trade that if you do not set your Men to Work, agreeable to the List of Prices which you will receive with this Note, by the ten of the Clock in the Fore noon of the 27th Inst. you may depend upon this, that no Small-ware Weaver in Lancashire will ever work for you any more.

The weavers' organization was powerful enough to "swear two masters out of the trade" and to force the employers into collective bargaining. Following a two-month strike the dispute was "amicably" settled in a joint meeting between five weavers and five manufacturers.[63]

Collective bargaining on lists of prices was typical not only of hand-loom weaving but of every other trade and industry in late eighteenth century Britain, most notably cotton mule spinning. Such a union demand, as a matter of fact, was at the core of early spinners' strikes in many British cotton towns. After all, when the mule spinners came to form their first societies they already had the weavers' experience to build on, and accordingly, they also demanded a standard list of prices. Moreover, "since no doubt many of the new spinners had been members of the weavers' societies," as aptly noted by S.J. Chapman, "to form spinners' clubs was but to follow custom—in some cases even to follow habit."[64] And indeed, in at least two cases the Lancashire spinners practically modelled their new organization on the weavers' unions.

In Oldham, the earliest spinners' union had essentially the same village association structure as the former organization of fustian weavers. In Manchester, on the other hand, the newly formed spinners' organization, like the older smallware weavers' association, was organized on a "shop" basis.[65] Unlike the fustian weavers who were widely distributed over the Lancashire countryside, the smallware weavers concentrated in Manchester and its outskirts and their "shop" was most probably the putting out warehouse of the merchant manufacturer. Each shop appointed a representative and when the representatives met in Manchester once a month they formed a "Trade's Society."[66]

The mule spinners, finally, were also recruited among the shoemakers and hatters—two of the best organized trades in Lancashire. By 1756 the journeymen shoemakers of Manchester and Liverpool were well organized; they struck against a reduction in wages in Liverpool in 1756 and for an advance in Manchester in 1772. Union tradition among the Manchester journeymen hatters was exceptionally strong. The hatters were preoccupied above all with maintaining control over entry into the trade, an issue over which bitter strikes erupted in the hatting trade of Manchester in 1777, 1780, 1783, and 1785, and Stockport in 1785.[67] Since the shoemakers and hatters, like the hand-loom weavers, were long-standing unionists, it is hardly surprising that they too carried over their craft union tradition from the cottage into the factory. Judging on the basis of the British case, we may thus conclude that former organizational experience was an important element in the rise of trade unions among first generation factory mule spinners.

THE UNITED STATES

Colonial Manufacture

American industrial development differs from the British in three fundamental ways. First, industrial activity in the United States prior to the birth of the factory was primarily organized in the form of household production. Second, American artisans specialized in the production for customers, not for the market. And third, craft organizations in colonial and early industrial America were confined to a few urban centers.[68]

In Britain, household manufacture remained a very important sector of the economy during the two centuries that preceded the industrial revolution, yet it operated alongside an ever-expanding system of capitalist domestic production. In the United States, on the other hand, the putting out system had scarcely appeared before 1790, the date in which the first American cotton mill was built. Furthermore, insofar as a slight development of capitalist production can be traced in the colonial period, this development took place in the manufacture of shoes and boots, not textiles or clothing.

In the North American colonies, distant markets for shoes in Boston, New York, and Philadelphia, as well as the West Indies and Europe, gave rise to an incipient development of capitalist production organized on a domestic basis. The transition from household production to putting out, from custom work to "market work," from the independent producer to the outworker employed by a manufacturer called a "cordwainer" who supplied material and sometimes tools—all these changes in the shoe industry occurred between 1750 and 1800, first in Massachusetts, and then in New Jersey and Pennsylvania.[69] How widespread was putting out before the rise of the "central shop" around 1800 is not exactly clear, however. Yet it could not have been nearly as extensive as in Britain, where such shoemaking firms employing as many as 500 domestic workers were operating in Glasgow and Warrington in the 1760s and 1770s. Consider the case of Lynn, Massachusetts—the largest American shoe manufacturing center in the second half of the eighteenth century. "There were but three men who conducted the business so extensively as to employ journeymen," noted a contemporary writer describing the shoe trade in Lynn in 1750;[70] apparently, the 80,000 pairs of shoes made in Lynn in 1767, or even the 175,000 pairs manufactured by some 400 Lynn workers in 1789[71] were the product of small independent cordwainers assisted by a few journeymen and apprentices. Consider next the case of Philadelphia, the leading artisanal city in eighteenth century America. On the eve of the Revolution, according to one study, fully one-half of Philadelphia's taxable shoemakers were masters, the rest were journeymen.[72] By contrast to Lynn, moreover, shoemaking in Philadelphia was organized almost entirely on a custom basis until after the Revolution.[73]

Far more typical than the shoe industry was the early growth of textile manufacturing, where the contrast between the British and American developments is all the more glaring. Unlike Britain, the production of yarn, cloth and clothing in eighteenth century America was almost exclusively a home industry. In Essex county, Massachusetts, in the beginning of the eighteenth century, it was estimated that scarcely one family out of forty did not manufacture its own clothing.[74] Time after time colonial and early American leaders emphasized the leading role of household manufacture, and their statements are instructive. In 1763 the governor of Massachusetts reported that "the poor labouring people in the country towns [wore] their common cloths principally of coarse homespun linens and woolens." According to a 1767 report of the governor of New York: "The custom of making...coarse cloths prevails in private families throughout the whole province." The cloth, however, was manufactured "for the use of the family *without the least design of sending any of it to market.*"[75] In 1791 Alexander Hamilton reported to Congress that in a number of districts surveyed throughout the United States, "two thirds, three fourths, and even four fifths of all the clothing of the inhabitants were made by themselves."[76] In 1810, Secretary of Treasury Albert Gallatin stated that "about two-thirds of the clothing, including hosiery, and the house and table linen, worn and used by the inhabitants of the United States, who did not reside in cities, [were] the product of family manufactures."[77] In 1820, a generation after the earliest American cotton mill had been erected, it was estimated that about two-thirds of the textile goods used in the United States were made by families.[78]

While early American farmers—who accounted for nearly 90% of the labor force in 1790[79]—were largely self-sufficient, the small city population along the coast received most of its supply of clothing from Britain. In 1721 the value of British textile imports to the North American colonies came close to $1,500,000; other articles—for example, furniture, nails, glass, lead, locks, and hinges—were listed in 1763 among the leading British imports to Massachusetts trading towns.[80] The importance of America as a "new" market for English goods in the eighteenth century is hard to exaggerate: British North America and the West Indies together bought 12% of the English domestic exports in 1699-1701, 20% in 1752-54, 37% in 1772-73, and 57% in 1797-98.[81] The English broadcloth was the most popular imported fabric used in the colonies; rarely was this expensive carded woolen fabric manufactured in America for sale. In 1772 the thirteen American colonies bought 20% of the total British export of woolen goods, in 1790 30%, and by the turn of the century the United States was taking as much as 40% of the British cloth export.[82]

Such a one-way trade across the Atlantic enhanced of course British capitalist development. But at the same time the flood of cheap British imports acted rather powerfully against the development of domestic capitalist production in the United States. The availability of mass-produced British goods in the urban markets of the New World was thus an important factor that encouraged American artisans to specialize in making goods "to order" rather than for general sale, thereby escaping a fierce competition from British imported wares.

In colonial United States, indeed, the small number of goods manufactured outside the home was the work of independent artisans. The one-man shop with perhaps a helper or two was the representative size of enterprise, and the craftsman labored mainly at turning out "spoken" or "bespoke goods"—articles made to the order of individual customers. Colonial craftsmen were engaged in a variety of specialized trades such as the manufacture of leather, clothing, and metal goods, and the making of straw hats, watches, and articles of wood such as chairs, clock cabinets, and other furniture[83]—practically all of which were important putting out industries in eighteenth century Britain.[84] Hence the contrast between the two economies. In Britain, pre-factory manufacture was the work of wage-earning artisans producing for vast and distant markets while much of the pre-factory industry that did exist in the United States outside the home was the product of self-employed artisans specializing in custom work.

American artisans in the eighteenth century were often called "tradesmen," "mechanics," "artificers," and "leather apron men." They were found in the rural villages and in the seaboard cities and towns, but their role in the economy was much more important in the urban areas. In the larger towns artisans specialized in custom work, they occasionally produced goods to keep on display in their shops, and more important, they often carried imported British wares as well, thus combining custom work with trade. The urban craftsman, it follows, was a customer artisan, an artisan shopkeeper, and an entrepreneur— the relative importance of each of these functions was mainly determined by wealth.[85]

Rural craft production, on the other hand, was organized around independent village craftsmen who were almost always engaged strictly in custom work and who were assisted by family members. Capitalist production dominated by market relations was largely nonexistent in the American countryside before the factory. Yet in the United States as in Britain, in New England as in Lancashire, it was in the rural areas, not the urban centers, where the early water-powered cotton mills were built. Thus, the contrast between a factory system *evolved* from a highly developed system of domestic manufacture as in Lancashire, and a factory system *imposed* directly on an economy characterized predominantly by household production as in New England, affected first the kind of labor that flowed into the early factories, and second, the extent to which early factory recruits— particularly mule spinners—were able to draw upon the experience, resources, and support of other artisans.

The Rural Craftsman in the Eighteenth Century

In eighteenth century New England rural craft production was organized around independent artisans who produced goods primarily for exchange, rather than for the market. They did not hire wage earners at all but relied almost exclusively on family labor, were often farmers as well as artisans, and nearly always engaged simultaneously in a variety of trades. The typical New England village craftsmen, in other words, operated within a household economy, an economy organized around individual households who produced first for themselves, then for exchange. In some cases rural craftsmen, for example, shoemakers and blacksmiths, produced for exchange *as well as* for commercial marketing, yet exchange relations between craftsmen and farmers predominated throughout the countryside.[86] In Pawtucket, Rhode Island, an ironworking village which in 1790 became the site of the first American cotton mill, Gary Kulik found a flourishing system of local exchange on the eve of the Revolution. Most of the sawyers, blacksmiths, and millers in the village, to name the principal groups of craftsmen, were working for local farmers taking their payments in grain, boards, and "country" goods.[87] Describing the American countryside in 1791 two French travellers observed: "The tailor and bootmaker go and do the work of their calling at the home of the farmer who requires it and who, most frequently, provides the raw material for it and pays for the work in goods. . . . They write down what they give and what they receive on both sides and at the end of the year they settle a large variety of exchanges. . . with a small quantity of coin."[88] Similarly, in Ulster County, New York, in the 1790s, payments in "wheat, rye, Indian corn, as well as cash, or *anything* that is good to eat" were acceptable to craftsmen. "Cash," as Michael Merrill persuasively argued, appeared to have been only one among many other means of exchange, and insofar as market relations did exist in the countryside, they were subordinated to barter transactions based on the use value of goods; that is to say, on what an item was worth to a specific individual.[89]

Equally significant was the absence of a free labor market in the countryside. Artisanal production for exchange severely limited the size of industrial undertakings, and as a result, the rural craftsman rarely employed anybody outside the confines of his own family members. In most cases, in fact, there was not even sufficient work for family members. The demand for manufacturing goods in the countryside was so limited that it was impossible for the rural artisan to specialize simply in one craft; rather, it was necessary to master a variety of trades, and in addition, to combine craftsmanship with farming.

In eighteenth century Rhode Island, to cite Kulik again, rural wage-earning artisans were largely nonexistent. Only a few blast furnaces, some forges, and a number of shipyards relied to some extent on wage labor, yet even in iron making, glass blowing, and shipbuilding—industries which were technically dependent on a centralized process of production—the predominant form of labor was family labor.[90] The history of a prominent iron making family in eighteenth century Pawtucket —the Jenckes—is a case in point. The Jenckes' iron works was a family-based enterprise. The business, however, could not support the entire family and therefore the Jenckeses operated a sawmill and a gristmill as well, cultivated extensive gardens, and raised livestock. But even such a diversification of business activities could not have provided employment for all, as evidenced by the large number of family members who migrated from Pawtucket generation after generation from the late seventeenth century onward. Even as late as the 1780s, following a considerable expansion of the Jenckes' enterprise, there was not sufficient work for the family to keep more than half of one generation busy in the village. The implication is clear. "It is entirely unlikely that wage laborers, or non-family apprentices, would have been taken on, when the business could not even support family members."[91]

It is equally unlikely that master craftsmen would have formed trade associations in the countryside so long as they operated within a barter economy. In the urban centers—Boston, New York, and Philadelphia—master craftsmen formed guilds in order to regulate prices as well as to restrict entry into the trade. Price regulation and entry control, as a matter of fact, were the keys for organizing trade guilds in the colonial city.[92] But why would the rural artisans be interested in price regulation when there was no established price system in the countryside? What could have been the craftsmen's incentive to organize in a period in which craft production was not yet subject to market forces? How, moreover, was it possible at all for the country artisans to develop an awareness of belonging to a particular craft tradition so long as they did not view their craft as defining? After all, insofar as craftsmen organized—whether in Britain or the United States, whether masters or journeymen—they did so along narrowly confined craft lines, and in relation to their common position in the market. That the relative absence of specialized crafts and a developed market economy in eighteenth century New England checked the growth of artisanal organizations is quite commonplace indeed.

The Rise of the Cotton Industry

More complex were conditions in the countryside during the period 1790-1830 —the pioneering phase of factory production. Here, it appears that the capitalist transformation of rural New England was, by and large, the product of cotton factory production. The rise of the cotton industry accelerated the growth of a market economy in three distinguishable ways: first, by expanding the market for yarn and cloth; second, by encouraging the rise of a free labor market; and third, by providing a growing market for related trades such as machine making. Furthermore, during the same period other rural handicrafts expanded as well. By the early 1830s, to judge on the basis of four New England rural communities— Pawtucket, Fall River, Oxford, and Dudley—non-factory craft production had also become predominantly market-oriented: local artisans hired wage laborers and produced goods for anonymous customers.

The four communities were factory villages as well. The first cotton factory was built in Pawtucket in 1790, and in Fall River, Oxford, and Dudley in 1813.[93] By 1832 Pawtucket had nine cotton mills, Fall River thirteen, and the two close-by townships of Oxford and Dudley had six and three cotton factories respectively.[94] In each of these communities mule spinners were employed in cotton mills. Located south of Boston, the four villages were quite typical of southern New England: from the 1800s until the 1840s the New England mule-spinning industry was largely confined to Rhode Island, Connecticut, and southern Massachusetts.

By contrast to Lancashire, mule spinning in New England was a factory trade from the outset. Although we know very little about the few mules introduced into New England as early as the 1800s, the available evidence indicates that the earliest mules—all imported or modelled on British construction—were installed directly in factories rather than experiencing any domestic use.[95] Large-scale introduction of mules into the United States occurred after 1812, at the time mule spinning in Britain had already become a factory industry.[96] American millowners, in other words, adopted the mule spinning technology only after the power-driven mule had taken over the British cotton industry; the domestic hand mule had already become obsolete by the turn of the century.

While the New England mule spinner "skipped" the domestic phase of the industry, the weaver certainly did not. Factory spinning and hand-loom weaving expanded simultaneously in New England after 1790. In hand-loom weaving putting out was used extensively to manufacture cloth for distant markets only after the earliest New England spinning mills had begun turning out yarn in large quantities, and prolonged until after the adoption of the power loom in the 1820s. Still, New England hand weavers like early factory mule spinners remained unorganized during at least the first four decades of the factory.

Why this was so may become clear by reexamining the link between cotton workers and rural artisans. Jonathan Prude's study of Oxford and Dudley is particularly illuminating in this respect. In 1832 about 300 individuals were employed in local stores and workshops in Oxford and Dudley. The majority were engaged in craft production: boot and shoemaking, textile machinery making, and the manufacture of chaises, nails, and leather goods. Most craftsmen were free wage earners employed by master artisans in small shops, though indentured apprentices were used as well.[97] Yet, despite the transition to free labor, the basic outlook of the rural craftsman remained unchanged. Country artisans had no awareness of belonging to an occupational tradition, no sense of craft community, and little dependency on each other. They did not share a collective way of life similar to that of urban journeymen.[98] Prude explains:

> Generally engaged in enterprises lacking any developed apprenticeship structures, generally employed by proprietors who themselves felt little sense of vocation toward their ventures, workers in the small businesses of Dudley and Oxford appear to have rarely identified with their jobs. . . . Wage laborers in local nontextile enterprises rarely viewed their work as defining or permanent. This is why, despite the spread of local handicraft shops, there was no local flowering artisanal culture between 1810 and the early 1830s. This was also why workers moved about. All but the most skilled appear to have repeatedly switched jobs. Even the most skilled commonly moved to other communities. Most of these workers did both.

Furthermore:

> Unsupported by the props of urban artisanal culture, even craftsmen— even those facing what may have been fairly stringent conditions within local machine and cordwaining shops—seem to have been quiet between 1810 and the early 1830s.[99]

A central feature of artisanal production in the countryside, we may thus conclude, was the underdevelopment of "craft consciousness." The tendency to repeatedly change jobs reflects both the low level of craft specialization in the rural villages and the availability of alternative employment in agriculture. Both elements are survivals from the eighteenth century agrarian economy, and both severely undermined attempts at craft solidarity.

The absence of craft unions in the countryside had, in turn, two profound implications insofar as the mule spinners are concerned. First, being unorganized, rural artisans neither inspired mule spinners to form unions, nor could they have provided substantial sources of support to spinners on strike. Second, to the extent that the mule spinners were recruited among the local artisans, they entered the mills with no prior organizational experience.

To begin with, the complete absence of strikes, let alone unions, among the early mule spinners of Oxford and Dudley reflects the lack of organization and militancy among the local artisans. Oxford and Dudley were not isolated cases; the same observation is evident among the mule spinners of Pawtucket, Webster, Fall River, Smithfield, and practically any New England community on which we have some detailed knowledge. Surely there were some differences in this regard between larger and older rural craft communities such as Pawtucket and newly established factory villages like Webster. For example, one attempt at organizing a mule spinners' union was recorded in Pawtucket in 1824,[100] but no such incident is reported to have occurred in Webster until after mid-century.[101] It is therefore quite plausible, as Kulik implies, that the presence of artisans in Pawtucket encouraged the local mule spinners to call a meeting.

Yet even the Pawtucket experience does not change the general picture: in early nineteenth century New England neither rural artisans nor factory craftsmen organized.

In addition, all the available accounts of the early New England cotton industry agree that mill workers were recruited from the rural areas. Some came from the immediate neighborhoods; more were recruited from the vast country areas surrounding the factory villages. This judgment is valid both for the small mule-spinning mills of Rhode Island, Connecticut, and southern Massachusetts, and the giant integrated throstle-spinning and power-loom weaving factories of northern New England.

The large-scale Lowell-type plants of northern New England relied on workers with no prior experience in industrial work: young unmarried daughters of relatively prosperous farmers. Southern New England mills, by contrast, recruited poor farmer families from the countryside typically through newspaper advertisements.[102] An early Connecticut millowner described his labor force as made up of "poor families. . . who have lived in retired situations on small and poor farms."[103] A southern Massachusetts employer during the 1820s collected his help among small farmers, agricultural laborers, and rural artisans.[104] The conclusion that emerges from recent studies of early New England mills that employed mule spinners—in Pawtucket, Webster, Oxford, and Dudley— reveals in fact that from the 1790s to the 1830s cotton factory workers, who were often recruited in families, came from a mix of farming and artisanal backgrounds.[105] Whether families of small farmers or farm laborers, independent artisans or wage-earning craftsmen, the characteristic feature of early factory recruits in southern New England was their rural origins.[106]

Rural New England, finally, stands in a sharp contrast to urban Philadelphia. While New England was the cradle of the American cotton industry, a large number of cotton factories were also erected in and around Philadelphia. Three mule spinners' strikes in the Philadelphia area reveal that the spinners, like other journeymen in the city, made concerted efforts to organize in opposition to their employers. Admittedly, the three incidents alone are insignificant in comparison to the massive strike waves recorded among the mule spinners of Lancashire during the same period. Nevertheless, they are suggestive.

In 1828 the mule spinners employed in Manayunk, Norristown, and other towns several miles around Philadelphia went on strike against a piece rates cut. Five years later, in 1833, a 20% reduction in wages triggered a strike among the mule spinners, throstle spinners, and power-loom weavers of Manayunk. Another wage strike among the cotton mill workers in the Rockdale district at the outskirts of Philadelphia erupted in 1836 and was led by the mule spinners—the "ringleaders" according to one employer. During the 1828 strike the United Beneficial Society of Journeymen Cordwainers held a meeting "to make a collection and to take such measures as may be deemed necessary for the relief and assistance of our brother operatives, the cotton spinners." Other Philadelphia trade unions proposed in a joint meeting to collect twenty-five cents from each member in support of the striking spinners. In 1833 two outstanding Philadelphia labor leaders— William Gilmore, a shoemaker, and John Ferral, a hand-loom weaver—joined the strike committee alongside the mule spinners and other tradesmen. The committee addressed an appeal to trade unions in other cities requiring information concerning their regulations, and formed the short-lived "Trades Union of Pennsylvania"—a union of all trades. During the 1836 strike, similarly, the painters, trimmers, glass cutters, white smiths, saddlers, cordwainers, and other crafts in Philadelphia struck for higher wages. The turn out of the Rockdale mule spinners should not be viewed in isolation from this larger strike movement: the spinners, who formed a Trades Union, "were acting in unison, if not in concert, with the striking craftsmen of Philadelphia," observed the historian of Rockdale.[107]

Even if only remotely similar to Lancashire, the Philadelphia experience thus confirms the importance of the artisan influence: artisanal strikes inspired mule spinners' strikes; artisanal organizations lent support to spinners' associations; and leading trade union activists from the ranks of artisans provided the spinners with experienced leadership. The major link between mule spinners and other craftsmen that underlay the transition to factory production in Britain was not completely absent in Philadelphia, though it was extremely fragile. In rural New England this link was missing.

Chapter 2
The Choice of Technology

On the whole, it may be said that the Americans are capable of rivalling the English in coarse and stout manufactures in which large quantities of the raw material are used...[but] in all other kinds of goods, in all which require either fine spinning or hand-loom weaving, the English possess, and must long continue to possess, a very great superiority.

Edward Baines,
History of the Cotton Manufacture in Great Britain
(London: Frank Cass, 1835), pp. 509-510.

A very large proportion of the cotton wool absorbed by the manufacture of America is made into domestic or other heavy fabrics, in which her advantages with respect to raw material tell with the greatest affect. Domestics comprehend a most important and extensive class of cloths used by the great mass of society for shirts, sheets, linings, and many other domestic purposes.

Andrew Ure,
The Cotton Manufacture of Great Britain
(London: Charles Knight, 1836), vol. I, p. xliv.

Three major technologies marked the transformation of the domestic cotton industry into a factory industry: throstle spinning, mule spinning, and power-loom weaving. All three had been invented in Britain and only later adopted by American manufacturers. In both countries, however, the power loom arrived only after spinning had already become a factory industry. Yet, while the two spinning technologies reached a level of perfection in Britain before they were introduced into the United States on a large scale, the power loom spread much faster in New England than in Lancashire.

SPINNING

The earliest cotton spinning machine in British and American factories had been the Arkwright water frame which was soon modified into the throstle. The first British cotton mill of modern type was erected by Arkwright at Cromford, Derbyshire in 1771. By 1795 there were some 300 throstle-spinning mills operating in Britain. The first American cotton factory—an Arkwright-type mill—was built by Samuel Slater, an English immigrant from Derbyshire, in 1790 at Pawtucket, Rhode Island. In 1814 there were about 250 cotton mills in the United States, and nearly all were throstle-spinning establishments.[1]

Mule spinning became a factory industry two decades after the arrival of the water frame—around 1790 in Britain and 1810 in the United States. The mule spread throughout the Lancashire region at a remarkable speed. By 1811, according to Samuel Crompton's census of the cotton industry, there were at least 650 mule factories and workshops in Britain and the spinning industry had already become overwhelmingly dependent on the mule.[2] As shown in Table 1, in 1811 Britain had thirteen mule spindles for every throstle and in 1831 the proportion of mule to throstle spindles was twelve to one. Both estimates, as noted in the table, are approximations. In the United States, on the other hand, the progress of mule spinning was much slower. The American mule did not displace the throstle, but rather the two machines spread simultaneously.

The first regional census of mule spindles in the United States appears in the McLane Report—a survey of American manufacturing authorized in 1832 by the secretary of treasury, Louis McLane. Although the McLane Report covers the eight most industrialized states in the union, it provides figures for mule and throstle spindles in New York only: of the 137,000 spindles in New York State in 1832 on which data are available, 51,000 or 37% were mounted on mules and 63% on throstle frames (only 13 firms with 20,000 spindles did not specify the type of spindle used).[3] Four years later, Secretary of Treasury Levi Woodbury estimated that in 1835 the total number of mule and throstle spindles in the United States was approximately equal. This proportion remained almost unchanged during the next thirty-five years, as indicated in Table 1.

The far greater dependency of Britain than the United States on mule spinning was a factor so important in the evolution of management, the emergence of craft control, and the rise of trade unions throughout the nineteenth century that the question of technological choice deserves more attention than it has thus far received. Given, however, the fact that the technological developments in the early cotton industry attracted more attention among contemporaries than any other aspect of its history, it is indeed disappointing that almost nothing is known about the ways in which American manufacturers reached their decisions on mules and throstles, as noted by David Jeremy in a comprehensive study of textile technologies.[4] Knowing more about Britain, we can nevertheless explore the issue in a comparative framework.

TABLE 1

Cotton Spinning Technology in Britain (1811-1831)
and the United States (1835-1870)

	Technology	
	mass production	artisanal
	unskilled women and/or children	skilled adult males
Britain		
spindles 1811 (1)	7% throstle	93% mule
spindles 1831 (2)	8% throstle	92% mule
United States		
spindles 1835 (3)	50% throstle	50% mule
spindles 1870 (4)	52% throstle (ring)	48% mule

Sources:
(1) G.W. Daniels, "Samuel Crompton's Census of the Cotton Industry," 108-11. As noted by S.D. Chapman, Crompton only counted throstle spindles where they existed alongside mules in the same factory and by definition he excluded rural areas where the Arkwright-type mill was still active. He therefore, no doubt, underestimated the number of throstle spindles. Yet it appears that even a fairly complete census of throstles would not have altered substantially the above figures. S.D. Chapman, "Fixed Capital Formation in the British Cotton Manufacturing Industry," in J.P.P. Higgins and Sidney Pollard, eds., *Aspects of Capital Investment in Britain, 1750-1850* (London, 1970), 73.
(2) Andrew Ure, *The Cotton Manufacture of Great Britain* (London, 1836), Vol. 2, 400-401. Factory inspectors' statistics during the 1820s and 1830s do not indicate the number of mule and throstle spindles. The above figures refer to Lanarkshire alone and according to Ure they are representative of the Scottish industry though in England the proportion of throstles to mules was somewhat higher. The overwhelming dependency of England on mule spinning is evidenced in Bolton where 580,000 mule spindles and 7,600 throstle spindles were in operation in 1833. P.P. 1834, XIX, *First Supplementary Report of the Factory Inquiry Commission*, 168.
(3) U.S. House of Representatives, *Cultivation, Manufacture and Foreign Trade of Cotton*. Letter from the Secretary of Treasury, Levi Woodbury. H. Document 146, 24th Cong., 1st Sess., 1836, 49. Woodbury does not provide percentages but states that in 1835 the mule was "equally as much used" in the United States as the throstle.
(4) U.S. Ninth Census. 1870. III, 596.

Broadly speaking, an employer's choice between throstles and mules rested on four types of considerations: skill supply, market demand, the cost of raw cotton, and efficiency. The first two, it will be clear in a moment, are derived directly from conditions that prevailed under the domestic system of production. The cost of cotton, on the other hand, was affected by the staple's quality and by the distance from the sources of supply, while efficiency was dependent on technological change over time, on the nature of the product, and on the cost of power.

Skills

The throstle frame, like the water frame, was a machine that worked on the principle of continuous spinning; it spun yarn by rollers. Continuous spinning was radically different from anything hitherto known in the cottage or even the workshop, though it did not necessarily require mechanical power from the start, as has previously been thought. A model of the 1769 Arkwright frame in the Science Museum of London makes it plain that the original machine could have been operated by hand: any visitor may try the machine by turning a handle outside the showcase. "It spins beautifully and shows that the water frame could have been built in small units, placed in cottages and turned by hand."[5] Partly because Arkwright restricted his original patent license to units of hundreds of spindles, but mainly because continuous spinning required vast amounts of power and therefore it was economical only when the machinery was erected in power-driven factories, neither in Britain nor in the United States was the water frame or its successor the throstle used as a domestic spinning machine. Instead, from the outset continuous spinning was a factory technology.

The technique of throstle spinning was based on direct substitution of labor by mechanical power. The throstle's technical advantage lay in its success to perform automatically on a continuous moving yarn three distinct operations that made up together the yarn production process: drawing, twisting, and winding. Hence, the only intervention in the spinning process required from operatives was to piece up yarns when they broke and to replace bobbins, tasks that could be learned in a few days of training. Typically, throstle spinning was a machine-tending job filled by women and children.[6]

In contrast to the throstle, the mule spun yarn intermittently. There was nothing in the design of the mule that made it dependent on mechanical power; in fact, the earliest machines were all turned by hand. But even when attached to power, the mule, unlike the throstle, still required manual assistance—the grip of the human hand remained essential. The mule spindles were mounted on a moving carriage. The movement of the carriage away from the rollers drew and twisted the yarn, while the next step, winding, was performed during the backward motion. Neither the backward motion of the carriage nor the winding process was mechanized. Rather, until about 1840, power was applied solely to the drawing and twisting motions, that is, the outward

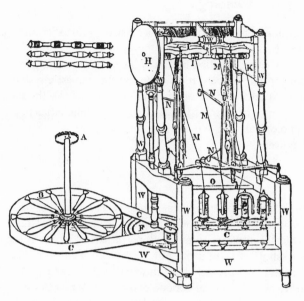

The original Arkwright water-frame spinning machine of 1769, containing four spindles.

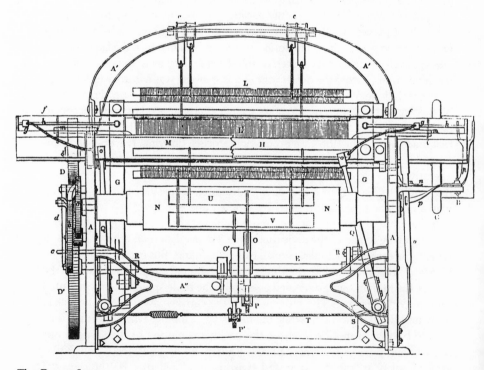

The Power Loom

Andrew Ure, *The Cotton Manufacture of Great Britain*. London, 1836.

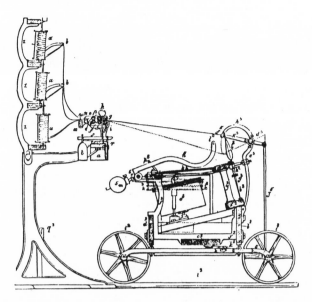

The Spinning Mule

Andrew Ure, *Dictionary of Arts, Manufacturers and Mines.*
London, 1839.

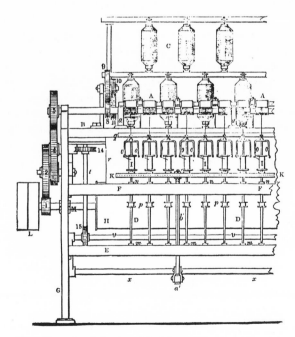

The Throstle Spinning Machine

Andrew Ure, *The Cotton Manufacture of Great Britain.*
London, 1836

movement of the carriage. Pushing the carriage back in a constant speed proportional to that of the rotating spindles while at the same time coiling the thread onto the spindle involved considerable skill, particularly since the mule specialized in spinning the high-quality yarn that was so desirable. With the left hand the spinner carefully regulated the winding of the thread into a cone-shaped package called a cop, with the right hand he varied the speed of the rotating spindles by turning the handle of a fly-wheel, and with his knee aided by the left hand he pushed the carriage back toward the frame. Pushing the carriage too slowly in relation to the speed of the spindles would break the yarn; pushing it too quickly would produce sagged yarn ends, slack winding and badly formed cops. The proper hand-and-eye coordination of these two simultaneous motions called therefore for great skill and dexterity. Moreover, spinning on mules required a good deal of strength as well because the carriage of spindles soon became very heavy. By the 1830s, a 1,400-pound or even 1,800-pound carriage was not uncommon in Lancashire.[7]

Far more important than the skill of running the mule was the knowledge required to maintain it. It is a commonplace of the history of technology that the first generation machines in the early factory age were so jerky and clumsy that they repeatedly broke under mechanical handling. In throstle-spinning rooms all maintenance tasks were performed by mechanics and overseers, the operatives themselves did nothing but spinning. In mule-spinning departments, on the other hand, the spinners were responsible for both driving the mule and ensuring that it functioned properly; for example, they would often replace broken bands, lubricate the machine, and readjust its moving parts. They were expected, in other words, to have an intimate knowledge of the machinery. Spinning on power-driven mules, according to Harold Catling, a leading authority on the British mule, required no more than three months learning time but "only to people brought up in the mule spinning room."[8] To maintain the equipment, however, would have required a training period of at least three years and perhaps even up to seven at any one time between the 1790s and mid-century.

In all likelihood, therefore, the possession of former industrial skills would have helped in mastering the mule. Such skills were abundant in eighteenth century Lancashire and no doubt encouraged the rapid growth of mule spinning. Apparently, artisans from other trades who became mule spinners were well acquainted with the mechanism of the mule. "The art of spinning with Crompton's machine," noted Andrew Ure in 1836,

> soon became widely known among work people of all descriptions, from the higher wages which it procured above those of other artisans; such as shoe-makers, joiners, hatters, etc.; many of whom were thereby induced to change their employment, and to become mule spinners. Hence it happened, among this motley gang, that if anything went amiss with their machine, each of them endeavoured to supply the deficiency with some expedient borrowed from his former trade; the smith introduced

a piece of iron, the shoemaker had recourse to leather, and the hatter
to felt; whereby valuable suggestions were obtained.[9]

Clearly, a former experience in any "pre-industrial" craft would have provided
a valuable pre-training for mule spinning. Since, however, Lancashire employers
offered mule spinners better wages than the ordinary rates for artisans, they
could secure much of the labor force needed despite the very rapid growth of
the industry.[10]

In the United States the shortage of skilled craftsmen ready to enter the mills
was likely to check the advent of the mule. Throstle spinning was a technology
suited for unskilled labor from the farm.

The first attempt to transfer the mule technology across the Atlantic was
abortive. The earliest known mule in the United States—a sixty-four-spindle
machine —was smuggled from Liverpool to Philadelphia in 1783 disassembled
in casks. Disguised as Wedgewood china, the casks were labeled "Queen's Ware"
to avoid the custom inspection necessary for the enforcement of the British laws
against the exportation of textile machinery. Once the machine arrived safely
in Philadelphia, a group of the city mechanics, among them textile machinery
builders, made concerted efforts to put the mule parts properly together but
they failed. They packed up the pieces in a box, put the box in storage, sold
it four years later, and eventually the disassembled mule was shipped back to
England.[11]

So complex was the skill of mule construction that it took another full decade
for its first successful installation in the United States. In 1796 several mules
of 120 spindles each were erected at the Globe Mill, Philadelphia.[12] A prominent artisanal city, Philadelphia became the leading American center of cotton
mule spinning during the next two decades. An incomplete 1814 federal survey
of "labor-saving machinery" recorded eighty-seven mules in the entire country, seventy-six of which were located in Pennsylvania.[13] At that date New
England millowners were just beginning to introduce mule spinning on a
relatively large scale.

The New England cotton industry developed along the lines of two
distinguishable sectors. A primary sector of core, large-scale "boarding house
mills" in the north that followed the plan worked out at Waltham and Lowell,
used the throstle. A secondary sector of small, peripheral "family mills" in the
south modelled on the pattern set up by Samuel Slater, "the father of the cotton manufacture of America," adopted the mule.[14] The Lowell system of boarding houses made a large number of young women from the countryside
available for short-term factory service of perhaps two or three years and thereby
encouraged the use of the throstle. Accordingly, throstle spinning was used
almost exclusively in any of the Lowell-type factories in northern New England
until the boarding-house system began to break down with the coming of immigrants in the 1840s. Henceforth mules were added but the throstle remained
the principal spinning machine.[15]

The rise of the Lowell mill system in New England since 1815 explains therefore why, in contrast to Lancashire where the mule superseded the throstle, the introduction of mule spinning in New England did not bring about a decline in throstle spinning. The sector of Slater-type mills in southern New England, it is true, shifted from the throstle to the mule, but this important change in technology had little to do with the availability of skilled labor. On the contrary, the difficulties of early Slater-type mills in collecting mule spinners were well attested both by their vigorous recruitment campaigns through newspaper advertising[16] and by the excellent wages they offered: in the 1820s American mule spinners received over 20% above the British rates.[17] Rather, the reason why small employers in Rhode Island, Connecticut, and southern Massachusetts were so attracted by the mule lies in the realm of market for yarn and cloth.

Markets

The decision to adopt one technology rather than another was largely dependent on the composition of market demand. The demand for low-quality textile goods in the United States, noted George Wallis, a British visitor to the New York Industrial Exhibition in 1853, "is said to run through every class of society." "Textile fabrics. . . are made more for appearance and less for actual wear and use, than similar goods are in England. . . . That sterling quality in make, which always forms so important an element in the judgement of the European customer, is comparatively unattended by the Americans."[18]

Across a whole range of commodities, not just the textiles, American consumers in the nineteenth century had more homogeneous tastes than the British, and these tastes furthermore concentrated on low-quality articles of short durability. Dominated by the tastes of rural households, the nature of consumer demand in the United States favored mass production methods.[19] In Britain, on the other hand, class distinctions were far more conspicuous than in the United States and consumers insisted upon a large variety of goods; in the words of Nathan Rosenberg, they "imposed their tastes on the producer in a manner which seriously constrained him with respect to the exploitation of machine technology."[20] The fact that consumer tastes favored variations in product design that were particularly suited to the perfection of craft technologies helps to account for the choice of mule spinning in Britain.

The contrast between throstles and mules reflects a broader and more fundamental difference between special-purpose and general-purpose machines. The more specialized the machine, the more general the goods, and the more likely is the technology to be oriented toward mass production.[21] Accordingly, throstle spinning may be viewed as a mass production technique: the throstle was designed to produce standard yarns which could be put for a variety of uses. Mule spinning, by contrast, was a preeminent craft technology; the mule was so constructed as to spin a wide range of diverse-quality yarns.

The throstle, in addition, was limited to spinning uneven and thicker yarns of "firm wiry quality," yarns suited for coarse cotton goods such as plain calicoes and velvets. Finer grades spun on the throstle would break in the winding pro-cess.[22] The mule, on the other hand, was first known as the "muslin wheel," muslin being the generic term for the finest cotton fabrics.[23] The mule succeed-ed in mechanizing fine spinning partly because the winding process, which required a sensitive touch, remained manual, and also because the mule's moveable carriage gave the thread a "stretch" which was essential for the pro-duction of fine, higher "counts" yarns. Because intermittent spinning required that drawing and twisting be performed separately from winding, the skilled mule spinner was capable of making full use of the machine potential and im-proving the yarn evenness (during the spinning stage) as well.[24]

The degree of fineness of the thread was expressed by the number of counts or the length of a single strand (measured by an 840-yard unit called a hank) that made up a pound of yarn. The higher the count, the finer the yarn. In the closing decade of the eighteenth century the British throstle spun yarns ranging from counts number 16 to 42 but mainly concentrated in the middle 20s. In the mid- 1830s yarn count no. 50 was regarded as perhaps the highest spun on throstles in Britain. The mule, by contrast, transformed the Lancashire industry so rapidly that by the turn of the century it was spinning counts up to 300. In Manchester alone at least nine mule-spinning firms were producing regularly counts over 200 in 1833.[25]

While fine spinning was an important advantage of the mule over the thros-tle, versatility nevertheless remained the crucial factor in the competition bet-ween the two techniques. Because it spun all kinds of yarns from the extremely coarse to the very fine, the mule was better suited for British manufacturers who produced a large variety of cotton goods for diverse markets both at home and abroad. Just as the British domestic demand was divided among wealthy customers desiring luxury goods and the poor who could afford only coarse fabrics, so was the British export trade divided among the European and American markets for high-quality cloth, and the Asian markets—mainly India—for cheaper goods. And just as market demand was heterogeneous, so did it fluctuate. The British cotton trade experienced rapid changes in market demand in two different manners. On one hand, the home market for expen-sive cloths was dependent on fashion, was affected by frequent changes in design, and as a result was chronically unstable. Faced with periodic reduc-tions in demand for high count yarns, Lancashire master spinners often swit-ched to coarser grades; in many cases the firm's ability to produce diverse-quality yarns was a matter of survival. Typically, during the two-year period 1795-96, McConnel and Kennedy, one of the largest mule-spinning firms in Manchester, sold more than twenty-eight different yarn counts ranging from no. 12 to 226. On the other hand, the overseas sector of the trade was even more risky. Whereas slow communication and transportation severely limited the effec-tiveness of market forecasting, a sudden suspension of trade in one market— Europe during the Napoleonic Wars or the United States during the War of 1812—required diversion of sales elsewhere and a quick shift from the manufacture of one article to another.[26]

"Flexible specialization" in such volatile markets, to use Charles Sabel's term, was an additional advantage of the mule over the throstle. The mule was well adjusted to rapid changes in market demand because the yarn count could be easily altered by changing either the speed of the draft rollers or the length of the roving (cotton sliver) entering the zone between the draft rollers and the carriage spindles.[27]

Flexible specialization revolutionized British foreign trade. Under the domestic system in the eighteenth century, Lancashire exported only three basic cotton products: fustian, checks, and printed (cotton and linen) cloths.[28] One way to increase exports was therefore to diversify the product. In addition, to compete successfully with Indian muslins, the mechanization of fine spinning was necessary.[29] The mule achieved both goals and by the 1790s "the cotton manufacturers were producing such a very wide range of cloths of different qualities and weights, that any attempt to subject them to common denominator would seem to be futile." At least twenty different types of cotton goods were exported from Britain in the 1790s. By 1805 from half to two-thirds of the total output of British cottons was dependent on foreign demand.[30]

Unlike the mule, the throstle spun a very limited range of threads so that its greater advantage lay in making standardized cotton goods, hence its relative success in New England. American manufacturers specialized in producing durable, cheap goods such as heavy shirtings, sheetings, jeans, and satinets that formed the bulk of the home market. Furthermore, since early American manufacturers scarcely produced any goods for export,[31] they responded to a demand that was both more predictable and more stable than that faced by British millowners. Contrasting the British and American cotton industries, James Montgomery, a British mill manager who acquired some experience in New England, noted in 1840 that American manufacturers did not have the "facilities to change the style of their goods." In the United States, he observed,

> a great proportion of the machinery . . . is fitted up as if never to be altered. The machine makers seem to proceed upon the supposition that their machinery is already perfect. The machines are calculated for only one kind of goods, and only one system of working. . . The machinery used in Great Britain is, in this respect, greatly superior to the American. There, every machine is so constructed, that all the parts can be adjusted with the greatest accuracy, to suit the various qualities of cotton . . . so as to make just such goods as will for the time being suit the market.[32]

Three different estimates, in 1816, 1817, and 1833, show that the average yarn count spun in Britain was about 40.[33] An 1833 survey of 170 cotton mills in the Lancashire region reveals that 85 mills, or one-half, spun an average yarn count no. 38 and finer, and nearly half produced coarser counts averaging in the upper 20s and 30s. Only 8 mills spun an average count below 20. The survey further indicates that the range of yarn spun by a typical Lancashire mill was rather broad.[34] In the United States counts finer than 20 were rarely spun until 1820, and even in 1840, according to James Montgomery, very few American mule spinning mills produced cotton goods made from no. 40 and above.[35] Consider the two following surveys. An 1816 Senate report noted that the 47 "cotton manufacturies" in operation in Bristol County, Massachusetts at that early date spun "yarn to average no. 12."[36] Similarly, 60 of the 75 Connecticut cotton mills surveyed in 1832 spun counts no.20 and under, and of the remaining 15 factories merely a single mill specialized in counts finer than no. 40.[37] In Providence, Whitestone (New York), and Philadelphia, cambrics and muslins made from higher counts (no. 45) were manufactured in 1830,[38] but apparently, even as late as 1854 no American mule spun yarn finer than no. 90.[39] In 1869 the average yarn count in the United States was 28.[40] In Britain, by contrast, fine master spinners produced counts up to 250 in 1815,[41] and in 1833 the Lancashire factory commissioner declared that 340 was the "highest number that ha[d] ever been reached. . .with the present machinery," namely the British mule.[42]

While the range of cotton goods manufactured in New England was far smaller than in Lancashire, there were important differences between the two mill systems, Lowell and Slater. The giant Lowell corporations specialized in the production of standardized, inexpensive coarse goods. The yarn spun by the Lowell-type mills was extremely coarse by British standards; the typical count was 14 and the standard fabrics were heavy, plain, white cloths. By the 1830s the Lowell corporation diversified, spinning higher counts which were necessary for the manufacture of cotton prints. Yet the standard yarn count remained below 20. According to an 1839 survey conducted by James Montgomery of the eight cotton corporations in Lowell at that time, four (Appleton, Lowell, Suffolk, and Tremont) spun counts 12 to 14 only, one (Lawrence) spun no. 14 to 30, two (Merrimack and Hamilton) spun no. 14 to 40, and only one— the Boott company—specialized in a wider range from 14 to 50.[43] A survey taken fourteen years later shows a range of yarn counts even narrower: of the eight cotton firms, all still at Lowell in 1853, four spun counts no. 13 to 14, three spun no. 14 to 30, and just one corporation manufactured "prints and sheetings no. 21 to 40."[44]

The glut of cheap durable cloths turned out by the Lowell corporations drove, in turn, the Slater sector to move up-market with the manufacture of finer yarns. The most practical way to do so was to adopt the mule. Slater-type mills, in other words, specialized in weaving more elaborate fabrics made from mule-spun yarn in order to escape what Caroline Ware described as the "most severe pressure of market competition."[45] The effect of these changes is clearly visible in the quality markets. The spread of the mule in many small mills in southern New England, New York (State), and Philadelphia was presumably responsible for much of the decline in British imports. Between 1815 and 1823 the annual declared value of white and plain muslins exported from Britain to the United States fell from 1,000,000 to under 50,000 sterling and remained at that level throughout the early 1830s.[46]

To be sure, Slater-type mills that moved up-market secured a higher margin of profit. Yet they were subject to fluctuations in demand caused by changes in fashion and therefore were forced to diversify and to develop a more flexible market orientation if they were to survive at all. Typically, the small "family" mill specialized in a wider range of products than the large "boarding house" plant. "Most of the cotton mills in Massachusetts and New Hampshire, built after the Waltham plan," Samuel Batchelder reminds us, "were generally adopted to the manufacture of a single article of sheeting or drilling . . . without any means of changing from one fabric to another."[47] Montgomery's survey indeed shows that not a single corporation in Lowell before 1840 manufactured more than three types of cotton cloth.[48] In Rhode Island, by contrast, as early as 1820 nine of the seventeen power-loom weaving firms made at least four types of cloth.[49]

Notwithstanding the diversification of Slater-type mills, there were still important differences between American and British mule spinning. The American mule was not nearly as advanced as the British, and consequently, the quality of American mule-spun yarn was not as high. In contrast to Britain where an entire piece of woven cotton cloth was ordinarily made up of mule-spun yarn, in most Slater-type mills until 1840 the mule was used almost exclusively for spinning filling (weft) yarn while the hard warp thread was spun on throstles.[50] Consider the case of New York State on which we have some aggregate data. Complete information on the number and kind of spindles used in 99 of the 112 cotton mills in the state of New York in 1832 is available in the McLane Report. Altogether, just three New York factories used the mule for both warp and filling, two of which spun fine yarn no. 40. A couple of large mills in Whitestone operated together 7,000 mule and 1,900 throstle spindles to manufacture yarn no. 40, and it is almost certain that most of their mules were used for spinning filling as well as warp. But the vast majority of New York factories that used mules, the report makes it plain, had roughly an equal number of mule and throstle spindles.[51] Typically, throstle-spun warp and mule-spun filling were used for power-loom weaving in these mills.

Finally, the terms "fine" and "coarse" used commonly by contemporaries convey a radically different meaning in the United States and Britain. The finest American-made yarn of the period would have still been regarded as coarse by British standards. According to one Philadelphia millowner the term "coarse" used in the United States in 1832 normally applied to "all goods made of yarns No. 20, and under"[52]—the typical product of the throstle. Samuel Stanway, by contrast, noted in 1834 that in Manchester coarse spinning ranged from count no. 1 to no. 90, and fine spinning from 90 upwards. In Lancashire in 1834, Factory Commissioner Edward Tufnell defined no. 80 and above as fine yarn, no. 40 and below as coarse, and all counts between 40 and 80 as medium.[53] Seven years later Factory Inspector Leonard Horner classified all Lancashire firms producing counts number "60 and finer than 60" as fine spinners.[54]

To sum up, the preceding analysis suggests that the early American cotton industry was divided into two sectors: a primary sector of core factories and a secondary sector of peripheral mills. The primary sector was composed of a small number of very large firms that employed special-purpose throstle-spinning machinery, produced standardized goods for the mass market, and satisfied the stable component of demand. At the fringe of the cotton industry hundreds of small competitive firms that made up the secondary sector flourished by responding to increases in demand and by supplying the changing variety of specialized goods. Facing fluctuating demand, these peripheral mills adopted the craft technology of mule spinning and embarked on the manufacture of more refined fabrics than those turned out by the core firms. What such an industrial dualism clearly implies is this: the early development of mass production in the United States was accompanied by the expansion, not the contraction, of craft production. The theory that underlies this argument has been proposed by Michael Piore and Charles Sabel,[55] but while the theory fits well the American case, it fails to account for the British development. The British cotton spinning industry, as every chapter of this book points out, has always been dominated by firms of one kind: craft-oriented mule-spinning firms.

Raw Cotton

"The cheapness of cotton in the United States," George Wallis noted in 1854, "caused it to be used for many of the purposes for which flax and hemp are alone employed in Europe." The American-made cotton sailcloth shown at the London Crystal-Palace Exhibition of 1851 is one example mentioned by Wallis. The cotton-cordage, cotton rope-rigging, and cotton-twine displayed at the New York Industrial Exhibition of 1853 are others.[56]

Wallis' observations were shared by others. Edward Baines, James Montgomery, Andrew Ure, and several of the witnesses before the Factory Inquiry Commission were all impressed by the competitive advantage of the United States as a cotton growing country. Like Wallis, they were concerned with two developments that had taken place in the early years of the nineteenth century: the increasing dependency of the British cotton trade on the import of American raw cotton and the growing competition in the American market between domestic cotton goods and British exports.

Britain's dependency on American cotton rose at a phenomenal rate. In 1790 the United States supplied just 1% of the British consumption of raw cotton and in 1795 4%.[57] By 1800 the United States superseded the West Indies as the world's leading exporter of raw cotton and supplied 27% of the British consumption; seven years later, in 1807, the American share in the British supply of cotton jumped to 71%.[58] Throughout the century Britain became so dependent on the import of American cotton that during major supply interruptions (the Embargo and War of 1808-14, the American Civil War) it could never obtain enough raw cotton elsewhere. Typically, over a period of forty years, from 1820 to 1859, Britain took 78% of its total import of raw cotton from the United States.[59]

The United States served, in turn, as a market for British cotton goods. Britain, however, became much more dependent on the United States for raw cotton than the United States on Britain for cotton goods because Britain did not grow cotton but American cotton textile production expanded at a very rapid pace. As early as 1816 New England cotton mills supplied close to 100% of the domestic market for low-quality plain cloths (shirtings and sheetings). During the 1820s the British were losing their share in the American market for medium-quality fancy goods (stripes, plaids, checks) as domestic manufacturers adapted the power loom to more sophisticated weaves and, in addition, began producing printed calicoes as inexpensive substitutes for British fabrics. After 1830 the British continued to supply about 20% of the American cotton goods consumption, primarily the most expensive shirting and prints made from high yarn counts number 50 to 150. Only a few American mills competed in this market before 1860.[60]

Increased competition with American cotton manufacturers alarmed British managers. Shortly after his return from the United States in 1840 James Montgomery reported: "In every description of goods in which the cost of raw material exceeds the cost of production the American manufacturers have a decided advantage over the British."[61] In 1840 the cost of raw cotton exceeded the cost of production for every type of cotton yarn produced in American factories and for well over half the yarn output of British cotton mills.

The proportionate cost of cotton depends on yarn count. The finer the yarn the greater are the cost savings on raw cotton because the proportion of cotton cost to total costs declines as the yarn count goes up. Montgomery estimated that the cost of cotton made up 65% of total spinning costs of yarns number 16 to 18 in a typical British factory in 1840.[62] The records of McConnel and Kennedy reveal that in 1819 the cost of cotton constituted 38% of total costs on count no. 100, 36% on count no. 150, 31% on no. 180; and just 30% on yarn count no. 200.[63] The switch from the manufacture of high counts to low counts, these figures imply, may double the cost of cotton from one-third to two-thirds of total costs. Fine spinning, in other words, saved cotton—an important consideration in selecting the mule in Britain where cotton was expensive.

Table 2 lists comparative cotton prices. It shows that in both Britain and the United States, cotton prices fluctuated widely from one year to another and that in both countries prices declined over time. It also shows that in every year from 1801 to 1835 save two—1801 and 1822—the American prices were lower than the British. The largest price differences are recorded during the hostilities of 1808-14 when the shipments of American cotton to Liverpool were severely curtailed, and the smallest during 1824-35. Significantly, between 1830 and 1835 American prices for upland cotton were at least 17% cheaper than British prices.

TABLE 2

American and British Prices for Upland Cotton 1801-1835 (prices per pound in cents)

Year	United States	Britain
1801	44.0	36.0
1802	19.0	32.0
1803	19.0	25.0
1804	20.0	28.0
1805	23.0	33.0
1806	22.0	36.0
1807	21.5	29.0
1808	19.0	44.0
1809	16.0	40.0
1810	16.0	31.0
1811	15.5	25.0
1812	10.5	33.0
1813	12.0	46.0
1814	15.0	56.0
1815	21.0	41.0
1816	29.5	36.5
1817	26.5	40.0
1818	34.0	40.0
1819	24.0	27.0
1820	17.0	23.0
1821	16.0	19.0
1822	16.5	16.5
1823	11.0	16.5
1824	15.0	17.0
1825	21.0	23.0
1826	11.0	13.0
1827	9.5	13.0
1828	10.3	13.0
1829	10.0	11.5
1830	10.0	13.8
1831	9.3	11.3
1832	10.0	13.3
1833	11.0	14.8
1834	13.0	17.0
1835	16.5	25.0

Sources: American prices for 1801-1835 and British prices for 1814-1835 are taken from U.S. Congress, House, *Cultivation, Manufacture and Foreign Trade* of Cotton, Levi Woodbury, 16. The British prices for 1801-1813 are from M.B. Hammond, *The Cotton Industry: An Essay in American Economic History* (New York, 1897), Appendix 1 (Woodbury does not provide average prices for these years, only high-and-low prices). Both Woodbury and Hammond note that the British prices are Liverpool prices and both express them in pence. Woodbury—one of our most reliable authorities on cotton prices during the period— tells us that the British prices "can easily be converted into cents, estimating the pound sterling at $4.80." I followed his advice and converted pence into cents by simply doubling the number of pence. Woodbury's American prices are U.S. export prices ("those at the places of exportation").

Lower cotton prices in the United States favored mass production techniques. American manufacturers bought raw cotton cheaper than their British competitors so that their greatest advantage lay in combining continuous (throstle) spinning and power-loom weaving in the manufacture of standardized, coarse, heavy cotton cloths. In Britain, by contrast, the expensive price of cotton encouraged employers to economize on raw material and to specialize in the production of high-quality mule-spun yarn and light expensive cotton fabrics. The mule, unlike the throstle, was capable of fine spinning and therefore better suited British millowners who sought to cut high cotton costs.

But the mule had another advantage over the throstle, namely flexibility in respect to the use of raw materials. Not only was the mule designed to spin a wide range of yarn counts from the finest to the very coarse but in addition, except for very fine counts, it was also capable of using many types of raw cotton, from the inferior to the very best. For any given yarn count spun on both machines, it was technically possible to use lower quality, cheaper cotton on mules than on throstles because intermittent spinning put less strain on the yarn than continuous spinning. The yarn spun on throstles had to be strong enough to withstand the continual drag of the bobbin, whereas no bobbins were used on the mule. Rather, mule-spun yarn was built directly onto the spindle in such a way that the winding process did not impose much stress. Actually, the mule was capable of spinning cotton as well as wool. Wool is made of extremely fragile fibers similar to the most inferior and least spinnable cotton, yet it could be spun intermittently. Not before the twentieth century was it possible at all to spin woolen (in contrast to worsted) yarns on a continuous spinning machine.[64]

The contrast between the quality of raw cotton used in the United States and Britain is unmistakable. Raw cotton was classified by staple and by grade with broad distinction between shorter and longer staples and between lower and higher grades. Staple refers to the length, strength, and fineness of the fibers and grade to their cleanness and color.[65] All through the nineteenth century American cotton manufacturers used superior grades and longer staples of cotton than did British millowners.

At the time the United States became the largest supplier of cotton to Britain, one type of American raw cotton—upland—emerged as by far the most important. "This was of tremendous significance to those in the trade; it meant that the search for a cotton to be used in the cheaper calicoes and muslins was over."[66] Upland was a short stapled cotton of unequal fibers, white, light, flimsy, and often dirty. It was inexpensive and produced strong, durable yarn. It was used in Britain after 1800 for all counts below 100 and, quite often, for filling counts no. 100 and finer.[67] But it was not used extensively in the United States until much later, not even in coarse spinning. In the United States, according to the McLane Report,

> previous to 1813, so imperfect was the machinery. . . in use, and so little skilled were the workmen. . . that No. 16 yarn could not be made from upland cotton but required a mixture of one-half long staple. Pernambuco was the principal long staple cotton used at the time, with occasionally a bale of Sea Island from South Carolina.[68]

Twenty years later, in 1833, James Kempton, a Connecticut cotton manufacturer, made a similar observation. In the United States, he told the Factory Inquiry Commission, warp yarn no. 16 was made "entirely of good cotton" while in Britain it was made of a mixture of cotton waste and "a small quantity" of upland.[69] Cotton waste spinning was a standard practice in nineteenth century Britain. It was one of the most effective methods undertaken by British millowners to downgrade cotton quality and thereby minimize their raw material cost disadvantage.

The extensive use of waste in Britain was limited to coarse- and medium-count spinning and resulted in low-quality products. It resulted nonetheless in substantial cost savings, because cotton waste accounted for 12.5% to 15% of Britain's raw cotton consumption.[70] The mix of waste and cotton tends to weaken the yarn and make it more breakable because waste consists of loose, broken filaments with very short staples similar to wool fibers. Hence the difficulty in spinning waste by itself. In the 1830s British millowners spun all counts up to 50 from a mixture of waste and cotton using perhaps 85% cotton and 15% waste in spinning count no. 40 (filling)[71] and a far greater proportion of waste in the manufacture of coarse yarns no. 16 and under. By the 1870s waste spinning became a highly specialized industry in Lancashire with a broad range of cheap and useful products.

Only the mule allowed British millowners to make maximum use of cotton waste. Waste yarn was so fragile that it required intermittent spinning on a specialized mule—"the cotton waste mule"—whose control mechanism was constructed on the principle of the woolen mule.[72] Waste was created in the cleaning and carding processes and was classified by type, quality, and price. "Strippings" from the cards and "blowings" from under the blowing machine were worth about one-half to two-thirds the value of raw cotton, while "droppings" from the blowing machine and "sweepings" from the floor of the carding room were sold for one-eighth to one-tenth the price of cotton. The enormous amount of cotton waste discarded by British millowners gave employment to some 500 waste dealers in 1875 and stimulated the growth of a satellite by-product industry of dozens of specialized small firms located in and around Oldham.[73] Cotton waste was soft, twisted, and bulky and was used in Britain for table covers, carpets, quilts, flannelettes, curtains, twills, cheap towels, cheap shirts, and upholstery for all types of furniture.[74]

There is no American parallel to the British waste industry. Nowhere in the United States was the practice of waste spinning as widespread as in Britain, and at no time did American cotton manufacturers rework a very large proportion of their cotton waste.[75] Waste weakens the yarn and therefore was not suitable for the throstle. It was perfectly suitable for the British mule but less so for the cruder American mule which required better cotton. Many of the Slater-type operators, furthermore, prided themselves on the high quality of their *coarse* yarns and were reluctant to spin waste on mules in order not to damage the reputation of their products.[76] Rather, in the 1830s American cotton manufacturers—both Lowell- and Slater-type operators—sold much of their waste in the form of batting (wads of cotton rolled up in paper) to rural families for the household manufacture of comforters.[77] Cotton waste was also sold to paper mills to be used in the manufacture of rag paper and to carpet factories for carpet fillings.[78] During the second half of the century, waste spinning gained more popularity, but it never attained such a prominent position as in Britain, nor did it become a highly specialized trade.[79]

Waste spinning was only one aspect of the mule's greater flexibility than the throstle. Versatility, as noted, was another. Spinning a wide range of staples and grades, the mule better suited British manufacturers who imported raw cotton from all over the world. Britain's dependency on the supply of raw material goes hand in hand with its dependency on the export trade: just as the demand for British cotton goods was divided among the European, American, and Indian markets, so was the British import of cotton divided among the North American, South American, and Indian markets. Like the export trade, furthermore, the foreign supply of raw cotton was unstable and unpredictable. A sudden suspension of supply from one source required manufacturers to direct purchases elsewhere and to shift quickly from the use of one type of cotton to another. Twice the British supply of cotton from the United States was cut off suddenly, and twice imports from elsewhere were used to substitute American cotton. During the Embargo and War of 1808-14, cotton crops from Brazil and India were used to replace the upland varieties while long-stapled cottons from the West Indies and Brazil were substituted for the finest Sea Island staples. During the Civil War, Egypt was the main British supplier of long-stapled cotton and India the chief source of Surat (an extremely short-stapled cotton, weak, coarse, and defective in color). Surat could effectively replace the American staple in spinning coarse yarns on mules, and more important, mules could be easily readjusted to spin much finer yarns from Surat than what had formerly been customary. By 1862 British millowners raised the highest counts spun from Surat from 24 to 50. Oldham, for example, depended totally upon American cotton but managed to adapt many of its mules to the spinning of Surat during the Civil War.[80]

The mule suited British millowners in still another way. It provided them with week-to-week flexibility in purchasing different qualities of cotton in what was the world's most developed market for raw cotton.[81] The Liverpool cotton market had a larger variety of staples and grades than any other cotton market in the world and as such allowed British millowners to make optimum use of cotton mixing.[82]

Mixing was a highly skilled craft in nineteenth century Lancashire, where "much of the success and profit of the cotton spinner depend[ed] on the skillful blending of dissimilar cottons, whereby one kind [was] made to conceal or supply the defects of the other."[83] Cotton mixing was a common practice in both Lancashire and New England, but was a craft in Lancashire alone. Touring the United States in the late 1830s, Montgomery noted the carelessness with which American managers mixed their cotton. By contrast to the British practice of "mak[ing] at least two mixtures of cotton, one for warp and another for filling," he found to his astonishment that in American mills both warp and filling were always spun from the same mixture.[84] Careful mixing in Britain served two purposes: economizing on the use of raw material and providing "a substitute for almost any particular kind of cotton."[85] Because they paid lower cotton prices and received their supply from domestic sources, American manufacturers were less concerned with material cost saving and less preoccupied with the need to develop supply substitutes than were British millowners.

British master spinners, to conclude, sought material supply flexibility. Paying relatively high cotton prices, they favored craft production and adopted the mule, a machine designed to get the most out of low-quality cotton. In the United States, on the other hand, the high quality of American cotton played an important role as a labor-saving device and favored mass production techniques. The American specialization in throstle spinning, accordingly, may be attributed to the high quality of American cotton and its relative cheapness.

Efficiency

Machine efficiency was dependent on technological improvements over time, on the type of yarn spun, and on the cost of power. In Britain during the 1790s, the productivity of mule spinning was as high as that of throstle spinning. Steady improvements in mule spinning during the next three decades more than doubled its labor productivity in terms of the number of operative hours required to process 100 lbs. of cotton.[86] By 1820, according to one estimate, the British mule produced (spindle for spindle) 20% more yarn per day than the throstle.[87] In the United States, continuous spinning on the throstle was faster and more productive than intermittent spinning on the mule. "Soon after the War of 1812," David Jeremy noted, "American throstles reached higher speeds...than English throstles and rivaled mules for productivity."[88] By the 1830s the improved American throstle clearly became more efficient per operative than the mule.[89]

One reason why continuous spinning was more economical in the United States than in Britain was the nature of the American product. Another was the quality of American cotton. The throstle was more productive than the mule in spinning coarse counts from high-quality cotton and therefore suited American manufacturers better. It is thus hardly surprising that the most important improvements in the mass production sector of the cotton-spinning industry originated in the United States. A comprehensive survey of all factory cotton- spinning patents issued by the U.S. Patent Office between 1790 and 1836 sheds some light on the issue. A total of forty-eight patents were issued during the period, forty in continuous spinning, five in intermittent (mule) spinning, and in three cases information is not available. Four of the five mule patents, furthermore, were only minor improvements.[90] In throstle spinning, on the other hand, the United States achieved a real breakthrough. In 1828 Charles Danforth of Rockland County, New York, patented the cap throstle which made it possible to increase the speed of spinning from 3000-4000 up to 7000 rpm. The invention of the "ring throstle" by John Thorpe of Providence, Rhode Island, in 1828 likewise led to significant increases in spinning speeds and to considerable reductions in the requirements for power, though the ring's general adoption was delayed until the second part of the century.[91] "I think in making coarse goods the machinery in America is better," Connecticut millowner James Kempton told a British Parliamentary committee in 1833, adding that he had never seen a throstle-spinning machine in Britain "equal to the best American throstles."[92] In 1830 a Scottish immigrant mule spinner at Rammapool near New York, who visited many cotton mills in "Paterson and other places," was just as convinced that the American mule spinning machinery was "quite inferior" to the British.[93] Hence the pattern of transatlantic transmission of technology: while the cap and ring throstle were American patents that were later adopted by British millowners, the power-driven mule and the self-acting mule were British innovations that were soon introduced into the United States. The notion that American manufacturers put their efforts in perfecting mass production techniques and British producers were preoccupied with improving craft technologies runs along every phase of the development of the early cotton industry, spinning as well as weaving.

The cost of power was an additional factor that was likely to induce British employers to use the mule. The mule required less power than the throstle, and power was cheaper in the United States than in Britain. In Lancashire, where water power was scarce and therefore expensive, the steam engine spread rapidly and major advances in productivity, especially on the mule, were largely derived from efficiency in the transmission of power. On the other hand, the American preference of water power over steam, especially in New England, was the result of the abundant supply of running water which cotton manufacturers exploited by building dams, reservoirs, and water wheels. In 1829 Zachariah Allen, a Rhode Island textile manufacturer, noted, "The manufacturing operations in the United States are all carried on in little hamlets which often appear to spring up in the bosom of some forest, gathered around the water fall that serves to turn the mill wheel. These villages are scattered over a vast extent of the country...instead of being collected together, as they are in England, in great manufacturing districts."[94] "It is, indeed, only after viewing the vast amount of labor expended in mining coal and transporting it to the furnaces of Steam Engines," wrote Allen on another occasion, "that an American can estimate the vast advantages possessed by the United States in the immense water power furnished by their innumerable rivers." In 1831 water power in New England was 40% cheaper than steam power in Manchester, England, according to Allen.[95] In a more recent analysis of comparative costs, one economic historian found that American power was nearly half as expensive as British power in the cotton industry in the 1830s.[96]

Unquestionably, the supply of low-cost water power in the United States checked the advent of the steam engine until the second part of the century. The 1832 McLane Report shows that the overwhelming majority of all spinning machines in American cotton mills, both mules and throstles, were still turned by water. In Rhode Island, for instance, just three of the 114 cotton factories that gave information derived their power from steam; the rest were water powered.[97] Challenging the accuracy of the McLane Report and examining the more complete 1838 Report on Steam Engines, Peter Temin has estimated that about 15% of the textile mills in existence in the United States in 1840 were using steam power.[98] Such a high figure for these early years does not, however, change the general picture: as late as 1867 fully three-quarters of the power in American textile mills was water power.[99]

Take the case of Britain now. As early as 1812 two-thirds of all steam engines in existence in Britain turned mules.[100] In 1838 more than 1,600 steam engines supplied 78% of the total horsepower used in British cotton factories, mostly for mule spinning, and by 1850 steam provided 86% of the aggregate power in British cotton factories.[101] In the Lancashire region the triumph of the steam-powered mule was even more impressive. In 1838 nearly 82% of the horsepower employed in Lancashire cotton mills was steam power, and by 1850 the proportion of water power employed in the cotton factories of the Lancashire region dropped to 11% making steam responsible for 89% of the total power.[102]

Why British mule-spinning mills were so attracted by the steam engine may be explained by the general shortage of water power, by the desire of manufacturers to concentrate production in a few urban locations within the Lancashire cotton region, and by the fact that the mule was particularly productive with steam. A mule driven by steam could be operated in a more uniform speed and thereby produce finer grades of yarn than by water power.

All estimates of the comparative requirements of power suggest that the mule had a decisive advantage over the throstle; the figures range from two to one to ten to one in favor of the mule. This broad range of figures reflects all different phases of development of the mule-spinning technology. Obviously, the more advanced the mule, the more fully mechanized it became, and the greater was its consumption of power. Yet unlike the automatic throstle, even the "self-acting" mule required some manual assistance so that it remained more energy efficient than the throstle. Andrew Ure estimated that one horsepower (steam) drove 500 mule spindles as compared to 180 throstle spindles in England in 1836; a ratio of two-and-two-thirds to one in favor of the mule. Robert Baird, an American cotton manufacturer writing fifteen years later, proposed a similar ratio: two-and-one-half to one in favor of the mule in 1851. Regardless of the type of machine used, furthermore, coarse spinning required considerably more power than fine spinning. In the middle of the nineteenth century, to cite a telling example, it was reported that one horsepower would drive twice as many mule spindles in spinning count no. 60 as in spinning yarn no. 25.[103] It is therefore quite plausible that the high cost of power in Britain encouraged cotton manufacturers to specialize in fine spinning, and conversely, the preference of coarse spinning in the United States was encouraged by the availability of cheaper power.[104]

While the mule required less power than the throstle, it entailed much higher labor costs. In England and the United States alike, a mule spinner in the mid 1820s received, on average, roughly three times the earnings of a throstle spinner, though wages were higher in the United States by about 20-25% for both categories of workers.[105] Cheaper power and expensive labor in the United States thus favored more power-intensive machinery run by unskilled machine tenders—the hallmark of mass production. In Britain, where power was scarce and the supply of labor was adequate, employers adopted a more labor-intensive, or rather "skill-intensive" technology, neglecting the use of fully powered machines.

WEAVING

Apart from spinning, power-loom weaving was the other major technology of manufacture which marked the transformation of the cotton industry to factory production. Mechanized weaving became operational for commercial use in Britain half a century after the earliest mills had gone into operation. As late as 1813 there were only 2,400 power looms in Britain and in 1819 just 14,000. During the 1820s British millowners introduced power looms for weaving coarser grades of cloth, but not until the 1830s did the mass expansion of the new technology occur. Between 1830 and 1844-45 the number of power looms in Britain climbed from 80,000 to 225,000, and in 1856 Lancashire had 344 weaving mills, 516 integrated spinning and weaving mills, and 591 mills engaged solely in spinning.[106]

New England cotton mills introduced mechanical weaving faster. In 1815,

TABLE 3

Cotton Spindles and Power Looms in
the United States and Britain

	1820		1831	
	United States	*Britain*	*United States*	*Britain*
Spindles	340,000	7,000,000	1,200,000	10,000,000
Power looms	1,700	14,000	33,500	80,000
number of looms per 1,000 spindles	5	2	28	8

Sources: The figures for Britain are taken from Thomas Ellison, *The Cotton Trade of Great Britain*, 65, 36. The American figures for 1820 are given by David Jeremy, *Transatlantic Industrial Revolution*, 277-78. Jeremy recorded a "minimum" of 1,665 power looms in the United States in 1820. The statistics for the United States in 1831 are taken from the census conducted by the Friends of Domestic Industry, *Address to the People of the United States*, 112.

twenty-five years after the first American cotton mill was erected, the earliest power looms were in operation in Waltham, Massachusetts. Five years later, in 1820, the United States had five power looms for every 1,000 cotton spindles as compared to only two power looms per 1,000 spindles in Britain. In 1831, as shown in Table 3, the United States had less than half as many power looms as Britain had, yet the ratio of looms to spindles was three-and-a-half times greater in the United States than in Britain. By 1832 the majority of New England cotton factories had already integrated power spinning and weaving.[107]

Why was the introduction of mechanized weaving in Lancashire so protracted as compared to New England?

Here again pre-factory production played a central role. In Britain, both the existence of a vast number of hand-loom weavers who experienced a sharp decline in earnings since the turn of the century, and the dependency of the industry on diverse quality markets, impeded the progress of the power loom. The relative absence of low-paid domestic weavers in New England and the specialization of the early mills in the production of standardized, coarse, throstle-spun yarn made from high-quality cotton, no doubt eased the mechanization of weaving.

Hand-loom weavers had probably formed the largest single group of industrial workers in Britain for some two hundred years before the coming of the power loom. The early transformation of spinning into a factory industry was followed by a growing demand for weaving; indeed, it was above all the loom, not the cotton mill, which attracted thousands of families. The number of cotton hand weavers in Britain rose from 108,000 to 240,000 between 1788 and 1820, remained almost unchanged until 1831, and then began to drop rapidly as the power loom gained popularity. Estimates of the total number of hand looms for cotton, wool, silk, linen, and flax in Britain in the late 1820s run from 500,000 to as high as 740,000.[108]

By the turn of the century, however, cotton hand-loom weaving had become an overcrowded occupation and wages began to fall. Frequent depressions pushed down wages between 1800 and 1820, but at the same time the over-supply of hand weavers grew so fast that employers not only refused to restore wages to their former level during good times but rather drove them lower and lower. An average of four different estimates of the piece rates received by Bolton muslin weavers shows a steep decline from thirty-four to ten shillings a week between 1795 and 1820.[109] The average weekly earnings of all kinds of cotton hand-loom weavers in Britain fell, according to George Henry Wood, from twenty-one shillings in 1802 to eight in 1820.[110]

In the United States, unlike Britain, the number of hand-loom weavers was so small that their labor was expensive. Philadelphia, the largest American center of handicraft industries, had perhaps no more than 4,500 hand-loom weavers in the late 1820s.[111] Rhode Island, another important center of hand-loom weaving, had only part-time weavers. Almost all Rhode Island weavers had supplementary sources of income and few had any difficulties earning a living as hand-loom opportunities diminished in the 1820s.[112] In comparing the economics of using hand-loom or power-loom weavers in the United States and Britain during the 1820s, two modern economists concluded in an article based on their examination of contemporary accounts that "American costs for unskilled labor and power looms were lower than the costs of hand-loom weavers, whereas British hand-loom weavers were generally cheaper than the new technology."[113] The choice between domestic and factory weaving, in other words, may be explained by contrasting labor supplies.

Labor supply nevertheless was only one factor. Equally important was market demand; the homogeneous demand for low-quality goods in the United States was another element in the sweeping victory of the power loom. The early power looms were too crude and too clumsy to be suitable for weaving anything but coarse yarns that were strong enough not to break under mechanical handling. Only low-count warps could withstand the strain imposed by the harsh beating of the shuttle.[114] American manufacturers specialized in coarse spinning and therefore were technically able to mechanize weaving rapidly, first in Lowell, then in Slater-type mills. But many of the Lancashire employers manufactured mule-spun yarn finer even than that turned out by the New England Slater sector, and therefore could apply power to only a very limited range of products. Of a list of twenty-five different kinds of cotton goods manufactured in the Lancashire region in the early 1830s, only four articles— stout prints, coarse calicoes, shirtings, and smallwares—were woven by power; the rest were still made by hand.[115]

Two other factors—the quality of cotton and the cost of power—mattered as well. The high quality of American cotton allowed manufacturers to introduce mechanical weaving with a technology cruder than the British technology. Finer grades and longer staples of cotton were stronger and less likely to break under the tension imposed by the motions of the loom and therefore enabled American manufacturers to experiment with power weaving sooner.[116] Similarly, the low cost of inanimate power in the United States facilitated the rapid mechanization of weaving. Just as American manufacturers preferred the automatic throstle to the semi-powered mule whenever market considerations permitted such a choice, so did they embark on power-loom weaving as fast as the new technology became operational for commercial use.

The power loom wove an entire piece of cloth automatically. Weaving by power was a continuous production technique strikingly similar to throstle spinning. The art of hand weaving consisted of three elementary motions: sending the shuttle that contained the weft through the warp threads, raising and lowering the alternate warp threads between each passage of the shuttle, and beating the weft thread against the edge of the cloth already woven. The power loom was designed to coordinate these three movements and drive them from a single source of power. While the loom was weaving, the operative was required simply to watch the machine and to perform one recurrent task: replacing empty bobbins with new ones. If the warp yarn broke, the machine would stop automatically, and the operative would have to tie the warp ends and restart the machine. Like throstle spinning, power-loom weaving required neither special skills nor a long training period, and therefore saved employers the high cost of hiring artisans. Typically, in Britain as well as in the United States, women and juveniles tended the power loom.[117]

VERTICAL INTEGRATION

Vertical integration of spinning and weaving was the final stage in the transformation of the cotton industry during the Industrial Revolution. The mechanization of weaving in the United States in 1810-15 enabled the Waltham company to integrate vertically, that is, to centralize all steps of production —cleaning, carding, spinning, weaving, and bleaching—within a single mill. Fifteen years after the completion of Waltham, around 1830, power looms were being installed in most new mills under construction and the vertically integrated mill remained the basic unit of cotton good production in the United States for the rest of the century. Judging on the basis of the McLane Report, by 1832 the vast majority of all northern mills had already integrated power spinning and weaving. In Rhode Island, for example, close to 90% of the mills enumerated in 1832 (107 out of 119) adopted power weaving to some extent while 10% specialized in spinning only. In New York, similarly, three-quarters of all cotton factories throughout the state (84 out of 112) were combined spinning and weaving establishments, and in Connecticut the figure is 87% (82 out of 94). In all three states, it should be noted, the typical spinning mill remained tiny, employing less than forty operatives and under 1,000 spindles.[118]

The British cotton industry never achieved such a high degree of integration. Actually, at no time during the nineteenth century were the majority of British cotton mills vertically combined. The integrated firm appeared in Britain later than in the United States and developed alongside separate, segregated spinning and weaving firms. In Lancashire in 1841 only 33% of all cotton factories were engaged in spinning and weaving, and in 1850—the year in which the integrated mill reached the zenith of its power—less than 38%.[119] In the English cotton industry the proportion of combined mills was lower, 31% in 1850, but they were considerably larger than the separate spinning and weaving establishments.[120] The continued proliferation of specialized firms and the growing geographical segregation of spinning and weaving in Lancashire[121] checked the movement towards vertical integration after it reached its peak in 1850. By 1896 the combined firms were outnumbered four to one by the separate spinning and weaving establishments.[122]

The movement toward vertical integration was influenced by the choice of spinning machinery. The separation of spinning and weaving was encouraged by the choice of the mule in much the same way as the preference of the throstle encouraged vertical integration. Throstle-spun yarn was much harder to transport than mule-spun yarn, and therefore throstle mills had a stronger incentive to integrate than mule mills. Filling (weft) yarn spun on mules was wound on the bare spindle in the form of cops designed originally to be shipped with no loss of shape to hand-loom weavers in the rural areas. Filling yarn spun on throstles had to be wound on heavy wooden bobbins which were expensive to transport. The choice of the throstle in the primary sector of the American cotton industry, accordingly, supported vertical integration because the yarn was spun and woven in the same mill and therefore could be handled conveniently on bobbins rather than being shipped away at high cost. The British dependency on mule spinning did not provide millowners with such an incentive; on the contrary, it encouraged specialization and supported the survival of the hand-loom weavers and the functional separation of spinning and weaving.[123]

The structure of the cotton industry was another element in the choice of vertical integration. The British cotton industry was dependent on two types of markets—one for yarn, the other for cloth—and both were diverse and unstable. Vertical specialization provided British millowners with the flexibility necessary to supply these markets. The chief characteristic of the American cotton industry, on the other hand, was the tight fit between spinning and weaving. American cotton manufacturers produced essentially for only one market—the standardized market for cheap cotton fabrics—so that vertical integration contributed to the efficiency with which they ran their mills.[124]

Consider the following figures. In 1830 more than 90% of the cotton spun in American factories was made into cloth in factories and less than one-tenth (in weight) was sold as yarn. In Britain, slightly over half the cotton spun in 1830, or 76 out of 145 million pounds, was made into cloth in mills; the rest was either put out to the countryside or exported. About one-third in value and one-half in weight of the total British export of cotton textiles in 1833-34 was in yarn.[125] Britain remained a major exporter of yarn all through the century, with hundreds of mills specializing in the production of wide ranges of counts. Many of the integrated firms in Britain, furthermore, did not consume all their yarn internally but rather sent part of it to market, hence retaining product flexibility. One Bolton mill, for instance, spun a wide range of yarn counts from 30 to 200, presumably wove much of the coarse yarn itself, and put the rest out to domestic weavers or to export. It is estimated that about one-third of the integrated firms in Lancashire in 1833 produced a significant proportion of their yarn under the same conditions enjoyed by the single-process spinning mill. In all these Lancashire firms flexibility was attained at the expense of efficiency.[126]

Flexibility was the rule in Philadelphia as well. In many ways, the Philadelphia experience resembles England's. Philadelphia had always been a center of mule spinning, had a few thousand hand weavers who survived well into the 1870s, had highly specialized cotton, cotton-wool and wool industries, and hardly any fully integrated establishments. As late as 1850, large quantities of yarn in Pennsylvania were produced "chiefly for the purpose of domestic manufacture by hand," and just as in Lancashire, there was a gross imbalance between factory spinning and weaving throughout the state. In 1850 the total amount of yarn spun and sold as yarn was *thirty times* larger in Pennsylvania than in Massachusetts.[127] "Immense quantities of yarn" were consumed in Philadelphia in the 1870s, at the time the city spinners could not supply more than about one-third of the needs of the fast-expanding weaving industry. In Philadelphia as in Lancashire, the movement towards vertical "disintegration" was clearly visible after mid-century, when dozens of spinning mills and hundreds of weaving operations were at work. The Philadelphia experience, so well described by Philip Scranton, shows how craft production coupled with the diversity of outputs and markets favored flexible specialization.[128]

SUMMARY

The decisive victory of the machine in America stands in marked contrast to the triumph of the craft in Britain. The foregoing analysis distinguishes two types of cotton factory technologies: intermittent and continuous, artisanal and mass production. Rooted in the domestic system of manufacture, mule spinning was essentially a handicraft technology adjusted to factory conditions. Throstle spinning and power-loom weaving, on the other hand, were mass production techniques that appeared first in factories where the application of water and/or steam power on a large scale was available.

Four factors were responsible for the rapid expansion of mule spinning and the sluggish diffusion of power-loom weaving in Britain: the availability of skill, market demand, cotton supply, and efficiency. A distinctive feature of the British economy had been the growth of industrial capitalism for two centuries before the breakthrough of the factory. The capitalist domestic system in Britain was dependent on the skilled labor of wage-earning artisans and on the existence of unstable markets both at home and abroad. Partly because domestic industrial skills in Britain were abundant, partly because the domestic textile industries were linked to unstable markets, and also because both the cost of raw cotton and the cost of mechanical power was expensive, British millowners incorporated craft into the factory, perfecting the mule—the most versatile of all spinning machines.

While the majority of British cotton factory workers in 1830 were employed in mule-spinning mills, most American cotton workers in 1830 labored in throstle- spinning and power-loom weaving departments. In the United States neither a dependent class of skilled craftsmen nor a network of putting out industries linked to distant markets was developed in the eighteenth century. Early American industrialists therefore responded to local conditions of skill scarcity, to a stable home demand for standardized coarse goods, and to a local supply of cheap cotton and cheap water power. Accordingly, they put their efforts in improving the mass production technologies of throstle spinning and power-loom weaving.

Chapter 3
The Management of Labor in the Early Mills

> In governing a Spinning Factory with propriety, it would be prudent for the manager, while guarding against too much *lenity* on the one hand, to be careful to avoid too much *severity* on the other; let him be firm and decisive in all his measures, but not overbearing and tyrannical; not too distant and haughty, but affable and easy of access, yet not too familiar. . . . Let him conduct himself so as to make [an] impression on the minds of all who are under him.
>
> James Montgomery,
> *The Theory and Practice of Cotton Spinning*
> (Glasgow: John Niven, 1836), pp. 269-70.

Two forms of factory management dominated the evolution of the cotton industry from its inception: subcontracting and foremanship. The first was the chief method of supervision used in craft production, namely mule spinning; the second, in mass production, namely throstle spinning and power-loom weaving. During the first half of the nineteenth century each technology was managed the same way in Britain and the United States.

From the outset manufacturers engaged in mule spinning managed by subcontracting. British and American mule spinners alike were autonomous craftsmen. Their functional autonomy rested on both their superior knowledge and the authority they exercised over other workers. Mule spinners had the prerogative to hire and fire, pay and supervise, train and discipline their own helpers. Throstle spinners and the majority of power-loom weavers, on the other hand, had no authority over other workers. Rather, employers in both countries differentiated operative from supervisory functions and subjected machine tenders to close supervision by foremen.

The similarity in the organization of craft and mass production between the United States and Britain leads to the conclusion that technology was a key variable in the choice of management in the early factory age.[1] Table 4 provides a summary presentation of the British findings that underlie this argument.

TABLE 4

Aspects of the Social Organization of Factory Production
in 225 Mills in the Lancashire Cotton Region 1833

	Technology	
	Craft Production (mule spinning)	Mass Production (throstle spinning)
1) Subcontract:		
children under 18 employed by operatives	88%	1%
2) Supervision:[1]		
ratio of overseers to workers	1:84	1:14
3) Age/Sex Composition:		
adult males employed	35%	10%
4) Forms of Wages:[2]		
a piece versus a daily wage	piece wages (spinner)	daily wages (spinner)
5) Wage Differentials:[1]		
average weekly earnings (shillings)	26 (spinner)	8 (spinner)

Source: Extracted from a Factory Commissioners' Report of 225 cotton mills in
Lancashire, Cheshire, and Derbyshire. *Parliamentary Papers* 1834, XIX, 136.

[1]Extracted from a smaller survey of 151 factories on which "complete returns"
are available selected from the original survey of 225 mills. *Parliamentary Papers*
1834, XIX, 125.

[2]Inferred from the questionnaire designed by the Factory Commissioner,
Parliamentary Papers 1834, XIX, 119ll-119mm.

Owing to the fragmentary nature of the American data it is impossible to
construct a comparable table, yet information extracted from American case
studies of individual mills conforms quite closely to the basic British pattern.
Again, to make the comparison more systematic, spinning is discussed first,
weaving next.

SPINNING

Subcontract

The method of subcontract in the cotton industry was to put a skilled mule spinner in charge of extensive machinery on the premise that he would recruit and pay his own assistants, children "scavengers" to clean the machine, and juvenile and women "piecers" to tie broken threads.

Subcontracting in the mule-spinning industry was not a new creation but, like many other artisanal industries in the nineteenth century, was a survivor from earlier forms of domestic production organized on the putting-out system. The mule spinner's position in the mill was not unlike that of the "undertaker" in the domestic weaving industry. Putting a mule spinner in complete charge of his assistants was a way of transferring the task of disciplining the new factory labor force from management to workers, a way of reducing the problems of mill management to that of a workshop size. Factory discipline under industrial capitalism was a problem faced by all employers so that the delegation of authority over other workers to artisans provided some solution. Subcontracting also solved recruitment problems and saved management all kinds of complicated labor cost calculations. Ordinarily management paid mule spinners by the quantity of yarn and spinners themselves decided who to employ, how many to employ, and how much to pay their employees.

That the spinner was "the sole patron and master" of his helpers seemed quite natural to Andrew Ure: "The spinners being. . . responsible for the quality of the yarn, must of course have the selection and hiring of their juvenile assistants."[2] Perhaps indeed subcontracting "was not a method of creating work discipline, but of evading it,"[3] as Sidney Pollard put it. It was a pre-factory method of industrial organization widespread in Britain as well as the United States; in both countries, in fact, many firms went through the process of transformation from one stage to another, putting out yarn for weaving and at the same time concentrating cotton spinning in centralized power-driven mills. Samuel Slater of Providence, Rhode Island, like Adam & George Murray of Manchester, England—to take just two examples—experienced the transformation in their own lifetime and in their own firms.[4] The survival of subcontracting in their spinning mills allowed them to share their risks with the mule spinners, to stabilize their labor costs, and to escape the most urgent need of factory management, namely, the direct supervision of workers gathered under one roof.

Subcontracting also facilitated the survival of family employment in the early mills. Mule spinners in both countries often employed their own children and the children of their relatives to assist them. Such an arrangement corresponded, of course, to the universal custom of apprenticeship in the domestic handicrafts where an artisan was expected to bring his sons up in a trade. As evident in the works of Neil Smelser on Lancashire, Anthony Wallace on Pennsylvania, and Barbara Tucker on southern New England, early millowners continued for years to recruit and pay workers on a family basis, and this practice was especially widespread in such factory trades as mule spinning where a long period of training was required. The subcontract system, Smelser insists, "perpetuated the traditional values of training children under paternal authority for an occupation." The survival of paternal discipline, it follows, postponed the need for creating factory discipline; the family system of labor relieved employers from the immediate problems of large-scale management.[5]

An 1833 survey of 67,800 operatives in 225 cotton factories in the Lancashire cotton region (Lancashire, Cheshire, and Derbyshire), or nearly one-third of the total employed in British cotton mills, shows that 88% of the 11,700 children under eighteen engaged in mule spinning were employed by operatives. Only 1% of the 1,200 children under eighteen in throstle spinning were employed by operatives.[6] No official statistics on subcontracting in American mills are available. Evidence drawn from case studies of individual mills, from employment contracts, and from company books, suggests nonetheless that during the 1820s and 1830s the practice of subcontracting among mule spinners was common in New England and Pennsylvania.[7] In Lowell—the largest American center of factory throstle spinning—the cotton corporations always employed workers directly.[8]

Supervision

Mule spinners scarcely required any supervision. The 1833 Factory Commissioners' Report of 151 mills in the Lancashire region provides detailed information on subcontract and supervision in the three main branches of the British cotton industry: mule spinning, throstle spinning, and power-loom weaving. Apparently, the higher the percentage of children helpers employed by operatives, the lower was the ratio of overseers to workers; alternately, the lower the percentage of helpers employed by operatives, the higher the ratio of overseers to workers.

The report shows that the average ratio of overlookers to workers in Lancashire cotton factories was six times as high in throstle as in mule spinning. An overlooker in the throstle-spinning department supervised an average of fourteen workers. His equivalent in the mule-spinning department was in charge of eighty-four workers (see Table 4). The ratio of overseers to workers in the American throstle-spinning industry was one to fifteen in 1840.[9] In American mule-spinning departments "the mule spinner was not subject to an overseer."[10] Owing to the small size of American factories during the 1830s, seldom would a mule-spinning department employ over eighty workers and therefore employers did not find it necessary to supervise mule spinners at all.[11]

Production in the mule-spinning department was organized in teams. In Britain in 1830, small teams of three to five workers ordinarily operated two mules of 300 to 600 spindles each, facing each other. One overlooker was in charge of some twenty to twenty-five such teams. The team consisted of a mule spinner who was in charge of two to three piecers ("big", "middle", and "little") and a part-time scavenger. The spinner performed the winding-on motion alternatively on each machine while the draw proceeded mechanically. At the end of each run of the carriage, when the mule was briefly motionless and during the few instants after the carriage started moving away toward the rollers in a winding motion, the piecers had to walk or rather "skip" along the mule, find the broken ends of threads and tie them together. The work of the spinner and his piecers is described in minute details and with exceptional clarity in the parliamentary reports of 1833:

> When at work the spinner stands between two mules, with his back to one and his face to the other, and the piecers stand on each side of him with their faces in the same direction as his. When the carriage of the mule comes towards him bearing the horizontal threads and spinning them all the while, he and his piecers are watching what threads require attention. . . .
> As soon as the carriage arrives at where the spinner is standing, it stops; a retrograde motion is given to it, and it returns to the back or the frame of the mule, gathering up on its spindles the threads which it has just spun. The piecers follow the carriage as it recedes, and piece or join all the threads that were broken. When the process is finished, then the carriage comes out again, and repeats the operation just described.
> . . . [But a]s soon as the spinner observes that carriage coming out again . . . he and his piecers turn their faces round to the other mule, and perform the same duties regarding that. The motions of the two carriages between which he and his piecers are standing, are so timed that one is always coming out whilst the other is going back, and thus no time is lost, and the spinner and piecers are able to manage two mules at the same time by merely turning their bodies round.[12]

Spinning on mules produced much waste from the cotton fibers which tended to accumulate on the working elements of the machine and had to be removed in frequent intervals. This was the task performed by scavengers. At the end of the winding process when the carriage was back at the frame, the scavengers had to duck and lay themselves low enough so that the carriage could pass over their heads in its outward movement. Once the carriage passed, the scavengers would "immediately raise themselves upon their knees" and start sweeping up the carriage top and clearing out cotton fibers and cotton dust from the space between the rollers.[13]

Piecers as well as scavengers were intensely loyal to the team leader, the mule spinner, "whose word was law in his little kingdom."[14] It was the spinner's responsibility to "apprise the piecer[s]" of what threads needed repair[15] and to make sure that the piecers would "seize the moment" and mend the broken ends each time the carriage was beginning to move backward. Otherwise, warned Andrew Ure: "they must remain idle till the completion of another act of stretching and winding on."[16] Overseers, as a matter of fact, hardly ever intervened either in the organization of work on a pair of mules, or in the enforcement of discipline. Close to 3,000 pages of evidence gathered by the Factory Inquiry Commission makes it quite clear that except in a few isolated cases British mule teams had never worked under the direct watch of overseers.

The American mule in the 1830s lagged far behind the improved British mule. In many American mills, especially around Philadelphia, either the entire machine was still manually operated, or only the rollers and spindles were turned by power. The mule spinner himself pushed in and pulled out the carriage by hand. For that reason the Philadelphia spinner and his helpers operated only one mule of up to 350 spindles before 1840. Mule spinning in Pennsylvania, furthermore, required more piecing than in Lancashire due to the inferior quality of the preparation of the roving (cotton slivers ready for spinning) and therefore a team of three to four workers was necessary for running a single mule.[17] But in advanced New England mills—just as in Britain—the mule spinner managed a pair of semi-automatic mules that stood parallel so that while one was running out by power the spinner was free to push the carriage of the other. Slater's company books show that nearly every mule spinner contracted between 1827 and 1837 operated two mules of up to 192 spindles each with the assistance of two to three helpers.[18] In factories that used longer mules the spinner-piecers team was larger; in the late 1830s each mule spinner employed by the Thorndike Cotton Manufacturing Company at Palmer, Massachusetts, was in charge of four to five piecers at a time.[19]

Mule spinners controlled the pace of production. The number of times the spinner put up and backed off the mule carriage determined the pace. Spinning by throstles, in contrast, involved a system of continuous production in which the speed of the machinery was set by managers. Neither machine tenders nor overlookers controlled the speed. Moreover, in mule-spinning rooms the activities of piecers and scavengers were closely coordinated with those of the spinner. Each mule or pair of mules was a self-contained, organic unit in which work was performed interdependently by the spinner and his helpers. In throstle-spinning departments each operative was assigned his or her particular machinery tending a given number of spindles. There was little interaction between operatives, who worked side-by-side independently, not interdependently.[20]

James Montgomery, the experienced mill manager from Glasgow, elaborated this point in his famous treatise on management. No other book on cotton mill management published before 1850 (with the possible exception of Ure's _The Philosophy of Manufactures_) had influenced the thinking of American managers more than _The Theory and Practice of Cotton Spinning; or the Carding and Spinning Master's Assistant_ by James Montgomery. Montgomery visited many mills in Britain as well as the United States and he also worked as a manager in both countries. The first edition of _Theory and Practice_ was published in Glasgow in 1832, a second edition appeared a year later, and a third in 1836. Not only was the book widely read in the United States, but in addition, a considerable number of American managers came from the ranks of British immigrants and as such they had already been exposed to Montgomery's ideas at home.[21]

Montgomery's theory of management was based on the notion that craft and mass production,"being rather different, require[d] somewhat different modes of government."[22] Unfortunately however, he did not contrast mule and throstle spinning but rather mule spinning and carding as the title of his book says. Nevertheless his remarks are suggestive. The process of carding—the crucial step of preparing the cotton for spinning—closely resembled that of throstle spinning insofar as the organization of work is concerned. Like throstle spinners, the vast majority of operatives in the carding department were machine tenders employed directly by management and subject to close supervision by overseers. The 1833 survey of 151 cotton mills in the Lancashire region indeed shows first, that the ratio of "carders and overlookers" to machine tenders ("Jack-frame tenders," "bobbin-frame tenders," and "drawing tenders") was one to ten, and second, that less than 6% of the children employed in the carding department were subcontracted by other operatives.[23]

"In the [mule] spinning department," Montgomery observed, "there are men who have the charge of their own work, and are paid only for what they do, and [are] responsible both for the quality and quantity of their work; they can also be made sensible of the consequences that would result from any degree of carelessness or negligence on their part; and hence it is not necessary that the spinning master should be always present." But this was not the case in mass production processes. "In the carding [and throstle-spinning] departments,"

> they are mostly women on set wages, whom it is difficult to make sense
> of their responsibilities, and the evils resulting from carelessness on their
> part; and, therefore, they require to be constantly looked over: hence,
> the...master should never be out of their view...as his very presence
> might prevent many faults that would otherwise take place.

What, then, are the qualities of a "good manager"? Are these qualities dependent on the type of technology used? To what extent?

In mule spinning, Montgomery advised, "the spinning master requires to act with prudence and caution—to be just and impartial—firm and decisive—always on alert to prevent rather than to check faults, after they have taken place." In mass production processes, on the other hand, "good discipline is of the very first importance." "The carding master must act with the utmost vigilance and promptitude, and sometimes with a degree of seeming severity, that is not necessary in the other [mule spinning]."[24]

Samuel Ogden, a Rhode Island cotton manufacturer who emigrated from Britain in 1806, shared Montgomery's perceptive views on labor management. "Every department in the card-room is diligently attended," Ogden told his fellow American manufacturers in a pamphlet composed in 1814, "and if any one neglects, or is slack in the performance of the necessary duty, the manager immediately discovers it: for there is scarcely a minute during working time, that his attention is not drawn to watch all parts of the work, but when detained to regulate a defect." "The rule of a good manager," Ogden declared, "is to be always walking to and fro in the room, or else standing in place where he can see the greatest part of the hands that are at work." Describing the carding room at some length he at once reminded his readers that work in throstle spinning was supervised precisely "by the same means and in the same manner" as in carding.[25] Any one of the Lowell cotton corporations may serve as an example of Ogden's managerial "rule." In a typical department in Lowell in the 1830s an overseer would sit on an elevated desk at one end of the room watching long rows of machines and operatives standing in the aisles between the machines, while a second hand would move about the room inspecting workers directly from close range.[26]

An important managerial innovation introduced by employers in the mass production sector of cotton spinning, we may thus conclude, was the complete separation of supervisory and operative tasks. Mule spinners worked while they supervised workers. Throstle-spinning overseers did not work at all but only supervised machine tenders. The employment of a specialized body of professional supervisors in throstle spinning (and carding) enabled employers, for the first time in the history of the industrial revolution, to transfer control over production from workers to management. The initial cost of the innovation, however, was rather high. The inculcation of work discipline among factory hands was much more of a problem in throstle- than in mule-spinning factories.[27] In the first management dealt directly with an aggregate body of factory proletarians on the shop floor. In the second management dealt with artisans alone.

Age and Sex Composition

Mule spinning was a male-dominated industry. The 1833 Factory Commissioner's Report shows that 77% of all workers employed in the mule-spinning departments of English factories were males. Only 30% of the operatives in throstle-spinning rooms were males. One in three operatives employed in mule spinning was a male above eighteen, in contrast to one in ten in throstle spinning (Table 5). Adult males held overseers' and mule spinners' positions. According to the 1842 Factory Inspectors' Report, mule spinners were generally men older than twenty-four years.[28]

Mule spinning was a male occupation for three reasons: the supervisory responsibilities of subcontracting, the sheer physical requirements of the job, and the unions' exclusionary policy.

To begin with, on the same grounds that men monopolized supervisory positions they dominated the skilled occupations in the mills.[29] The underlying assumption of employers was that operatives would better comply with a male than a female authority. Since mule spinning involved a degree of authority over other workers, employers excluded women. And furthermore, because

TABLE 5

Age and Sex Percentages of 72,561 Workers
Employed in the Spinning Departments of
English Cotton Mills, 1833,
Broken Down by Industry

	Throstle Spinning	Mule Spinning
Male above 18	10	35
Male under 18	20	42
Total male	30	77
Female above 18	39	8
Female under 18	31	15
Total female	70	23
Total male and female	100 (7,709)	100 (64,852)

Source: Extracted from the Factory Commissioners' Report of the "Estimated Number of Persons Employed in the Cotton Mills of England," *Parliamentary Papers* 1834, XIX, 138.

---

mule spinners in the early mills exercised their authority by means of corporal punishment employers were even more reluctant to delegate women control over helpers. A widely held view in early industrial Britain was that "boys about twelve or thirteen" were "beyond [women's] control."[30]

"Each [spinner] enforces obedience in his own way,"[31] one Manchester millowner said, yet unmistakably, child beating and the threat of the strap were the universal methods of enforcing discipline in British mule-spinning mills up to the 1830s. Child helpers from nine to fifteen were "licked" regularly by their employers the mule spinners, for coming "too late in a morning," for "having [their] ends down" (leaving threads untied), and for being "negligent" and "inattentive" in general.[32] Physical discipline was frequent: "six and eight times a week" for piecers, "six and eight times in a day" for scavengers.[33] The younger the child the more likely he or she was to get beaten. One employer considered corporal punishment "the best punishment for boys" but did not allow it for girls. Juveniles above the age of fifteen were punished more often by fines than by whipping.[34]

A point worth emphasizing is that the strap was the visible symbol of the spinner's authority at work regardless of whether or not he actually used it. "The spinners in general have taws [leather straps] with a view to show their authority more than to punish the children," noted a Glasgow mule spinner in 1833, and his fellow spinner at the same mill conceded that he had a strap "three feet long and with heavy ends" in order "to keep the piecers to their work," but he never used it though he might "threaten the young workers to do so." Similarly, the mule spinners of Manchester kept their straps hanging in view for all, piecers and scavengers alike.[35]

Here again paternal authority in the factory reflected authority relations in the family; the adult male spinner was a disciplinarian both at home as a father and in the mill as a subcontractor. Children in early nineteenth century British society were "corrected" (i.e., beaten) everywhere they were—in the family, at school, in the mine, or on the shop floor—and everywhere we look the strap is associated with a male, not a female authority. Factory Commissioner Edward Tufnell thought that the "corrections" mule spinners gave their assistants should never be "more than [what] a father ought to give his refractory child."[36] Henry Houldsworth of Glasgow could tolerate physical punishment among the mule spinners in his establishment so long as it did not exceed "the degree usually inflicted by a parent on a child, or a master on his scholar."[37] "I don't mean to say that children are not beaten by spinners in factories," a Manchester machine maker stated his opinion, "but it is my decided conviction...that a child is beaten ten times more at school than he is in a factory."[38] Spinners apparently disciplined their own child assistants in much the same way as they disciplined the children of others, especially since the needy parents who sent their children into the mill often preferred a "correction" to an outright dismissal of a child, provided of course "he deserved it."[39]

As far as one can tell from the testimonies collected by the Factory Inquiry Commission, discipline was certainly a problem faced by the few women skilled workers who did operate small mules. "How do they manage to keep the boys at work,"one of the commissioners asked, "since they cannot correct them?"[40] The answer is threefold. In Manchester, women mule spinners often used the carrot rather than the stick, reward rather than punishment, positive incentives rather than deterrents;[41] nevertheless, it was the adult male overseers, not the women, who were responsible for "keep[ing] the boys in order."[42] In Scotland women mule spinners had always preferred girls to boys as assistants,[43] while in the Midland and Scotland alike women occasionally operated mules that were so small that no helpers whatever were needed.[44]

But all these solutions were far from satisfactory. Small mules were not as productive as large ones, putting overseers in charge of piecers would have undermined the subcontract system, and a large-scale hiring of female rather than male piecers is hard to imagine given the nature of the craft and its apprenticeship rules. In short, that the supervisory responsibilities of the trade barred women from the mule is hardly astonishing.

Yet there was another factor, namely, the strength requirements of the job. Remember that although power was applied to the outward movement of the mule carriage the spinner still had to return the carriage by hand. By any standards the carriage was enormous. A medium-size mule in the 1830s had 350 spindles arranged in a single row on a forty-five- to fifty-foot carriage weighing close to 1,400 pounds. Typically, a British coarse spinner who was in charge of a pair of mules with 350 spindles each had to drive the carriage of each mule back and forth alternatively 2,500 times in twelve hours, or three-and-a-half times per minute.[45]

No wonder that John Sutcliffe, a civil engineer writing in 1816, regarded mules carrying 300 spindles "unfit for any but men to work them."[46] Equally understandable is the factory commissioner's conclusion in 1833: "A woman can spin, and many do, but she is not so capable of managing two mules as a man is." The employment of women on mules, the commissioner goes on, has been on the decline in the Lancashire district, but "a change in machinery can bring them back to this occupation to-morrow."[47] It never did. Despite the introduction of the celebrated self-acting mule around mid-century, men retained their monopoly over the trade for reasons we shall explore in the following chapter.

Perhaps there is no better way to assess the importance of physical strength as a barrier for women's employment on mules than to examine which kind of mules women actually operated. Scottish employers, we know, hired women mule spinners more frequently than English employers did, and one likely explanation is that the average yarn count spun in Scotland was higher than in England (though it did not approach the finest Manchester grades).[48] As a rule, the coarser the yarn the more arduous was the task of spinning on mules because the speed of the carriage was much faster in coarse than in fine spinning. Fine spinning involved no more than one round trip per minute for each carriage, medium count spinning required two round trips, and coarse involved three to three-and-a-half trips a minute.[49]

Regardless of the type of mule used, however, all machines operated by women were small. In Scotland in the early 1830s women operated two mules of up to 240 spindles, 120 on a carriage. Occasionally a team of two women mule spinners would manage together a large pair containing over 400 spindles. In New Lanark, Robert Owen had two kinds of mules: those carrying 84 to 120 spindles each, for women, and those large mules of 352 spindles each, worked by men.[50]

The final barrier for the employment of women on mules was union policy. There is a great deal of evidence that British mule spinners' unions maintained men's control over their craft by excluding women from membership and by opposing their employment on mules.

The earliest British mule spinners' unions in the 1790s had enrolled women. By 1830, however, there were no female members in the vast majority of local societies of mule spinners. Strikes by the men spinners over the employment of women on mules were quite common in early nineteenth century Britain and they occasionally involved a good deal of violence. During the 1818 Manchester strike several mills that employed women mule spinners were set on fire, and in Glasgow in 1824 and during the 1830s violence erupted in a number of instances in which the male union members attempted to prevent women mule spinners from entering the mills. In 1829 the newly formed national federation of cotton spinners prohibited women from joining the men's trade unions, though it encouraged them to set up their own organizations, and in 1870 women members were again expelled from local mule spinners' societies throughout Britain.[51]

"The chief reason" for the exclusion of women, one mule spinner said, was "to prevent the lowering of wages."[52] Women engaged in a man's trade were "the most dangerous enemies of the artisan's Standard of Life," wrote the Webbs at the close of the century, and in the same vein, William Lazonick recently argued that the prevailing notion of "fair wages" in early industrial Britain was paternalistic, not universalistic: men were entitled to higher wages than women merely because men were expected to support families, regardless of whether or not they actually did so. Similarly, all women were bound to accept "women's wages," even women who in fact practiced a "male trade," even women who actually headed families.[53] The entry of women into mule spinning was thus perceived by the men spinners as a threat to the status of their trade, as an attempt on the part of the employers to turn the craft into a low-paid women's occupation. Opposition to the employment of women was further intensified by continuous technological improvements throughout the century which led to chronic unemployment problems among the adult male spinners.

Like the few women mule operators, only a small number of women served as assistants to mule spinners. The majority of helpers in the mule-spinning department were males under eighteen. Scavengers were children of both sexes from nine to thirteen.[54] Piecers were the largest category of workers employed in the mule room. Mule spinners preferred to employ male rather than female piecers for two reasons. First, a minority of piecers served as apprentices to mule spinners; these were men between fifteen and twenty known as "big piecers."[55] Because the men spinners opposed the employment of women on mules they limited apprenticeship to males only. The second consideration in favor of employing males was the physical labor involved in piecing on mules. The piecer, as noted, was required to run back and forth along the mule's rail, following the moving carriage, twelve hours a day. A piecer engaged in fine spinning had to walk about ten miles a day, but in coarse spinning he had to "run as hard as [he] could." Addressing a former Manchester piecer in 1833, Factory Commissioner Tufnell inquired: "Of the...thirty or forty miles which piecers at coarse factories have to go a day, how much of it do you think they have to run?" "Why," the witness replied, "I should allow them to run about one-fourth of it, and the other quick walking. Sometimes standing, but only for a moment."[56] The race after the carriage was so exhaustive, the evidence suggests, that the mule spinners preferred hiring male rather than female piecers, a choice that tells us more on the men's prejudices against females than on the actual capacities of men and women. Yet in one important respect the hiring of young male piecers made sense from the spinners' viewpoint: during the long working day the spinners would now and then take a break and have the piecers themselves operating the mules and pushing those heavy carriages with their muscles.[57]

By contrast to mule spinning and piecing, to proceed, throstle spinning was a female-dominated occupation (see Table 4). The 10% adult males employed in the industry were mostly overseers, while the 70% women and girls (and the 20% males under eighteen) were machine tenders.[58] Tending the throstle did not require any physical strength, just attentiveness and endurance; hence it was a job perfectly suited for low-paid women and juveniles. Constantly on her or his feet alongside the machine, the operative had to stop the appropriate spindle each time the thread broke. This task, repeated endlessly during the day, involved three distinct steps: standing on one leg and raising the other on tiptoe, pressing the knee of the raised leg against the revolving spindle, and using both hands to knot the broken ends.[59] Throstle spinners were neither employed by other workers, nor did they hire any helpers, and the absence of subcontracting in the industry is undoubtedly one reason why child beating was not nearly as widespread in throstle as in mule spinning.[60] Like other unskilled occupations, throstle spinning in Lancashire remained a non-union job during most of the nineteenth century.[61]

Finally, mule spinning in America was an occupation segregated by age and sex. The nine mule spinners employed by Slater in 1840 in his Webster, Massachusetts mill were all men, as were the ten mule spinners employed in 1832 in the Riddles' mill at Rockdale, Pennsylvania.[62] Occasionally, to be sure, women operated small mules. They did so in Pawtucket as early as 1805, in Nashua, New Hampshire, off and on between 1827 and 1843, and in numerous mills throughout Massachusetts and Rhode Island soon after the Civil War.[63] It is not clear to what extent women and girls were employed as helpers on mules, but it is almost certain that the vast majority of piecers, who also served as informal apprentices in American mills, were young men.[64] In a typical throstle- spinning department at Lowell, by contrast, fully 93% of all employees in 1838 were women; the remaining 7% were men overseers.[65]

The similarity between early British and American mule-spinning mills is also evident in the methods of enforcing discipline. Speaking before a Pennsylvania Senate Committee in 1837, a Pittsburgh mule spinner stated: "Children are sometimes punished with the strap—I think it necessary—some of the boys are obstinate and idle." Another operative, an immigrant from Lancashire, reported that "a slap on the head with the open hand, and sometimes a strap" were among the principal means of enforcing discipline in Pennsylvanian mills (in addition to wage docking and outright dismissals), though he did not consider such punishments to be "severe." A Baltimore-born mule spinner who had been employed in four different Pennsylvanian cotton factories within a period of nine years described the punishment by whipping as "frequent," adding: It is the "person having charge of the children" who "inflicts the chastisement." One of his former employers conceded that "severe whipping" had been a common practice in early Pennsylvanian factories, but since "it was found not to be the best mode of management, [it] has been, in a great degree, abandoned." Child beating as a "mode of management" was surely abandoned by the millowners and their agents but not by the subcontractors. Pennsylvanian mule spinners during the 1830s continued to subject their child helpers to occasional slapping and strapping, though certainly not to the extent that did mule spinners in Lancashire and Scotland.[66]

Unfortunately, no Senate investigation on the employment of children in factories (comparable to the Pennsylvanian one) was conducted by either the Rhode Island or the Massachusetts legislature during the 1830s. This is not to imply, of course, that the use of physical discipline in the early mule-spinning mills of these states was not pervasive. On the contrary, a New England overseer with thirty-three years experience testified in 1870 that "years ago" factory children had been subject routinely to "corporal chastisement"; evidently, the use of "strips of leather fourteen inches long, four inches wide, three-eighths of an inch thick—sometimes tacks were inserted"—was quite "promiscuous" in the early cotton mills of Rhode Island.[67]

The Form of Wages

Mule spinners, like other artisans, were paid in proportion to output. Throstle spinners, on the other hand, were almost always paid by time.

According to the 1833 Factory Commissioners' Report, 52% of the 61,600 operatives employed in 225 cotton mills in the Lancashire region (for whom the method of payment is known) were paid by piece and 48% by day.[68] All overseers and mule spinners received piece wages. Throstle spinners, piecers, and scavengers received daily wages. Likewise, American mule spinners were paid by the number of hanks (a hank equalled 840 yards) their machine turned out during the payroll period, and from their own wages they paid their helpers by the day. American throstle spinners earned a daily wage independent of their output.[69]

Wages in the British domestic industries in the seventeenth and eighteenth century were customarily tied to tasks, not directly to time. As shown by E.P. Thompson, there was little demarcation between "work" and "life" in pre-industrial Britain.[70] Labor and leisure were intermingled and tasks were generally assigned for a week or a fortnight within which the working day might be lengthened or shortened. Hand-loom weavers, for example, were paid by the piece of cloth they wove; hence they could regulate their own pace of work. Mule spinners, who had worked in the cottage before moving into the factory, were paid by the quantity of yarn they spun, setting their own work rhythm.

And their work rhythm was "very irregular." Working at home or in a small workshop, the hand mule spinner "ha[d] the command of his time." He would drink the first day or two of the week, and try to make it up by working very long hours towards the end of the week. "I have seen them working all night on a Friday night," a Manchester millowner recollected, and another master spinner, referring to Manchester in the 1790s, noted that the mule spinners' custom of spending the first two or three days of the week in public houses was typical of "all trades where the wages [were] high and the work carried on in private houses." With the coming of power-driven factories, however, the spinners no longer could work day and night as they pleased, but only during engine hours while the machinery was running. Nevertheless, despite the far greater regularity of attendance in factories, the method of payment by results prevailed.[71]

Payment by results in the early cotton factories was introduced in order to ease recruitment as well as to increase output. Everywhere artisans responded better to payments in proportion to output than to direct day wage incentives and that is probably one reason why early factory masters adopted this domestic custom in mule spinning along with the subcontract system.[72] Subcontract and the piece rate went hand in hand: nearly all the child helpers at a typical British or American cotton mill in the 1830s were subcontracted by operatives who worked by the piece;[73] the vast majority were employed by mule spinners.

No contemporary writer on management understood the significance of payments by results better than Samuel Ogden. Nearly a century before Frederick Winslow Taylor launched the campaign for scientific management, Samuel Ogden, the British immigrant millowner and mule manufacturer in Rhode Island,[74] had advised American millowners to adopt the piece rate system, arguing that incentive wages were the key to increased productivity. Ogden's convictions resemble Taylor's ideas so closely that the following paragraph written by Ogden in 1815 might as well have been written by Taylor himself:

> Place two men to work in one room and at one sort of work, and employ one by the day and the other by the piece, and you will find that the day man is a slave to time more than [to] his work, and that the piece man is actively industrious at his work, and *takes no note of time*, unless it be to think it short, when work, he had allotted out to do is not completed. Take the weekly amount of wages paid to each one, and the quantity of work each one has done, and you will find that the . . . piece-man by working four days in a week, will earn more than the day man's wages amount to for six days.

He then asks rhetorically,
"Who is a greater slave than he who is a slave of time?"
"Who would be a slave to time that can earn more by fair industry?"[75]

The ideological implications are clear enough: "Those who work at the cotton business are free." In mule spinning, Ogden accordingly proceeded, the method of payment in proportion to output was used "to induce and not to compel the work people" because only by means of "open and liberal inducements" was it possible to achieve "such an extraordinary degree of exertion." "One man works two mules, and during working time there is a continual strife throughout a room to gain a strech [a round trip of the carriage] at him who spins at the next pair."[76]

Ogden's assertion that the piece rate system brought about "an almost un-paralleled degree of voluntary industry"[77] in the mule room is certainly correct insofar as the spinners are concerned. But there was nothing voluntary in the work of piecers and scavengers. Spinners paid their helpers by time, not by results, so that the helpers had no incentive to boost output. Corporal punishment and the threat of the whip were among the means used by the mule spinners to drive their assistants harder and harder.

Machine tenders in mass production processes, according to Ogden, received daily wages. As physical discipline was not pervasive either in carding or in throstle spinning, how, then, was management able to keep up production, or in Ogden's words, "to bind the workman to his duty?" In carding, we are told, the overseers calculated the speed as well as the potential output of each machine and the operatives were expected to process a given quantity of cotton in a day's work. In throstle spinning, too, no machine would "fall short" and no defect would remain undetected because the overseers were always aware of the speed of the spindles, the count of the yarn spun, and the proper "twist" required, and thereby they controlled both quality and quantity.[78]

Ogden's perceptive observations thus lead to the conclusion that the form of wages was an important element in workers' control. A daily wage received by machine tenders reflected the low level of skill required and the limited control over production provided by the job. Payments by results to artisans and overseers meant, on the other hand, an autonomy from management supervision.[79] The mule spinner regulated the speed of the machinery so that his earnings fluctuated according to his own work pace. He paid his helpers a *fixed* sum from his earnings regardless of how hard they worked. The throstle-spinning overseer neither regulated the speed nor paid his subordinates. He was nonetheless responsible for quality as well as output. When the yarn broke the operative had to stop the appropriate spindles, tie the broken ends, and restart the spindles again. It was the overseers' task to speed up this part of the production process.

Wage Differentials

"All the available wage statistics," wrote S.D. Chapman, "confirm that the mule spinner was the best paid artisan in the cotton industry."[80] The 1833 Factory Commissioners' survey of 151 cotton mills in Lancashire, Cheshire, and Derbyshire, shows that the net average weekly earnings of mule spinners were over three times as high as those of throstle spinners, five times the earnings of piecers, and almost nine times the pay of scavengers. Mule spinners were also better paid than overlookers in the throstle-spinning departments. The mule spinner's weekly pay, after deduction of his assistants' wages, was inferior only to that of his own overseer (Table 6).

As in Britain, factory craftsmen in the United States were much better paid

TABLE 6

Net Weekly Pay of Operatives Employed in Mule and
Throstle Spinning Departments of 151 Cotton Mills
in Lancashire, Cheshire, and Derbyshire, May 1833,
Broken Down by Major Jobs

Department	Job	Net Weekly Pay
Mule Spinning	overlooker	29 shillings
	spinner	26
	piecer	5
	scavenger	3
Throstle Spinning	overlooker	22
	spinner	8

Source: *Parliamentary Papers* 1834, XIX, 138.

than machine tenders. Aggregate data on wages broken down by departments
and major jobs are not available for the American cotton industry during the
1830s. Data extracted from case studies of individual mills indicate that a Pennsylvanian mule spinner earned in 1832 about 9.00 dollars a week, or more than
seven times as much as his own helper ($1.25) and over two-and-a-half times
the earnings received by a New England throstle spinner ($3.50) in 1836.[81] A
New England mule spinner took in the late 1830s a weekly wage bill of about
9.50 dollars, more than the earnings received by an overseer in the carding
($9.00), weaving ($8.50), or throstle-spinning ($7.50) rooms.[82]

These wage statistics show that all the poorly-paid jobs in the mill were held
by women and children machine tenders and helpers. The well-paid jobs were
all held by adult male artisans and supervisors. The mule spinner's position
in early British and American factories, then, closely resembled that of an
overseer not only in terms of authority over other workers, but also in terms
of economic benefits. Among all other categories of mill operatives, early factory artisans were privileged workers.

Conclusion

Reviewing the five aspects of the social organization of factory production:
subcontract, supervision, age and sex composition, the form of wages, and wage
differentials, it is evident that during the first round of industrialization differences in the management of labor between American and British cotton-
spinning factories *were not all that great*. Employers in the American mule-
spinning industry adopted British managerial techniques in much the same way

as they imported British machinery. Production was organized in small autonomous teams headed by a spinner. Mule spinners were adult male artisans who subcontracted their helpers, were independent of management supervision, were paid in proportion to productivity, and received excellent wages.

British and American cotton manufacturers who adopted the mass production technique of throstle spinning also introduced similar employment policies. In both countries employers recruited women and juvenile machine tenders, subjected them to close supervision by male overseers, and paid them low daily wages independent of output.

Managerial strategies of throstle-spinning firms remained essentially unchanged all through the century. The resemblance between British and American management of continuous spinning processes at the start of the century is indeed apparent at the end of the century as well. But this was not the case in mule spinning. In managing intermittent processes the American experience after mid-century stands in marked contrast to the British.

During the second part of the nineteenth century, British mule spinners managed to retain *intact* their autonomous position in production despite the introduction of improved machinery. American mule spinners failed. Since the 1840s American employers subjected the spinning craftsman to the absolute rule of the foreman. Employers took away from mule spinners their most important right—the right to supervise their own helpers—and gave this function to the foreman. Losing both his autonomy and his authority over other workers, the American mule spinner became a mere "machine minder"; his status became that of a factory operative. The chapters that follow discuss these far-reaching developments in detail.

WEAVING

"Much of the older system," Sidney Pollard observed, "was left in the interstices of the new factory organization, making adjustment easier and postponing to some extent the development of modern management techniques."[83] The invaluable 1833 British report shows that of the three factory techniques, mule spinning was organizationally the closest to the domestic industry, throstle spinning was the farthest from it, and power-loom weaving fell somewhere in between.[84] The social organization of power-loom weaving thus represents an intermediate case between the cottage and the factory. The position of the factory weavers in the mill was superior to that of throstle spinners but still far inferior to that of mule spinners.

A minority of employees in the weaving department had achieved a degree of authority in production, employing their own assistants. They were either adult male dressers who performed the highly skilled task of sizing the warp yarn and who were assisted by juvenile piecers or the few men weavers who were in charge of four looms at a time and who received assistance from one child tender. Most factory weavers in Britain in the 1820s and 1830s tended just two looms.[85] Of the estimated 23,500 children under eighteen working in the power-loom weaving rooms of English cotton mills in 1833, 29% were employed by other operatives and 71% directly by management;[86] the respective figures for mule spinning were 88% and 12%.

The majority of power-loom weavers, like all throstle spinners, were machine tenders who did not subcontract labor, required a considerable degree of supervision, were women and juveniles, and received relatively low wages. The 1833 parliamentary report shows that the average ratio of overlookers to operatives was three times as high in power-loom weaving as in mule spinning, but only half as high in weaving as in throstle spinning.[87] Power-loom weaving, according to Factory Commissioner Cowell, was "the greatest single field for the employment of adult females" in the Lancashire cotton industry. From the outset power-loom weaving was regarded as a "woman's job" so that the wages of men who entered the occupation were "of course regulated by those of women," the commissioner stated.[88] The average weekly pay of factory weavers in 1833 was eleven shillings, or two-fifths the earnings of mule spinners, though three shillings above the rates received by throstle spinners. Such a wage differential between loom and throstle tenders may be attributed in part to the lower proportion of children under eighteen in factory weaving (33%) than in throstle spinning (51%).[89] Still, the single clear-cut difference between the social organization of the two mass production processes was the universal practice of employers to pay loom tenders by the piece and throstle tenders by the day.[90]

Throstle spinners were paid by time and weavers by task for two probable reasons. First, a daily wage was an innovation of factories. Payments by results were universal in the putting out industries and were introduced into the early factories for all classes of operatives who had equivalents in the earlier domestic industry.[91] Since the gap between the throstle and the traditional spinning wheel was so wide, throstle spinning was regarded as an entirely new occupation. Accordingly, operatives were paid by the day. Power and hand weaving, on the other hand, were for a long transitional period complementary to each other and in many cases actually combined. Consequently, millowners who employed both domestic and factory weavers were encouraged to pay the latter in proportion to output simply as a matter of convenience in calculating labor costs. Equally important, however, was the fact that employers based their wage policies on the skill requirements of the job. Although power-loom weaving was a machine-tending occupation, it required a more frequent intervention in the production process than throstle spinning, and payment by results was important incentive to increase output.[92]

The resemblance between British and American management of power-loom factories provides additional evidence of support to the importance of technology in the social organization of production. As in England, American loom tenders in the 1830s were mostly women[93] who were subject to considerable control by management (a ratio of one to twenty-three supervisors to workers in a typical Lowell mill[94] as compared to one to twenty-eight in

Lancashire), earned slightly better wages than throstle spinners ($4.00 as compared to $3.50 a week)[95] but far below the rates of mule spinners, and were always paid in proportion to output.

Yet there were important differences between the two American mill systems. First of all, virtually all weavers and dressers employed in Lowell-type plants were women, whereas a minority of power-loom weavers and nearly all dressers employed by Slater-type firms (in New England as well as Pennsylvania) were adult males. Second, while the Lowell-type corporations always paid workers directly, the scant evidence we possess shows a few cases of factory weavers in Slater-type mills who subcontracted helpers. Barbara Tucker's examination of the Slater's company books conveys nonetheless the impression that insofar as the subcontract system was used in the weaving departments of American mills, it could not have been as widespread as in Britain, and more important, it did not survive the 1840s. Beginning in the 1830s and throughout the 1840s, management in Slater's mill at Webster, Massachusetts, was making systematic efforts to put an end, once and for all, to the practice of subcontracting in both mule spinning and power-loom weaving, thus eliminating "the last vestiges" of the domestic organization of production.[96]

Chapter 4
The Survival of Craft Control in Britain

Like the crossbow, the stagecoach and the square-rigged clipper ship, the mule burst upon an astonished world, had its brief hour of glory and is now eclipsed. To coming generations it may seem incredible that such a machine, with a carriage 150 feet long and carrying 1,300 spindles in a single row, could ever have been built. It will seem even less credible that in Lancashire alone there were once nearly 50,000,000 mule spindles, each accelerated to 10,000 rpm before being stopped and reversed with infinite precision four times a minute throughout a fifty-six hour week. Soon there will be only a few drastically shortened remnants of this great army of awe-inspiring machines standing lifeless in our museums to remind us of what has been.

> Harold Catling,
> *The Spinning Mule*
> (Newton Abbot, Devon: David and Charles, 1973), pp. 192-93.

The survival of mule-spinning technology in Britain for nearly two centuries is indeed amazing: in no other country did the mule play such a critical role for so long a period.[1] The success of British mule spinners in retaining control of their craft intact over a period of about 180 years, from the two closing decades of the eighteenth century when the mule had first gone into operation until almost the demise of the industry in the 1960s, is even more remarkable. Craft control had always been the distinctive characteristic of British mule spinning.[2]

To understand how this process actually did occur we need first to know more about the technology. Far-reaching technological innovations were introduced during the first hundred years in which the mule was used as the principal cotton-spinning machine by British manufacturers. Broadly speaking, the spinning mule had gone through three major phases of development. The hand mule had first appeared in the late 1770s, the power-driven mule was taking over the industry by the turn of the century, and between 1840 and 1880 the self-acting mule was steadily making its progress. With each successive stage a number of hand motions were subject to mechanization, yet even the improved "self-acting" machine was not fully automatic.

The entire yarn production process—drawing, twisting, and winding—was performed manually on the hand mule. The rollers, spindles, and carriage were connected to a large handle cranked by hand. Turning the handle, however, involved a great deal of skill and dexterity because the speed of the moving parts required frequent correction in order to spin and wind even-count yarn without breaking the thread.[3]

When the mule was first attached to power only the spindles and rollers revolved automatically. The spinner had to pull out and push in the carriage by hand. But even when power was applied to the running of the carriage in the more advanced mules, it was limited to the outward run. Driving the carriage back manually in a speed proportional to that of the spindles, while at the same time coiling the thread into a conoid shape, required, as noted, hand, eye, and knee coordination that only long and rigorous training could provide. It required physical strength as well, for the mule became heavier and heavier. The original mule invented by Samuel Crompton contained fewer than 30 spindles; hand mules had from 100 to 130 spindles in the 1780s[4] and by 1792 the average number of spindles on a Lancashire mule was 160.[5] In 1795 the mule manufacturing firm of McConnel and Kennedy wrote one of its customers: "It is difficult to fix what number of spindles may be most profitable as what was thought best only two years ago is now thought too small. 216 [spindles on a mule] is made to run as light now as 144 used to do then." In 1795 McConnel and Kennedy were already making water- and steam-powered mules with 180 to 288 spindles each.[6] Power-driven mules increased in size to more than 300 spindles by the turn of the century, 600 spindles in the 1820s, and up to 800 or even 1,000 by the late 1830s.[7] Apart from the steady enlargement in the size of machines, employers further intensified the labor of spinners by putting each operative in charge of two power-driven mules operating simultaneously.

The next step in the mechanization of mule spinning was the invention of the self-acting mule. The self actor was patented in 1825 by Richard Roberts of Sharp Roberts and Co., Manchester. From the early 1830s the new machine was manufactured for commercial use, but not until after 1840 was it introduced into British cotton spinning factories on a large scale.[8]

Writing in 1835, Andrew Ure, a vocal advocate of employers' interests, declared: "The effect of substituting the self-acting mule for the common mule is to discharge the greater part of the men spinners, and to retain adolescents and children." An automatic mule would have reduced the production costs because the expensive skill of craftsmen would no longer be necessary. In addition, replacing adult males with women and juveniles would have solved labor problems caused by the militant spinners' unions. In the same year, the editor of the *Journal of the Franklin Institute* brought the self-acting mule to the attention of American manufacturers, pointing out, similarly, that one advantage of the new machine was to "render [millowners] independent of the working spinners whose combinations and stoppages of work [had] often been extremely annoying to the masters." Contrary to employers' expectations, however, adult males managed to fully retain their position as mule spinners in Britain as well as in the United States.[9]

Admittedly, the self actor did not live up to the claims of its inventor; it did not become perfectly automatic. But at the same time the self-acting mule greatly diminished the skill of the spinner by eliminating many of the skill requirements of the job.

Spinning on power-driven mules required continuous attendance of the mule spinner, draw by draw, round-trip of the carriage after round-trip. Two draws a minute in fine spinning, four draws a minute in coarse spinning—the mule spinner had to push the carriage, vary the speed of the spindles, and regulate the winding carefully during every draw on each of the two mules, twelve hours a day. Spinning on self-acting mules, by contrast, required no manual assistance during most of the working day. For one thing, the self actor drove the carriage mechanically back and forth on the rail. For another, it synchronized automatically the speed of the moving carriage and the speed of the rotating spindles. It thus relieved the spinner both from the sheer physical effort required to push the carriage back in, and from the complex task of coordinating delicately the speed of the carriage and that of the spindles.[10]

The remaining problem inhibiting the complete automation of the mule lay in the winding motion. A quadrant nut or a quarter wheel was designed by Roberts to synchronize automatically the speed of the spindles in inverse proportion to the diameter of the cop and in direct proportion to the inward speed of the carriage. Despite Roberts' promises, however, two aspects of the winding process were not mechanized. First, for the first few minutes in which the cop was beginning to be formed the spinner had to adjust the quadrant nut during nearly every draw. As the cop diameter enlarged, the need for adjustments fell, and when the cop bottom reached near completion, adjustments were needed for only one in every twenty draws. Once the cop bottom was completed, manual adjustments were no longer needed. Altogether, about ninety adjustments were required on the self-acting mule during the first four hours of a twenty-hour winding cycle in which a set of cops (yarn no. 80's) was being completed. On the power-driven mule, by contrast, the manual regulation of the winding was necessary for each and every draw, that is, 1,500 to 3,000 times a day. Furthermore, "the actual making of adjustments [on the self actor] was simplicity itself," as evidenced by the practice common among British mule spinners to place an experienced child helper near the mule's control mechanism and have him make the adjustments in response to the agreed hand signals of the spinner.

Second, to prevent snarling, the spinner had to manually delay the rise of the "faller" (a wire used to guide the thread) during the last few inches of the winding for each run of the carriage in the last stages of the cop formation. The manual regulation of the faller was needed only during the critical last hour of the total twenty-hour winding cycle. During most of its running time the mule was completely self-acting.[11]

Although the adjustment of the quadrant nut required attentiveness, and although the regulation of the faller demanded a certain degree of dexterity, both of these operations could be taught in a relatively brief period of training. By no means did their execution constitute any longer a highly skilled craft, as had been the case with the hand mule and, to a considerable extent, with the power-driven mule as well.[12] Yet "self-actor minders" claimed craft status on the basis of these operations. Moreover, even when it became technically feasible to mechanize these manual tasks further (by way of reducing the number of adjustments of the quadrant nut from ninety to five, for example), the British spinners still retained their craft control untouched. As late as 1892, James Mawdsley, secretary of the Amalgamated Association of Operative Cotton Spinners, was firmly convinced that "no two spinners will manage a pair of mules alike."[13]

This rather peculiar British experience raises immediately a number of questions. What did craft control concretely mean? Which aspects of the job did it involve? How was it possible to exercise these controls at all without practicing a craft?

In analyzing these problems, it is helpful to distinguish among three types of controls that correspond to three dimensions of a given job. The first is *control over the production process*. This means the ability of workers to direct themselves and to direct others. It is, in other words, the craftsman's autonomy at work. The second is *control over recruitment*. To regulate entry into the occupation craft unions incorporated elaborate apprenticeship regulations into their rules. *Control over piece rates* represents the third dimension. The ability of workers who are paid by results to insure themselves against increases in output with no corresponding raises in wages might be called piece rates control. A craft union would typically bargain with employers on a "standard list of prices."

THE PRODUCTION PROCESS

"The functional autonomy of craftsmen," observed David Montgomery, "rested on both their superior knowledge...and the supervision which they gave to one or more helpers."[14] The "superior knowledge" of British mule spinners steadily eroded during the nineteenth century. Their supervisory functions, on the other hand, scarcely diminished. From the days mule spinning had first become a factory trade until after the decline of the industry in the twentieth century, British spinners had the prerogative to subcontract their own helpers. Supervision thus became a distinctive feature of the craft and it survived long after the skill itself had dissipated.

"The spinner has from one to six juvenile assistants according to the magnitude of his spinning machine," wrote the factory commissioner of the Lancashire District in 1834.[15] The number of assistants, however, was dependent not only on the size, but on the type of the mule machine as well. In general, the longer the mule and the finer the yarn spun, the more helpers were required to assist a spinner. Longer mules carried a large number of spindles with a large number of threads to watch, and accordingly, more piecers were needed to manage the threads. Fine spinning, similarly, required more piecing than coarse spinning because fine, high count yarns were more likely to break under mechanical handling. For a given number of spindles, then, a fine mule spinner would ordinarily employ more helpers than a coarse spinner.

The typical hand mule in the 1780s—a single machine of one-hundred spindles—was so small that the operative spinner hardly required any assistance. He could perform much of the piecing and cleaning himself. The application of steam power steadily enlarged the size of machines yet the small mule survived well into the nineteenth century. As late as 1841, to give one example, the mule spinners in one Manchester coarse-spinning mill did not employ any helpers at all; evidently, their power-driven mules were "all short."[16]

This, of course, was not a typical case. In much the same way, four, five, or six helpers to a spinner was rather exceptional; the increase in the number of assistants during the 1820s and 1830s has been exaggerated by both Andrew Ure and Neil Smelser.[17] By 1833, it is true, power-driven mules varied enormously in the number of spindles from some 200 to 800 each, or 400 to 1,600 for a pair,[18] but the most commonly used machine in British factories had from 300 to 400 spindles each.[19] To operate a pair of mules with a total number of 600 to 800 spindles, a spinner would require the assistance of two piecers and a share of the services of one scavenger.

These figures are derived from the factory commissioner survey of 1834. Altogether, 3,797 operative mule spinners gave supervision to 8,404 assistants, 7,157 piecers, and 1,247 scavengers, a ratio of 2.2 helpers to spinners in 151 Lancashire cotton mills. In towns specializing in coarse spinning, for example, Oldham, Brinnington, and Hyde, the proportion was lower, 1.6 or 1.7 helpers to a spinner. In Manchester and Bolton—the chief centers of factory fine spinning—the ratio was higher: 2.5 assistants per spinner. More complete returns from seventeen Bolton mills show an even higher proportion: 3.12 to 1 in 1833. At that date, a Bolton fine spinner and his three helpers managed together an average number of 732 high count cotton threads on two mules.[20]

The mule spinner had complete shop floor control over his helpers. So jealously did the spinners guard their autonomy that any employer who attempted to challenge their control faced the immediate threat of a strike. In Glasgow in 1824 the spinners in one large mill went on strike demanding the removal of an overlooker who was abusing their piecers, and in 1822 the spinners at another factory near Glasgow struck work calling for the dismissal of an overlooker and two managers who were "too vigilant." The dismissal was

rejected; nonetheless both overlooker and managers were publicly reprimand-
ed by the employers upon the insistance of the mule spinners.[21]

Minders had the same prerogatives as spinners. From the outset self-actor
minders supervised two helpers on a pair of mules. Notwithstanding a steady
increase in the size of machinery, the basic unit of production—a team of three
workers on a pair of self actors—remained unchanged[22] In 1833 the pioneering
self actors had from 360 to 480 spindles. In the 1870s the number of spindles
mounted on a self actor was from 720 to 960. By 1910, 1,080 spindles was the
usual size of a single self-acting spinning machine.[23] Partly because the self actor
relieved the minder of the need to push the carriage back by hand, and also because the adjustment of the quadrant nut and the manipulation of the guide wire
were limited to brief periods during the first and last stages of the cop formation,
the minder was now free to do a great deal of the piecing on the new machines.
Since self-actor minders assisted in piecing, and since, moreover, the early self
actors were suited for coarse spinning and therefore did not require as much
piecing, the minder could now manage a pair of larger and faster machines with
only two helpers. Harold Catling, son of a minder and a former mule piecer,
describes the organization of work in factories that adopted the new technology:

> There was a clear division of responsibilities for the running of each pair
> of mules. From the main access alley to the headstock of each mule of
> the pair was known as the minder's half. Beyond the headstock was the
> big piecer's half. Normally the minder was assisted in the routine task
> of piecing by the little piecer, but the big piecer was expected to keep his
> half up unaided. Menial tasks such as floor sweeping and weft carrying
> were done for both halves by the little piecer.[24]

Like his forerunner the spinner, the minder was in complete control of production. Each pair of self actors was a self-contained, autonomous unit of work
directed by a minder. The minder's control of production rested on his privilege
of setting the speed of the machinery and on his autonomy from management
supervision. Working the hand mule or the semi-power mule, the spinner
regulated the speed of the carriage with his muscles. Tending the self actor,
he regulated the speed of the carriage with mechanical power. "The English
spinner does not need overlooking the same as the German," wrote G. Schulze-
Gaevernitz in 1895 in his comparative study of the cotton industry, noting that
one overlooker was in charge of 60,000 to 80,000 mule spindles in Britain as
compared to 10,000 to 20,000 in Germany. A typical Oldham mule room with
70,000 spindles mounted on thirty pair of mules gave employment to thirty
minders, sixty piecers, and only one overlooker, a ratio of one foreman to ninety
workers at the close of the century.[25] In the mid 1890s a larger spinning department with forty pair of mules employed forty minders, eighty piecers, and two
overlookers, a ratio of one supervisor to sixty operatives organized in twenty
work teams.[26]

Like the early mule spinners, moreover, minders, not overlookers or

managers, gave orders to piecers. Any attempts on the part of management
to interfere with the minders' shop-floor authority over piecers—two such cases
in 1888 are cited by Lazonick from *Cotton Factory Times*[27]—were fiercely opposed by the unions. The minders, in addition, challenged management's
prerogative of hiring overlookers: when in 1870 a Lancashire millowner fired
an overlooker sympathetic to the minders, the union struck immediately in
order to force the employer to reinstate the man.[28] The minders' success in defen-
ding their autonomy, we shall see below, was rooted in the control their union
exercised over recruitment.

RECRUITMENT

Early friendly societies among domestic textile workers were preoccupied
with maintaining the traditional seven years apprenticeship, a custom codified
in the 1563 Elizabethan Statute of Apprentices for "any art, mistery, or manual
occupation."[29] Apprenticeship was a method of formal instruction, but far more
important, it served as a means to restrict acquisition of skills, thereby preven-
ting job competition, wage depression, and unemployment. In their early attempts to impose apprenticeship regulations the mule spinners followed the examples of hand-loom weavers and other organized groups of domestic
workers.[30]

The 1792 and 1795 rules of the Stockport and Manchester spinners' societies,
as well as the 1796 rules of the Oldham society, included strict apprenticeship
regulations. In 1792 the Manchester spinners prohibited anyone who learned
to spin elsewhere from working in Manchester unless he paid 10.5 shillings to
the Society.[31] The Oldham and Manchester unions' rules of 1795-96 required
members to withhold information on earnings from non-members in order to
discourage outsiders from entering the trade. It was "an original device," commented Sidney Chapman, "for stopping apprentices at the source."[32] To
guarantee their control over recruitment by way of selecting journeymen exclusively from their own apprentices, the Manchester spinners further attempted in 1810 to fill each vacancy from a list of three names submitted to the
employer.[33] In the 1820s other local unions demanded that vacancies be filled
only from names submitted by the union.[34] One witness before the Factory
Inquiry Commission was particularly impressed by the Glasgow mule spinners who had organized themselves into a "close exclusive societ[y]" and staged
sporadic strikes at individual mills during the early 1820's in order to exclude
"obnoxious" spinners.[35] By an 1830 resolution of the Grand General Union of
the Operative Cotton Spinners of England, Ireland, and Scotland, a spinner
"acting contrary" to the union's apprenticeship rules had to pay a fine of "Half-
a-Guinea" for the first offense, "one Guinea" for the second offense, and for
the third, "be expelled [from] the Society, and have his name exposed throughout
the trade."[36] In the 1820s and 1830s, evidently, mule spinners' district societies
had close to 100% organization in British cotton towns.[37]

The mule spinner's apprentices were his piecers. Initially, on the small mules, every piecer was an apprentice designated for future spinning. The increase in the number of piecers on the large machines, however, upset this system; and the spinners, after unsuccessful attempts to resist the introduction of longer mules, solved the problem by refusing to recognize all piecers as "learners."[38] To prevent piecers from competing for jobs on which journeymen were dependent, spinners restricted apprenticeship status to one assistant—the big piecer— thus creating a situation whereby unapprenticed, unskilled piecers would not attain a spinner position. One way to limit the number of apprentices was to exclude women from spinning but not from piecing. Restricting the rights to learn to spin to family members was another method, as evidenced in the 1830 resolutions of the Grand General Union.[39] "This association binds and obliges every one of its members," says one of the regulations, "to refrain from instructing any individual in the art of spinning, except such as are sons or brothers of a spinner." Furthermore, "such persons can only be admissible, by having served [the spinners] as piecers; and individuals having admissible piecers may not take advantage of their neighbour, they are strictly prohibited from allowing such piecers to spin in their absence, they must follow their draws, and overlook them in all their instructions and practice."[40]

This elaborate rule was designed not so much to restrict *instruction* as to limit the *actual right to spin*. Why else would "admissible piecers" be "strictly prohibited" from spinning without supervision? After all, operating the power-driven mule in 1838 did not require as much skill as working the hand mule in the 1790s. And with the rapid diffusion of the self actor after 1838, an observant piecer could acquire the skills of spinning without much learning. Control over entry into the occupation became therefore an essential element in the strategy of the mule spinners' unions to protect their craft status. Typically, the "right to a trade" was a family heritage—an exclusive privilege granted by fathers to their sons and relations.[41]

In Britain, moreover, the slow pace of technological change was conducive to retaining craft control. The self-acting mule had appeared in the 1830s but was not used for fine spinning until the 1860s.[42] In 1870 the self actor was still limited to spinning yarn counts in the 50s and under; it did not entirely supercede the power-driven mule until after the mid 1880s.[43] Spinning on power-driven and self-acting mules was thus complementary and often actually combined; the operators of both kinds of machines were found in the same factory and even in the same department.[44]

Spinners and minders not only worked side by side in the same mills but also enrolled in a combined union. Early minders joined mule spinners' societies during the 1830s and 1840s and became subject to their union rules. In 1842 the minders participated in the formation of the Association of Operative Cotton Spinners, Twiners, and Self-Actor Minders of the United Kingdom. However, to protect their threatened craft as well as their high wages, the old mule spinners expelled the new minders from their ranks in a number of local unions. Later the minders formed their own organization; they adopted first the rules of the mule spinners and then in 1870 assumed their title also: The Amalgamated Association of Operative Cotton Spinners and Twiners. By 1880 the small number of spinners who still operated power-driven mules joined the minders' federation.[45] In 1910 (as in 1868) there were nine unionists for every non-union man among the Lancashire self-actor minders.[46]

The minders, like the spinners, converted the subcontract system itself into a system of recruitment control. Union seniority rules replaced the old apprenticeship regulations; the self-actor spinners (as the minders were now called) created a promotion ladder and enforced the selection of new recruits exclusively from the ranks of their own helpers in a strict order of seniority at the individual mill. At any one time during the nineteenth century piecers outnumbered spinners and therefore not every piecer had a chance of promotion. At the end of the century piecers outnumbered spinners by three to one.[47]

Subcontracting was not only a system of recruitment but also a system of unequal wages. In 1871 self-actor spinners received from twenty-four to thirty shillings a week while big piecers earned from nine to sixteen shillings.[48] The big piecer, almost invariably an adult male, was "roughly as efficient as the minder." Tending together a pair of self actors the spinner and the big piecer performed, by and large, an identical task, namely piecing up broken threads. "I am inclined to think that had it not been for the policy of the spinners," wrote Sidney Chapman in 1900, "the two adults on the mule would be receiving wages more nearly alike than they are today."[49] The wage differentials between big piecers and spinners in the 1900s were as wide, if not wider, as they had been in the 1870s. In 1906, for example, spinners collected forty to forty-seven shillings per week and big piecers sixteen to eighteen.[50]

STANDARD PIECE RATES

While the craftsman's autonomy and apprenticeship regulations were firmly established from the pioneering days of the industry, the regulation of "fair prices" was an issue over which the unions fought time and again during the nineteenth century. Collective bargaining between unions and employers on a "Printed List of Prices" had first appeared in the 1820s, but not until after 1850 did the mule spinners' unions achieve effective control over the regulation of wages.

Hand-mule spinners, like hand-loom weavers, had first worked in cottages, buying raw material from cotton manufacturers and selling back their finished products, as the early entrepreneurial experience of Robert Owen and Peter Drinkwater suggests.[51] The pioneering mule workshops and factories merely reproduced the capitalist domestic system under a single roof: spinners often owned their own mules, renting space and power, buying carded cotton, and selling their yarn at set prices to their suppliers—the mill owners.[52] To deal with masters on prices, mule spinners customarily combined. The earliest known

The MANCHESTER LIST of PRICES for spinning upon Mules of different Sizes.

	Spindles, 300.	Spindles, 312.	Spindles, 324.	Spindles, 336.	Spindles, 348.	Spindles, 360.	Spindles, 372.	Spindles, 384.	Spindles, 396.	Spindles, 408.	Spindles, 420.	Spindles, 432.	Spindles, 444.	Spindles, 456.	Spindles, 468.
	s. d.	s. d.	s. d.	s. d.	s. d.	s. d.	s. d.	s. d.	s. d.	s. d.	s. d.	s. d.	s. d.	s. d.	s. d.
Nº 80	0 5	0 5	0 4¾	0 4¾	0 4¾	0 4½	0 4½	0 4½	0 4½	0 4¼	0 4¼	0 4¼	0 4	0 4	0 4
– 85	0 5½	0 5½	0 5¼	0 5¼	0 5¼	0 5	0 5	0 5	0 4¾	0 4¾	0 4½	0 4½	0 4½	0 4½	0 4½
– 90	0 6	0 6	0 5¾	0 5¾	0 5¾	0 5½	0 5½	0 5½	0 5¼	0 5¼	0 5	0 5	0 5	0 5	0 5
– 95	0 6¾	0 6¾	0 6½	0 6½	0 6¼	0 6¼	0 6	0 6	0 5¾	0 5¾	0 5½	0 5½	0 5½	0 5½	0 5½
– 100	0 7½	0 7½	0 7¼	0 7¼	0 7	0 7	0 6¾	0 6¾	0 6½	0 6½	0 6¼	0 6¼	0 6¼	0 6¼	0 6¼
– 105	0 8¼	0 8¼	0 8	0 8	0 7¾	0 7¾	0 7½	0 7½	0 7¼	0 7¼	0 7	0 7	0 6¾	0 6¾	0 6¾
– 110	0 9¼	0 9¼	0 9	0 8¾	0 8¾	0 8½	0 8½	0 8¼	0 8¼	0 8	0 7¾	0 7½	0 7½	0 7½	0 7½
– 115	0 10¼	0 10¼	0 10	0 9¾	0 9¾	0 9½	0 9½	0 9¼	0 9	0 8¾	0 8¾	0 8½	0 8½	0 8½	0 8½
– 120	0 11½	0 11¼	0 11	0 11	0 10¾	0 10¾	0 10½	0 10¼	0 10	0 9¾	0 9¾	0 9½	0 9½	0 9¼	0 9¼
– 125	1 0¾	1 0½	1 0¼	1 0¼	1 0	1 0	0 11¾	0 11½	0 11¼	0 11	0 10¾	0 10½	0 10½	0 10¼	0 10¼
– 130	1 2¼	1 2	1 1¾	1 1½	1 1½	1 1¼	1 1	1 0¾	1 0½	1 0¼	1 0	0 11¾	0 11¾	0 11½	0 11½
– 135	1 3½	1 3¼	1 3	1 2¾	1 2¾	1 2½	1 2¼	1 2	1 1¾	1 1½	1 1¼	1 1	1 0¾	1 0½	1 0¼
– 140	1 5	1 4¾	1 4½	1 4¼	1 4	1 3¾	1 3½	1 3¼	1 3	1 2¾	1 2½	1 2¼	1 2	1 1¾	1 1½
– 145	1 6½	1 6¼	1 6	1 5¾	1 5¼	1 5	1 4¾	1 4½	1 4¼	1 4	1 3¾	1 3½	1 3¼	1 3	1 2¾
– 150	1 8	1 7¾	1 7½	1 7¼	1 6¾	1 6½	1 6¼	1 6	1 5¾	1 5¼	1 5	1 4¾	1 4½	1 4	1 3½
– 155	1 9½	1 9¼	1 8¾	1 8½	1 8	1 7¾	1 7½	1 7¼	1 7	1 6½	1 6¼	1 6	1 5¾	1 5½	1 5
– 160	1 11	1 10½	1 10¼	1 10	1 9½	1 9¼	1 9	1 8½	1 8¼	1 7¾	1 7½	1 7¼	1 7	1 6½	1 6
– 165	2 1	2 0¾	2 0¼	2 0	1 11½	1 11	1 10¾	1 10¼	1 10	1 9¾	1 9½	1 9	1 8¾	1 8¼	1 8
– 170	2 3¼	2 3	2 2½	2 2	2 1½	2 1	2 0¾	2 0¼	2 0	1 11¾	1 11½	1 11	1 10½	1 10	1 9½
– 175	2 6	2 5½	2 5	2 4½	2 4	2 3½	2 3¼	2 2¾	2 2¼	2 2	2 1½	2 1	2 0¾	2 0¼	1 11½
– 180	2 8¾	2 8¼	2 7¾	2 7¼	2 6¾	2 6¼	2 6	5¼ 2	2 4¾	2 4¼	2 3¾	2 3¼	2 3	2 2½	2 2

20th March 1829. (Signed) G. E. AUBREY.

Parliamentary Papers, 1834, XIX. *First Supplementary Report of the Factor Inquiry Commission.*

The Mule Spinner and His Helpers at Work

The spinner has just turned around to push the carriage of the other mule, while the piecer, still busy tying broken ends on the carriage of the mule on the left, is ready to join the spinner in a moment. When the carriage of the mule on the left will come out again, the scavenger will duck and let the machine pass over his body so that he can clean the carriage from within. The drawing shows only one-half of each mule, and there was at least one more piecer employed on the other half, beyond the headstock. There is one misleading thing about the drawing, however: the ''gentleman'' with the stick, overlooking the mule. A typical mule room with 20-25 pairs—just like the one in the drawing—had only one overlooker. How could he supervise more than one pair at a time?

Andrew Ure, *The Philosophy of Manufacturers*. London, 1835.

record of a mule spinners' union, that of the Stockport Society in 1785, shows that members were prohibited from working "under the usual prices."[53]

The "usual prices" were regulated by custom.[54] Insofar as the size range of yarns spun was comparatively small, the piece rate system was relatively simple. A single price or piece rate was determined and held by custom over a producing district. With the rapid mechanization of mule spinning, however, the mule reached a degree of fineness by the end of the century that was four or five times as high as two decades earlier. Expressed by trade conventions, the mule spun yarn with counts number 80 in the 1780s, 180 in 1795, and 300 by 1800.[55] At the same time the number of spindles on a single mule steadily increased, doubling the size of machines between 1780 and 1800. The result was a wide range of mules of different sizes that spun diverse types of cotton threads. The determination of wages was no longer a simple matter, and therefore a "list" was required.

The first district wage list for mule spinning of which record survives appeared in Bolton, a center of factory fine spinning, in 1813. There are scattered references to lists in Bolton, Manchester, Oldham, and Glasgow between 1823 and 1826, and by 1830 the district price list became the rule in many cotton towns. The Bolton list of 1813 clearly embodied the principle of prices varying with the quality of yarn, but it is not certain whether it also included a scale of rates according to the size of machines. In 1823 the Bolton employers drew up a new list based explicitly on the principle of reduced price rates on "larger wheels"—mules having greater number of spindles. Soon adopted by employers in Manchester and other towns, this principle was at the core of most mule spinners' disputes in the following decade.[56]

The 1829 "Manchester List of Prices for Spinning upon Mules of Different Sizes" is printed in the 1834 Factory Commissioners' report of the Lancashire District. Prices on the list fall as the number of spindles increases, and rise as the count number (fineness) goes up. The smaller was the mule and the finer the yarn spun, the higher was the wage received by a mule spinner for producing one pound of yarn.[57]

The list is based on a standard rate. First, a standard price rate was fixed for a typical unit of output of a mule of a typical size. Next, variations from the standard product expressed by the number of counts and by the number of spindles were graded systematically. Then, for each point of variation from either the standard product or the standard machine, adjustments were made by additions or subtractions. Collective bargaining between employers and spinners was mainly concerned with fixing the standard rate.

The standard list of prices guaranteed spinners a minimum wage, and more important, it provided a measure of protection against arbitrary cuts in the piece rate. Employers could not change unilaterally any of the rates without revising the entire list. Production gains due to technological improvements and market fluctuations were the two main causes that led employers and unions to negotiate new standard rates. Yet, while collective bargaining took the form of violent strike waves during the 1820s and 1830s, the 1850s and 1860s were marked by a decline in strike activity as a result of close cooperation between management and workers in setting the standard price list.

In the 1820s and 1830s spinners operated power-driven mules. The sheer physical effort required from a spinner to push back the heavy carriage made mule spinning one of the most laborious occupations in early nineteenth century Britain. A witness before the Select Committee on Combinations of Workmen reported in 1837-38 that driving a 1,400 pound carriage with 336 spindles "5,000 times in 12 hours" (or 2,500 times each carriage of the pair) required "an energy of 160 lbs., or the same mechanical exertion which would raise 160 lbs. . . . over the distance of six feet in three seconds." The manual manipulation of the faller, or guide wire, likewise involved "a considerable force."[58]

The power-driven mule in the 1830s represents the most advanced stage of the old technology. While the carriage became steadily heavier during the four decades in which the power mule was perfected, the basic manual tasks remained unchanged, and therefore the spinner, still pushing back the carriage by hand, had to work harder and harder.

This is precisely why mule spinners so vigorously opposed employers' attempts to reduce prices on the longer mules. Employers, as noted, drew up lists of prices based on the principle of reduced rates on larger machines. Spinners, on the other hand, demanded a uniform rate "on all sizes of wheels" subject to variation only according to the quality of yarn. The 1823-24 Bolton strike, the gigantic "long wheel" strikes that erupted throughout the Lancashire region in 1829-30—particularly the 1829 Manchester strike and the Ashton under Lyne strike of 1830—as well as the 1836-37 Preston strike and the Glasgow strike of 1837, were all fought over this issue.[59] The mule spinners unions, nonetheless, were defeated. They were forced to accept the new principle of reduced rates on longer mules, and during the next decade they redirected their efforts from piece rates control to wider political issues such as shorter hours and Chartism.

When the self-acting mule began taking over the industry, control over wage rates once again became a major preoccupation of unions: by mid-century spinners demanded price lists more than anything else. A seven-month strike over this issue took place in Preston in 1853-54, and although the mule spinners lost the strike, their demand for a self actor spinning list was granted five years later.[60] By 1864 Arthur Arnold could declare that a "standard list of prices for spinning. . . [was] published in most of the chief centers of the manufacture."[61] Price lists for self-actor minders first appeared in Blackburn in 1853, then in Bolton (1858), Preston (1859), Ashton (1860), Bury, Burnley and Stockport (1867), and Hyde (1872). All these wage lists were based on *exactly* the same principles of the older lists for spinning on power-driven mules. They were composed of two scales: the number of spindles and the number of counts. Yet since the self actor was a more efficient machine than the older mule, a new list was now taken as the standard; hence the piece rates of minders were lower than those of mule spinners.[62]

Self-actor minders exercised a great deal of control over wage rates. They were, above all, protected against any arbitrary reduction of wages due to the business cycle. "The standard list of prices," wrote Arnold, "is not affected by fluctuation in wages, any rise or fall being accomplished by the addition and subtraction of a percentage agreed to by employers and employed ."[63] A testimony given by a Lancashire immigrant spinner before a U.S. Senate Committee in 1883 illustrates the extent to which collective bargaining was institutionalized in the British cotton industry after mid-century. "In England," pointed out the spinner, "both the Secretary of the Manufacturers Board and the Secretary of Spinners' Association have their eyes on the market all the time, and if there is a change in the market, the secretaries will ask through each other for a corresponding change in wages."[64] Similarly, the secretary of the North Lancashire Cotton Manufacturers' Association reported in 1892 that a large number of costly strikes were avoided as a result of the "perfectly good understanding" between the representatives of employers and spinners.[65] "Speaking as a trade-union secretary of nearly twenty years' experience," Thomas Ashton, head of the Oldham spinners, wrote in a letter addressed to the American consul in Manchester in 1884, "I have come to the conclusion that strikes are ruinous modes of settling differences between employers and employed, and... the best plan is for employers and employed to agree upon a rule of wages as a standard, and let the general state of trade afterwards govern such rate of wages up or down, always allowing reasonable profits to capital."[66] By 1893 the Brooklands Agreement was signed by representatives of the spinners' amalgamation and the employers' federation.

The Brooklands Agreement was described by Charles Macara, an employer who had participated in drafting it and shortly thereafter became the president of the Master Cotton Spinners' Federation, as "the most complete treaty between capital and labour that has ever been framed,"[67] and as "the greatest stroke of industrial statesmanship ever made."[68] The agreement had two major provisions. First, it limited cyclical fluctuations in wages to just one adjustment in any year of no more than 5% of the standard earnings, and second, it set up an elaborate grievance procedure to solve disputes. Its effects were to routinize industrial conflict through conciliation, to "incorporate" union officials into the conciliation procedure, and to avoid strikes at almost any cost, as James Mawdsley, the spinners' general secretary, noted in 1897: "The fact that we have got through a whole year without a single strike...proves that the working arrangements now in force have been of immense value to all concerned."[69] In the same year Sidney and Beatrice Webb published their classic study, *Industrial Democracy*, in which they express a similar view:

> The machinery for Collective Bargaining developed by the Cotton [Spinning] Operatives, in our opinion, approaches the ideal. We have, to begin

with, certain broad principles unreservedly agreed to throughout the trade. The scale of remuneration, based on these principles, is worked out in elaborate detail into printed lists, which... automatically govern the actual earnings of the several districts. The application, both of the general principles and of the lists, to particular mills and particular workmen, is made, not by the parties concerned, but by the joint decision of two disinterested professional experts, whose whole business in life is to secure, not the advantage of particular employer or workmen by whom they are called in, but uniformity in the application of the common agreement to all employers and workmen. The common agreements themselves are revised at rare intervals by representative joint committees, in which the professional experts on both sides exercise a great and even a preponderating influence. The whole machinery appears admirably contrived to bring about the maximum deliberation, security, stability, and promptitude of application.[70]

The Webbs overstate the case, however. Although the wage lists protected the spinners' earnings from being eaten away during depressions, the lists were not as effective against piece rate cuts made due to technological improvements. Nor were the lists effective against the phenomenon known as "bad spinning"— the employers' cost-cutting practice of using low-quality raw cotton which made it harder to keep the mules in motion without frequent breakages in the yarn. Bad spinning disputes were numerous and bitter in the 1880s and the Brooklands Agreement was supposed to have settled them through its multi-level grievance and conciliation system. But it did not. Rather, the grievance procedure allowed management to use inferior cotton without the fear of strikes while the grievance was being settled so that, in practice, the agreement failed to protect minders from piece rate cuts resulting from frequent yarn breakages.[71] Nevertheless, self-actor minders were scarcely affected by such reductions (or by reductions due to technological change) because they were able to pass on the increased workload to their helpers. The conclusion that follows elaborates this point.

CONCLUSION

Craft control in Britain was entrenched so deeply in customary union rules that no technological change could seriously undermine it. Deskilling, in fact, did not result in the loss of control but rather in its consolidation. It resulted, moreover, in a close cooperation between spinners and millowners: during the second half of the nineteenth century British mule spinners reached an accommodation with their employers.

Mule spinners in Britain converted the subcontract system into a system of entry control and unequal wages, forming what might be called an aristocracy of labor. Labor aristocracy in the British mule-spinning industry was not a new phenomenon emerging in the early 1850s, as John Foster has claimed in an influential study of Oldham, Shields, and Northampton, but was as old as the mule-spinning industry, dating back to the late eighteenth century. Even the term itself was not as new as Eric Hobsbawm—the initiator of the recent debate on labor aristocracy—once had supposed. Members of the Select Committee of 1837-38 commonly referred to the cotton mule spinners as an "aristocratic class amongst the labouring population," or plainly, "the aristocracy of skilled labour."[72]

Mule spinners were aristocrats on four different counts: authority at work, economic benefits, ability to exclude outsiders, and life style. Their authority at work was reflected by their privilege to direct helpers and by their autonomy from management supervision. The economic benefits they received were first and foremost a reward for their managerial responsibilities, not for their scarce "skills." On the shop floor their unions excluded from membership all other operatives; in the larger community "their status was recognized by the best rooms in some public houses being marked 'Mule Spinners Only'."[73]

Employers locked into competition and confronted with powerful unions neither challenged the spinners' aristocratic position, nor did they try to undermine the spinners' control. Instead they intensified labor on the larger and faster machines. Between 1865 and 1885, according to one estimate, the typical self-acting minder and his piecers experienced a stretch-out of 12-30% and a speed-up of 15-20%.[74] The gains in productivity were the most substantial in fine spinning: in one mill, for instance, the number of operatives required to manage 1,000 spindles dropped from 7.5 to 3 between 1850 and 1885.[75] To be sure, the provisions of the standard price lists ensured self-actor minders that a larger output as a result of harder work would lead to higher earnings. Still, the increase in wages fell short of the growth in productivity. By the mid 1890s the Lancashire minder was in charge of 15% more spindles than twenty years earlier and the machinery ran 12-15% faster, but his weekly wage bill increased by only 8-10%.[76] Nevertheless, the minders, by contrast to their forerunners the mule spinners, did not oppose the intensification of labor. Furthermore, unlike the older spinners' societies which resisted technological change (mule spinners often opposed the introduction of larger mules), the unions of minders were the most ardent supporters of any improvements in the self-acting mule technology.[77]

This important difference in the attitudes of spinners and minders may be explained by contrasting the actual tasks they performed. The mule spinner who underwent a great deal of stretch-out during the 1820s and 1830s had to work much harder pushing the heavy carriage with his muscles. The workload of piecers, on the other hand, was hardly affected by lengthening the mules. Ordinarily, the growing demand for piecing was met by adding more assistants. The self-actor minder, in contrast, was above all a supervisor who also assisted in piecing; his major operative task—thrusting the carriage—was completely mechanized. The growth in the size and speed of self actors, their application to fine spinning, and the widespread use of inferior cotton, all increased first and foremost the demand for piecing. But the minder could now pass on much of the increased workload to his piecers. Moreover, unlike the spinner, the minder did not usually hire additional helpers to meet the augmented workload; two piecers on a pair of self actors became the norm. As a result of all these changes the minders developed a conciliatory attitude toward employers: they cooperated with management in raising productivity on the self-acting mule. The decline in militancy of the British mule spinner after mid-century, in other words, was rooted in the shift of his *primary* responsibility from that of an operative to that of a supervisor.[78]

The decline in militancy, however, was a relative decline. The 1850s, 1860s, and early 1870s were by no means a period of industrial harmony, yet conflict was localized—there were no industry-wide struggles—and furthermore, the exceptional violence of the Industrial Revolution greatly diminished.[79] It is during these decades, moreover, that British mule spinners' unions developed a growing interest in emigration. By seeking to reduce the oversupply of spinners through emigration, the unions essentially identified their interests with the prosperity of their employers. The fact that the spinners' unions continued to advocate emigration and to operate emigration funds during most of the second half of the nineteenth century was thus another aspect of their conservative outlook.

Emigration, finally, was a selective process. Lancashire spinners' unions assisted above all their most experienced members and leaders—the typical victims of strikes—in immigrating to the United States. Such a policy contributed further to the conservative outlook of British mule spinners' organizations at home, and at the same time enhanced the militancy of American unions abroad.

Chapter 5
Immigration to the United States

Q. If the workmen in Glasgow are as well off as they were fifteen years ago, why do they emigrate?

A. In the spinning trade the emigration arises from its being a very profitable business to the operatives; and they are aware that a great excess of hands would have the effect of reducing wages; the combination therefore prefer the pecuniary sacrifice of sending as many of such excess away as is necessary to enable them to keep up the wages of those remaining; some of those sent to America are now returning.

Henry Houldsworth of Scotland
Report from the Select Committee for Manufactures, Commerce, and Shipping
Parliamentary Papers, 1833, VI, p. 311.

"Much of the skilled labor in the early mills," Caroline Ware observed, "was quite normally English and Scotch"; cotton mule spinners, apparently, were among the principal emigrants from the British Isles.[1] Scattered references to British immigrant mule spinners in the United States appear in the Pennsylvania Senate Journal of 1837-38 and in several case studies of the early New England cotton industry. More systematic data on immigration between 1770 and 1830 can now be found in David Jeremy's *Transatlantic Industrial Revolution*. Using British Customs' passenger lists, registration returns of the U.S. Department of State, and American ships' passenger lists, respectively, for three successive periods, Jeremy shows that in 1773-75 22 spinners left Britain for the United States, between 1809 and 1813 70 British spinners arrived in the United States, and during 1824-31 427 British spinners entered American ports.[2]

Jeremy's figures, however, neither allow us to estimate the actual number of *cotton mule* spinners, nor do they tell us whether immigrants changed jobs in the United States, nor whether immigrants went back to Britain after a short stay in America.

To be sure, the twenty-two spinners who arrived in the mid 1770s could not possibly have been mule spinners because the British mule was invented in 1779.[3] But in all likelihood, most spinners who emigrated in the early 1810s and late 1820s worked mules. Three circumstantial clues lead to this conclusion. First, very few spinners who specialized in fibers other than cotton—for example wool—arrived from Britain to the United States during 1810-30.[4] Second, a cotton mule spinner would customarily describe himself plainly as a "spinner" or sometimes a "cotton spinner" but would rarely use the term "mule spinner."[5] And third, mule spinning was an adult male occupation while throstle spinning—the alternative technique of cotton yarn production—was an occupation filled by women and children. Since 96% of the immigrant spinners recorded in 1809-13 and at least 71% in 1824-31 were men over nineteen, they were most probably mule and not throstle spinners.[6]

The number of British immigrant mule spinners who continued to practice their craft in the United States is much harder to estimate.[7] Given, however, the rapid growth of the American mule-spinning industry in the 1820s, the small number of British spinners who arrived during the period fell short of the American demand. Furthermore, some of the immigrant spinners returned to Britain, as evidenced in their testimonies before the parliamentary committees of the 1820s and 1830s. Jeremy has estimated that British immigrants could not have supplied much more than perhaps a quarter of the American need for adult male textile workers in the 1820s (and that, without considering reverse migration.[8] In Fall River in 1826, for example, native-born workers still accounted for nearly 94% of the 612 cotton mill operatives.[9]

During the next twenty-five years the proportion of British immigrants among American mule spinners climbed steeply. On the one side, the changing conditions of the British cotton industry during the period led a growing number of mule spinners to seek emigration; on the other, the rapid growth of the mule-spinning trade in the United States provided thousands of British cotton workers with alternative employment opportunities. As a result, an increasing number of spinners emigrated to the United States during the 1830s,[10] more came from Lancashire in the early 1840s,[11] and in spite of the growing prosperity in mid-century Britain, adult male textile workers were the leading group of industrial emigrants from England and Scotland who arrived in the port of New York between 1846 and 1854.[12] According to British government statistics cited by Charlotte Erickson, between 1862 and 1885 there were 11,668 spinners and weavers who left the United Kingdom, 83.7% of whom sailed to the United States.[13]

Who were the British emigrant mule spinners to the United States? To answer this question it is useful to distinguish between three types of causes or conditions that drove British spinners to seek employment across the Atlantic. The first was *technological unemployment*. The steady increase in the size of power-driven mules, the pairing of two mule machines together, and their replacement by the still larger and more productive self actors, eliminated many mule spinners' positions. At the same time, the apprenticeship system trained far more spinners than the number of available jobs. The second inducement for emigration was temporary *unemployment as a result of depressions*. The so-called "cotton famine"—the complete stoppage of raw cotton supply from the United States during its Civil War—created the most severe problem of unemployment in the British cotton industry during the nineteenth century; hence it precipitated emigration. *Blacklisting of militant unionists by British employers* was a third major impetus to emigration. British mule spinners' unions provided "victimized" members funds for emigration.

Technology, market conditions, and union policy were not mutually exclusive but rather complementary. Technological change created chronic unemployment problems in the British cotton industry from the early 1820s throughout the century. The cotton famine was responsible, directly and indirectly, for much of the emigration during the 1860s. The encouragement of emigration by British mule spinners' unions was most pronounced between 1850 and 1880. Ordinarily unions assisted blacklisted members and strikers, and occasionally, the temporarily unemployed as well.

TECHNOLOGICAL UNEMPLOYMENT

Mule spinning in Britain generated an oversupply of spinners in three different ways. First, fully apprenticed piecers, that is, adult piecers qualified to spin, outnumbered by far spinners' vacancies even during periods of most rapid expansion. This is because British mule spinners typically remained in their lucrative craft for life while apprentices served a maximum of seven years, and most often less than that. Second, unapprenticed piecers also acquired the skill of spinning, although *informally*, and when they reached the age of eighteen or twenty, they too were looking for better employment. A third source of oversupply was the enlargement of machines. Longer, more productive mules displaced spinners and at the same time increased the demand for piecers, thus aggravating further the problem of spinners who were unable to find employment in their occupation.

"The nature of the trade" is such that it "breeds up more persons to the business than can be supported by it," wrote Godfrey Lushington in 1860, referring to Lancashire in the 1830s. "Each spinner requires three piecers, who must be little children in the ages nine to fourteen; these therefore must be changed every four years; and when they leave him they normally take to the spinning trade, of which they have already acquired some experience."[14] Unemployment among adult piecers who could not attain mule spinners' positions was already a problem by the early 1820s; according to one employer, "boys from 16 to 20" were "too big for piecing," and since they were not allowed to spin, they were seldom employed.[15] By the 1830s and early 1840s, however, unemployment reached such a critical point that experienced spinners were losing their jobs.

In Manchester in 1831 there were between 700 and 1,000 "legally" apprenticed journeymen spinners who were out of work, and in Glasgow at least 200 in 1833.[16] In one Bolton mill in 1841, 20 of the 80 piecers employed were fully grown men who were "obliged" to take piecers' jobs.[17] In the same year Factory Inspector Leonard Horner reported that because of difficulties in finding better jobs, adults were filling piecers' positions; they could no longer become mule spinners at the age of eighteen but only at age twenty-five and older.[18] Two years later he was speaking of hundreds of men between the ages of twenty and thirty, "in the full vigour of life," who were employed as mule piecers.[19]

One reason why the effects of technological improvements on the employment of spinners culminated around 1840 was the introduction of doubledecked mules. "For every 300 spindles added to a machine by the method of yoking the wheels," to quote Lushington again, "a man was dismissed—a hardship not only to the man thus dismissed but to others; for it threw more hands into the labour market, already overstocked." The practice of "yoking the wheels," known also as "coupling" or "doubledecking," was a method of converting two small mules into a larger one by simply connecting them with one headstock (control mechanism) and thereby regulating their motion with a single movement. As a result of doubledecking, the spinner found himself in a position not unlike that of "a horse who ha[d] at the same time to draw two carts yoked to one another."[20] Since doubledecking became widespread in Britain at the time each spinner operated a pair of mules, under the new arrangement he would work four mules in two connected pairs. "By *coupling* mules, and thus throwing out of work *half* our spinners," one Manchester employer boasted, his firm succeeded in bringing about a "great reduction in the price paid for spinning in 1841, as compared with 1836." In another Manchester establishment, the owner cut the number of mule spinners by 40% between 1828 and 1840, while in one Bolton mill twenty-six spinners in 1841 were turning out the same amount of yarn as thirty-five had done in 1837. In still another Manchester factory in 1841, twenty-five mule spinners were doing the same amount of work of forty-six spinners in 1834.[21]

Case after case discussed by the factory inspectors in 1841 makes it plain that the coupling of mules represents a rather short-lived attempt of employers to render the old technology more productive in face of competition from the self-acting mule. The coming of the self actor by no means solved the problem, for the self-acting mule still required two piecers on a pair of machines, both eager to join in turn the ranks of mule spinners. Indeed, the augmented pool of big piecers waiting for promotion remained a chronic problem of the craft in Britain well into the twentieth century.

Consider the findings of the Royal Commission on Labour in 1892. According to the testimony of James Mawdsley, leader of the cotton spinners' unions and a member of the commission, the employment cycle in the mule-spinning trade at the end of the century was a three-phase process: a fourteen- or fifteen-year-old boy would enter the factory as a little piecer, a year or two later he would either quit or be promoted to the position of a big piecer, and at the age of twenty-one, after serving five years as a big piecer, he would become fully apprenticed. Every six years, in other words, each mule spinner would complete the training of one piecer qualified to take charge of a pair of self actors. But spinners, according to Mawdsley's considered opinion, held their jobs for an average period of twenty years, so each spinner trained at least three piecers during his entire career in the mill. What, then, was the fate of the other two piecers? Some, we are told, "remain[ed] piecers all their lives with an occasional attempt at spinning in case of the sickness of a spinner." Others drifted into "miscellaneous" unskilled occupations, for example, portering, hawking, or working as laborers in foundries. They were not likely to find skilled positions because all other high-paying craft jobs in nineteenth century Britain had their own forms of apprenticeship.[22]

Others considered emigration. Typically, unemployed spinners who decided to leave Britain preferred to emigrate to areas where their customary skills were much needed. New England was such a place. Favorable accounts of the employment opportunities in the United States reached England and Scotland as early as the 1820s through letters written by emigrant spinners to their friends and relatives.[23] An event of great significance was the publication in Glasgow in 1840 of a volume titled *A Practical Detail of the Cotton Manufacture of the United States*, by James Montgomery. Strongly urged by a number of friends to write an account of his lengthy trip to the United States, Montgomery thought that the information he collected would be "not altogether uninteresting" to many British cotton workers.[24] Montgomery's book presented the American trade in most appealing terms, reporting, for instance, that wages were higher in the United States than in Britain.[25] The volume was widely read and extensively reviewed[26] in England and Scotland in the early 1840s and it undoubtedly accelerated the movement of emigration among the highly literate mule spinners.[27]

During the 1840s the mule-spinning industry in New England was still decentralized over many small villages and towns throughout the rural areas of Rhode Island, Connecticut, and southern Massachusetts. In 1850, for example, twenty-two Rhode Island cotton towns had an average mill population of 560 workers each.[28] Fall River, situated on the Massachusetts-Rhode Island state line, was larger. Although still a small town, in 1850 Fall River had eight combined mule-spinning and weaving cotton mills which gave employment to 1,500 workers, only 68 of whom were adult male spinners.[29] The ratio of spinners to all cotton workers in Fall River was typical.[30]

The exact proportion of American mule spinners who were British immigrants is unknown. On the local level, however, such information can be extracted from the 1850 and 1860 manuscript schedules of the United States population census. According to federal census figures, 49 of the 68 adult male cotton spinners employed in Fall River in 1850 were born in Britain, and 15 in Ireland. Altogether, 94% were British and Irish. In 1860 Fall River cotton mills gave employment to 164 adult male spinners. Sixty-four percent were English and Scottish, nearly 33% were Irish, and a mere 3% were native-born, as shown

TABLE 7
Ethnic Background of Adult Male Spinners
Employed in Fall River, July-August 1850,
June-July 1860.

Country of Birth	1850[1]	1860[2]
Britain	72.1%	64.0%
Ireland	22.1%	32.9%
United States	5.9%	3.0%
Total Cases:	68	164

Sources: United States, Federal Manuscript Census of Fall River, 1850: Microcopy 432, Roll 308; 1860: Microcopy 653, Roll 491.

Notes: 1) The 1850 census records only the occupation of men age eighteen and older. It is plausible that nearly all these adult male spinners worked mules, but we do not know. The census enumerators used alternatively three job titles: "spinner," "cotton spinner," and "mule spinner." Spinners in mills other than cotton appear as "wool spinner," "flax spinner," etc.

2) In 1860 the census recorded both male and female occupations. Of the total of 188 cotton spinners employed in Fall River in 1860, 164 were adult males older than seventeen and 24 were women, juveniles, and children. Apart from one woman and a sixteen-year-old boy described as "mule spinner," the remaining 22 women and child spinners probably tended throstles, for it is very unlikely that a ten-year-old boy, a girl age twelve, or even a woman age twenty, to give three typical examples, would operate mules. Unfortunately, the 1870 manuscript census (Fall River, Lowell) did not employ specific job titles but rather the general classification "work in cotton mill." There is no way, therefore, to estimate even roughly the proportion of British-born mule spinners on the basis of the 1870 census.

in Table 7. Daniel Walkowitz arrived at similar figures in his study of Cohoes, New York—another town of factory mule spinning. In 1860, of the male spinners employed in Cohoes, 58. 3% were British, 25% were Irish, and 16.6% were American-born.[31]

The census statistics conceal, however, the fact that a large proportion of the Irish mule spinners had emigrated from Lancashire and Scotland. Before the famine of the mid 1840s, Irish immigrants moved predominantly to Britain, not the United States. In 1833 native-born Irish accounted for almost 60,000 people in Manchester and Liverpool, with some 30,000 to 40,000 more scattered in the smaller towns of the Lancashire county. Glasgow alone had 25,000 Irish residents in 1825 and 35,000 in 1833.[32] Though peasants when they arrived, many became mill operatives.[33] And "while those who subsequently came to America generally remained Irish in religion and sentiment," comments Rowland

Berthoff, "at least their economic role in Fall River, derived from Lancashire rather than Mayo, rested on an English foundation."[34] Walkowitz too notes, again and again, that many Irish mule spinners in Cohoes had prior experience in English cotton factories.[35] Similarly, a study of Bolton mule spinners who received funds for immigration to the United States between 1880 and 1905 shows that 32% were of Irish origins.[36]

Like Fall River and Cohoes, New Bedford, Massachusetts, was also a mule-spinning town. A center of fine spinning, New Bedford was known in Lancashire as the "Bolton of America."[37] The earliest factory operatives in New Bedford came largely from England after 1846,[38] and British immigrants completely dominated the mule-spinning departments of New Bedford mills all through the second half of the century.[39] In Webster, Massachusetts, to give one last example, two-thirds of the mule spinners employed in 1860 were foreign born, the majority probably British.[40]

But all these factory mule-spinning towns remained relatively small until the massive influx of Lancashire workers during the decade that followed the Civil War. Between 1865 and 1872 Fall River's expansion was the most remarkable; its mill population grew from 3,300 to 14,000, surpassing that of Lowell—the largest cotton manufacturing city in the United States up to that date.[41]

THE COTTON FAMINE

Before the Civil War between two-thirds and three-quarters of the British consumption of raw cotton came from the United States. By August 1861 this supply was entirely cut off.[42] In Manchester alone bankruptcies totalled 1,193 between 1861 and 1864.[43] In coarse-spinning towns that were the largest consumers of inferior-quality American cotton, for example, Preston and Blackburn, production virtually came to a standstill. In other towns production sharply declined and only a minority of factories remained open. In July-October 1862, of the total 361,000 cotton mill workers in Lancashire and the adjacent parts of Cheshire and Derbyshire, or 82% of all British cotton operatives, 59,000 were fully employed, 120,000 were working short time, and 182,000 were unemployed.[44]

Early in 1863 British cotton workers began to seek relief for emigration. Public funds, however, were available for passage money only to the British colonies. "The United States afforded the only opening for large numbers," noted John Watts, a member of the Central Relief Committee at the time, "and the British legislature does not send emigrants beyond the boundaries of the empire."[45] Colonial grants supplemented by funds raised by local emigrant aid societies in the large cotton centers provided two-thirds of the cost of "removal," and the rest was paid by the emigrant. Yet only a few sailed to the colonies.[46]

"The distinctive characteristic of cotton-spinners," wrote the London *Economist* in 1863, "is *to do one thing perfectly*, and the distinctive requirement for a backwoodsman or an Australian labourer is to be able *to do many* things tolerably." Therefore, concluded the *Economist*, mule spinners were not likely to emigrate to areas where their highly-skilled craft was not needed.[47] Although no government funds were employed to promote American immigration, spinners who desired to leave indeed favored the United States despite the fact that the Civil War was being fought there.

Discussing emigration in the first four months of 1863, Factory Inspector Alexander Redgrave reported: "The most flattering accounts are forwarded from America." Some of the Lancashire immigrants in the United States, he added, were sending free tickets to their friends at home, an arrangement which relieved the local emigration agents from the need to provide aid.[48] Free tickets were sent from Fall River. An advertisement of a steamship agency printed in one of the town's newspapers in 1865 says: "Steerage $35. Those who wish to send for their friends can buy tickets here."[49] To make it easier for the Fall River operatives to bring over their friends and relatives, another local agency specialized in arranging free trips by rail from Scotland and Lancashire to the port of embarkation in the British Isles.[50]

From the annual reports of the emigration commissioners it is easy to see that the worst year of the cotton famine—1863— was also the peak year of immigration to the United States. The total number of spinners and weavers sailing from Britain to American ports during the Civil War was as follows: 93 in 1861, 462 in 1862, 1,518 in 1863, 763 in 1864, and 666 in 1865. In all, nearly 4,700 spinners and weavers left Britain between 1861 and 1865, three-quarters of whom went to the United States, and the rest to British North America and to Australia.[51]

"America," wrote Arthur Arnold, the government inspector of public works in Lancashire during the crisis, "was generally the El Dorado which the [Blackburn operatives] wished to reach." In the early months of 1863 the Blackburn cotton workers appealed for assistance from the New York Relief Committee for immigration to the United States.[52] In the same year American ship companies were advertising passages across the Atlantic for four pounds a person.[53] Their unions bankrupt and their lifetime savings lost in the severe depression, spinners who desired to emigrate appealed for aid from the United States. In January 1863 the Spinners' and Minders' Association of Preston sent a petition to the New York Chamber of Commerce for transportation expenses and for employment in American cotton factories.[54] At the end of the year the cotton manufacturers of New England, aided by other industrialists, established the Foreign Emigrant Aid Society in Boston. Its recruiting agents visited Lancashire cotton towns regularly. A second labor recruiting agency—the American Emigrant Company—was organized in March 1865 in Hartford, Connecticut. A congressional act that legalized the importation of contract labor was approved by the president on July 4, 1864. Though the Act to Encourage Immigration failed to generate a massive inflow of skilled workers coming on pre-paid passages, it certainly did something to alleviate the shortage of labor in the fast-expanding cotton industry of New England. Agents who belonged to the two American agencies contracted 284 workers between July 1864 and December 1865, among them Blackburn operatives bound to Fall River,[55] and others on behalf of two New Hampshire cotton firms, the Amoskeag and Stark mills in Manchester.[56] More came under the "guidance and protection" of the agencies than on contract.[57] Agents of the cotton mills in Holyoke, Massachusetts, dispatched 200 skilled spinners and weavers from Scotland in 1865[58], and in the same year the Granite Mills in Fall River imported 120 Scottish operatives.[59] Between 1864 and 1866 agents representing cotton companies in Lowell, Lawrence, and Salem were sent to Britain to secure workers.[60] In 1864 the American Linen Company of Fall River, a firm heavily dependent on cotton mule spinning (notwithstanding its name),[61] signed an agreement with the American Emigrant Company which stipulated that the former would pay for the steerage passages of the British operatives recruited on its behalf. The immigration law of 1864 allowed employers to deduct the passage money from the immigrant's prospective wages, and typically, the American Linen Company withheld up to three-quarters of the monthly earnings of the operative until his or her passage was fully paid.[62]

All these recruitment activities show that British operatives did not abandon their interest in emigration when employment conditions began to improve in 1864-65. To be sure, in 1864 textile workers were reported as returning from the United States to Lancashire,[63] a practice not uncommon among recent immigrants in other American industries.[64] Yet despite this reverse migration, the overall number of British cotton workers in American factories steeply increased in the post-Civil War years as a result of rapid industrial growth.[65] Once again, Fall River is a case in point. Between 1865 and 1875 Fall River saw a *fivefold* increase in spindles from 240,000 to 1,250,000. During the same decade the number of English residents in the city rose by nearly 500% from 1,800 to 8,700.[66] By 1878, 4,500 British-born workers were employed in Fall River's cotton mills, nearly half of them adult males.[67] Between 800 and 1,000 were mule spinners.[68]

The growing interest of British mule spinners in emigration was reflected in their unions' policy during the famine and shortly thereafter. In May 1863, Secretary Mawdsley and eighteen delegates representing fifteen local mule spinners' unions met in Manchester and proposed to establish the Cotton Districts Emigration Society, a national association whose goal was to encourage "a continuous stream of emigration. . .at all times."[69] Soon after the worst of the famine was over, in September 1864, a resolution passed by the Associated Operative Cotton Spinners of Lancashire, Cheshire, Yorkshire, and Derbyshire, expressed the new outlook explicitly: "It is only by emigration that the position of the working classes can be improved." The resolution called for each member "to promote to the utmost of his power the emigration movement" in order "to vindicate an equitable price for spinning on coupled mules."[70] The unions thus saw emigration as a means to strengthen their bargaining power with employers, in the words of the London *Times*, "as the grand panacea for the evils of short time and low wages."[71] Union leaders practically accepted their employers' viewpoint and looked upon labor and capital as partners, not adversaries.[72] They fully acknowledged the benefits of the capitalist system, they tried to avoid, as much as they could, any violent confrontations with the employers, and in advocating emigration, they encouraged first and foremost the departure of militant members.

BLACKLISTING

At least one Scottish mule spinners' union adopted emigration benefits early. In 1833 there were between 600 and 800 mule spinners in Glasgow, 200 to 300 of whom were unemployed. The abundant supply of labor in the city led the union to devote some of its funds for emigration, thereby reducing membership by nearly 100 in three years. "Conceiving that in America they can get provisions almost for nothing," emigrant spinners sailed to New York. Union benefits were paid directly to the emigration agent with an additional sum received by the spinner upon his arrival in the United States. Occasionally, the spinner's wife and children—who normally travelled separately later—also received assistance from union funds.[73]

A "Small Paper Book titled 'Emigration'" was found in the committee room of the Glasgow spinners in 1837 and its content is described in the parliamentary reports on combinations. Again, the oversupply of spinners was "choking the labour market" and the union adopted an emigration scheme as a remedy. A two-year membership was required in order to qualify for a "lot by ballot." The "fortunate candidate" received as much as 10 pounds and was prohibited from spinning in Glasgow for three years. Each fortnight, three unemployed and two working spinners received emigration aid from the committee.[74]

The Glasgow case, however, was rather exceptional. Apparently, in the 1820s and 1830s most Lancashire unions had not yet adopted emigration schemes: according to Sidney and Beatrice Webb[75] it was only from the mid 1840s that funds for emigration began to appear, off and on, in the accounts of large British trade unions. An allowance of two pounds per emigrant spinner was included, for example, in the 1849 rules of the Bolton Society.[76] During the 1853-54 thirty-week strike in Preston, to mention another case, the spinners encouraged the emigration of all members who desired "to leave a land of oppression for one of freedom."[77] The balance sheet of the union's expenditure during the strike shows that a rather modest sum of 110 pounds was spent on "emigration and removing," yet at least 62 of the 847 mule spinners and self-actor minders in Preston were reported to have emigrated by the end of the strike.[78] In another dispute fifteen years later, a strike against wage cuts during the depression of 1869, the Preston spinners adopted the emigration scheme immediately in order not to exhaust their resources on relief. The strike started in March 1869, and by the middle of May the Spinners' and Minders' Association of Preston claimed to have sent off 100 members to the United States. In May-June the spinners were sending off eight members per week. During the strike, furthermore, the spinners' committee invited a New York agent to Preston to speak in trade union meetings on employment opportunities in the United States, and to discuss "a plan for a more numerous deportation of . . . members." In the same year, as a result of severe unemployment, 1,000 Blackburn spinners and weavers applied for emigration assistance in a single month. Only a few received benefits. The spinners, however, received much greater assistance than the weavers owing to the financial strength of their union. The mule spinners of Blackburn augmented their emigration fund in two ways: first, by voting 500 pounds from general unions; second, by doubling the weekly membership dues. In May 1869, consequently, the Blackburn union arranged to send off between 60 and 70 spinners to America, and in June the union aided at least 50 more members.[79]

Preston and Blackburn, like Fall River, specialized in spinning low counts coarse yarns made from American raw cotton.[80] Fall River therefore soon became a major destination of emigrants from these two factory towns. The Preston and Blackburn immigrants in Fall River were apparently militant unionists. Many of the Fall River mule spinners, according to the Massachusetts Bureau of Labor, came "from the Preston and Blackburn districts of England, bringing their inherited distrust of the employer, and accompanied by their old leaders, who were not long in establishing [t]here the customs and regulations of their craft."[81] The leaders of the 1875 Fall River strike, notes Philip Silvia, were "haunted by the grim memory" of the unsuccessful struggle in Preston.[82] "The rough 'Blackburn' operative of Old England" had hundreds of representatives in Fall River in the 1870s, the *Fall River Herald* of June 23, 1879, tells us, and the *Fall River Daily* of the same day reports that the organizers of the 1879 city-wide strikes were recent emigrants from Blackburn and Preston, the two "hot-beds of trades-unionism and communism."

The immigrant spinners who came to Fall River, as well as to other New England centers of cotton mule spinning, had been among the most militant union activists while still living in Lancashire. Speaking before a parliamentary committee in 1889, John Burnett, labor correspondent to the Board of Trade, explains:

> In the case of the Cotton Spinners' Society the [emigration] benefit is intended solely for members who have become marked men, or as the society terms them "victims," for taking an active part in the society's business, or who have been prominent in any trade dispute. The rule is as follows: "In the event of any member of this association being in receipt of the society's funds as a victim, and being wishful to emigrate to some foreign country, he shall be allowed to do so, and to receive one-half the pay he is entitled to at the time he wishes to emigrate."[83]

Examining the emigration rules of twelve local mule spinners' societies in the Lancashire region between 1866 and 1891, Charlotte Erickson arrived at

TABLE 8

Age Distribution of Adult Male Spinners
Employed in Fall River, June-July 1860,
Broken Down by Country of Birth.

Age	Country of Birth		
	Britain	Ireland	United States
18-19	3.8%	16.7%	20.0%
20-29	34.3%	51.9%	60.0%
30-39	42.9%	27.8%	20.0%
40 and over	19.0%	3.7%	
Total Cases	105	54	5

Source: United States, Federal Manuscript Census of Fall River, 1860.

similar conclusions. Her findings are twofold. First, the amount of money a local trade union provided for the emigration of each member was dependent on the number of years that member had been paying his contributions to the union. Since several-year membership was required in order to receive maximum emigration assistance, longstanding and experienced unionists were the first to emigrate.

Critical for understanding the role played by Lancashire unionists in industrial America, this observation may be independently confirmed by checking federal census records. British-born mule spinners, we learn from the United States census, were rather older, experienced workers. In Fall River, for example, nearly one-fifth of the British immigrant spinners in 1860 were age forty and older, as shown in Table 8.[84] Similarly, in Cohoes, New York, the male English cotton workers were older than the Irish, the French Canadian, and the American-born operatives, according to both the 1860 and 1880 federal censuses.[85]

The second point Erickson makes refers to the emigration benefits of unemployed union members. Among unemployed members who were drawing "out of work" pay, strikers and "victims" received the largest grants. The Oldham mule spinners' union, for example, granted a four-year member who became unemployed an emigration benefit of 2 pounds and 10 shillings, a striker 3 pounds, and a victim 3 pounds and 10 shillings. The Stockport cotton spinners allowed striking and victimized members to draw the emigration benefit within the first seven weeks they were receiving relief, while the unemployed members could draw the benefit only during the first five weeks. "The provisions the textile unions made to assist members to emigrate in times of dispute," concluded Erickson, "aided their most faithful members first and provided most generously for persons sacrificed for trade union activities." Although the union rules did not include stipulations as to the destination of members, the benefits assisted above all spinners who immigrated to the United States.[86]

The militancy displayed by British mule spinners in the United States is indeed hard to imagine without their former commitment to trade unionism in Lancashire. Every strike of any importance in the American mule spinning industry was organized by British-born workers, particularly recent immigrants. The Fall River strikes of 1850-51, 1868, 1870, 1875, 1879; the 1867 and 1877 New Bedford strikes, the 1875 strikes in Newburyport and Lowell; as well as the 1880 and 1882 Cohoes strikes, were all led by British immigrant mule spinners.[87] Furthermore, prominent New England labor leaders had formerly been trade union activists in Britain, as the three following examples suggest. Robert Howard had served as the principal officer of the Stockport spinners' society for two years before he sailed to the United States in 1873 at the age of twenty-nine. After working five years as a mule spinner in the Flint Mills at Fall River, he became in 1878 the secretary of the Fall River Mule Spinners' Union, and in 1885, the organizer and first leader of the National Mule Spinners' Union in the United States.[88] John Golden, a Lancashire mule spinner who had left England after being blacklisted for union agitation, served nine years as the treasurer of the mule spinners' union in Fall River, and in 1903 became the president of the United Textile Workers of America and held office for eighteen years until his death in 1921.[89] And Thomas O'Donnell, who served in 1901 as secretary of both the Fall River Mule Spinners' Association and the National Spinners' Association, began to work in the mule room of a British mill when he was nine years old. In 1873, at the age of twenty-one, he left for Fall River where he took part in organizing the general strike of 1879 and consequently lost his job and was forced to leave the city for five years.[90]

SUMMARY

This brief survey of immigration leads to two inescapable conclusions. First, mule spinning in America was firmly in British hands. Not only the leadership, but the vast majority of mule spinners in a typical New England cotton town in the third quarter of the nineteenth century were British and Lancashire Irish. Fall River led the way: from 1850 onward, close to 100% of the town's mule spinners were British and Irish.

It is for that reason that we examined the background of these immigrants, reaching the second conclusion, namely, that many of the British spinners who moved from Lancashire to New England had been committed trade union activists. This is also why the industrial war that tore Fall River apart in the 1870s is incomprehensible unless one fully appreciates the role played by the British unionists.

But while former trade union experience contributed to the militancy of the Fall River spinners, equally important, the remainder of this book argues, was the attitude of the American manufacturer. The contrast between the British and American systems of management was the underlying theme of the Fall River contest. From the standpoint of the American employer, control over production, recruitment, and piece rates was the sole prerogative of management. It was such a conception of management which evoked so much resistance on the part of British mule spinners in industrial New England.

Chapter 6
The Break-Up of Craft Control in the United States

As for myself, I regard my work-people just as I regard my machinery. So long as they can do my work for what I choose to pay them, I keep them, getting out of them all I can. What they do, or how they fare, outside of my walls, I don't know, nor do I consider it my business to know. They must look out for themselves, as I do for myself. When my machines get old and useless, I reject them and get new, and these people are part of my machinery.

A Fall River mill agent,
1855, Massachusetts Senate Document no. 21, 1868, p. 23.

We were surprised to find in a democratic country like America, that the men had so little power and were to such a large extent the docile instruments of energetic employers. The "bosses," as the foreman and managers of factories are called, drive the men to an extent that employers would never dream of attempting in this country. There are trade unions, but they do not seem able to protect the men in this respect. The "bosses" have the faculty of "driving" the men and getting the maximum amount of work out of them, and the men do not seem to have the inclination or power to resist the pressure. American manufacturers thus get the greatest possible service out of their plant.

A British traveler to the United States,
Wade's Fibre and Fabric,
(Boston), 15:373 (April 23, 1892), p. 101.

The break-up of craft control in the United States coincided with the transition to the self actor. The self-acting mule technology was first transmitted to the United States from Britain, and then spread rapidly among hundreds of mule-spinning mills throughout the northern states. Two elements encouraged American employers to subject the mule spinners to the rule of foremen: the sheer speed of the diffusion of the new technology and the relative weakness of trade unions. The role of technology, the rise of the foreman, and the importance of unions are the topics covered in this chapter.

THE TRANSFER OF TECHNOLOGY

In 1840 William Davol put the first self-acting mule in operation at the Annawan Mill, Fall River. "It was the wonder of the town," noted Henry Earl, the historian of Fall River, "and was visited and examined by the whole community."[1] A year later the company of Hawes, Marvel, and Davol began manufacturing the new machine, and within the next four years American machinery builders from New York, Rhode Island, Massachusetts, and New Hampshire were busy constructing at least three different types of self actors. Between 1845 and 1850 the number of self-acting mules installed in American mills rose at a phenomenal rate: by 1850 the United States had two-and-a-half million cotton spindles, one million of which were mounted on self actors.[2]

The story of William Davol's efforts to secure the British self actor is worth telling, even if only to show how nothing had changed in the business of technology transfer from Britain to the United States during a period of close to sixty years. Like the first hand mule in 1783, the earliest self actor in 1840 was smuggled from Britain. But unlike the first attempt that was a failure—no Philadelphia machine builder had been able to put the pieces of the hand mule together—the second was an immediate success, a contrast which tells us something of the progress of the mechanical skills in the United States between the early 1780s and 1840.

During his trip to England in 1838 to inspect the latest British improvements in cotton machinery, Davol bought from Sharpe and Roberts one of their self actors and the American patent rights. Because of the parliamentary prohibition on the export of machinery, the British refused to sign a contract; rather, Davol reached a verbal agreement with a "mysterious agent" who promised to ship the mule clandestinely as soon as possible; the freight being 70% of the machine's cost payable upon its arrival at New York. Sailing back to the United States, Davol waited impatiently for nearly two years—he often wrote letters of inquiry to the British firm but received no reply—until an invoice of small metal ware packed in broad thin cases arrived at the New York custom house for a Fall River order on a ship embarking from Havre, France. The Roberts' self actor reached Fall River disassembled with "every considerable piece of iron or wood...sawn into bits a few inches in length." Davol had no difficulty in fitting the bits together. Soon thereafter and all through the 1840s, his company introduced a number of small improvements to adapt the machine to the American needs, and proceeded with the manufacture of self-acting mules with a total capacity of 280,000 spindles. Davol's success was a turning point in the history of mule spinning in America. Here is how Henry Earl, the impassioned admirer of Fall River industrialists, describes the event in his *Centennial History of Fall River*:

> No sooner had the merits of the self-acting mule and its production in
> Fall River become known, than an instant demand for it sprang up in

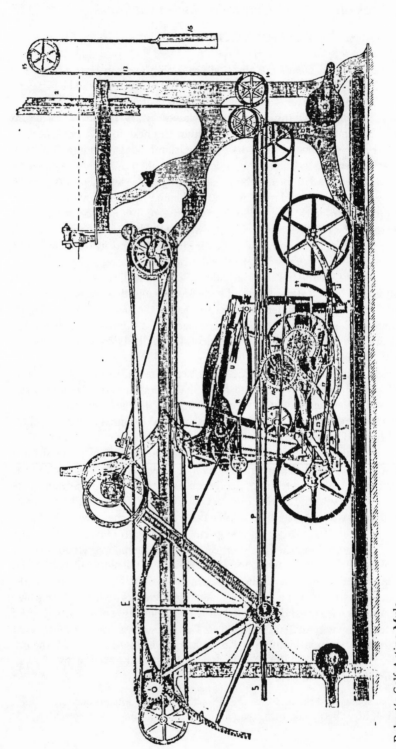

Robert's Self-Acting Mule

Evan Leigh, *The Science of Modern Cotton Spinning*. Manchester, 1873.

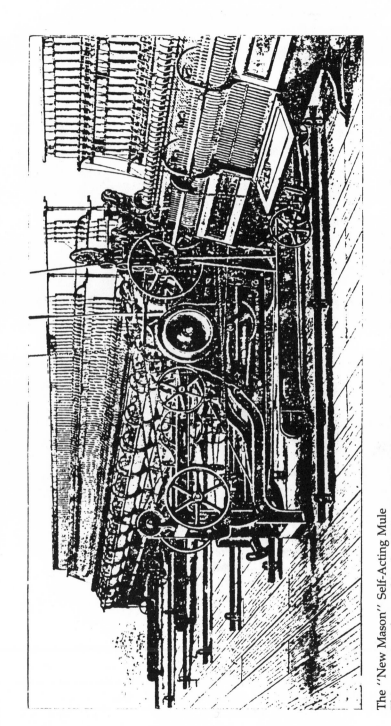

The "New Mason" Self-Acting Mule
This was manufactured in the 1880s, at a time when the American mule spinning industry was already fast declining.

Wade's Fibre and Fabric. Boston, 30 October 1886.

The New England Mule Spinner
"They work almost in a nude state—with bare feet, and all their ordinary garb stripped off, with the exception of a light undershirt and a pair of light working drawers."

Wade's Fibre and Fabric. Boston, 21 November 1885.

The New England Back-Boy
"Perhaps of all the situations in the mills followed by children, none is so harassing and dangerous as that of the back-boy, who keeps the roving in on the spinning mules. His labors are onerous, and he requires more strength, tact, and intelligence than children employed in other departments."

Wade's Fibre and Fabric. Boston, 28 November 1885.

all directions. Manufacturers of cotton machinery resorted to every possible device to possess themselves of the patterns, many of them sending their draftsmen to inspect and furtively carry away working sketches of them; while one builder, bolder than the rest, declared openly that he had come with his designer to secure drawings of the whole machine. He was told he could have the patterns and a right to manufacture by paying a royalty, but warned at his peril not to infringe the patent.

This default of success was succeeded by attempts to break down the patent through claims of previous invention, similarity to other machines, and various kindred subterfuges, until finally, discovering that they could not accomplish their purpose covertly, the cotton manufacturers and machine builders combined openly to wrest the advantages, profits, and control of the new machine from the patentees.[3]

Whether any American mechanic invented the self-acting mule independently of Roberts is impossible to say. Yet two things are clear. First, all types of self actors used in American cotton mills were similar in design to the Roberts machine, and second, no self-acting mule was manufactured for commercial use in the United States until after 1840. William Mason, the experienced machine builder from Taunton, Massachusetts, had begun experimenting with his own self-acting mule in 1837 and up to 1843 he continued "to persevere and improve it."[4] The Mason mule had the essential features of the Roberts self actor with one notable exception: it used devices other than the quadrant arm to control the winding-on motion.[5] Less efficient and therefore less widespread than the Roberts and Mason mules was the Smith or "Scotch" mule patented by William B. Leonard, an agent of the Matteawan Company of New York, soon after 1840.[6] In 1845 at least six large machine shops in the North Atlantic states were manufacturing self-acting mules: Hawes, Marvel, and Davol of Fall River; the Mason Machine Works in Taunton; the machine shops of the Locks and Canals Company in Lowell; the shops of the Amoskeag Manufacturing Company in Manchester, New Hampshire; the Matteawan Machine Shop in Fishkill, New York; and the Franklin Foundry Company in Providence, Rhode Island.[7] By 1850 the triumph of the self actor in the United States was uncontested; the older hand-driven and power-driven mules all but disappeared.

THE PACE OF TECHNOLOGICAL CHANGE

While the self-acting mule took over the American cotton industry within a decade, the transition from the power-driven mule to the self actor in Britain lasted over forty years. There are two plausible reasons why the pace of technological change in the two countries was so remarkably different, why American manufacturers adopted the new technology so much faster than the British.

In the first place, the attitude of British and American employers toward innovations was markedly different. The American manufacturer would try anything new, and he would try it thoroughly. He would invest in an improved machine even before the machine was properly tested, taking a risk the British manufacturer was not even likely to consider. "The attitude of Lancashire manufacturers towards novelties is decidedly skeptical," noted one English inventor of textile machinery. "Each wants to see the new thing well tested by somebody else before he tries it." An American employer installs perhaps fifty or one-hundred new machines at a time, he goes on,

> and having done so he recognises that his reputation is more or less staked on their success. If any defects or difficulties appear in their working, he applies all his resources to overcome them, and he watches very closely to see that everybody else who has anything to do with them tries to make them a success too. The result, in nine cases out of ten, is that the preliminary hitches are overcome and success is achieved. The English manufacturer, on the other hand, will put in, or allow you as a favour to put in, four or eight [machines], probably everybody in the place will regard them with suspicion, every hitch in their working will be set down against them as an inherent defect, and perhaps in the end they will be thrown out as useless, and the manufacturer will see in their "failure" merely a justification of his reluctance to have anything to do with them.[8]

Reflecting on his own experience, the English inventor may have exaggerated when he gave this account to T.M. Young, a correspondent to the *Manchester Guardian* who was on a tour in the United States at the turn of the century. Making the very same point, Young was more careful:

> Some English manufacturers are, of course, more intelligent and more enterprising than many Americans, but when every allowance has been made for the differences in their situations the conclusion is hard to resist that the average English manufacturer is more conservative—more cautious, if you will—and more liable to reject a good thing because it happens to be new and hitherto untried, than the average American manufacturer.[9]

The second reason why the self-acting mule spread in the United States with a remarkable ease and speed was the nature of the American product. As noted, initially the self-acting mule was limited to coarse spinning. Because American manufacturers specialized in coarse spinning, and because the range of yarn counts spun in American cotton mills was much narrower than that spun in Lancashire factories, it was technically feasible to complete the transition in the United States faster than in Britain. In very rough terms, four-fifths of all mule spindles in operation in the United States in 1850 were mounted on self actors.[10] Granted that no reasonable employer would have scrapped well-functioning mules (unless he had compelling reasons to do so), that the self actor was quite an expensive piece of machinery, and that the average length of service of a mule machine was about twenty-five years,[11] how was it possible to complete the transition in only one decade? The answer, undoubtedly, lies in the widespread practice of machinery conversion. An employer wishing to spin on a self actor was not bound to purchase a whole new machine, but just the headstock, that is, the part containing the mule's control mechanism. In the 1840s the self-acting mechanism sold for about 20% of the price of a complete mule.[12]

THE RISE OF THE FOREMAN

The speedy diffusion of the self-acting mule in American cotton mills went hand in hand with the transition from subcontracting to foremanship. In Britain, we have seen, the employment of minders alongside spinners in the same plant made it easier for millowners to organize production on self actors in exactly the same way they had done on power-driven mules. The rapid pace of technological change in American factories produced the opposite effects. The sheer speed of the transition in the United States was likely to encourage employers to revolutionize management once and for all. American manufacturers did not have to deal with spinners employed alongside minders to the same extent that British employers did, and they were therefore freer to experiment with new methods of supervision.

The self actor transformed the social organization of mule spinning in America in two fundamental ways. First, it drastically reduced the number of helpers. Second, employers transferred the authority over helpers from mule spinners to overseers, placing the spinner himself under close supervision.

What the transfer of control from spinner to overseer concretely meant may be illustrated by contrasting the management of labor in American and British mills after mid-century. To assert that in New England the mule spinner assumed the role of the Lancashire big piecer while the overseer performed a task similar to that of the Lancashire mule spinner is certainly not far from the truth. In much the same manner as the Lancashire self-actor minder was first and foremost a supervisor, so also was the New England mule-spinning overseer. And while the Lancashire self-actor minder passed on the increased workload to his helpers, particularly the big piecer, so did the New England overseer intensify the labor of the spinners under his supervision.

The self actor spun yarn intermittently, not continuously, and consequently managers could not set the speed of the machinery, as in throstle spinning, but each mule spinner established his own pace. One of the ways open to management to gain control over speed was therefore to place a foreman close to the spinner and his helper(s) who pushed continuously for increases in output. Furthermore American employers no longer had to bargain with subcontractors but simply dictated the terms of employment to machine tenders, giving management greater control over labor costs.

"If I were asked to attempt in a single sentence a definition of 'the improved management of the Americans'," Young concluded his report on the American cotton industry in 1902, "I should say it is this: Unceasing study and close analysis of the costs of production, and unresting endeavour to diminish any and every element in them by any departure from existing routine."[13] Nowhere was the "departure from existing routine"—that is, from the British way of doing things—more conspicuous than in the management of mule spinning.

The self actor worked faster, broke fewer threads, and held more spindles than the common mule.[14] Common mule spinners in the United States were assisted by two to three helpers and operated either a single medium-size hand-driven mule or a pair of smaller power-driven mules. Self-actor minders, or mule spinners, as they were called in the United States, operated a pair of large mules with only one child assistant. The minders were regarded as "the hardest worked of any class"[15] and that is probably why employers excluded women. Robert Howard, leader of the Fall River mule spinners, contrasted the work done by British and American self-actor minders:

> [In England] they give a man a pair of mules...and they give a man an assistant to work between the mules with him, and also an assistant to work on the back of the mules; but in this country, it is a very peculiar fact...that *however large the mules may be, no matter how many spindles they may contain*, the employers will not come down to the same policy adopted in England. They insist on one man running the mule with only one little assistant to go behind it [my emphasis].[16]

In other words, American employers provided the self-actor spinner with a little piecer known as a "back boy" who was responsible for ancillary tasks such as creeling (replacing empty bobbins with full ones), cleaning, and sweeping. The spinner himself was responsible for the tasks of the minder and the big piecer—tasks assigned to two adult mule workers in Britain. In some Fall River mills by the 1880s employers cut further the number of helpers by half; just one back boy divided his services among two mule spinners. In Lowell and New Bedford, too, the cotton corporations reduced the number of assistants so that under the new arrangement two back boys served three spinners at the turn of the century.[17]

By the early 1840s management in Slater's Webster mill put an end to the subcontract system. Henceforth overseers hired, disciplined, and paid helpers.[18] During the 1850s mule-spinning overseers in the Pepperell mills in Biddeford, Maine, "were given almost complete authority to hire, train, fire and make out the payroll for the workers in their rooms."[19] A mule spinner employed in one Massachusetts mill reported in 1871 that overseers, not spinners, "chastised" back boys.[20] In the vast majority of Rhode Island mills in the late 1870s back boys were paid "direct[ly] out of the office," but overseers had the sole prerogative to authorize the pay, as well as to hire and discharge all their subordinates.[21] In the large cotton factories of New Hampshire in the early 1880s overseers hired and fired all their workers, mule spinners and helpers alike,[22] and in Lowell at the end of the century mule spinners neither recruited helpers nor paid them.[23] A survey conducted in 1891 by the U.S. Commissioner of

Labor tells the same story. The commissioner examined thirty-eight cotton textile establishments in the northern district of the United States, thirty of which employed mule spinners. In one establishment the spinners paid their back boy helpers, in another, the helpers were paid partly by the spinners and partly by the firm, and in the remaining twenty-eight cases, the helpers were paid solely by the firm, presumably through the overseers.[24] In Fall River overseers assumed control over helpers, though here the evidence is seemingly ambiguous because the mule spinners continued to recruit and pay their back boy assistants.[25] Fall River employers in fact encouraged this practice[26] while at the same time they transferred the authority over helpers from spinners to overseers, as Thomas Ashton, secretary of the Oldham spinners, observed during his visit to Fall River in October-December 1902: "The overseer in the [mule] spinning department...has full management...with power to discharge any person employed therein." Asked on the same occasion to contrast the supervisory requirements in the United States and Britain, Ashton replied: "In the cotton industry there is more 'overlooking' in America than in England."[27]

American observers held the same view. "There is one peculiarity about English factory or mill life," wrote Henry Blair, Chairman of the U.S. Senate Committee on the Relations between Labor and Capital in 1883. "The number of overseers is fewer; there are fewer men 'on the staff.'"[28] In Britain, one overseer was in charge of twenty to twenty-five mule spinners' work teams in the early 1830s, and this proportion changed little with the triumph of the self actor. In the American mule-spinning industry, by contrast, the advent of the self actor coincided with increased supervision. In Fall River, for example, one self actor foreman was in charge of four subforemen known as "second hands" or "section hands, "each supervising directly perhaps nine minders and six to twelve helpers.[29] In typical New England mill in 1885 an overseer earned $25, a minder $10, and a helper $2.70 per week.[30] Overseers and minders were paid in proportion to output. Back boys received a daily wage.

One task performed by the American foreman and his assistants was maintenance. In Britain, we are told, "many of the duties...which otherwise might require the care of an overlooker" were delegated to the minder, who, like his predecessor the mule spinner, was expected to have an intimate knowledge of the machinery under his direction.[31] In the United States, on the other hand, the foreman and his subforemen were responsible for repairing broken straps and bands, for adjusting and readjusting the mule's moving parts, and for making all the alterations in the mule necessary for shifting from the manufacture of one yarn count to another.[32] The American minder himself did almost nothing but piecing. He was practically reduced—in British eyes— to "a piecing up machine."[33]

But the main function of the foreman was supervision, not maintenance. Investigating labor and capital in the American cotton industry, the Senate Committee of 1885 paid close attention to the contrast between British and American mills in this respect. Testimonies heard before the committee reveal, in fact, how alien, indeed incomprehensible, was the notion of craft autonomy to American managers. James McIntosh, a sketch maker for calico prints who had emigrated from Scotland first to Rhode Island and then to Manchester, New Hampshire, was interviewed by Henry Blair in October 1883. McIntosh was a cotton factory craftsman *par excellence* and his general outlook was shared by many of the British immigrant spinners.

Blair: Do you think that the same English help will do more with fewer overseers than with the many?

McIntosh: I should think so.

Blair: They will do more work, you think?

McIntosh: I should think they would do it more comfortably.

Blair: Do you think they would accomplish more work in the day than if taken, as in this country, and put under a larger number of overseers?

McIntosh: Well, I can only answer that by a general remark, that where men act from a sense of necessity or duty, or whatever it may be, the work will be done, overseer or no overseer, and the great thing is to train men to that habit. As far as my experience with the best men has gone, they say when they begin in the morning, "I shall accomplish so much—I shall get over so much ground by such and such a time"; and they work by a "stint" that they lay down themselves. I think that is a better state of mind for a workman to be in than to have the constant impetus given by the presence of foremen.

Blair: Do you think that the man likes to be trusted?

McIntosh: Yes; that is just it.

Blair: It is a compliment to his better nature?

McIntosh: Yes.

Blair, however, was not all that interested in either the "comfort" or "happiness" of workers. He was preoccupied first and foremost with individual output and that is why he was so skeptical, so suspicious, of any operative working "without the sense of being overseen."[34] Instead, he adopted the standpoint of American management, namely, that to get the work out was the most important function of the foreman.

Always paid in proportion to the quantity of yarn spun by the mules under his supervision, the New England foreman always attempted to increase production, "grinding" and "driving" the spinners "almost beyond human endurance."[35] The foreman would watch the mules closely, pushing the minder to drive the carriage back immediately at the end of each run. He would not let a machine stop for more than a few seconds.[36] A mule spinner from Danvers, Massachusetts, noted that the reason why the spinners had always preferred "to work by the job" was to escape supervision, but with the triumph of the self actor: "piece-work does not save us from being driven."[37] In 1888 the cotton manufacturers of Rhode Island insisted that it was "impossible to incorporate

into the system of factory management any check upon th[e] absolute authority of the overseers,"[38] and in Fall River in the 1870s a foreman who did not
push his help was immediately discharged. "There is no redress here and no
appeal," the spinners of Fall River complained. "The by-word is 'If you don't
like it, get out!' " "They are more tyrannical here in Fall River than they are
in England. I always thought they were tyrants at home, but found out differently when I came here." It is the "unhealthy spirit of competition that is
the ruin of the working class," shrewdly noted another operative; "they call
it 'grinding'; but who do they grind? Is it not to beat the other mills?" So hard-
pressed were the spinners of Fall River, one witness maintained, that even a
minor grievance could easily trigger a strike just in order to "secure a relaxa-
tion of labor," to gain a "resting spell." An English immigrant spinner in Fall
River observed:

> There is a slate in every room, upon which each man's name is written,
> and the amount of work done is entered opposite the names, so that every
> operative knows the exact amount of work his neighbor is accomplishing,
> and is constantly striving to exceed him. . . . In England each of us had
> a book in which our work was entered, and we alone knew what the
> amount was. [In Fall River] the Board of Trade drives the agent, the agent
> drives the superintendent, he drives the overseer and the overseer drives
> the operative. They drive us and we drive each other.[39]

All this driving implies, of course, a higher rate of speed and a larger output
per mule of a comparable type (yarn count) and size (number of spindles) in
the United States than in Britain. In addition, the use of better-quality cotton
in the United States than in Britain permitted American manufacturers to run
their machinery faster with only a moderate increase in yarn breakage.[40] Actually, as early as 1850, when the first generation self actors had just been put
into operation in American factories, a Connecticut writer on mill management observed that in spinning coarse counts (number 14 and up to the 30s)
mules in the United States ran faster and turned out a larger amount of yarn
than mules in Britain. As early as 1850, moreover, the Fall River employers
had already speeded up the self-acting mule machinery, and from 1870 onward speed became a recurrent grievance of the New England spinners in Fall
River and elsewhere.[41]

Not only did American manufacturers run their machinery faster but they
also operated longer hours. In 1839 the length of the work week in cotton mills
was 72 to 78 hours in the United States and 69 hours in England.[42] By 1879
the working hours were reduced to 66 a week in Rhode Island and 56.5 in Britain.[43] The legal day's work in Massachusetts at that date was 10 hours, but
overseers often violated the law and drove the machinery 10.5 or even 11 hours
a day, "stealing time"—a standard practice throughout large parts of the state.[44]
Two decades later, in 1902, the work week was still 3 to 5 hours longer in the
cotton factories of the North Atlantic states than in Britain.[45]

Hard driving, lastly, was thought to have shortened the working lives of American operatives. Evidently, New England mule spinners quit work at an earlier age than Lancashire spinners. Such was the impression of American as well as British commentators. A correspondent for the *Outlook* magazine visited New Bedford in the spring of 1898 to prepare an article for a twelve-part series— "America's Working People." Going through the mule-spinning departments and other rooms in the mills he was struck by the absence of "old men." Asking the leader of the local mule spinners' union "why do the men drop so young?" he was told: "The strain of work wore men out...and their fingers were no longer nimble enough to keep up with work demanded."[46] Similarly, Thomas Ashton of Oldham, writing four years later, was convinced that the "hurry-scurry system" of work to which American spinners were subject from youth was the main reason why they were thrown out of work at an earlier age than the English. This, he tells us, was the opinion of all the British immigrant workers with whom he talked about the subject.[47]

THE ROLE OF UNIONS

Perhaps no other factor contributed to the rise of the foreman in American mills more than the absence of trade unions. In a striking contrast to Lancashire and Scotland, there is no evidence of union militancy among early American mule spinners. The first mule spinners' union in New England was organized in Fall River in 1850. By that date the introduction of the self-acting mule was well under way, and the subcontract system had already disappeared from many mills.

Admittedly, the scant evidence we possess reveals traces of short-lived union associations among Philadelphia and Rhode Island mule spinners before mid-century. As noted in chapter 1, three mule spinners' strikes around Philadelphia, in 1828, 1833 and 1836, show that the spinners made collective efforts to form a union, and another early attempt at organizing a mule spinners' union was recorded in Pawtucket, Rhode Island, in 1824. But these efforts were minimal, if not negligible, by any British standard. British mule spinners, recall, formed "the most powerful, extensive, and best organized Union in the Kingdom" in the early 1830s when the new minders were beginning to join their ranks.[48] Local spinners' unions in the United States during the 1830s, on the other hand, were so rare, and were so difficult to form, that a British immigrant mule spinner who had gone to the United States "for the purpose of establishing combinations there" came back home convinced that the American spinner was unorganizable. He found "the works so scattered in small vicinities that it was impossible to attain the object."[49]

Consider the British experience once again. The early modern history of trade unionism in Britain reads like the history of the mule spinners' unions. In 1810 a mule spinners' strike in the Lancashire region put 30,000 workers out of work for four months. Edward Tufnell described it as "the most extensive and persevering strike that has ever taken place."[50] According to evidence given by a Manchester spinner who outlined the extent of the "combination," a comprehensive federation of local societies of mule spinners covered the entire Lancashire region.[51] In 1818 Manchester experienced a general strike of all trades. Leading the strike movement the Manchester spinners initiated the formation of a "Union of all Trades called the *Philanthropic Society*"—the first attempt at a general federation. And in the course of the 1829-30 gigantic strike wave in Lancashire cotton towns, at the time "the tendency to turn out seemed to partake...the character of a mania," the mule spinners set up the "National Association for the Protection of Labour," again, a federation of all trades. The association enrolled 150 separate unions from twenty different trades and provided substantial funds to support the striking spinners.[52]

The three Lancashire strikes of 1810, 1818, and 1829-30 occurred over the issue of wages, not craft control. Yet the militancy displayed by the mule spinners' unions and the support they received from diverse trades were likely to make employers cautious in challenging the spinners' autonomy when the improved self actor was first introduced around 1830. Since control over recruitment was well grounded in the work rules of British mule spinners' unions, any attempt on the part of employers to do away with the subcontract system would have amounted to costly battles with the unions. John Doherty, former secretary of the Manchester spinners and a national labor leader, understood this point all too well. Asked by a parliamentary committee in 1838 "what advantage" would "any trade derive...from combination," he answered: "The masters knowing the combination is in existence, are slower to propose a change of terms to the men, believing there will be a resistance."[53]

In the United States, in contrast, the subcontract system had nothing to do with customary union rules. American employers introduced this system simply as a managerial technique borrowed from British cotton mills. Craft autonomy in the United States was merely a privilege handed down by management: early American mule spinners did not develop the organizational means necessary to protect this privilege in face of rapid technological change. Spinners, to be sure, were often recruited from among the piecers,[54] yet they failed to convert subcontracting into apprenticeship. They lacked, in fact, any *formal apprenticeship* so characteristic of early British spinners. Referring to the Pennsylvanian mule spinners during the 1830s, Anthony Wallace explains:

> Among the factory skills, mule spinning came closest, perhaps, to a craft but it was a craft learned informally, and often quickly, by a youth who first familiarized himself with the machine by working for a few weeks as a piecer, and then, under the instruction of an experienced spinner, by trying out the machine himself. The mule spinner was the employer of his piecers and scavengers; but they were certainly not apprentices.[55]

Given an informal instruction with no clear career lines rather than the traditional seven-year apprenticeship common in Britain, Wallace hesitates to call mule spinning in the United States a "craft." The failure of American mule spinners to monopolize their skills and to restrict entry into the trade clearly undermined their craft status. For spinners to be able to retain their autonomy, and hence their control over production, adoption of formal apprenticeship rules as in Britain was quite crucial, but since American mule spinners had not formed trade unions until mid-century, they could not have incorporated apprenticeship rules into the subcontract system. As a result, employers were able to dismantle both systems—subcontracting and apprenticeship—without creating serious training problems and without evoking too much resistance on the part of mule spinners.

Yet the spinners did resist. Apparently, the first strike of any importance in the American mule spinning industry occurred over the issue of control. In 1850-51 the mule spinners employed in seven of the eight cotton mills in Fall River formed a union and staged a six-month general strike which involved 1,300 workers. Although a cut in piece rates triggered the strike, a careful reading of the evidence suggests that the main issue over which the strike occurred was not wages but the spinners' loss of autonomy from management supervision. According to the 1880 Report of the Massachusetts Bureau of Labor, "It was asserted that within a few years previous to the strike...[n]ew machinery had been introduced by which more yarn could be spun in a given time." The striking spinners complained about the "numerous petty tyrannies and unjust actions on the part of the overseers"—actions which probably resulted from changes in the methods of supervision that came about with the introduction of the self-acting mule.[56]

Nearly all the striking spinners in Fall River were immigrants from Lancashire. When exactly they had arrived in Fall River, and whether or not they had formerly enjoyed the status of autonomous craftsmen in the United States, we do not know. Nevertheless, one thing is certain: unions, like strikes, were introduced into the New England mule-spinning industry from the outside by British immigrant spinners.

Until the end of the Civil War, however, unionization did not spread outside Fall River. The 1850-51 Fall River strike was an isolated event; it did not inspire unions or strikes in other New England towns, nor was it followed by subsequent strikes in Fall River. Defeated in the strike, the Fall River Spinners' Union survived throughout the 1850s, though its existence was precarious.

The massive expansion of the mule-spinning industry soon after the Civil War coincided with the formation of local unions elsewhere, and with a sharp rise in militancy, especially in Fall River. The sources of this militancy were twofold: the recent arrival of longstanding British unionists on the one side, and the determination of American employers to oppose unions at all costs, on the other. The encounter between Lancashire militant unionists and Fall River "mill Czars," the following chapter proposes, erupted in an all-out struggle over control.

Chapter 7
The Struggle over Control

Those of my countrymen who still conceive of America that its principal features are prairies and forests. . . had better step over to Massachusetts, and take a look around. I venture to think that before they had been in the city of Fall River long enough to get themselves known to the police, they would have some of their ancient notions knocked out of their heads.

Ben Brierley,

Ab-O'th'- Yate in Yankeeland: The Results of Two Trips to America (London: Simpkin, 1885), p. 217.

A member of the Massachusetts House of Representatives sent in 1881 a letter to the state Bureau of Statistics of Labor asking: "Why is it that the working people in Fall River are in constant turmoil when at Lowell and Lawrence they are quiet?" Subsequently the bureau conducted a massive inquiry. It concluded that the main cause of the labor troubles in Fall River during the 1870s was the recent influx of British immigrant cotton workers who brought with them their Old Country tradition of labor militancy.[1]

This explanation was generally accepted by later historians. Rowland Berthoff, Clifton Yearley, Charlotte Erickson,[2] and Philip Foner[3] emphasized the growth of militancy in New England textile centers of British immigrants, as well as in other American industries dominated by British-born workers such as mining, the metals, pottery, stonecutting, and the building trades.

As we have seen in so many ways, a longstanding militant tradition among British immigrant spinners certainly contributed to the eruption of labor struggles in the United States. Yet union tradition alone does not provide a sufficient explanation for the growth in militancy. An additional factor was the difference in employment conditions between Britain and the United States. British employers had granted mule spinners complete control over their craft. American employers challenged the spinners' job control. The roots of militant strikes in the New England mule-spinning industry, accordingly, are to be sought in the changing status of the craft worker who moved from Britain to the United States. When the British immigrant spinner first entered the American factory he was about to lose much of his craft status. The Fall River disputes of the 1870s, it follows, can be better understood as an attempt of recent Lancashire immigrants to retrieve "the rights of the craftsman" that they had formerly possessed in the Old World.

The mule spinners' struggle for job control was thus distinctly different from that of other groups of American craftsmen; for example, iron molders and machinists. Whereas molders and machinists struggled to *retain* their craft control, mule spinners fought to *regain* control. Employers in the iron industry and machine production did not challenge the craftsmen's job control until after the Civil War. When they did so in the 1870s and 1880s, molders and machinists struck to preserve the achievements they had already won. In this sense, strikes to retain control were defensive. The mule spinners, on the other hand, fought to retrieve their customary rights, hence their strikes were offensive in nature. Establishing their Lancashire unions in Fall River, British mule spinners sought to regain control through union recognition.

The conventional interpretation of the Fall River events does not, however, lead to this conclusion. Actually, the three major strikes in Fall River during the 1870s were all reported to have occurred over wage demands. Yet, "since wages stand for more than can be bought with them," K.G.J.C. Knowles reminds us, "wage strikes tend to be symbolic of wider grievances."[4] In Fall River, undoubtedly, wages were not the real issue but rather what Edward Shorter and Charles Tilly call "a mobilizing device."[5] The question in Fall River was not "a question of dollars and cents," as one mill treasurer put it, "but a question as to who shall rule."[6] Citing the example of Fall River, David Montgomery captured the essence of these struggles when he wrote: "Strikes over wage reductions at times involved thinly disguised attacks by employers on craftsmen's job controls."[7]

THE STRIKES

Collective bargaining in any branch of the American cotton industry was unknown until 1886. Between 1873 and 1879 the Fall River spinners saw a reduction of 45% in their weekly earnings, partly as a result of trade depression and partly as a consequence of speed-up and stretch-out.[8] Not being bound by any agreement on a uniform list of prices, and moreover, refusing any contact with the representatives of the spinners' unions, New England employers reduced wages arbitrarily time and again during the 1870s. Wage cuts triggered strikes. The most bitter disputes occurred in Fall River—"the Manchester of America."

Three strikes erupted in Fall River in the 1870s, those of 1870, 1875, and 1879. None was successful. Throughout the decade, the mule spinners' union was the only body of organized workers which had a continuous existence in Fall River.

The 1870 Fall River strike erupted shortly after management had announced a general reduction of wages and lasted nine weeks. Employers reduced the piece rates of mule spinners by 7.5% to 8%, the wages of other operatives by 10%. The spinners led the strike, and they apparently gained a good deal of support from other classes of operatives, though many still opposed the strike. All in all, a strike of 430 mule spinners put out of work some 7,000 operatives— the entire body of Fall River's mill population at the time.[9]

Between 1870 and 1875 Fall River's cotton factory population more than doubled from 7,000 to nearly 15,000, largely as a result of an unprecedented mill building boom during 1871-72. Expansion was followed a year later by a nationwide business depression that equally affected the cotton trade. Consequently, the Fall River firms announced two wage cuts of 10% each in 1873 and 1874, and cotton corporations in Holyoke, Chicopee, Blackstone, and other New England towns imposed similar reductions.[10] A convention of union delegates from the northeastern spinning districts was held in Fall River in Spring 1874 and resolved that with the first improvement in trade the Fall River spinners would demand a restoration of wages to their former level, and if denied it, would strike. "Thus," in the words of Robert Howard, "Fall River was selected as the battlefield for the textile workers of New England,"[11] a strategy not unlike that of the Lancashire cotton spinners who in 1853 had turned Preston into "the battlefield in strikes for all England."[12]

Two major strikes were staged by the Fall River workers in 1875 and both were the product of the combined efforts of three unions: the older spinners' organization and the recently formed weavers' and carders' unions. A partial six weeks "turnout" during the winter that spread slowly among some 3,000 to 4,000 operatives, or a fifth to over a quarter of the total mill work force, was followed by an eight-week general strike and lockout of 15,000 workers in the summer. The first was hailed as a success; employers restored a 10% wage cut during a brief trade revival in March, only to enforce an equal reduction in August, thus precipitating a general strike.[13] The outcome of the general strike was a complete triumph of capital over labor. The newly organized unions among the weavers and cardroom operatives did not outlive the strike, the reduction remained in force, the entire leadership was blacklisted, and most devastating of all, any of the strikers who reapplied for work, mule spinners and all, were compelled to sign the "Infamous Document":

Agreement

We will not, while in the employ of the said corporation, belong to or be influenced by the action of any association or combination whose members are subject to the will of the majority in the matter of wages or any other subject connected with the free right of any person to work for whom and at such rates as they [sic] may see fit.[14]

Like the weavers and carders, most members of the mule spinners' union eventually signed the pledge, though they by no means considered it binding, as they made very clear to their overseers. In 1876 the Spinners' Union of Fall

River remained the only organized body of cotton workers in the city.

The Fall River strike of 1879, like the one in 1870, was a mule spinners' affair. As a result of a trade depression in 1878 the Fall River cotton corporations posted a 15% wage cut in March and during the following summer most factories were running only half time. When market conditions began to improve early in 1879 the Spinners' Union sent petitions to the employers asking to restore 10% of the reduction. "The petitions met with a cold and haughty refusal." Likewise, manufacturers declined to meet a delegation from the spinners' association. To enforce their demand the mule spinners took an informal vote and decided to strike, but only after their proposal to refer the case to a board of arbitration was rejected. With two-thirds majority vote by ballot in favor of striking, the spinners left the mills, but again, not before they gave a two-weeks notice for the advance. When the notice expired on June 26, from 800 to 1,000 spinners went on strike, forcing 14,000 out of work.[15] The struggle was long, lasting three-and-a-half months, and according to the *Labor Standard*, a workers' weekly published in Fall River since 1876, "aid for the strikers ha[d] come in as never known before in any strike in America."[16] Altogether, $25,000 were raised from trade unions in forty-eight different towns all over the United States.[17] Typically, inexperienced French-Canadian immigrants who were prone to damage the machinery were hired as mule spinners and housed in barrack-like tenements within the confines of the mill gates. Significantly, employers furnished many of the strikebreakers with firearms, particularly revolvers, and in at least one case a spinner was struck by bullets fired by strikebreakers.[18] "Every day our men are getting more desperate," wrote the secretary of the spinners' union in the tenth week of the strike. "I keep prevailing upon them to keep the law, but my efforts are unavailing."[19] By the twelfth week of the strike, 104 spinners were arrested.[20] At the end of the sixteenth week the mule spinners yielded.

THE EMPLOYERS

"The unions declare how many apprentices a boss may take on," reports the *New York Journal of Commerce* in its review of the 1875 Fall River strike, "what kind of work shall be given out to hands, how many hands should be put on certain jobs, what materials shall be used in manufactures, prohibit the employer from discharging or hiring a man without consultation with their committee, and force him in fifty ways to surrender all his business into their keeping."[21] Fall River employers viewed the strikes as above all endurance contests with the union. They regarded entrepreneurial freedom as the uncontested right of the American employer and therefore opposed any accommodation with the mule spinners' union that might have implied the slightest notion of recognition. They "did not desire any outside interference," as one Fall River worker put it, "as they thought themselves qualified to manage their own business."[22] They refused to meet with the representatives of the striking spinners because they did not wish "to surrender [their] property and [their] business to be managed by strangers."[23] They opposed arbitration. To prevent strikes by referring disputes to arbitration was one of the rules of the Benevolent and Protective Association of the United Operative Mule Spinners of America from its inception, soon after the Civil War.[24] Similarly, British trade unions strove persistently for arbitration all through the third quarter of the nineteenth century.[25] When the *Fall River Daily* found it advisable in 1875 to call for arbitration, it reminded the manufacturers that the system of arbitration adopted in Britain had been quite instrumental in solving labor disputes and there was no reason why it would not work well in Fall River, too. After all, the newspaper concluded: "As long as capitalists in America persist in importing or employing the shrewd operatives from Lancashire, Eng[land], they cannot expect them to forget or refuse to use the intelligence acquired at home, after they get here."[26] Still, Fall River employers insisted that running a business in the United States was a different matter: "Such means [arbitration] of settling disputes between employers and employed are not in consonance with the methods of doing business in this country and we do not propose to inaugurate the Plan."[27] One treasurer's announcement during the 1879 strike, that he would oppose arbitration even if the mills had to remain shut down for an entire year, was typical.[28] An editorial printed in the pro-management *Boston Herald* provides perhaps the best summary description of the ideology that underlay the anti-union attitude of the Fall River employers. "The American idea tends to individualism," declared the newspaper, adding,

> We regret exceedingly the development in this country, of a class which shows any lack of ability to better its conditions in this American way. Men employ labor for the purpose of gain; men work for wages. It is a matter of business.... There is no protecting and dependent class in this country. Good relations may be maintained between employers and employed by mutual justice and honesty; but when we come down to the question of rights, it is for the employers to say what wages he [sic] will pay, and for the employed to say whether he will work for such wages or not. On these terms alone can the workingmen maintain their dignity and avoid falling into the dependent condition of the operative class in England. Let us stand by the American idea with equal rights for all under the law.[29]

Again and again, Fall River manufacturers claimed that the main issue over which the strikes occurred was control, not wages. "I think the question with the spinners was not on [sic] wages," the treasurer of the Durfee Mills, one of the largest Fall River concerns, testified before the Massachusetts Bureau of Labor in 1871, "but whether they or the manufacturers should rule. For the last six or eight years they have ruled Fall River." He believed the 1870 dispute was a "question of power" rather than a matter of four or five cents a day, because the spinners were ready to go back to work immediately if employers would make "any compromise whatever." A sound judgment. The position of the Spinners' Association is stated in their address to the manufacturers: "We believe that the question in dispute can be more amicably settled if you will condescend to appoint five of your number to meet an equal number of spinners, and discuss the question pro and con, and if you can prove to us that there is a just cause for the reduction, we are willing to submit to it." Characteristically, the proposal was treated with "silent contempt"; employers were resolutely determined to have nothing to do with the union at all. "I might as well throw my property away," said the Durfee Mills' treasurer, as "submit to their ruling.... I will never do it."[30]

"Employers had plainly intimated that it was not a question of money but of discipline," a Fall River worker said of the 1875 contest. They could easily afford a 10% increase when production was booming in the winter, he continued, but their real purpose was to break up the union's control as soon as market conditions would permit a lockout.[31] "If the help want to control us and our capital," warned a representative of the manufacturers' Board of Trade, "it is manifest that they have undertaken a serious task; serious especially for themselves." The employers, he promised, would suspend production for a while, and then hire strikebreakers and armed guards to protect them, and reopen the mills.[32]

Similarly, the main objective of employers in 1879 was not merely to save 10% in labor costs, nor even just to win the strike, but rather "to make strikes impossible in Fall River in the future," as the Board of Trade publicly stated. And as the editors of the *Fall River Daily Herald* put it, for the employers the main issue was "mastery," and the key question was "rule or ruin"; for the spinners it was essentially a battle over "the recognition of their manhood."[33]

In 1879 the employers hired strikebreakers on a scale larger than ever before. They were less experienced and less skilled, yet much better paid than striking spinners. The millowners provided strikebreakers with food, shelter, and police protection, gave them a 50% wage hike, and in addition, paid scab labor-recruiters $10 a head. The "Mill Czars in order to rule," thus concluded the *Labor Standard*, "paid more than double wages." Evidently, the 1879 strike alone caused the employers a loss of over two million dollars.[34]

Such a determination on the part of the employers to vanquish the mule spinners at all costs raises an interesting question: how could the employers sustain the losses? What was the source of their power? Why, furthermore, did every strike in Fall River result in a complete victory of capital over labor while strikes in Lancashire during the same period ended occasionally in a victory or a partial victory of the strikers?

The answer can be found in the cohesiveness of the employers. Fall River employers, like manufacturers in other New England cotton towns, were unified. Lancashire employers, by contrast, were sharply divided by competition.[35]

Fall River cotton corporations were organized in a Board of Trade which, according to the *Labor Standard*, was "practically composed of the various members of. . . seven families. . . who [were] all agents, treasurers, clerks and directors."[36] The *Standard* provides a partial list of interlocking directorates of Fall River mills, and despite management's denial of these allegations,[37] evidence for the period 1873-78 derived from other sources confirms that 41 members of 7 families held 100 of the 259 directorships and 52 of the 102 top offices (president, treasurer, chief clerk, and agent) in 32 Fall River cotton corporations.[38] Eleven members of a single family—the Borden family—held 30 directorships and 22 top offices in 18 different corporations,[39] and 9 members of 7 leading families filled the positions of 55 directors and 29 corporate officers: 13 presidents, 8 treasurers, and 8 chief clerks, as shown in Table 9.[40]

Intercorporate linkages in Fall River extended beyond the cotton industry. Corporate directorates show that the top officers of Fall River mills met regularly on the boards of the Fall River railway and steamship companies, the Fall River Manufacturers' Mutual Insurance Company, the Manufacturers' Gas Company, and on the large boards of the Fall River banks.[41] Occasionally they also served as the principal officers of these companies and banks. Charles P. Stickney, for example, served in 1876 as both president and treasurer of the Fall River Steamboat Company and at the same time held nine directorships and one presidency in Fall River cotton mills.[42] Thomas Borden served in 1879 as chief clerk of the city's Old Colony Steamboat Company while he was holding four directorships and five other top offices in Fall River cotton corporations. And John Brayton, who served in 1879 as both president of Fall River's First National Bank and as chief clerk of Fall River, Warren and Providence Railroad Company, was in addition, president and director of two cotton mills and a board member of four other mills.[43]

Actually, financial control of every important aspect of business activity in the city had been firmly in the hands of the leading families long before the expansion of the 1870s. The Fall River city directory shows that every name listed in Table 9, save that of John P. Slade, also appeared ten years earlier in the 1864 directory as an officer and/or director of at least one cotton manufacturing firm. In 1864 as in 1875, members of the leading cotton families already dominated the boards of the Fall River banks and transportation companies.[44] Being fully aware of all these developments, the Massachusetts Bureau of Labor commented in 1882: "Financial ability and not technical knowledge of goods is what is required to make a successful Fall River mill owner. No new blood has been introduced into Fall River manufacturing circles. The mills have bred in and in."[45]

The concentration of control, and to a large extent ownership, of some thirty or forty Fall River firms in the hands of seven related families[46] surely contributed to employers' victories in strikes. Contrary to the employers' claims that the Board of Trade was simply an advisory body with no power to enforce its rulings,[47] the evidence suggests that the board succeeded in suppressing competition between firms to an extraordinary degree. The board fixed wages, regulated prices, controlled output, and held production costs at the

TABLE 9

Top Positions in Thirty Fall River Cotton Corporations
Held by Nine Individuals, 1873-1878

	President	Treasurer	Clerk	Director	Total	No. of Corporations
Borden, Jefferson	3	1	1	5	10	5
Borden, Richard	1	2	2	7	12	8
Borden, Thomas	2	3	2	5	12	5
Durfee, Nathan	3			7	10	7
Chace, S.A.	1	2	1	6	10	6
Davol, Stephan	1			6	7	7
Slade, John P.			1	4	5	4
Brayton, John S.	1		1	6	8	6
Stickney, C.P.	1			9	10	9
Total	13	8	8	55	84	57

Source: Silvia Lintner, "A Social History of Fall River, 1859-1879," 27. Lintner extracted
the figures from a letter found in William N. Bogle, Scrap Book, in the Fall
River Historical Society. She notes that internal evidence places the letter
between 1873 and 1878. See footnote 40.

---

minimum by constantly comparing the costs of individual mills.[48] In addition,
to track down strike agitators, to blacklist them, and to ensure that no Fall
River mill would ever employ them again, the Board of Trade established what
one manufacturer called a "secret service," adding: "The black list is directed
mostly toward the members of the Mule Spinners' Union, for they cause us
the most trouble."[49] The board used the blacklist "to guard against strikes."
It also provided generous assistance to individual employers during strikes, and
most important, the Board of Trade was powerful enough to impose and coordinate general lockouts in which time after time the employers outlasted the
spinners.

The corporate interlock, it should be noted here, was not a feature unique
to Fall River but a characteristic of Lowell, Lawrence, and other New England
cotton towns as well. Admittedly, the proportion of individuals who held more
than one corporate position (of either a director or an officer) in 1881 was higher
in Fall River (49%) than in Lowell (35%) or Lawrence (27%). It is also true
that neither in Lowell nor in Lawrence did any individual hold more than 6
positions, while thirteen of the Fall River industrialists did so. Accordingly,
the average number of corporate positions filled by an individual was 1.55 in
Lowell, 1.41 in Lawrence, and 2.52 in Fall River.[50] Yet despite these differences,

the Lowell and Lawrence employers, like the Fall River employers, were unified. Because the number of textile firms in Lowell (16) and Lawrence (12) was far smaller than in Fall River (38), and because the average size of a corporation in Lowell (870 employees) and in Lawrence (910 employees) was more than twice as large as in Fall River (395 employees)[51], the industry in each of these two factory towns was sufficiently monopolized, and the corporations were closely enough connected to suppress competition, to facilitate cooperation, and to oppose any attempt at unionization. In Lowell, for instance, in order to defeat a partial strike by the mule spinners in 1875, the corporations managed to enforce a lockout of all the mule-spinning departments in town for six weeks until the spinners yielded.[52]

Lancashire millowners, by contrast to New England employers, were divided by conflicts of interest, conflicts between spinning and weaving firms, between different cotton districts, between large and small employers, and between firms of different structure. For one thing, the representative size of enterprise in the British cotton industry remained small and the typical firm was the family-owned concern, not the public corporations.[53] In addition, while New England cotton manufacturers almost always integrated spinning and weaving, the increasing separation of these two processes in Lancashire meant that the industry was easily accessible to the small capitalist, and competition was intense.[54] Beginning in the early 1870s, moreover, in a growing number of Lancashire cotton towns, most notably Oldham, there developed a fierce competition between two sectors of the industry: the newly established joint stock companies known as the "limiteds" and the older family firms.[55] Ownership of these joint stock companies was widely spread among many small investors, hence competition increased in yet another way. Joint stock companies were not confined to Oldham but were also founded in Rochdale, Ashton, and Stockport, and in six similar spinning centers in Lancashire.[56] Divided by competition, Lancashire employers sought an accommodation with the unions. As a result, they adopted a far more conciliatory attitude toward the resolution of labor disputes than that of the New England manufacturers.

THE OLDHAM COUNTER-EXAMPLE

Nowhere is the question of corporate control more vital for understanding labor relations than in the contrast between Oldham and Fall River. In many ways, the resemblance between these two factory towns in the 1870s is striking. Oldham was the largest mule-spinning center in the world; Fall River was the leading mule-spinning center in the United States. Both mill towns specialized in coarse spinning with yarn count numbers concentrating in the lower- and mid- 30s.[57] Both underwent a phenomenal expansion in the early 1870s—a "mania" of mill building. Between 1870 and 1875 the number of cotton manufacturing companies in Fall River rose from 21 to 33.[58] In Oldham during the same period some 50 or 60 new spinning mills went into operation bringing the total up to 180 or so.[59] In both cases, furthermore, the new mills raised capital by issuing stocks to the public so that their size was not limited by the capacities of the individual employer.

Yet there were differences. On the one hand the Oldham corporate model was characterized by low share denominations and many shareholders; on the other, corporate control in Oldham was further decentralized as a result of a remarkable arrangement whereby each shareholder, no matter how many shares he or she held, had the right to one and only one vote.

As far as the *Fall River Daily* could ascertain in its 1875 investigation of the "Manufacturers' Side of the Story," no Fall River operatives owned any stocks in the mills. "There was nothing to hinder them from owning stocks," the newspaper assures us, except, of course, for the fact that the value of a single stock of a Fall River cotton corporation was $100, far beyond the reach of any mill operative, including a mule spinner. In Oldham, by contrast, the spinning companies limited their shares to $25 each, so that the better paid, skilled operatives could invest their family savings in the mills.[60]

The total amount of capital the Oldham spinners invested was rather slight, however. Much of the stock ownership in the limited liability firms was in the hands of private millowners who sought to extend their control to the new companies. Like the Fall River capitalists, the Oldham industrialists attempted to do so by means of interlocking directorates, and they actually managed to place individual members of prominent families on several corporate boards of the limiteds.[61] But in contrast to the Fall River practice, the voting rules of the Oldham companies ensured that no single shareholder, no single family, not even a group of families would be able to seize control over the industry and stifle competition. As Albert Shaw, the American consul in Manchester, expressed it, the rules "allow[ed] *the man* not the *money* to vote."[62]

The Fall River cotton manufacturing corporations adopted the modern principle of joint stock which assumed that the company was a union of capital, not of people. Accordingly, votes were weighted in proportion to the number of shares held so that a relatively small group of large investors could easily outvote the majority of shareholders. The Oldham's radical principle of "one man one vote," which by the way extended to women shareholders as well, prevented the consolidation of control by a few individuals. On the one hand, the allotment of equal votes in Oldham led to high rates of attendance in quarterly meetings, to meticulous supervision of directors and top officers by the shareholders, and to the election of mule spinners to corporate boards of directors.[63] But on the other, it led to growing divisions among many small investors, to their inability to unify in opposition to the unions, to their desire for accommodation and reconciliation, and in turn, to the resolution of labor disputes in a peaceful and orderly manner.[64]

THE INTERPRETATION OF THE STRIKES

Corporate control and craft control went hand in hand; the contrast between Fall River and Oldham extended from one realm of control to another. In Fall River in 1870, in contrast to Oldham, control over recruitment, production, and piece rates was firmly in the hands of management. Management itself decided who to employ, what kind of work the spinner would do, how many helpers he would employ, how fast he would work, and the amount of wages he would receive. Such a measure of control provided the Fall River manufacturers with a great deal of freedom to change the terms of employment according to the business conditions of the industry. Consequently, during the slumps of the 1870s Fall River employers recruited a growing number of unorganized spinners, cut the number of helpers, increased supervision, stretched out and speeded up the machinery, and reduced wages arbitrarily. All these changes led directly to the strikes. Nonetheless, the main issue over which the strikes occurred was union recognition.

But why was recognition so crucial? What were the fundamental goals the spinners attempted to achieve had they succeeded in forcing employers into some form of union recognition?

These goals may be understood in terms of the three aspects of craft control mentioned in the foregoing discussion of Lancashire. The struggle for recognition was a struggle for craft control, and with each successive strike an additional aspect of control became a major preoccupation of the union. In 1870 the mule spinners fought above all to control recruitment. In 1875 the union resisted not only the employer's authority to regulate hiring, but even more so, his control over the production process. The battle for control over production led to the demand for collective bargaining on a standard list of piece rates: from 1879 onwards the Fall River Spinners' Union insisted more upon price lists than upon anything else.

The mule spinners' organization in Fall River, as in other New England towns, was a craft union modelled on the Lancashire example. Ideally, union membership was a prerequisite for entry into the occupation. But insofar as employers refused to recognize the union, the spinners found it extremely difficult to exercise effective control over entry. Still, this type of control was of paramount importance in order to prevent employers from hiring scabs.

"I . . . object to their saying who shall work and who shall not work," protested the Durfee Mills' treasurer in his instructive testimony before the Massachusetts Bureau of Labor in 1871. Apparently, one of the main causes leading to the 1870 strike was the recent practice of the Fall River manufacturers to employ "boys and girls" on small mules, thereby displacing the adult male unionists. Opposing this policy, the spinners refused to work alongside the unorganized workers. Moreover, in the course of the strike itself, reported the treasurer, Fall River managers hired "a great many people from out of town, but when they came they were threatened, intimidated, and induced to go back."[65] Although one-sided, this is a valid observation. On the basis of evidence collected from spinners, treasurers, police officers, and the mayor of Fall River, the Massachusetts Bureau of Labor concluded that the mule spinners indeed were "likely to make it uncomfortable for one of their own number who betrayed,"[66] and it was such a conduct that evoked the greatest opposition among employers. "It is the spinners that cause all the agitation and stop the mills," said another employer, "but they go too far when they order out men whom they call 'scabs' and 'knob-sticks'."[67] Yet to exclude scabs was to enforce solidarity—a critical element in the mule spinners' efforts to control hiring. After all, the powerful position of early spinners' unions in Lancashire was largely dependent on their ability to exclude knobsticks, and that in exactly the same fashion as in Fall River. "The spinners would trouble only their own class," is the remark of the treasurer of the Fall River Tecumseh Mills in 1870: "It is their own mates that they intimidate and no others."[68] Since the mules supply the necessary yarn, a general mule spinners' stoppage, whether in Lancashire or Fall River, would sooner or later put out of employment the weavers, dressers, calico printers, and preparatory workers; in short, the entire mill work force.[69] There was no need to "trouble" other workers.

Control over hiring and close supervision were interrelated. Both were the functions of the foreman. Supervision, however, encroached upon the functional autonomy of the spinner and it is of little surprise that no other issue evoked so much bitterness among the Lancashire mule spinners in Fall River as the conduct of the overseers. An immigrant mule spinner who worked twenty-two years in England and six in the United Stated complained in 1870 that the American overseer was more "authoritative and overbearing" than the British, and that the "liberties" enjoyed by the spinners were greater in England.[70] "There was more *freedom from restraint*" in Lancashire factories, related another mule spinner: "We could sing and talk." In Massachusetts, on the other hand, there was no escape from "tyrannical driving": "We are driven all we can possibly bear and have to strain any nerve to give satisfaction."[71] By 1875 hard driving reached a critical point. The spinners' opposition to "the tyrannical conduct of the subordinate officers in the mills" and to the "numerous unreasonable rules and requirements" instituted by the treasurers overshadowed all other issues over which the Fall River strike of 1875 occurred.[72]

Just as the mule spinners resisted increased supervision, so they insisted on keeping their extra help. A recurrent complaint during the 1870s was the new arrangement enforced by Fall River employers under which the spinner had to oil and clean his own pair of mules—tasks formerly done by boy helpers. The helper performed these tasks while the spindles were in operation, so that the mule spinner did not have to stop the machinery. But since the Fall River spinners had no control over helpers, employers could intensify their labor by simply depriving them of the service of scavengers.[73] As a result, the spinners of Fall River were "required to do in the same time a larger amount of work than elsewhere," concluded a special report of the Boston Committee of the

Labor Council in 1875.[74]

An "Appeal of the Fall River Spinners to the Workingmen of America" sheds some light on the strike of 1879. The Appeal raised two major complaints. Once again, the spinners resisted stretch-out and speed-up. But in addition, they now demanded some form of control over wage rates.[75] Autonomy at work would have provided the spinners with a degree of control over production and thereby freed them from the tight grip of the foreman whose chief task was to "drive" and "grind." Likewise, a written agreement on wages rather than a verbal promise; that is, a price list, would have protected the spinners both from arbitrary wage cuts during depressions and from unrenumerated increases in output, and would have put an end, once and for all, to the notorious practice of the Fall River employers to adjust and readjust the standard piece rate according to the pace of production of the fastest working spinners.[76]

Both points were the subject of state and federal investigations.[77] The 1879 strike, "the most bitterly contested struggle that ever occurred in the annals of Fall River industrial history,"[78] led directly to these hearings, and the two reports contain valuable information on what the strike was all about. "Speed," testified one mule spinner, "is an absolute science in Fall River and what the superintendents and overseers do not know about it, you may rest assured is not worth knowing."[79] "I have been nine years in Fall River," said another spinner, "and have never worked anywhere else, except in England, where we worked at high speed but not to the extent practiced here." He continued that, whereas in Fall River the mule's carriage of spindles made four "stretches" or round trips per minute, in England three-and-a-half trips a minute was the rule in spinning the same yarn count.[80] "It is drive, drive, drive," charged Robert Howard, "It is a continual race from morning till night, and there is not one man in twenty not brought up in the business who could follow a mule spinner from the beginning of his day's work to the end, even considering nothing but the walking."[81]

Just the walking? Yes, indeed. All estimates agree that mule spinners covered twenty to forty miles in a day's work following the carriage that slid back and forth on the rail. As a rule, spinners as well as piecers always worked in their bare feet. They were required to do so to avoid slipping on the oily floor and tripping over the gigantic mule machine while it was in motion. The distance an operative had to walk depended on the quality of the yarn spun and on the type and size of the mule. In spinning low counts the carriage moved faster than in fine spinning; accordingly, it was estimated that by the end of the nineteenth century coarse spinners walked twice as far as fine spinners.[82] Likewise, the self-acting mule was larger and faster than the power-driven mule, and hence it required more walking. A board of commissioners appointed by the British government to investigate the matter found that in the 1830s when the carriage of the power-driven mule made only two trips per minute (in fine spinning), an operative walked a distance of between eighteen and twenty-five miles in a twelve-hour day.[83] In Fall River in the 1870s, with four round-trips per minute, a mule spinner on a pair of self actors walked in his bare feet from twenty-five to thirty-nine miles in an eleven-hour day.[84] Since each of these machines traveled sixty-four inches back and forth, four times per minute, and since piecing up yarns involved an incessant race after the carriage, it is no wonder that work in Fall River was so arduous. Furthermore, because the average yarn count in the United States was coarser than in Britain, American mule spinners generally worked harder than the British. But most telling of all is the fact that the rate of speed was largely a matter of control: in New England the manager controlled the speed while in Lancashire the mule spinner himself did so. A visitor to Fall River in 1881 thus reported that the superintendent in the mule spinning room would "stand by timing with his watch the fearful action of the machinery to see if it were going at full speed," a practice not uncommon in the 1870s also.[85]

Notwithstanding the speed-up of the machinery, finally, Fall River employers were reluctant to hire "spare hands" who would assist individual mule spinners here and there, and would occasionally substitute them altogether for a few moments at a time. As a result absenteeism was high. Five regular vacancies in a mule-spinning department was the norm in Fall River on the eve of the great strike. "The speed at which mules have been driven during the past few years," the Spinners' Association charged in 1879, "without the assistance of any spare help, renders it next to impossible for a spinner to work continuously, often having to lose from three to five days per month in order to restore his wasted powers, consequence of excessive toil."[86] To insure themselves against speed-up, as well as against stretch-out and wage cuts due to the business cycle, the spinners of Fall River demanded a price list.

Robert Howard, then secretary of the Fall River Spinners' Union, led the strike of 1879, and testified four years later before a Senate committee. Only a "standard list of prices, and a uniform rate of work in all the mills," which could guarantee the spinner "a fair week's wage for a fair week's work," he told the committee, would have prevented the strike.[87] Howard saw the Oldham "speed list," just adopted in 1876, as the model.

Like Fall River, Oldham in the second part of the nineteenth century became a rapidly growing center of coarse spinning and, since speed had advanced considerably more on the coarse than on the fine counts, the Oldham spinners demanded a list based partly on the principle of speed. The Oldham list of 1876 differs from the older Lancashire lists in two respects. First, all other Lancashire lists adjusted the piece price according to the size of the mule and the count of the yarn produced. The Oldham list alone determined its piece price by reference to the size and speed of the machinery. The speed of the carriage was directly related to the fineness of the yarn so that output on mules of different sizes could be measured by reference to speed rather than to yarn count.[88] More important was the allowance for "quick speed" made by the Oldham list. The "quick speed" clause granted a wage increment for every additional second above the "standard speed"—three draws or round trips of the carriage in fifty seconds.

The advantage in production arising from "quick speed" was to be divided equally between spinners and employers.[89]

The "quick speed" clause is what Robert Howard had in mind when he demanded a price list for the spinners of Fall River. A list similar to the one adopted in Oldham would have guaranteed the Fall River spinner "so much for every inch that the mule traveled." "A list like the Oldham list [he explained] would give more satisfaction to the men and also more satisfaction to the manufacturers themselves; because the men would then know that there would be no way whereby they could be cheated out of their honest earnings, and that knowledge would be a great preventative of strikes. If the manufacturers would only give themselves time to sit down along with the best of the men— let three and three meet—and draw off a list, much trouble would be avoided." In addition, Howard continued, such a list would specify "the proportionate share that each party was entitled to" when profits were soaring during prosperity and vice versa in a slump. He even went as far as suggesting that once a uniform list was agreed upon, the union would not allow its members to go on strike until every grievance had been thoroughly investigated, adding that in "ninety-nine cases out of a hundred" a dispute would be settled without a recourse to a strike.[90] The demand for a price list remained the major preoccupation of the Fall River union in the years following the defeat of 1879.

THE OUTCOME OF THE STRIKES

Collective bargaining on a price list, as a matter of historical fact, was an act of union recognition. The event was a landmark; it took place for the first time in the history of the American textile industry in Fall River in 1886.[91] To avoid strikes employers eventually consented to negotiate a spinning list with the union, yet the Fall River list differed markedly from the Oldham one.

A revised version of the Fall River list—or "sliding scale" as it was often called in the United States—is printed in *Wade's Fibre and Fabric*, a Boston trade journal, in September 1888. It is a list based simply on broad ranges of spindles (up to 1,150; 1,151 to 1,300; and 1,301 to 1,600 spindles on a mule) and counts, that is, on the length of the mule and the quality of the yarn, not on speed.[92] A few months after this list was adopted, in response to the spinners' complaints, the Fall River Board of Trade agreed to frame a new list with finer gradations according to the number of spindles (a reduction for every additional 12 spindles on a mule) and yarn count (an advance for every additional count number), but the board utterly rejected any provisions for increases in speed that resulted from improved technology.[93] Further attempts of the Fall River union to negotiate a speed list failed.[94] Indeed, when Thomas Ashton, secretary of the Oldham spinners, visited Fall River in 1902, he discovered to his astonishment that the same piece rates were paid for spinning "whether the mules [ran] quick speeds or slow speeds." "In many instances," Ashton said, "I found that the spinners were paid standing wages, and when I inquired the reason for this, I was told it was because the standard list did not provide for the counts of yarn being spun." The Fall River price list covered a limited range of yarn counts numbering 18 to 50 only.[95]

One fundamental reason why the Fall River spinners failed to negotiate a comprehensive speed list was the growing weakness of their union organization. At the time the first price list was adopted in Fall River, in 1886, the bargaining power of the Fall River spinners had already diminished as a result of what was perhaps the most serious and far-reaching offensive of the employers: the introduction of new spinning machinery that would replace mules. Technological change, of course, did not occur overnight, and to avoid costly stoppages employers entered into agreements with the mule spinners. But at the same time, the steady diffusion of the improved ring-spinning technology guaranteed the downfall of the union in the long run. This is how the Fall River manufacturers undermined the mule spinners' union over the course of the next three decades.

"Ever since 1853," reflected a member of the New England Cotton Manufacturers' Association in 1883, "we have spun our filling on frames. . . . The ring frame was not as perfect at the time as it is today . . . but we concluded it was worth the trial to get rid of this nuisance of mule-spinners that could succeed at any time in stopping the work."[96] The ring was an improved throstle. It was invented in the United States in 1828 in order to increase the speed of spinning without causing frequent breakage to the yarn. Its perfection, however, was not completed until the early 1880s.[97] Yet, Fall River employers invested large sums in ring spinning after 1870.

Ring spinning, like throstle spinning, was a machine-tending job filled by unorganized women and juveniles. "We never employ men when we can get women," testified a Fall River treasurer before the Massachusetts Bureau in 1881, "because [women] cause less trouble by striking, or by finding unnecessary fault." Accordingly, he proceeded, his firm was replacing old mules with rings whenever possible and adding rings when new machinery was required. "We would rather employ a woman or a boy when they are able to do the work for which we now have to engage men," said another manufacturer, and concluded that the improved ring spindle would "do the work required fully as well as the mule." By the 1880s the transition to ring spinning was well under way. A Fall River manufacturer explains:

> It is the mule spinners that cause all the trouble and to obviate this the mules are gradually being done away with, and the day is not far distant when mules will be remarkable only for their entire absence. The system of frame or ring spinning is being rapidly adopted; and, as the frames can be run exclusively by women and boys, the men will soon be left high and dry, and must look for some other employment.[98]

What exactly the role of the Fall River strikes was in promoting technological change is impossible to say. But as Lars Sandberg noted, "The desire to break the power of the union...did have at least some effect in encouraging the adoption of ring spinning."[99] The ring was more efficient than the mule.[100] It produced stronger and more durable yarn but not quite as soft and smooth as mule-spun yarn—the typical product of Fall River. Ring spinning, therefore, "will be brought about very gradually," predicted a Fall River writer in 1879, "unless manufacturers are compelled to resort to it at once in self-defense." "Capital will not permit itself to be hampered by labor unions," he proceeded, "when it can easily relieve itself by the aid of the inventive genius of the mechanic." Fall River capitalists acted accordingly.[101] Shortly before the 1879 strike broke out several mill agents met and proposed to replace four or five pairs of mules in each mill with ring frames and thereby reduce the number of mule spinners by 100 to 200.[102] During the strike itself the board of directors of the Troy company voted to discontinue the use of 10,000 mule spindles, and to install ring spindles instead. In the same year, two other Fall River firms—the Flint and Osborn Mills—were reported to have installed new ring frames "to take the place of mules." [103]

Fall River employers, as a matter of fact, embarked on ring spinning soon after they had defeated the 1870 strike, and the effects of technological change on production were already becoming visible during the 1879 strike. To be sure, manufacturers still invested in mules (the ring was not yet suited for spinning higher counts yarns), but the relative share of the mule-spinning industry in Fall River sharply declined after 1870. According to the manuscript schedules of the federal census of industry, 484,000 of the 540,000 spindles in operation in Fall River in 1870, or nearly 90%, were attached to mules; the rest were "frame spindles" — the generic term for throstles and rings. Of the twenty cotton firms enumerated in the 1870 census, fourteen spun yarn solely on mules, and of the remaining six only one large firm, the American Linen Company, installed an approximately equal number of mule and frame spindles.[104] A survey taken a decade later, in 1881, shows a 17% decline in the relative proportion of mule spindles: 946,000 of the 1,302,000 spindles in Fall River on which data is available, or 73%, were mounted on mules, and 27% on frames. Of the twenty-nine firms that gave information in 1881 (only six corporations with 193,000 spindles did not specify the type of spindle used), five specialized in mule spinning only, twenty-four combined mule and frame spinning, eleven of the combined firms had nearly an equal number of mule and frame spindles, and one big firm, the Pocasset Manufacturing Company, was largely dependent on frames.[105]

It is truly revealing that the Pocasset corporation was able to run five-sixths of its machinery in 1879 despite the strike.[106] The King Philip Mills, which employed only 15 mule spinners in 1879, also did not close down during the strike but continued to spin yarn on ring frames. And so did other combined firms: "Some of the corporations employ ring-spinning to a greater or less extent, and were thus able to continue to run a portion of their machinery."[107] Firms that owned ring-spinning machinery were likely to be less affected by the strike not only because the ring spinners remained at work, but also because the weavers and other operatives engaged in interdependent processes were not necessarily forced to stop as a result of yarn shortages. "Such lessons are not lost upon the manufacturers," the Massachusetts Bureau of Labor tells us in its summary of the strike, warning that the replacement of mules by rings would "inevitably be hastened by an unwise use of [union] power."[108] Significantly, within the next twenty-five years, 1879-1904, the proportion of mule spindles in Fall River fell from 73% to 24%.[109] The total number of mule spinners in the city declined from 1,000 in 1879 to 350 in 1909.[110] Once again, the removal of mules culminated during strikes. In the course of the gigantic Fall River general strike of 1894 mill agents were reported to be "throwing out [all] but precious few mules."[111] More mules were replaced by ring frames during subsequent strikes in 1898 and 1904.[112]

The Fall River events were repeated elsewhere,[113] and mule spinners were eventually displaced by the new technology. In a remarkable testimony given before the U.S. Industrial Commission in 1899, a former Massachusetts spinner related his experience: "I have . . . observed . . . the substitution of ring spinning for mule spinning"

> . . . throughout the whole of my career in the mills from the time I first took charge of a pair of mules until the time my last pair was broken up. . . . We were shorn of our locks, Sampson-like, and our machines were made junk of shortly afterwards. We are out. . . . The mules are being broken up, and my opinion, formed years and years ago, is that they are broken up not because it is the opinion of the employer[s] that they can do better work with the ring frame at all, but because the fact is appreciated that the mules require men to operate them, and men coming together in the room and consulting each other, are more easily organized. The mule spinners are organized, and some of the employers consider it is dictation to have committees come from the organization and tell them they would like to have such things done or not done. My feeling about tearing out mules is that it is done to crush the power of the operatives to devise and put in working order the means that would bring about better conditions for them [the employers].[114]

In 1870 the United States had 7 million spindles, 48% of which were mule and 52% ring spindles. By 1905, of the total number of 23 million spindles in the United States the proportion of mule spindles was 23%. In England, by contrast, 83% of the 48 million spindles at work in 1909 were attached to mules.[115]

The advantage of replacing mules with rings was greater in the United States than Britain for a variety of reasons. One factor was the cost of transportation. The vertical specialization of the Lancashire cotton industry ruled out the introduction of ring spindles for weft in the vast majority of mills owing to the prohibitive cost of shipping ring weft. Because spinning and weaving in New England was integrated in the same plant, American employers did not have to consider this extra cost in choosing between rings and mules.[116] In addition, the labor cost advantage of rings over mules was lower in Britain than the United States[117] while the cotton cost advantage of mules over rings was lower in the United States than in Britain. The ring, like the throstle, required better quality cotton than the mule (for spinning a given yarn count) so that the relative cheapness of raw cotton in the United States encouraged the transition to ring spinning. Lastly, the ring was limited to coarse spinning and therefore British employers who were more dependent on fine spinning than American manufacturers could not make a large-scale switch to the new technology.[118]

Rather than adopting the more efficient machine, Lancashire employers cooperated closely with the mule spinners to raise productivity on the mule. The mule spinners, in turn, passed on the increased workload to their piecers.[119] The fact that the mule spinners of Lancashire managed to retain their craft control intact as well as to expand their supervisory responsibilities, enabled them to raise productivity by driving their helpers harder and harder.[120] In New England by contrast, the struggle of British immigrant spinners to take control, to establish in New England the craft autonomy they had known in Britain, and to resist the intensification of labor, hastened the diffusion of the alternative ring-spinning technology.

Chapter 8
Cotton, Coal, Iron, and Steel

One consequence of nineteenth-century competitive capitalism was the consolidation of job control by many groups of workers in the major British industries. During the long mid-Victorian boom, Britain's atomistic firms opted for collective accommodation with [the] unions...rather than jeopardize their individual fortunes through industrial conflict.

> Bernard Elbaum and William Lazonick,
> *The Decline of the British Economy*
> (Oxford, Clarendon Press, 1988), p. 4.

The emergence of monopoly capitalism was characterized by the interaction of technical progress and new forms of industrial organization and market control. American producers were at the forefront of this development. British industry was increasingly its victim.

> Bernard Elbaum and Frank Wilkinson,
> "Industrial Relations and Uneven Development:
> A Comparative Study of the American and British Steel Industries,"
> *Cambridge Journal of Economics*,
> vol. 3, no. 3 (September, 1979), p. 276.

This study examined technology and labor relations in the cotton mule-spinning industry and showed how the American experience differed from the British one. It contrasted labor-management cooperation in Britain with industrial conflict in the United States, the triumph of craft control in Britain with the breakup of craft control in the United States. It concluded that the relative power of unions, the divisions among the employers, and the pace of technological change were all important elements in the mule spinners' ability to retain their craft control. It demonstrated, in addition, how intense labor struggles in the United States led to the demise of the mule-spinning industry while industrial peace in Britain helped the industry survive well into the twentieth century.

One problem that arises from such a narrow-appearing case study is that of generalization. How does the study of the cotton industry relate to the history of technology and labor in other industries? Were the developments depicted above unique to cotton mule spinning or were they also found in other British and American industries? Were they found, for example, in the two other great staple industries of the nineteenth century, coal and iron (later steel)?

This chapter argues that they were. The essential developments that took place in the British and American cotton mule-spinning industry during the nineteenth century occurred in the coal, iron, and steel industries as well. There were, to be sure, significant differences among these industries in terms of technology and labor relations. Still, the basic line of argument presented above in respect to the mule spinners is also valid when applied to the coal miners, the ironworkers, and the steelworkers.

Cotton was the earliest factory industry in Britain and the United States, it was at the core of the first industrial revolution, and it continued to expand all through the nineteenth century. Coal, iron, and steel expanded later and played a critical role in the industrialization of both countries during the second half of the nineteenth century. By the end of the Civil War, cotton, coal, iron, and steel were the leading industries on both sides of the Atlantic.

Consider the following British statistics. In 1865 cotton, coal, iron, and steel made up together about 16% of Britain's Gross National Product (GNP) and in 1907 close to 14%. According to the 1907 Census of Production, cotton accounted for over 2% of the British GNP, coal for 5%, and iron and steel for 6.4%.[1] Coal mining was the largest employer with close to half a million workers in 1880 and over a million in 1909. Cotton gave employment to 480,000 operatives in 1880 and just under 580,000 in 1907.[2] In 1875 cotton accounted for 32% of all British exports, iron and steel for 12%, and coal for only 4%. In 1900 the figures were 24% (cotton), 11% (iron and steel), and 13% (coal). Taken together, the three staple industries accounted for close to a half of Britain's domestic exports in both 1875 and 1900.[3]

By 1900 the three British industries were heavily unionized. The cotton mule spinners were the first to organize and the first to bargain collectively on price lists. Next, union recognition in the iron industry resulted in the introduction of collective bargaining on "sliding scales" around mid-century, and the same developments took place in the steel industry in the 1860s and in the coal mining industry during the 1870s. In all three British industries, collective bargaining led to reconciliation between employers and unions. It also led to the unions' encouragement of emigration of militant members, to a massive departure of British unionists to the United States, and to a steep increase in the number of American spinners, miners, ironworkers and steelworkers who were British immigrants.

British immigrants played a key role in American labor struggles. Militant strikes in the American cotton, coal, and iron and steel industries erupted at the end of the Civil War and continued for more than two decades. Many of these strikes were fought over the issue of control. Control struggles, to be sure, took somewhat different forms and occurred at different times in cotton mule spinning, coal mining, and iron and steel making. Yet in each of these industries, employers won the battle over control.

The struggle over control in the mule-spinning industry took place during the 1870s and culminated with the Fall River strike of 1879. From 1879 and throughout the 1920s trade unionism in the American mule-spinning industry was losing ground steadily and irreversibly. The battle over control in the anthracite coal-mining industry was fought in the fields of eastern Pennsylvania between 1868 and 1875 and ended with the utter destruction of the union. The turning point was the 1875 general strike of Pennsylvania anthracite coal diggers. The union's defeat in 1875 was so devastating that for the next forty-five years, until 1920, the anthracite coal operators managed to resist any demand for union recognition, though the bituminous coal companies, it should be noted, signed the first interstate collective bargaining agreement with the United Mine Workers in 1898. The struggle over control in the iron and steel industry was the longest. It lasted over twenty-five years from the end of the Civil War until 1892. It resulted in early union defeats—and victories—among the iron-workers and steelworkers in the 1870s and 1880s, and reached its apex in the Homestead Strike of 1892—the decisive battle over control in the American steel industry. The Homestead strikers were defeated and their union crushed. It took American steelworkers nearly half a century to rebuild their union into a centrally controlled nationwide organization that could match the power of the steel corporations.

RECONCILIATION AND ACCOMMODATION

The British mule was an extremely complex piece of machinery. Before the transition to the self actor, mule spinning was a highly skilled job which required coordination, dexterity, stamina, and strength. Mule spinners were responsible for quality control, for machine maintenance, and most important, for frequent mechanical adjustments of the mule's parts during the spinning and winding processes.

Iron making and coal mining, like mule spinning, were craft industries. Puddlers were the most important category of skilled craftsmen employed in iron making. They were responsible for refining "pig" iron to wrought iron. They employed craft skills to steer and shape the molten iron, metallurgical know-how to distinguish between variable qualities of hot and molten iron, and exhaustive physical labor. Other craftsmen, rollers, heaters, and shinglers, required a similar combination of technical knowledge, metallurgical judgment, physical strength, and endurance in the production of semi-finished and finished iron products.[4]

Miners working at the coalface, or hewers as they were called in northern England, were an elite group of skilled craftsmen among all coal workers. They were in charge of blasting the coal at the face. The miner drilled a hole at the face of the coal, filled it with powder, set a safety fuse, lit it, and moved away to safety. All these decisions—when and where to drill the hole, place the powder, and set and light the fuse—required knowledge and judgment. The miner, in addition, was subject to severe physical constraints because he often worked at a near-vertical breast and had to pass through low and narrow tunnels to get to the coalface.[5]

Cotton mule spinners, skilled ironworkers, and miners were subcontractors. In the cotton industry, mule spinners subcontracted piecers and scavengers. In the iron industry, craftsmen subcontracted unskilled helpers to handle materials between stages of production. "Forehand" puddlers and shinglers employed from one to two "underhands" while rollers and heaters employed teams of laborers. Helpers were hired and fired, paid and supervised, trained and disciplined by their contractors. Like the mule spinners, skilled ironworkers received payments in proportion to output (based on tonnage) and paid their helpers time rates.[6]

Subcontracting in the British coal industry was not as widespread as in iron making or cotton spinning, yet it survived well into the second half of the nineteenth century. In the northeastern coal fields of Northumberland and Durham, the miners employed their own "putters"—laborers engaged in hauling the coal.[7] In many of the Midland fields, the "butty" system prevailed. A subcontractor, called a butty, hired his own group of colliers and contracted with the owners to deliver the coal from one section of the mine.[8]

The subcontract system went hand in hand with a promotion ladder. In cotton, coal and iron, a promotion ladder that led from the less skilled to the more skilled replaced the traditional system of formal apprenticeship. Just as the big piecer was promoted to a cotton spinner, so was the iron "underhand" promoted to a puddler and the haulage worker to a coal miner.

Early trade unionism in the cotton, coal and iron industries was built on apprenticeship. There were no permanent organizations of iron and coal workers before mid-century, only temporary associations. Between 1800 and 1850 short-lived unions emerged among the puddlers in Staffordshire and among the miners in the northeast of England, the Midlands, Scotland, and Wales.[9] An example of such an organization was the Friendly Society of Coal Mining, established in Lancashire in 1830 with branches in Staffordshire, Yorkshire, Cheshire, and Wales. The rules of the Society, like those of early mule spinners societies, included restrictions on entry into the trade; for example, members were prohibited from instructing nonunionists in the art of coal mining. Typically, the Society failed to win the employers' recognition and collapsed within a year.[10]

Permanent district societies among miners and ironworkers appeared during the third quarter of the nineteenth century. In the 1850s and 1860s miner unions were established in Northumberland, Durham, Yorkshire, and South Wales, and unions among ironworkers emerged in Staffordshire and in the northeast of England.[11] These unions resembled mule spinners' societies in several respects: they were all regionally based, they adopted price lists or sliding scales, they entered into collective agreements with the employers, and, due to conservative leadership, they tried to avoid strikes at almost any cost.

They tried to avoid strikes and ensure industrial peace through their participation in arbitration and conciliation boards. The most famous of all nineteenth century boards was the Board of Conciliation and Arbitration for the Manufactured Iron Trade of the North of England. The board was established in 1869 by a joint agreement between the Associated Iron and Steel Workers of Great Britain, led by John Kane, and the North of England Ironmasters Association, led by David Dale.[12] Massive strikes and lockouts in the iron industry during 1862-68 convinced employers and unions to set up the board.[13] Composed of equal numbers of representatives of employers and workers and headed by national union officials, the board prohibited strikes and lockouts, became the prototype of all such arbitration boards during the nineteenth century, and achieved a remarkable degree of industrial peace in the British iron and steel industry after 1869.[14]

Similar developments occurred in the coal industry. Joint committees of arbitration and conciliation among coal miners were established in Northumberland in 1871, in Durham in 1872, and in West Yorkshire in 1873. Altogether, 75,000 miners in the Northeast and 40,000 in Yorkshire were covered.[15] The joint committees were preoccupied above all with wages. They adjusted wages up and down according to the selling prices of the product (coal), an arrangement which clearly benefited the employers because most arbitration awards took place during depressions and most resulted in reductions. A survey of arbitration in five industries between 1865 and 1896 shows thirty-four wage-arbitration cases in iron and twenty-one in coal. Of the thirty-four cases in the iron industry only nine resulted in wage advances, and of the twenty-one awards given in coal mining, nineteen resulted in wage reductions, two in no change, and not a single one in an advance.[16]

Wage arbitration awards were determined by price lists or sliding scales. In the cotton industry, as noted, district price lists appeared very early. By 1830 most British cotton towns had mule spinning lists and by 1870 most had self-actor spinning lists. The cotton spinning list was revised up and down according to the "state of the trade," that is, the market price of cotton yarn. The same principle—the principle that "prices should rule wages"[17]—was applied to collective bargaining on sliding scales in the coal, iron, and steel industries.

The first sliding scale in the iron industry—the Thorneycroft Scale—was negotiated in Staffordshire in 1848 as a result of a strike by puddlers at the Thorneycroft mill. It established a "shillings for pounds" formula whereby the puddling wages varied with the price of iron at the rate of one shilling for every price change of one pound per ton. In 1863 the "shillings for pounds" formula covered all workers in the iron industry of South Staffordshire, the rule being that wage rates for skilled occupations were linked to the base puddling rates.[18] The North Iron Board of 1868 and the Midland Iron and Steel Board of 1887 both settled wage disputes on the basis of mutually agreed sliding scales.[19]

Likewise, the arbitration boards in the coal industry used sliding scales to determine wages. Sliding scales in coal mining appeared later than in iron making, first in Staffordshire (1874) and South Wales (1875), and then in Durham (1877), Northumberland (1879), and West Yorkshire (1880).[20]

The acceptance of sliding scales by the unions reflected the new spirit of accommodation embraced by their leaders. It reflected, furthermore, the incorporation of top union officials—many of whom obtained managerial or governmental posts later in their careers—into the capitalist economy. The incorporation of union leaders persuaded employers, in turn, that union recognition could bring about industrial peace and hence prevent grievances from turning into costly disputes. Union officials everywhere—in cotton spinning, coal mining, and iron and steel making—acted as mediators of conflicts between employers and employed, advocated conciliation, and did their utmost to reduce the number of stoppages. A formalized procedure of conciliation had a disciplinary effect on the rank and file whose militancy often threatened the officials' own authority. One way union officials dealt with dissident members was to encourage their emigration to the United States, where plenty of job opportunities were available. Unions of spinners, miners, ironworkers, and steelworkers assisted, first and foremost, their most loyal members—the typical blacklisted strikers—in immigrating to the United States.

IMMIGRATION TO THE UNITED STATES

The movement of immigration among British mule spinners was the topic of chapter 5. The chapter distinguished three types of causes that induced British mule spinners to immigrate: technological unemployment, unemployment as a result of severe depression (above all the cotton famine), and the blacklisting of militant union activists by British employers. Because employment opportunities in the American cotton industry were growing, most immigrant spinners moved to the United States. Typically, well over 50% of the mule spinners employed in the leading cotton towns of the United States after 1850 were immigrants from Britain.

Admittedly, there was nothing analogous to the cotton famine in either the British coal mining or iron industries. It is also true that the proportion of British immigrants among American coal miners and ironworkers was not quite as high as among the mule spinners. Still, British immigrants made up a large proportion of American coal miners and ironworkers throughout the nineteenth century.

As early as the 1820s crowds of English miners were reported to have arrived at the coal fields of eastern Pennsylvania, and in the 1830s and 1840s Welsh colliers settled in central New York State, Pennsylvania, and Ohio. In 1848, according to one observer, nearly all American miners were foreign-born, "principally from England and Wales, with a few Irish and Scotchmen." Thousands of English and Welsh miners came to Pennsylvania anthracite coal fields during the 1860s. Many others from Scotland, Durham, and Staffordshire arrived at the bituminous fields of western Pennsylvania, Maryland, West Virginia, Ohio and Illinois. Travelling in the United States in 1869, Alexander McDonald, leader of the Scottish miners, found 7,000 British colliers in Maryland, 3,000 in Pennsylvania, 2,000 in Illinois, and "large colonies" in Ohio. Thousands emigrated from the Durham coal region between 1879 and 1881. In 1881 alone it was estimated that 3,000 Durham miners departed. Most came to the United States. A careful tally of British official statistics shows that 106,000 miners emigrated from Britain between 1862 and 1885, 71% of whom sailed to the United States. By 1888 42% of the underground miners employed by one Pennsylvania coal company were British: 29% Welsh, 12% English, and 1% Scotch.[21]

Early American ironworkers, like spinners and miners, came from the ranks of British immigrants. Welsh ironworkers made up the majority of skilled workers in the new iron centers of Pennsylvania in the 1850s, and English and Scottish immigrants arrived at Pennsylvania iron and steel towns during the Civil War and for two decades later. A new Pittsburgh steel mill erected in 1866 hired its skilled workers among immigrants from Sheffield, Birmingham, and Manchester. In 1879 many British puddlers and rollers came to Pittsburgh under contract to American companies. A year later, in 1880, British immigrants accounted for 36% of the 22,400 ironworkers in Pennsylvania and 46% of the 9,500 ironworkers in New York State.[22]

One reason why spinners, miners, and ironworkers left Britain was the encouragement and assistance they received from their unions. Off and on between 1850 and 1880 British trade unions promoted emigration. "By thinning the labour market you enhance the value of the British workman," John Kane, president of the Ironworkers Association of the North of England, noted in 1865, and this view was typical of trade unionists in other industries, notably cotton and coal. In 1863, at the height of the cotton famine, James Mawdsley, secretary of the cotton mule spinners, signed a circular saying, "A large emigration of factory workers is now absolutely essential.... The importance of emigration has been felt...even in the most flourishing state of trade." Emigration among coal miners was looked upon as a solution to the problems of overproduction, unemployment, and low wages. Accordingly, during the hard times in the mines, between 1863 and 1865, union leaders like Alexander McDonald were touring the mines preaching the cause of emigration. McDonald travelled to the United States three times, in 1867, 1868, and 1876, visiting "the entire mines from the Atlantic to the Pacific" so that he could advise British miners where to go in America. He spoke in meetings and submitted reports urging prospective emigrants to contact local trade unions in the United States. Other trade unionists, William Crawford of the Durham miners and John Burt of the Northumberland miners, also travelled to the United States for the purpose of advising emigrants.[23]

The most extensive efforts at union emigration were made in times of conflict. In the cotton industry, mule spinners' societies on strike adopted emigration

schemes immediately in order not to spend all their resources on relief. In the
iron and mining industries, too, unions turned to emigration schemes in times
of disputes, often working closely with recruiting agents of American industry.
In a circular issued to members on February 1, 1865, John Kane explained the
union's philosophy:

> Instead of exhausting our funds on strikes and defending ourselves against
> the tyrannical conduct of the employers, as manifested in what is becom-
> ing quite a common practice—viz., lockouts, we would advise the
> workmen to put out with grievances, rally round the standard of union,
> pay their money, but not grudgingly, so that we may be enabled, with
> your approval, to carry out an extensive scheme of emigration.[24]

Six weeks later, in the middle of March, a nationwide lockout of puddlers
led the two locked out unions—the Iron Workers' Association of the North
of England and the Associated Ironworkers of Staffordshire—to adopt emigration programs. An agent of the American Emigrant Company—a labor-
recruiting agency financed by American iron manufacturers—was invited to
Gateshead, headquarters of the northern union, and according to John Kane,
500 applications for emigration were received by the end of the second week
of the lockout. In 1868, faced with wage reductions, the Associated Ironworkers
of Staffordshire organized an emigration scheme at once and appealed to the
American consul in Birmingham for assistance. One American mining company arranged with Alexander McDonald, president of the miners' union, to
assist locked out Scottish miners to immigrate to the United States.[25]

The vast majority of these strikes and lockouts took place in the 1860s, before
the formation of arbitration and conciliation boards. They resulted in the
blacklisting of leaders and activists who were often made victims of the disputes
and were deprived of their jobs. Victimized members who sacrificed for trade
union activities were the first to emigrate. Cotton mule spinners' societies granted
victims larger emigration benefits than unemployed members or strikers.
Similarly, coal miners' unions aided their most loyal members first. In 1864,
a delegate meeting of the Durham Miners' Association resolved "that all men
who were 'sacrificed' for taking an active part in the union would be entitled
to the first claims upon the funds of the society if they chose to emigrate."[26]
The Durham miners granted large emigration benefits to victimized members:
in 1881, for example, one local union in Durham refused to strike on behalf
of eight miners who were dismissed but granted each of them fifty pounds.
Several South Wales colliers viewed the emigration fund primarily as a means
to aid victims to leave the country.[27] Thomas Halliday, a miners' union official, explained the unions' position in testimony before the Select Committee
on Coal in 1873:

> Chairman: Your going down to Wales was the first attempt, was it not,
> that had been made to settle disputes between masters and

	men by agents of the colliers such as yourself?
Halliday:	I am told that in 1864...those who took the leading part in the union have had to go to America; in fact many are now in America of those who used to take a very important part in the interests of Wales.
Chairman:	Do you mean to say when these disputes took place in 1864, and after that time, the men who led the disputes and communicated with the masters were taken advantage of, and obliged to leave the country?
Halliday:	Quite so: They tell me that very good men indeed try to get work and could not; supposing that a man had been on strike, and the strike terminated, if he went to a neighbouring valley he was followed there, and was told that he could not have work there.
Chairman:	He was treated as a leader of the men?
Halliday:	Yes, and had to leave the country; in fact, he preferred that to going north.[28]

Victimized miners left the country, sailed to the United States, moved into American mines, helped organizing unions, and staged militant strikes. Like Lancashire cotton spinners, English, Welsh, and Scottish miners were experienced trade unionists who carried their union tradition across the Atlantic.

In coal as in cotton, unions and strikes in American industry were British affairs. The first union in Pennsylvania anthracite fields was organized in 1849 by an Englishman, John Bates, with the help of Welsh, English and Irish assistants. William Clachan, an immigrant Scottish union leader, led a strike in 1850 among the Maryland bituminous (soft) coal miners, many of whom were Scots. The first attempt at a national miners' organization was made in southern Illinois in 1861. Two British miners who were also former Chartists, Daniel Weaver of Staffordshire and Thomas Lloyd of Wales, established the American Miners' Association, with Weaver as the elected president and Lloyd as secretary. The association survived for seven years and then collapsed as a result of strikes in 1867-68. By 1868 the center of miners' unionism moved back to eastern Pennsylvania. John Siney, a Lancashire Irishman, helped organize the first enduring miners' union in Schuylkill County in 1868 in a wake of a successful wage strike which he led. The Workingmen's Benevolent Association of St. Clair—the nucleus of the county-wide union—originally had sixteen charter members, all but two of whom were immigrants from Britain. Siney enlarged his organization and in 1873 formed the Miners' National Association with the assistance of two Scottish miners, John James and Daniel McLaughlin. The two were close associates of Alexander McDonald, president of the Scottish miners, before immigrating to the United States. James modelled the constitution of the Miners' National Association after McDonald's Scottish organization. McLaughlin led the Illinois State Miners' Union, served successively as president, treasurer, and chief of the Executive Board of the National

Federation of Miners and Mine Laborers (a forerunner of the United Mine Workers) and later became a vice president of the American Federation of Labor. When the United Mine Workers of America was founded in 1890, its first president, John Rae, was a former Scottish collier, and its first secretary, Robert Watchorn, a Derbyshire miner.[29]

British immigrant ironworkers were not as militant as British coal miners or cotton spinners; nevertheless, they played an important role in the unionization of the American iron and steel industry. John Edwards, a Welshman who had trade union experience in the iron mills of England and Scotland, became president of the Sons of Vulcan in 1868 and served for several terms. John Jarrett emigrated from Wales in 1861, worked as an iron puddler in Pennsylvania, and in 1867 went back to Britain and stayed there for four years. While working at the puddler's trade in England he became acquainted with John Kane, who instructed him "in the principles of trade unionism." Returning to the United States, Jarrett became vice president of the Sons of Vulcan, helped merge it with three other unions to form the Amalgamated Association of Iron and Steel Workers in 1876, and from 1880 to 1883 served as second president of the Amalgamated Association. Another British immigrant, William Martin of Scotland, had served as secretary of the Iron and Steel Role Hands Union in 1875-76 and as first secretary of the Amalgamated Association for twelve years, from 1878 to 1890. Closely associated with Edwards, Jarrett, and Martin was Thomas Jones, a Welshman who had organized unions and led strikes in Scotland before emigrating to the United States in 1862. He first became the secretary of the heaters of Bridgeport in South Chicago, then was fired and blacklisted for two years, and in 1872 established the Associated Brotherhood of Iron and Steel Heaters, Boilers, and Roughers of the United States. Jones was the union's first president and a key negotiator in the merger of the Sons of Vulcan, the heaters, the rollers, and the nailers' unions to establish the Amalgamated in 1876.[30]

All these examples show that many of the immigrant miners and ironworkers had been committed trade unionists. Their British union tradition and the American conception of management were difficult to reconcile, however. Whether in cotton spinning, coal mining, or iron and steel making, American manufacturers were determined to oppose trade unions at all costs. The clash between British immigrant workers and American employers, this book has suggested, contributed to the breakout of control struggles in the cotton mule-spinning industry. The same is true, to some degree at least, in the coal, iron, and steel industries as well.

THE STRUGGLE OVER CONTROL IN THE UNITED STATES

The battle over control in the cotton industry was centered in Fall River, took the form of three general strikes (1871, 1875, 1879), and touched on three aspects of craft control: control over production, recruitment, and piece rates.

The Fall River spinners, like the spinners in other New England cotton towns, were defeated. They were defeated because the employers were unified. An inspection of inter-corporate linkages in Fall River, Lowell, and Lawrence showed that in each of these towns the cotton industry was sufficiently monopolized to ensure the employers victory in strikes. A subsequent examination of the Lancashire cotton industry led to the opposite conclusion. Lancashire cotton manufacturers were divided by intense competition so that they sought reconciliation and accommodation with the unions.

British coal owners and iron masters also sought reconciliation. Their American counterparts sought confrontation. The remainder of this chapter is devoted to the analysis of control struggles in the coal, iron, and steel industries of the United States.

Coal Mining

In 1870 the coal-mining industry of the United States was concentrated in two regions within Pennsylvania. Of the 95,000 coal miners enumerated in the 9th census, 70,000 were employed in Pennsylvania. The census divides the miners into two categories according to the type of coal they cut: 53,000 hewed anthracite and all worked in Pennsylvania; 42,000 dug bituminous, 17,000 of whom labored in Pennsylvania. The anthracite industry was highly concentrated in the eastern part of the state, in and around Schuylkill County some fifty miles northeast of Philadelphia. The bituminous coal industry was scattered in the western part of the state around Pittsburgh. The anthracite industry was organized in relatively large units of extraction averaging over 230 miners per establishment. The average number of miners employed in a bituminous colliery in 1870 was 31.[31]

It is hardly surprising, therefore, that the first powerful trade union organization among American coal miners was formed in the anthracite coal region of eastern Pennsylvania. Like the mule spinners of southern New England, the miners of eastern Pennsylvania organized themselves in local societies. By 1870 the Miners' and Laborers' Benevolent Association (M&LBA) of Schuylkill County had 20,000 members registered in twenty-two district societies.[32]

The Schuylkill coal miners went on strike in 1869, 1870, 1871, and 1875. The 1869 strike was general, lasted two months, and ended in a compromise. The miners' demand for a sliding scale was granted, but their demand for control over hiring was rejected. Actually, many small strikes over the unjust discharge of union members, the hiring of strikebreakers, and the discharge of "obnoxious" bosses erupted in 1869 in individual collieries. In addition, the miners struck to control production: a typical work stoppage in 1869 occurred over the issue of the miner's "right" to his gangway, that is, the union control over the allocation of places in the mine.[33]

The 1870s Schuylkill strikes, like the Fall River strikes of the 1870s, were all reported to have occurred over wages. But unmistakably, control over piece rates rather than wage demand was the real issue. Attempts by the coal companies to revise the sliding scale downwards, that is, to lower the floor under which wages could not fall, triggered the 1870 and 1871 strikes. Both ended in a compromise which was clearly favorable to the employers, both seriously weakened the union, and both were a prelude to the great showdown of 1875.

"There is no war with the miners' union as such," says a joint statement which the employers drafted during the 1871 strike. "The only issue involved is the right to control our own property." "We grant the men...the right to combine," the statement proceeds, "but we deny the rights to dictate who [we] shall employ, or who [we shall] discharge, how we shall sell or dispose of our property, or to determine the amount of our production, or to...give direction in the management of our operations."[34] While the strike was going on, the coal, iron, and railroad companies of Schuylkill coal region met and resolved: "We are united in opposing any interference by the workmen...with the management or control of our works, and we will insist on the abandonment of their claims to such control."[35]

The immediate causes of the 1875 strike were a 10%-20% wage cut and the removal of the minimum wage. But the larger issue was the life of the union, as observed by both employers and unionists as well as the correspondents covering the strike. "It is well known that the coal market can afford to pay last year's prices," a local correspondent wrote to the *Miners' Journal*, "but it seems that the wage...question is not the trouble, but the disbanding of the M&LBA."[36] It was not a "fight...over the question of wages but over the question of who shall manage the mines,"[37] the mine owners declared, and in the same vein, a M&LBA leader described the 1875 contest as a war against the union.[38]

Reluctant to settle the strike, the employers demanded that the union "give up all control of the mines."[39] They refused to meet with the union representatives even once. What they really wanted was to break the union, and they did so by starving the miners into submission. The "long strike" of 1875 lasted six months, the miners were defeated, their union dead, and wages were reduced to 26% below the 1869 basis. By 1877 the average wage of eastern Pennsylvania miners fell to 54% below the 1869 level.[40] A year later, an anonymous writer published the union's obituary under the title "After the Long Strike":

> Well, we've been beaten, beaten all to smash,
> And now, sir, we've begun to feel the lash,
> As wielded by a gigantic corporation,
> Which runs the commonwealth and ruins the nation.[41]

"The gigantic corporation which runs the commonwealth" was what Marvin Schlegel called "America's first Cartel."[42] It was a combination of coal and iron companies, canal companies, and railroad corporations which controlled much of the anthracite mining industry in eastern Pennsylvania. The combination regulated competition among firms, reconciled business interests, and pulled together its immense resources to weaken and defeat the union. In essence, the coal combination of eastern Pennsylvania was similar to the cotton combinations of Fall River and other New England mill towns, as the following account suggests.

In 1868 only a minority of collieries in eastern Pennsylvania were controlled by large corporations. By 1873 virtually the entire industry was dominated by six powerful corporations—all but one were common carriers as well, owning canals and/or railroads. The largest corporation was the Reading Railroad, renamed the Philadelphia and Reading Coal and Iron Company in 1871. One important reason why the Reading Railroad went into the business of coal mining, the historian of *St. Claire* assured us, was to crush the coal miners' union.[43]

To begin with, in 1869, following the union's partial success in the general strike, the Schuylkill coal operators reorganized the Anthracite Board of Trade under the leadership of the Reading Railroad. The board suppressed competition, regulated wages and prices, enforced long "suspensions" to maintain high coal prices, and coordinated lockouts. Three years later, the six corporations formed a cartel and divided the anthracite coal market among themselves according to fixed percentages. The largest share—26%—was in the hands of the Reading corporation.[44] In 1875 the Reading Railroad, headed by Franklin Gowen, used its enormous resources to defeat the strike and Gowen could report to his stockholders that "the company rid itself of the last vestiges of trade unionism."[45] Nearly two decades later in 1893, after acquiring other railroads, the Reading owned or controlled 70% of all anthracite shipments in Pennsylvania, still opposing unionism successfully.[46] Finally, in 1903 the coal and railroad corporations of eastern Pennsylvania accepted the award of the Anthracite Commission set up by President Roosevelt to regulate labor relations in the industry; nonetheless, they adamantly refused to recognize the UMW or deal with its representatives for another seventeen years, until 1920.[47]

Contrast now Britain with the United States. Everywhere in Britain the family-owned concern was the representative form of enterprise; everywhere we look the typical operator owned one or two collieries employing no more than a few hundred workers. In the Midland in the 1870s the average pit gave employment to 150 colliers and the average operator owned 1.5 pits. In Scotland in the 1880s the miners were still working in pits of 100 to 200 hands and the typical owner had one or two collieries. The Durham mines were larger. In the early 1860s the average Durham pit employed over 200 hewers and by 1884 the typical Durham owner ran more than two pits, each employing 300 colliers. In South Wales 1.6 collieries per firm was the norm in the 1870s.[48]

The coal industry of South Wales closely resembled that of eastern Pennsylvania. The South Wales coal industry was famous for its anthracite, it developed rapidly during the 1860s and 1870s, it was nearly equal in size to the eastern Pennsylvania industry, and it became highly unionized during the early 1870s. In 1871 the number of workers employed in the South Wales coal industry came close to 58,000; the corresponding figure for eastern Pennsylvania was 53,000 in 1870. Over 20,000 South Wales colliers were union members in 1873 compared to some 20,000 in eastern Pennsylvania in 1870.[49] In both South Wales and eastern Pennsylvania the miners staged three large-scale stoppages between 1870 and 1875. Still, the outcome of the strikes was markedly different.

The miners of South Wales reached an accommodation with their employers. They struck in 1871, 1873, and 1875, and were never defeated. The Amalgamated Association of Miners in South Wales struck for twelve weeks in 1871 until the coal owners agreed to submit the dispute to arbitration. The final settlement not only avoided the reduction that the owners sought but actually gave the miners an advance. In 1873 the South Wales union struck again to oppose a wage reduction. The strike was successful, although the union accepted a token 5% wage cut for a period of five days. The strike of 1875 involved 50,000 coal workers and resulted in a compromise. The union accepted a 12.5% wage reduction for three months but at the same time it reached an agreement with the owners that future wages should be governed by a sliding scale supervised by a joint conciliation board of representatives of employers and miners. The mine owners welcomed the sliding scale agreement because they were eager to prevent stopages and give stability to the industry. The union leaders favored reconciliation and accepted the sliding scale because such an arrangement put an end to the employers' arbitrary control over wages and because it enhanced the leaders' own status and respectability as board members alongside the representatives of the employers. The sliding scale agreement regulated industrial relations in the South Wales coal industry throughout the century. It was renewed eight times, in 1880, 1882, 1887, 1890, 1892, 1893, 1895, and 1898.[50]

The mine owners of South Wales, like the cotton mill owners of Lancashire, were unable to defeat the union because they were divided by competition. Ownership of the South Wales industry in 1873 was divided among 256 coal mining firms, the majority of which—183—owned but a single colliery. Of the remaining 73 firms, 40 owned 2 collieries each, 17 owned 3 pits, 5 owned 4 pits, 10 owned 5 to 8 pits each, and one large firm owned 12 collieries. In addition, there developed in the 1870s a cut-throat competition between the newly established limited companies and the old family firms; in 1875 nearly half the total coal output extracted in South Wales was controlled by limited liability companies. More important, member firms of the Coal Owners Association of South Wales accounted in 1873 for less than three-fourths of the industry's output. In the same year, the four largest coal mining firms in South Wales produced just 16% of the total output of the region and the eighteen largest firms accounted for only 28% of the output.[51] Such market shares were far too small to facilitate monopolistic control over the industry. Divided by conflicts of interests, South Wales coal owners failed to form an association powerful enough to promote cooperation, enforce solidarity, coordinate lockouts, defeat strikes, blacklist union activists, and keep unions out.

Iron and Steel

As in Britain, the formation of trade unions among American ironworkers was followed by a flood of militant strikes. The strikes were fought over the issue of piece rates' control, were led by the Sons of Vulcan, the powerful organization of puddlers, and took place in and around Pittsburgh—the main center of the American iron industry. To avoid costly battles, the employers agreed to relinquish control over wages. Accordingly, the first recorded sliding scale in the United States was signed in Pittsburgh, Pennsylvania, in 1865 by representatives of the ironmasters and of the Sons of Vulcan.[52]

The sliding scale linked the puddling rate to the selling price of iron. The union divided its jurisdiction to districts with all districts governed by the same scale. By 1876, at the time the Amalgamated Association was formed, all districts west of the Allegheny Mountains, from Pittsburgh to the Midwest, had scales for puddling.[53]

From the outset, collective bargaining on sliding scales was the Amalgamated Association's main preoccupation. Each year during the union convention, delegates drew up price scales for boilers, puddlers, heaters, and rollers, endorsed them in the convention, and presented them to the ironmasters. Unlike British trade unions, however, the Amalgamated rejected arbitration as a method of settling disputes; thus, differences over scales between the union and the employers often led to strikes and lockouts. Over time, union power increased dramatically until it peaked on the eve of the Homestead strike. Membership in the Sons of Vulcan more than doubled from 1,500 to 3,000 between 1867 and 1874, and membership in the Amalgamated rose more than sixfold from 3,800 to 24,100 between 1877 and 1891. Not until 1934 did membership in the Amalgamated match the 1891 record.[54]

Ironworkers and steelworkers, like cotton mule spinners, staged three types of control strikes, each corresponding to a different dimension of a given job. They struck first and foremost to control piece (tonnage) rates, but they also struck to control production and hiring. It is impossible to estimate the exact number of strikes staged by the puddlers over the issue of collective bargaining on a sliding scale; evidently, strikes over scales are lumped together in the Vulcan records with other wage strikes—a total of sixty-nine between 1867 and 1875. Strikes that occurred over the issue of job control and over workload and strikes against the discharge of union members, against the employment of strikebreakers, and for the dismissal of unpopular bosses are also lumped together in the union's records. Classified as strikes "for administration of works," they totaled sixteen between 1867 and 1875.[55] During the depression of 1874-76 three rollers' strikes and three heaters' strikes involved "administration of the works."[56]

The puddlers won more strikes than they lost. Of the eighty-seven strikes of all kinds staged by the Sons of Vulcan between 1867 and 1875, twenty-eight resulted in a union victory, twenty-two were terminated in favor of the employers, twenty-one ended in a compromise, and in sixteen cases the outcome is unclear. The Amalgamated, by contrast, lost sixty-one strikes and won twenty-eight during the first ten years of its existence, from 1876 to 1885.[57]

The Amalgamated defeats coincided with the rapid increase in steel production. During the 1870s and 1880s almost the entire steel output of the United States was made up of pig iron converted to steel with the Bessemer technology. Hot air blown from the bottom of the Bessemer converter kept the iron molten and refined without the need of direct application of heat and without the need of puddling. In 1872 just 4% of the total U.S. output of iron was converted into steel, in 1880 28%, and by 1892 over 50%.[58] Steel was produced in two kinds of mills: iron mills converted to steel, like the Cambria Works in western Pennsylvania, and mills designed from the start to produce steel, like Carnegie's Edgar Thompson Works at Braddock, Pennsylvania. Both types were much larger than the older iron mills: in 1880, for example, the average capacity of a Bessemer mill was nearly ten times that of an iron rolling mill.[59] Under the Bessemer technology only a large-scale operation was efficient.

Steel mills proved hard to organize. Initially, the economic boom that followed the end of the depression in 1878 led to a massive drive of unionization among steelworkers, to the formation of many new steel lodges, and to the Amalgamated's successful adoption of a sliding scale for steel. The scale, however, was negotiated separately with each steel lodge alone. Following the economic downturn of 1882, iron and steel prices steeply declined, tonnage rates dropped, and many strikes resulted. During 1881-85 the Amalgamated was involved in thirteen large-scale steel strikes and lockouts and lost all but two.[60] Within one year—mid-1882 to mid-1883—the iron and steel industry experienced twenty-one strikes and lockouts; nearly all were defeated.[61] Between 1882 and 1885 the Amalgamated lost ninety lodges, at least twenty-five of which were in the steel industry, and union membership fell by more than 10,000.[62] Only three of the fifteen steel rail mills operating in 1885 did not require their employers to take the "iron clad oath" of nonunionism.[63]

The steelworkers' defeats were followed by defeats among the ironworkers. A general puddlers' strike in the Pittsburgh district in the spring of 1882 was aimed at retrieving the wage losses of the 1870s and was met with a resolute determination of the employers to crush the union. The employers locked out over 150 iron rolling mills—nearly the entire industry west of the Alleghenies from Pittsburgh to Illinois—and within five months the strikers reported back to work with no pay raise and with many of their lodges broken.[64] The 1882 lockout was followed by subsequent defeats among the ironmasters during the hard times of 1883-85.

The revival of the steel industry in the late 1880s was accompanied by an unprecedented resurgence of unionism, however. So rapidly did the

Amalgamated recover that between 1886 and 1891 union membership tripled from 7,200 to 24,100, the number of lodges rose from 106 to 290, and the number of union delegates climbed from 121 to 294. In 1891, on the eve of the Homestead strike, every fourth eligible worker was enrolled in the Association.[65]

But the Homestead strike changed everything. Homestead was one of the best-organized plants in the United States; it won a scale in a bitter strike in 1882—a rare victory at the time. Homestead was also the only powerful stronghold of the Amalgamated in the Pittsburgh area—the most dynamic sector of the steel industry. Carnegie's other great steel mills around Pittsburgh—Edgar Thompson and Duquesne—were nonunion: the Amalgamated lost control of Edgar Thompson in 1885 and failed in its attempts to organize the Duquesne mill after it had opened in 1889. The Homestead strike, furthermore, demonstrated how a powerful union may be defeated by a giant corporation. Indeed, with the union's defeats at Edgar Thompson, Duquesne, and finally Homestead, the Carnegie Company assumed the leadership in the struggle against trade unionism.[66]

Other steelmakers followed Carnegie. After 1892 the union had been driven from one mill after another, and by 1900 not a single steel mill of any size in western Pennsylvania recognized the Amalgamated. In 1901 the Amalgamated was defeated in a general strike against the newly organized U.S. Steel Corporation, and during the following years many of the Amalgamated lodges fell without a struggle. In 1909 the U.S. Steel Corporation posted an open-shop notice at its twelve remaining union mills, in 1919 the steelworkers were defeated again in a massive strike, and by 1929 membership in the Amalgamated was reduced to 8,600, slightly above the 1886 figure.[67]

The decline of the Amalgamated stands in stark contrast to the rise of trade unionism among British steelworkers. Unlike the Amalgamated, British trade unions survived the transition from iron to steel. British ironworkers' unions had begun recruiting steelworkers as early as the 1860s, and as steel superseded iron, new trade unions were established for the specific purpose of organizing the steelworkers; for instance, the British Steel Smelters' Amalgamated Association was founded in 1886 and the [Scottish] Associated Society of Millmen was formed in 1888. The outcome was a resurgence of unionism. Between 1897 and 1913 membership in British ironworkers and steelworkers' unions jumped from 21,000 to about 80,000, and in 1917 several of these unions joined together to form a single nationwide organization: the Iron and Steel Trades Confederation.[68]

Why, then, were the steelworkers more successful in Britain than in the United States? What were the reasons for the resurgence of unionism in the British steel industry? Why, on the other hand, did the Amalgamated fail to survive the transition from iron to steel successfully?

These questions have been addressed earlier in respect to the cotton mule spinners. One recurrent argument of this book is that union strength was affected by two key elements: competition among firms and the pace of technological change. On the one hand, the more competitive structure of the British than the American cotton industry weakened British employers substantially in their struggle against the unions. On the other hand, the much slower pace of technological change in the British than the American cotton industry facilitated the survival of craft unionism in Britain.

These findings apply with equal force to the British and American steel industries.

In the United States, the transition from iron to steel was accompanied by the emergence of large corporations. Over time, these corporations became vertically integrated and secured monopolistic control of the industry. As early as 1879 all the Bessemer plants in operation in the United States had some business links with the railroads, usually through common ownership or interlocking directorates, and many formed pools to control output and prices.[69] Using their vast financial resources to capture a larger and larger share of the market, the steel companies managed to increase cooperation, reduce competition, weaken the unions, and gain control of labor costs. Competition virtually ended in 1901 with the formation of the U.S. Steel Corporation—a holding company representing, among other firms, the two giants of the industry, Carnegie and the Illinois Steel Companies. Two-thirds of the American steel output in 1901 was produced by U.S. Steel and 54% in 1911.[70] Typically, American steel corporations were multiplant firms. Operating both union and nonunion plants, they were able to defeat strikes by maintaining full production in their nonunion plants while strikes were going on elsewhere. The Carnegie company used this tactic during the Homestead strike and U.S. Steel used it during the strike of 1901.[71]

In Britain, in contrast, the transition from iron to steel was accompanied by growing competition. Steel production was scattered in numerous small plants which were vertically disintegrated. Many of the British companies, moreover, were family firms operating on narrow margins and specializing in either iron rolling, steelmaking, semi-finishing or finishing.[72] Weakened by intensified competition, British steelworkers were unable to oppose the unions successfully. Rather, they reached an accommodation with the unions and introduced into the steel industry the very same procedure of collective bargaining used in the iron industry, namely, arbitration and conciliation in joint boards composed of representatives of employers and unions. The result was a long period of industrial peace that lasted until the 1960s.[73]

Industrial peace in Britain was also encouraged by the slow pace of technological change. In steel as in cotton, British visitors to the United States were greatly impressed by the high level of mechanization of American industry,[74] and in iron rolling—just as in cotton ring spinning—the British lagged far behind the Americans. The introduction of ring spinning in New England, the foregoing chapter suggested, steadily eroded the position of the organized mule spinners. Spinning on ring frames was a machine-tending job filled by unskilled and unorganized women, and ordinarily, American cotton corporations combined mule and ring spinning in the same plant so that they were able to defeat mule spinners' strikes by maintaining full production on rings. The speedy mechanization of iron rolling in the United States, similarly, rendered traditional craft skills obsolete, hence undermining the base of the Amalgamated power. Here is how David Brody describes the process:

> Earlier, rolling mills had required highly skilled men to catch and pass hot steel through the rolls. At every point rollers, roughers, and heaters had manually handled the metal. They were men of long experience and at a premium in America. Each new device that mechanized a different procedure undermined their favored position. . . . The head roller, whose knowledge and experience remained essential, gradually took on the functions of supervisor. The mass of rolling men slipped into the ranks of the semiskilled.[75]

But because semiskilled workers were easier to replace than craftsmen, these changes in the rolling technology weakened the bargaining power of the union. At the Edgar Thompson Works in 1885, for example, the Carnegie Company displaced dozens of craftsmen on the heating furnaces, the rail trains, and elsewhere, and subsequently, the union's two lodges at the plant were disbanded.[76]

The process was reversed in Britain. The increasing obsolescence of iron-rolling technologies contributed to union strength in two ways. First, skills remained more critical in Britain than in the United States and therefore the British iron and steel unions were comparatively harder to defeat than the Amalgamated. Second, the mechanization of iron rolling in Britain was such a slow and uneven process that the new semiskilled operatives managed to capture the craft status of their predecessors, the skilled rolling hands.[77]

They did so in much the same way as British self-actor minders captured the status of mule spinners. In the British cotton mule-spinning industry, we have seen, the sluggish pace of technological change was conducive to retaining craft control; it discouraged employers from experimenting with new methods of supervision. In the American cotton industry, on the other hand, the speedy transition from one mule technology to another encouraged employers to do away with craft autonomy, to subject the mule spinners to the rule of foremen, to turn the spinners into machine tenders, and in turn, to undermine the craft basis of their union power.

In the United States, finally, the speedy transition from one kind of mule to another was followed by a transition from mule to ring spinning. The first large-scale introduction of ring frames in the United States occurred during the 1870s at the time the mule spinners were striking for control. The mule spinners' struggle to regain control, this book concluded, accelerated the diffusion of the alternative ring-spinning technology and thereby hastened the demise of mule spinning in America.

Appendix 1
Note on the Quantitative Uses of Data on Wage Strikes

The three Fall River disputes entered the official history of strikes in the United States as wage strikes. The Massachusetts Bureau of Labor under the direction of Carroll Wright conducted in 1880 a survey of "Strikes in Massachusetts" from 1830 to 1879—one of the earliest attempts in the United States to gather official strike statistics on a state level. In tabulating the results according to the "original" causes of strikes, the bureau lumped the three Fall River strikes together with 115 other strikes under the heading: "To secure better wages."[1] And so did the U.S. Bureau of Labor seven years later. The U.S. Bureau of Labor was established in 1884 under the direction of Carroll Wright. Its Third Annual Report compiles strike statistics in the United States between 1881 and 1886. In addition, the volume contains a detailed supplement of strikes and lockouts in the United States prior to 1881. While the authors of the U.S. report did not simply duplicate the figures from the 1880 Massachusetts tables but rather read the descriptions that preceded the tables, they still categorized the 1870 and 1875 strikes in Fall River as strikes "against a reduction" and the 1879 strike as "for an increase of wages."[2]

Similar considerations guided the U.S. Commissioner of Labor in classifying strikes by causes in three successive reports: 1894, 1901, 1907. "Frequently there are strikes in which the initial spark is perhaps some minor friction that bears no relationship to what is later alleged to be the cause," John Griffin wrote in his analysis of the 21st Annual Report of the federal Bureau of Labor summarizing strike activities in the United States from 1880 to 1905, and rightly concluded that "the habit of striking first and formulating the demands later will distort, to a certain extent, the statistics on causes."[3] The following quotation from the 21st Annual Report[4] illustrates how unreliable indeed the statistics on causes are:

> By far the greater number of strikes included under the cause "for increase of wages" were thus literally reported, but under this cause are also

included strikes for adoption of a new scale, for adoption of union scale, for a change from piece to day work, etc., in which the object of the strike really was to secure an increase of wages.

How did the authors of the report know what "really" was the object of the strike? Perhaps the same considerations that led the U.S. Bureau of Labor in 1887 to conclude that the real issue in Fall River in the 1870s was wages also guided the judgment of the commissioner of labor in 1907? Perhaps, furthermore, these considerations also guided many labor historians—particularly of the John Commons' school, who, in their efforts to emphasize the conservative nature of American trade unionism, pointed repeatedly to the marketplace as the primary locus of industrial conflict and as a result continued to view strikes in economic terms?

My study of the Fall River strikes therefore casts doubt on the validity of all such quantitative studies of causes of strikes based on the U.S. government statistics for 1880-1905. If the Fall River case is typical, and there is no reason why it should not be so, then at least in late nineteenth-century America, it is extremely likely that the yearly percentages of wage strikes were lower than the official figures disclose. David Montgomery, to take a notable example, has analyzed the data on "wage strikes" collected by Griffin from the 21st Annual Report.[5] Montgomery, like Shorter and Tilly[6] and other historians writing today, is aware of course that wage demands were not necessarily the issue, yet given the nature of his source he cannot possibly know in most cases what the real struggle was all about. This is not to deny the importance of quantitative studies, just to highlight their limitations. Such limitations can nevertheless be overcome in the future by supplementing quantitative research with a growing number of local case studies of strikes. To unveil the real issue over which a strike occurred, an in-depth analysis is indispensable. This book attempts to make such a contribution.

Appendix 2
Fall River, Lowell, and Lawrence

The contrast between labor relations in Fall River and those in Lowell and Lawrence that so puzzled the member of the Massachusetts House of Representatives who, as noted at the beginning of chapter 7, requested an official inquiry in 1881, may be explained on technological grounds.

To begin with, the three Massachusetts cotton towns had many things in common. The mule spinners of Lowell and Lawrence, like the majority of the New England mule spinners, were Lancashire immigrant unionists. The Lowell and Lawrence corporations, like the Fall River firms, were hardly divided by competition, and hence employers were powerful enough to defeat the unions. The three towns, moreover, were all mono-industrial: 80% of Fall River's industrial capital in 1875 was invested in textile mills, the figures for Lawrence and Lowell are 80% and 78%, respectively. Similarly, 89% (15,000) of those employed in Fall River in 1875 worked in textile mills, as compared with 83% (10,900) in Lawrence and 76% (13,900) in Lowell.[1] Furthermore, in the three factory towns the cotton corporations extended their control beyond the shop floor into the larger community, mainly in the form of company housing: mill tenements in Fall River and factory boarding houses in Lowell and, to a lesser degree, in Lawrence.[2] Why, then, despite all these similarities, did Lowell and Lawrence remain quiet in the 1870s? Why did Lowell and Lawrence, in contrast to Fall River, experience no general strikes?

It was precisely because frame spinning played a far greater role in Lowell and Lawrence than in Fall River. Mule spinning accounted for less than half of the total yarn output in Lowell and Lawrence in the 1870s, and therefore no work stoppage in either town could come even close to a general strike, as the following example suggests. The Lowell mule spinners went on strike in 1875 in solidarity with the Fall River strikers. This was the largest strike that Lowell saw in the decade. Although the number of mule spinners in Lowell was by no means insignificant—304 mule spinners and more than 320 boy helpers left the mills for six weeks—employers managed to run the mills using

TABLE 10

Mule and Frame Spindles in Five American Cotton Towns, 1870

	Mule Spindles	*Frame (ring and throstle) Spindles*
Fall River	90%	10%
Lowell	26%	74%
Lawrence	43%	57%
New Bedford	59%	41%
Cohoes	56%	44%

Sources: For Fall River, Lawrence, and New Bedford, see United States Federal Manuscript Census of Barnstable-Hampden Counties, Massachusetts, Manufacturing, 1870. For Lowell (Middlesex County) see master copy of the Schedules of the 1870 federal census, Massachusetts State House, Boston, in conjunction with New England Cotton Manufacturers' Association, *Statistics of Cotton Manufactures in New England, 1866* (Boston, 1872), 16-17. The 1870 census of Lowell is very incomplete—the number of mule and frame spindles is given in only three of the eight cotton mills enumerated—and therefore the 1866 statistics are used as well. It should be noted, however, that these figures probably underestimate the proportion of mule spindles in Lowell in 1870 because a considerable number of mules were installed in Lowell between 1866 and 1870. For Cohoes see Evan Leigh, *The Science of Modern Cotton Spinning*, vol. 1, 127-28. The Cohoes figures refer to the 70,000-spindle Mastodon Mill in 1870 which was, by far, the largest owned by the Harmony Mills—the single cotton manufacturing company in Cohoes at the time. Leigh notes that the spinning machinery used by the Mastodon Mill was typical of other mills owned by Harmony. See also William Bean, *The City of Cohoes: Its Past and Present History, and Future Prospects* (Cohoes, New York, (1873), 15-29.

---

ring spinning. Actually, all through the strike the Lowell factories were still producing *over half* their normal capacity and therefore the strike could not have been nearly as effective as the Fall River one.[3] And in principle, the same is true of Lawrence, as well as other American cotton towns, for example, New Bedford and Cohoes. Fall River, in fact, was the only large cotton town in the United States at the end of the Civil War in which spinning was done almost exclusively by mules, as shown in Table 10.[4] It was also the single American cotton town which experienced an industrial war during the 1870s. Lowell, Lawrence, New Bedford, and Cohoes, on the other hand, were combined ring- and mule-spinning towns, and this fact helps to explain why, despite several wage reductions during the 1870s, they all escaped the labor troubles of Fall

River. Indeed, once the yarn production process was divided between unskilled, unorganized, and undemanding ring frame tenders, on the one side, and the highly unionized Lancashire immigrant mule spinners, on the other, general strikes were unlikely to erupt unless the skilled formed alliances with the unskilled. This important development in the American cotton industry was just beginning in the 1880s.

Notes

INTRODUCTION

1 Jonathan Prude, *The Coming of Industrial Order: Town and Factory Life in Rural Massachusetts, 1810-1860* (New York, 1983); Barbara Tucker, *Samuel Slater and the Origins of the American Textile Industry, 1790-1860* (Ithaca, 1984); Gary Kulik, "The Beginning of the Industrial Revolution in America: Pawtucket, Rhode Island, 1672-1829" (Ph.D. dissertation, Brown University, 1980); Philip Scranton, *Propriety Capitalism, The Textile Manufacture at Philadelphia, 1800-1885* (New York, 1983); Cynthia Shelton, *The Mills of Manayunk: Industrialization and Social Conflict in the Philadelphia Region, 1787-1837* (Baltimore, 1986).

2 Michael Piore and Charles Sabel, *The Second Industrial Divide: Possibilities for Prosperity* (New York, 1984), 19. For a similar version of the argument with a more extensive bibliography see Charles Sabel and Jonathan Zeitlin, "Historical Alternative to Mass Production: Politics, Markets and Technology in Nineteenth Century Industrialization," *Past and Present*, no. 108 (August, 1985), 133-176.

3 Piore and Sabel, *The Second Industrial Divide*, 19.

4 Referring to Lowell, Edwards describes "technical" control in the following way: "What the Boston manufacturers discovered, of course, was that continuous-flow production permitted them, rather than their workers, to establish the pace of work. The spindles...could be set to operate at a given rate, and the attending workers could be forced to keep up. The first element in controlling labor...was handled mechanically." But such a system did not dispense with the need of close supervision as Edwards mistakenly implies. Rather, direct supervision by foremen was necessary to ensure adequate performance standards so that actual control was vested in the foreman, not the machinery (see chapter 3). Richard Edwards, *Contested Terrain: The Transformation of the Workplace in the Twentieth Century* (New York, 1979), 113. See also William Lazonick's critique of Edwards, "Technological Change and the Control of Work: The Development of Capital-Labour Relations in US Mass Production Industries," in Howard Gospel and Craig Littler, eds., *Managerial Strategies and Industrial Relations* (London, 1983), 130-32.

5 Karl Marx, *Capital: A Critique of Political Economy* (1867; reprinted, New York, 1967), vol. 1, 435-36; Andrew Ure, *The Philosophy of Manufactures: or an*

Exposition of the Scientific, Moral, and Commercial Economy of the Factory System in Great Britain (1835; reprinted, New York, 1967), 367; Samuel Smiles, *Industrial Biography: Iron Workers and Tool Makers* (1864; reprinted, London, 1876), 268; Edward Tufnell, *Character, Object and Effects of Trades' Unions with Some Remarks on the Law Concerning Them* (1834; reprinted, New York, 1972), 108.

6 Harry Braverman, *Labor and Monopoly Capital: The Degradation of Work in the Twentieth Century* (New York, 1974); David Montgomery, *Workers' Control in America: Studies in the History of Work, Technology, and Labor Struggles* (New York, 1979), 10-27.

CHAPTER 1

1 D.C. Coleman, *Industry in Tudor and Stuart England* (London, 1975), 16, 25-26. *The Economy of England 1450-1750* (Oxford, 1977), 49-50.

2 Phyllis Deane, "The Output of the British Woolen Industry in the Eighteenth Century," *Journal of Economic History* 17:2 (June 1957), 209-10, 212-13, 215-16, 220.

3 See John James, *History of the Worsted Manufacture in England* (London, 1857), 238.

4 Ibid., 234-35, 239; see also Deane, "The Output of the British Woolen Industry," 211.

5 Coleman, *The Economy of England,* 12.

6 David Landes, *The Unbound Prometheus: Technological Change and Industrial Development in Western Europe from 1750 to the Present* (1969; reprinted, New York, 1972), 50.

7 E.P. Thompson, *The Making of the English Working Class* (1963; reprinted, New York, 1966), 270-74.

8 Parliamentary Papers (henceforth P.P.) 1806, III, *Minutes of Evidence Taken before the Committee on the Woollen Manufacture of England,* 446.

9 M.T. Wild, "The Saddleworth Parish Registers as a Source for the History of the West Riding Textile Industry During the Eighteenth Century" *Textile History* 1 (1968), 221-23.

10 Emphasis added. P.P. 1806, III, 8.

11 P.P. 1806, III, 5, 13, 129, 175, 220. See also Thompson, *The Making of the English Working Class,* 271; William Ashley, *The Economic Organization of England: An Outline History* (1914; reprinted, London, 1949), 145-46; Paul Mantoux, *The Industrial Revolution in the Eighteenth Century: An Outline of the Beginning of the Modern Factory System in Britain* (1928; reprinted, New York, 1965), 61; and Dorothy George, *England in Transition: Life and Work in the Eighteenth Century* (London, 1931), 47-53.

12 Herbert Heaton, *The Woollen and Worsted Industries From the Earliest Times Up to the Industrial Revolution* (1920; reprinted, Oxford, 1965), 313.

13 P.P. 1806, III, 13.

14 See R.G. Wilson, "The Supremacy of the Yorkshire Cloth Industry in the Eighteenth Century," in N.B. Harte and K.G. Ponting, eds., *Textile History and Economic History* (Manchester, 1973), 237-38.

15 Julia de Lacy Mann, *The Cloth Industry in the West of England from 1640 to 1880* (Oxford, 1971), 90-91.

16 Wilson, *op. cit.*, 239.

17 Alfred Wadsworth and Julia de Lacy Mann, *The Cotton Trade and Industrial Lancashire, 1600-1780* (1931; reprinted, Manchester, 1965), 39.

18 Ibid., 14-23, 145-48; Richard Guest, *A Compendious History of the Cotton Manufacture* (1823; reprinted, London, 1968), 12; Coleman, *The Economy of England*, 162.

19 Wadsworth and Mann, *Cotton Trade*, 23-25, and see map p. 79; Edwin Butterworth, *Historical Sketches of Oldham* (Oldham, 1856), 85.

20 S.D. Chapman, *The Cotton Industry in the Industrial Revolution* (London, 1972), 13. For a more detailed description of the working of the system see Wadsworth and Mann, *Cotton Trade*, 78-91.

21 See George Daniels, *The Early English Cotton Industry with Some Unpublished Letters of Samuel Crompton* (Manchester, 1920), 56.

22 Ibid., 56.

23 Wadsworth and Mann, *Cotton Trade*, 211; Daniels, *English Cotton Industry*, 23, 28.

24 T.S. Ashton, *An Economic History of England: The 18th Century* (London, 1955), 99; Ashley, *Economic Organization of Britain*, 145.

25 S.D. Chapman, *The Early Factory Masters: The Transition to the Factory System in the Midlands Textile Industry* (Newton Abbot: Devon, England, 1967), 23-24. See also Daniels, *English Cotton Industry*, 28.

26 Sidney Pollard, *The Genesis of Modern Management: A Study of the Industrial Revolution in Great Britain* (Cambridge, Mass., 1965), 32; see also pp. 35-37.

27 Ashton, *Economic History of England*, 101.

28 W.H.B. Court, *The Rise of the Midland Industries 1600-1838* (London, 1938), 210.

29 Dorothy George, *London Life in the XVIIIth Century* (New York, 1926), 184-85.

30 "The Case as it Now Stands between the Clothiers, Weavers, and other Manufacturers with Regard to the Late Riot in the County of Wilts," by Philalethes (pseud.), 1739. Reprinted in *Labor Problems Before the Industrial Revolution: Four Pamphlets* (New York, 1972), 2:14.

31 Arthur Young, *Tours in England and Wales* (selected from the *Annals of Agriculture*, 1776-1797; reprinted, London, 1932), 140.

32 Daniels, *English Cotton Industry*, 29.

33 Wild, "The Saddleworth Parish Registers," 221.

34 Butterworth, *Historical Sketches of Oldham*, 101.

35 Wadsworth and Mann, *Cotton Trade*, 314-316.

36 William Radcliffe, *Origins of the New System of Manufacture Commonly Called "Power Loom Weaving"* (Stockport, England, 1828), 59.

37 S.J. Chapman, *The Lancashire Cotton Industry* (Manchester, 1904), 3.

38 Michael Anderson, *Family Structure in Nineteenth Century Lancashire* (London, 1971), 37-38; Bryan Roberts, "Agrarian Organization and Urban Development," in J.O. Wirth and R.L. Jones, eds., *Manchester and San Paulo: Problems of Rapid Urban Growth* (Stanford, 1978), 85, 102.

39 S.J. Chapman, "Some Policies of the Cotton Spinners' Trade Unions," *Economic Journal* 10 (December 1900), 467; Ashton, *Economic History of England*, 233; H.A. Turner, *Trade Union Growth, Structure and Policy: A Comparative Study of the Cotton Unions in England* (Toronto, 1962), 56. See also Butterworth,

Historical Sketches of Oldham, 113.

40 John Kennedy, "A Brief Memoir of Samuel Crompton, with a Description of his Machine Called the Mule, and of the Subsequent Improvement of the Machine by Others," *Memoirs of the Literary and Philosophical Society of Manchester,* 5 (1831), 355-56.

41 See Butterworth, *Historical Sketches of Oldham,* 128, 209, 247-49.

42 George H. Wood, *The History of Wages in the Cotton Trade During the Past Hundred Years* (London, 1910), 112, 14, 32; Duncan Bythell, *The Handloom Weavers: A Study of the English Cotton Industry During the Industrial Revolution* (London, 1969), 275.

43 Wood, *History of Wages,* in conjunction with P.P. 1834, XIX, *First Supplementary Report of the Factory Inquiry Commission,* part I, 125.

44 See Neil Smelser, *Social Change in the Industrial Revolution: An Application of Theory to the British Cotton Industry* (Chicago, 1959), 202; and Wood, *History of Wages,* 138 .

45 John Kennedy, "Observations on the Rise and Progress of the Cotton Trade in Great Britain, Particularly in Lancashire and the Adjoining Counties," *Memoirs of the Literary and Philosophical Society of Manchester* 3 (1819), 129, 127.

46 Gilbert French, *The Life and Times of Samuel Crompton* (Manchester, 1862), 57.

47 Michael Edwards, *The Growth of the British Cotton Trade, 1780-1815* (Manchester, 1967), 182, 186; Chapman, *Lancashire Cotton Industry,* 60-61; Smelser, *Social Change in the Industrial Revolution,* 109-16.

48 P.P. 1816, III, *Select Committee on the State of Children Employed in the Manufacturies of the United Kingdom,* 234-35, 252.

49 Edwards, *British Cotton Trade,* 204.

50 French, *Life and Times of Samuel Crompton,* 84; Butterworth, *Historical Sketches of Oldham,* 128.

51 Webb Manuscript on Trade Unionism, vol. 34, 116, quoted in Smelser, *Social Change in the Industrial Revolution,* 315.

52 James Butterworth, *A Complete History of the Cotton Trade, Including also that of the Silk, Calico Printing, and Hat Manufactures with Remarks on their Progress in Bolton, Bury, Stockport, Blackburn, and Wigan* (Manchester, 1823), 37.

53 Ashton, *Economic History of England,* 231; Elie Halevy, *A History of the English People in the Nineteenth Century,* vol. 1: *England in 1815* (1913; reprinted, New York, 1961), 325-26.

54 Thompson, *The Making of the English Working Class,* 420-21.

55 See Chapman, *Lancashire Cotton Industry,* 181.

56 Beatrice and Sidney Webb's view is given in the first chapter of their classic, *The History of Trade Unionism* (London, 1894). For a summary critique of their view see R.A. Leeson, *Travelling Brothers: The Six Centuries' Road from Craft Fellowship to Trade Unionism* (London, 1979), ch. 16.

57 Quoted in James, *History of the Worsted Manufacture,* 232.

58 Ibid., 262-63. Woolen workers in eighteenth century Britain were more strike-prone than any other group of tradesmen. Of the 383 labor disputes reported in Britain between 1717 and 1800, 64 occurred among combers, spinners, and weavers

in the woolen trade—nearly twice the number in any other trade or industry. C.R. Dobson, *Master and Journeymen: A Prehistory of the Industrial Revolution 1717-1800* (London, 1980), 24-25.

59 See Ephraim Lipson, *The Economic History of England*, vol. 1: *The Middle Ages* (1915; reprinted, London, 1959), 308-439; Dorothy George, "The Combination Laws Reconsidered," *Economic Journal* (*Economic History Supplement*), 1:2 (May 1927).

60 James, *History of the Worsted Manufacture*, 232.

61 Daniels, *English Cotton Industry*, 40-42; and see also Wadsworth and Mann, *Cotton Trade*, 344.

62 Daniels, *English Cotton Industry*, 45-52; Wadsworth and Mann, *Cotton Trade*, 346-51, 361-66.

63 The quotations are from Wadsworth and Mann, *Cotton Trade*, 371-73; see also Daniels, *English Cotton Industry*, 53-54.

64 Chapman, "Some Policies of Cotton Spinners' Trade Unions," 467.

65 Turner, *Trade Union Growth*, 56-57.

66 Daniels, *English Cotton Industry*, 44; Wadsworth and Mann, *Cotton Trade*, 344-45.

67 Wadsworth and Mann, *Cotton Trade*, 366-83.

68 One may use the concept of proto-industrialization to capture the essential differences between pre-factory Britain and the United States. Increasingly used by social scientists, this concept refers to rural craft production which developed in symbiosis with commercial agriculture, which was typical of a given region, which was directed towards the international (or national) market, and which implies the subsequent proletarianization of the village and small town population. While several European countries underwent proto-industrialization during the seventeenth and eighteenth centuries, none had done so to the extent that Britain did. See Peter Kriete, Hans Medick, and Jurgen Schlumbohm, *Industrialization before Industrialization: Rural Industry in the Genesis of Capitalism* (1977; translated by Beate Schempp, Cambridge, England, 1981); Charles Tilly, "Flows of Capital and Forms of Industry in Europe, 1500-1900," *Theory and Society*, 12:2 (June 1983); Maxine Berg, Pat Hudson, and Michael Sonenscher, eds., *Manufacture in Town and Country before the Factory* (Cambridge, England, 1983), especially ch. 1; and Maxine Berg, *The Age of Manufactures: Industry, Innovation and Work in Britain 1700-1820* (Totowa, New Jersey, 1985), ch. 3. For two critical accounts of the proto-industrial theory see D.C. Coleman, "Proto-Industrialization: A Concept Too Many," *Economic History Review*, 2nd Series, 36:3 (August, 1983), and Rab Houston and K.D.M. Snell, "Historiographical Review: Proto-Industrialization? Cottage Industry, Social Change, and Industrial Revolution," *Historical Journal*, 27:2 (June 1984).

In the American countryside, by contrast, the level of proto-industrial production was negligible by any British standards. This is why some American historians are reluctant to use the "European" term proto-industrialization to describe the putting out system in New England. See, for example, Thomas Dublin, "Women and Outwork in a Nineteenth-Century New England Town: Fitzwilliam, New Hampshire, 1830-1850," in Steve Hahn and

Jonathan Prude, eds., *The Countryside in the Age of Capitalist Transformation: Essays in the Social History of Rural America* (Chapel Hill, North Carolina, 1985), 53-54.

69 John P. Hall, "The Gentle Craft: A Narrative of Yankee Shoemakers" (Ph.D. dissertation, Columbia University, 1953), 73-125; Blanche Hazard, *The Organization of the Boot and Shoe Industry in Massachusetts Before 1875* (Cambridge, Mass., 1921), 24-41; Victor Clark, *History of Manufactures in the United States*, vol. 1: 1607-1860 (New York, 1929), 443-44; Susan Bloomberg, "Industrialization and Skilled Workers: Newark, 1826 to 1860" (Ph.D. dissertation, University of Michigan, 1974), 19-20; Dorothy Brady, "Comment," in David Gilchrist, ed., *The Growth of the Seaport Cities 1790-1825* (Charlottesville, Virginia, 1967), 95.

70 Quoted in Hall, "Gentle Craft," 73.

71 Rolla Tryon, *Household Manufactures in the United States, 1640-1860* (Chicago, 1917), 200; Hall, "Gentle Craft," 76.

72 Billy G. Smith, "The Material Lives of Laboring Philadelphians, 1750 to 1800," *William and Mary Quarterly*, 3rd Series, 38:2 (April 1981), 197.

73 Sharon V. Salinger, "Colonial Labor in Transition: The Decline of Indentured Servitude in Late Eighteenth Century Philadelphia," *Labor History*, 22:2 (Spring 1981), 190.

74 Tryon, *Household Manufactures*, 65-66.

75 Emphasis added. Quoted in Clark, *History of Manufactures*, vol. 1, 207, 209.

76 Alexander Hamilton, "Manufactures" (1791), reprinted in Thomas Cochran, ed., *The New American State Papers, Manufactures* (Wilmington, Delaware, 1972), vol. 1, 55.

77 Albert Gallatin, "Manufactures" (1810), reprinted in *New American State Papers, Manufactures*, vol. 1, 126.

78 Clark, *History of Manufactures*, vol. 1, 438.

79 Alfred Chandler, *The Visible Hand: The Managerial Revolution in American Business* (Cambridge, Mass., 1977), 51.

80 Clark, *History of Manufactures*, vol . 1, 109, 111, 208; Court, *The Rise of the Midland Industries*, 206-9.

81 Coleman, *The Economy of England*, 138; Phyllis Deane and W.A. Cole, *British Economic Growth 1688-1959: Trends and Structure* (1962; reprinted, London, 1967), 34.

82 Herbert Heaton, "Benjamin Gott and the Anglo-American Cloth Trade," *Journal of Economic and Business History*, 2:1 (November 1929), 146-47; "Yorkshire Cloth Traders in the United States 1770-1840," *Publications of the Choresby Society*, 37 (1941), 226-27.

83 Chandler, *Visible Hand*, 51-52; Carl Bridenbaugh, *The Colonial Craftsman* (New York, 1950).

84 See Ashton, *Economic History of England*, ch. 4; Coleman, *Industry in Tudor and Stuart England*, ch. 3 and especially p. 23; Pollard, *The Genesis of Management*, 31.

85 For Philadelphia see Charles Olton, *Artisans for Independence: Philadelphia Mechanics and the American Revolution* (Syracuse, New York, 1975), ch. 3; Sam

Bass Warner, *The Private City: Philadelphia in Three Periods of Its Growth* (Philadelphia, 1968), 6-8; Richard G. Miller, "Gentry and Entrepreneurs: A Socioeconomic Analysis of Philadelphia in the 1790's," *Rocky Mountain Social Science*, 12:1 (January 1975), especially 74; and Smith, "The Material Life of Laboring Philadelphians." For Philadelphia as well as Boston and New York see Gary Nash, *The Urban Crucible: Social Change, Political Consciousness, and the Origins of the American Revolution* (Cambridge, Mass., 1979), especially ch. 5.

86 Hall, "Gentle Craft," 100-1.

87 Gary Kulik, "The Beginning of the Industrial Revolution in America: Pawtucket, Rhode Island, 1672-1829" (Ph.D. dissertation, Brown University, 1980), 43.

88 Quoted in Kulik, "Beginning of the Industrial Revolution," 47.

89 Michael Merrill, "Cash is Good to Eat: Self Sufficiency and Exchange in the Rural Economy of the United States," *Radical History Review*, 4:1 (Winter 1977), 57. For more examples that illustrate the importance of this system of local exchange in the rural North see James Henretta, "Families and Farms: Mentalité in Pre-Industrial America," *William and Mary Quarterly*, 3rd Series, 35:1 (January 1978), 15-16.

90 Kulik, "Beginning of the Industrial Revolution," 22-23; see also Bridenbaugh, *Colonial Craftsman*, 38-46.

91 Kulik, "Beginning of the Industrial Revolution," ch. 1; the quotation is from p.42. A check of some fifteen account books of New England shoemakers from the period before 1800 leads to similar conclusions. Ten of the fifteen shoemakers undertook lines of business other than shoemaking. These activities included such trades as tanning, butchering, blacksmithing, shipbuilding, glass setting, weaving, and brickbuilding, in addition to running sawmills and gristmills, and fishing. Furthermore, almost all the accounts show evidence of farming as well as stock raising. A journal of a cordwainer from Redding, Massachusetts, written between 1788 and 1793, makes it plain that in the winter he spent most of his days working in his shop while during the summer the production of shoes steeply declined as he spent whole days farming. Off and on during the long working day he also took time off to look after his cows and pigs. Hall, "Gentle Craft," 62-73, 95, 104-7.

92 In 1718 the Philadelphia cordwainers and tailors requested in a joint petition to the Common Council the permission to incorporate by a charter. Ian Quimby, who examined this petition, suggests that the cordwainers and tailors probably intended to control the grant of municipal freedom, namely, the English policy of granting the right to practice one's trade within the city limits *only after* the new tradesman had been admitted by the guild. But there is no evidence, according to Quimby, that the petition ever became law. When the Philadelphia cordwainers eventually founded a relatively permanent organization in 1760 under the cover of a Fire Company, they attempted to restrict entry into the craft by limiting membership to those who served "a regular apprenticeship." The Philadelphia tailors, by contrast, organized in 1771 primarily in order to control the prices of cloths and the wages of journeymen. Given, however, the widespread use of unfree labor in the colonial cities, urban craftsmen (who often employed apprentices, indentured servants, and slaves) were preoccupied above all with prices, not wages. Attempts at price fixing are thus recorded among the Philadelphia carpenters from 1724 onwards, the coopers in 1742, and the wheelwrights in 1763,

among the New York carpenters in the 1760s, among the Boston booksellers and barbers in 1724, and the tanners in 1747. Ian Quimby, "The Cordwainers Protest: A Crisis in Labor Relations," *Winterthur Portfolio*, 3 (1967), 85-86, 90; John Commons, "American Shoemakers 1648-1895: A Sketch of Industrial Revolution," *Quarterly Journal of Economics*, 24 (November 1929), 40-44, 82-83; Olton, *Artisans for Independence*, 13-16; Oscar T. Barck, *New York City During the War of Independence* (New York, 1931), 17; Bridenbaugh, *Colonial Craftsman*, 144-46; Nash, *Urban Crucible*, 118, 324.

93 For Fall River: Henry Earl, *A Centennial History of Fall River, Mass.: Comprising a Record of Its Corporate Progress from 1656 to 1876 with Sketches of Its Manufacturing Industries* (New York, 1877), 13-16. For Oxford and Dudley: Jonathan Prude, *The Coming of Industrial Order*, 49.

94 For Pawtucket and Fall River see Louis McLane, "Documents Relative to the Manufacture of the United States" (1833), reprinted in *New American State Papers Manufactures*, vol. 3, 164-67, 170-79. For Oxford and Dudley see Prude, *Industrial Order*, 60.

95 William Bagnall, *The Textile Industries of the United States*, vol. 1: *1639-1810* (Cambridge, Mass., 1893), 222, 445; Samuel Needles, "The Governor's Mill and the Globe Mills, Philadelphia," *Philadelphia Magazine of History and Biography*, 8 (1884), 378; "Textile Material Again," *Bulletin of the Business Historical Society*, 6:3 (May 1932), 6-7; Clark, *History of Manufactures*, vol. 1, 427; Caroline Ware, *The Early New England Cotton Manufacture: A Study of Industrial Beginnings* (Boston, 1931), 205. Anthony Wallace and David Jeremy, "William Pollard and the Arkwright Patents," *William and Mary Quarterly*, 3rd Series, 34:3 (July 1977), 417-18; Kulik, "Beginnings of the Industrial Revolution," 169; Prude, *Industrial Order*, 48.

96 David Jeremy, *Transatlantic Industrial Revolution: The Diffusion of Textile Technologies Between Britain and America, 1790-1830's* (Cambridge, Mass., 1981), 90; George Gibb, *The Saco-Lowell Shops: Textile Machinery Building in New England, 1813-1949* (Cambridge, Mass., 1950), 32.

97 Prude, *Industrial Order*, 69-70.

98 Typically, the journeymen society in early industrial America was an urban phenomenon. Journeymen printers, for example, were among the first American craftsmen to organize; between 1794 and 1825 printers in seven cities extending from Boston to New Orleans formed over a dozen typographical societies. Nevertheless, the country printer remained unorganized during the period. See Rollo Silver, *The American Printer, 1787-1825* (Charlottesville, Virginia, 1967), 14-15; Milton W. Hamilton, *The Country Printer, New York State 1785-1830* (1936; reprinted, Port Washington, New York, 1964), 89.

Journeymen organizations in early American cities were mutual aid societies with significant recreational, fraternal, and beneficiary functions, but just as in Britain, their primary goal was control over recruitment and wages, as a few examples may illustrate. The 1802 constitution of the Philadelphia Typographical Society denied membership from any person who had not served the required period of apprenticeship. In 1810 the New York Typographical Society went as far as closing the trade to adult males by setting age limits for beginning apprenticeships. The Journeymen Cordwainers of Baltimore, too, had a special article in their 1806 constitution referring to apprenticeship: "No member of this society shall teach or instruct any apprentice for any employer in this city or precincts there of under the penalty of being excluded." As a result, the society generally managed to maintain closed shops through the occasional use of the strike. The New York Society of Journeymen Shipwrights and Caulkers was formed in 1804, among other things, in order to prevent employers from hiring "scab" labor. Its constitution threatened to expel any members "who intrude on the regular business, and underwork the established wages of the members of the Society." An 1800 strike of the New York printers likewise showed how critical control over hiring was in enhancing strike solidarity: soon after employers recruited strikebreakers, or "rates" as the strikers later called them, the journeymen printers changed the constitution limiting membership to those who served a three-year apprenticeship. The Philadelphia Journeymen Shoemakers, to give one last example, resolved in 1805 to fine any member of their society who "turned scab" sixteen dollars, a substantial sum given an average journeyman's weekly wage of six to nine dollars at the time. Silver, *American Printer*, 20, 16-17; Charles Steffen, "Between Revolutions: The Pre-Factory Urban Worker in Baltimore, 1780-1820" (Ph.D. dissertation, Northwestern University, 1977), 177; Richard Twomey, "Jacobins and Jeffersonians: Anglo-American Radicalism in the United States, 1790-1820" (Ph.D. dissertation, North Illinois University, 1974), 188-89.

Journeymen's efforts to control the established prices were equally important, and here, too, the evidence is abundant, and the resemblance to early British trade unions is striking. The Philadelphia Journeymen Cabinet and Chairmakers adopted in 1794 a "Book of Prices" on which standard piece rates for all work were to be based. By means of a strike, the details of which are lost, the journeymen managed to force the masters into collective bargaining; the result was a mutual agreement signed in 1796 by three employers and three workers on a revised edition of the price book. Similarly, in 1800 the New York printers went on strike and won the first complete price list adopted by American printers. When the Philadelphia Typographical Society was formed two years later, its members drew up a price list addressing their employers: "Our object is, to have one uniform price established." In 1815 the Washington printers claimed that their newly organized society had two objectives: "first, benevolence, second, the establishment of a regular system of prices." Early shoemakers societies also included demands for minimum prices in their constitutions. An 1805 strike of the Philadelphia journeymen shoemakers was thus an attempt "to regulate the price of labour of others as well as their own," as one council for the prosecution put it in a well known conspiracy trial that followed and led to the conviction of the strike leaders. See Sharon Salinger, "Artisans, Journeymen, and the Transformation of Labor in Late Eighteenth Century Philadelphia," *William and Mary Quarterly*, 3rd Series, 40:1 (January 1983), 79-80; Quimby, "The Cordwainers Protest," 91; Silver, *American Printer*, 15, 19, 24; and John Commons et al., eds., *Documentary History of American Industrial Society*, vol. 3: *Labor Conspiracy Cases* (1910; reprinted, New York, 1958), 68, and see also pp. 61-248.

99 Prude, *Industrial Order*, 71, 133.
100 Kulik, "Beginning of the Industrial Revolution," 369; "Pawtucket Village and the Strike of 1824: The Origins of Class Conflict in Rhode Island," *Radical History*

Review, no. 17 (Spring 1978), 26-27.

101 Barbara Tucker, "Samuel Slater and Sons: The Emergence of the American Factory System, 1790-1860" (Ph.D. dissertation, University of California, Davis, 1974), 214.

102 Ware, *Early New England*, 199-200; Peter Coleman, *The Transformation of Rhode Island, 1790-1860* (Providence, R.I., 1963), 230; Gary Kulik, "Pawtucket Village and the Strike of 1824," 13-14.

103 George White, *Memoir of Samuel Slater, the Father of American Manufactures, Connected with a History of the Rise and Progress of Cotton Manufacture in England and America* (Philadelphia, 1836), 127.

104 Tucker, "Samuel Slater and Sons," 168.

105 For Pawtucket see Kulik, "The Beginnings of the Industrial Revolution," 201-2. 204-5; "Pawtucket Village and the Strike of 1824," 13-14. For Oxford and Dudley: Prude, *Industrial Order*, 92-98. For Webster: Tucker, "Samuel Slater and Sons," ch. 5. The sources of labor supply in the cotton mills of rural Delaware were similar. See William Sisson, "Bell Hours: Work, Values and Discipline in the American Textile Industry, 1787-1880" (Ph.D. dissertation, University of Delaware, 1985), 85.

106 To be sure, skilled British immigrants were also present among early New England mill workers. Immigration is the topic of chapter 5. It is sufficient to note here that however scarce was the skill of mule spinners in America, however difficult it was to train mule spinners locally, in all indications, up to the late 1830s, New England employers recruited mule spinners mainly among native-born Americans.

107 For the 1828 strike see John Commons et al., *History of the Labor Movement in the United States*, vol. 1 (1918; reprinted, New York, 1946), 418-19. For a conspiracy trial that followed this strike see Commons et al., eds., *Documentary History*, vol. 4: *Labor Conspiracy Cases*, 265-68. For the 1833 strike see William Sullivan, *The Industrial Worker in Pennsylvania 1800-1840* (1955; reprinted, New York, 1972), 104, 146-47, 224; and Shelton, *The Mills of Manayunk*, 135-49. For the 1836 strike see Anthony Wallace, *Rockdale: The Growth of an American Village in the Early Industrial Revolution* (1978; reprinted, New York, 1980), 356-59, 367, 355.

CHAPTER 2

1 For Britain see S.D. Chapman, *The Cotton Industry in the Industrial Revolution*, 30. See also John W. McConnel, *A Century of Fine Cotton Spinning: McConnel & Co. Ltd., 1790-1906* (Manchester, 1906), 29, and Butterworth, *Complete History of the Cotton Trade*, 100. For the United States see Tench Coxe, "Digest of Manufacture" (1814), reprinted in *New American State Papers: Manufactures*, vol. 1, 247-410. But many of the mills included in the Digest were short-lived. See "A List of Locations of American Textile Mills, 1808-1818," *Textile History Review* 4:1 (January 1963), 46-51; and Clive Day, "The Early Development of the American Cotton Manufacture," *Quarterly Journal of Economics* 39: 3 (May 1925), 464-65.

2 George Daniels, "Samuel Crompton's Census of the Cotton Industry in 1811," *Economic Journal (Economic History Supplement)*, 2 (January 1930), 108. For a detailed list of ownership and size of fifty-five of the mills enumerated by

Crompton—all located in and around Bolton and Oldham—see Katrina Honeyman, *Origins of Enterprise: Business Leadership in the Industrial Revolution* (1982; reprinted, New York, 1983), 182-84.

3 McLane, *New American State Papers*, vol. 6, 88-98.

4 Jeremy, *Transatlantic Industrial Revolution*, 91.

5 R.L. Hills, "Hargreaves, Arkwright, and Crompton. Why Three Inventors?" *Textile History* 10 (1979), 123.

6 Andrew Ure, *The Cotton Manufacture of Great Britain*, vol. 2, 120-47; *A Dictionary of Arts, Manufactures, and Mines* (London, 1839), vol. 1, 364-66; James Montgomery, *The Theory and Practice of Cotton Spinning or the Carding and Spinning Master's Assistant* (Glasgow, 1836), 163-76; S.J. Chapman, *The Lancashire Cotton Industry*, 53-55; Julia de Lacy Mann, "The Textile Industry: Machinery for Cotton, Flax, Wool, 1760-1850," in Charles Singer, E.J. Holmyard, A.R. Hall, and Trevor Williams, eds., *A History of Technology* (Oxford, 1958), vol. 4: *The Industrial Revolution, 1750-1850*, 291; W.E. Morton and G.R. Wray, *An Introduction to the Study of Spinning* (1937; reprinted, London, 1966), 149-55; David Jeremy, "Innovation in American Textile Technology during the Early 19th Century," *Technology and Culture* 14:1 (January 1973), 48; Hills, "Hargreaves, Arkwright, and Crompton," 123.

7 Abraham Rees, *The Cyclopaedia or Universal Dictionary of Arts, Sciences and Literature*, 39 vols. (London, 1819), vol. 22, "Manufacture of Cotton"; P.P. 1837-38, VIII, *Reports from the Select Committee on Combinations of Workmen*, 306-7; Ure, *Cotton Manufacture*, vol. 2, 148-74; *Dictionary of Arts*, vol. 1, 366-70; Montgomery, *Theory and Practice*, 177-95; Godfrey Lushington, "Abstract of the Evidence on Combinations of Workmen, taken before a Select Committee of the House of Commons in 1838," in National Association for the Promotion of Social Science, *Trades' Societies and Strikes* (London, 1860), 390-91; Chapman, *Lancashire Cotton Industry*, 68; Morton and Wray, *Introduction*, 143-46; Mann, "The Textile Industry," 287-90; Harold Catling, *The Spinning Mule* (Newton Abbot: Devon, England, 1970), 34; William Lazonick, "Industrial Relations and Technical Change; the Case of the Self-Acting Mule," *Cambridge Journal of Economics* 3:3 (September 1979), 234-36; Hills, "Hargreaves, Arkwright, and Crompton," 125-26.

8 According to information given by Harold Catling to David Jeremy. See Jeremy, *Transatlantic Industrial Revolution*, 30, 301.

9 Ure, *Cotton Manufacture*, vol. 1, 272.

10 Kennedy, "A Brief Memoir of Samuel Crompton," 335; C.H. Lee, *A Cotton Enterprise, 1795-1840: A History of M'Connel & Kennedy, Fine Cotton Spinners* (Manchester, 1972), 114-15; Morris David Morris, "The Recruitment of An Industrial Labor in India, with British and American Comparisons," *Comparative Studies in Society and History*, 2:3 (April 1960), 326.

11 Joanne L. Neel, *Phineas Bond: A Study in Anglo American Relations, 1786-1812* (Philadelphia, 1968), 56, 65. The shipment from Liverpool included two spinning jennys, one carding machine, and one "Hallwood." Jeremy has correctly identified the hallwood as a mule. See David Jeremy, "British Textile Technology Transmission to the United States: The Philadelphia Region Experience, 1770-1820," *Business History Review* 47:1 (Spring 1973), 39-40.

12 Bagnall, *Textile Industries*, vol. 1, 222-25. According to Bagnall (pp. 185-86) a cotton mill in Hurlgate, New York, had a mule as early as 1794.

13 Coxe, *New American State Papers*, vol. 1, 197.

14 James Montgomery, *A Practical Detail of the Cotton Manufacture of the United States of America; and the State of the Cotton Manufacture of that Country Contrasted and Compared with that of Great Britain* (1840; reprinted, New York, 1968), 147. All cotton mills in the United States before the War of 1812, notes Batchelder, "were built after the plan first introduced by Slater, with very little modification." Samuel Batchelder, *Introduction and Early Progress of the Cotton Manufacture in the United States* (Boston, 1863), 56.

By contrast to the family mill, the boarding house plant was giant. According to the McLane Report, which is the earliest attempt to enumerate every cotton mill in existence in the United States, there were 470 "cotton factories" in New England in 1832 (see Day, "Early Development of American Cotton Manufacture," 452). Based on the McLane Report, Caroline Ware (*Early New England Cotton Manufacture*, 191, 202) estimated that in 1832 about half of New England cotton factory workers were employed in "family" mills, and that the "aggregate labor force" in boarding house mills "amounted to somewhat less than half the total number of mill workers" in these states. This statement, cited recently by Jonathan Prude (*The Coming of Industrial Order*, 276), is misleading. A close scrutiny of the Report reveals that only 28% of the cotton mill operatives in New England in 1832 were employed in Lowell-type mills. The fifteen boarding house mills enumerated in the McLane Report (Maine: the Saco Company; New Hampshire: the New Market, Exeter, Upper, Cocheco, Great Falls, Nashua, and Jackson companies; Massachusetts: the Taunton, Chicopee, Appleton, Lowell, Merrimark, Hamilton, and Boston manufacturing companies) gave employment to 9,500 of the total 34,000 New England cotton mill operatives in 1832. McLane, *New American State Papers*, vols. 3-5. The relative proportion of workers employed in Lowell-and Slater-type mills in Massachusetts in 1832 is revealing:

	no. of cotton factories	no. of operatives
Lowell Sector	7	4,800
Slater Sector	185	9,200
	192	14,000

McLane, *New American State Papers*, vols. 3-4.

15 U.S. Senate, *Report on Conditions of Woman and Child Wage Earners in the United States*, 19 vols., S. Doc. 645, 61st Cong., 2nd Sess., 1910, vol. 9: *History of Women in Industry in the United States*, by Helen Sumner (reprinted, New York, 1974), 53.

16 Ware, *Early New England Cotton Manufacture*, 209. See examples of newspaper advertisements in Gary Kulik, Roger Parks, and Theodore Penn, eds., *The New England Mill Village, 1790-1860* (Cambridge, Mass., 1982), 408, 411.

17 Zachariah Allen, *The Science of Mechanics as Applied to the Present Improvements in the Useful Arts in Europe, and the United States of America* (Providence, R.I., 1829), 347. For a modern evaluation of Allen's comparative wage statistics, see Nathan Rosenberg, "Anglo-American Wage Differences in the 1820's," *Journal of Economic History* 27:2 (June 1967), 221-29. "In this country," reported the directors of one New England cotton corporation in 1827, "the expense of employing mule spinners and the extreme difficulty of obtaining good and faithful ones have caused the mule to fall into general disuse in the larger factories." Quoted in Paul F. McGouldrick, *New England Textiles in the Nineteenth Century: Profits and Investment* (Cambridge, Mass., 1968), 36.

18 George Wallis, "New York Industrial Exhibition: Special Report to the House of Commons" (1854); reprinted in Nathan Rosenberg, ed., *The American System of Manufacture* (Edinburgh, 1969), 304.

19 See Nathan Rosenberg, *Perspectives on Technology* (Cambridge, 1976), 286-87; *Technology and American Economic Growth* (New York, 1972), 39-51; Charles F. Sabel, *Work and Politics: The Division of Labor in Industry* (1982; reprinted, New York, 1984), 31-41; and Piore and Sabel, *The Second Industrial Divide*, ch. 2.

20 Rosenberg, *Technology and American Economic Growth*, 44.

21 For the important distinction between special and general purpose machines see Sabel, *Work and Politics*, and Piore and Sabel, *The Second Industrial Divide*.

22 Ure, *Dictionary of Arts*, vol. 1, 366; Clark, *History of Manufactures in the United States*, vol. 1, 426. Running a model of the 1775 water frame in the North-Western Museum of Science and Industry, R.L. Hills understood "immediately why it was impossible to spin fine yarns or softly twisted yarns on the water frame. Quite simply the pull [caused by the friction of the bobbin] is so great that they would have broken." "Hargreaves, Arkwright and Crompton," 121.

23 Daniels, *English Cotton Industry*, 117.

24 Jacob Bigelow, *Elements of Technology* (Boston, 1829), 351-52; Catling, *The Spinning Mule*, 118; Jeremy, "British Textile Technology Transmission," 28.

25 The figure for the mid 1830s is from Montgomery, *Theory and Practice*, 177; for the other estimates see S.D. Chapman, "Fixed Capital Formation in the British Cotton Manufacturing Industry," 77; Ure, *Cotton Manufacture*, vol. 2, 141-42; Chapman, *The Cotton Industry in the Industrial Revolution*, 21; and P.P. 1834, XIX, 119 pp-23, 190.

26 On the home market for cotton goods see Edwards, *The Growth of the British Cotton Trade*, chs. 3 and 4. On the overseas market see Lars G. Sandberg, "Movements in the Quality of British Cotton Textile Exports, 1815-1913," *Journal of Economic History* 28:1 (March 1968), 4, 16, 18, 20; D.A. Farnie, *The English Cotton Industry and the World Market 1815-1896* (Oxford, 1979), ch. 3 ; Edwards, *Growth of the British Cotton Trade*, ch.9; Thomas Ellison, *The Cotton Trade of Great Britain* (1886; reprinted, New York, 1968), ch. 5. For sales of yarn by McConnel and Kennedy see McConnel, *A Century of Fine Spinning*, 45-47. The sales were for the home market as well as for export.

27 Jeremy, *Transatlantic Industrial Revolution*, 26, 301.

28 By 1779 an additional type of cotton fabric known as "Manchester" was manufactured in Lancashire for export. See Wadsworth and Mann, *The Cotton Trade and Industrial Lancashire*, 146.

29 British made muslins competed with East Indian muslins in Britain, Western Europe, and India itself. Initially, in the 1810s the British cotton cloth imported to India was of a very high quality. By 1823, however, the value of British exports of plain calicoes to India surpassed that of muslins and thereafter the cloth quality of Indian imports from Britain deteriorated rapidly. At the same time there was a considerable

improvement in the quality of British cotton goods going to home consumption, to Western Europe, and to the United States during the first half of the nineteenth century. Overall, the home trade catered to a wealthier market than the foreign trade. Because higher counts yielded the greatest profit margin, the home trade was also more profitable. Edwards, *Growth of British Cotton Trade*, 40-42; Farnie, *The English Cotton Industry*, 101, 132; Sandberg, "Movements in the Quality of British Cotton", 17-18, 20.

30 Edwards, *Growth of the British Cotton Trade*, 25, 247, 27, in order.

31 After 1828 the value of cotton goods exported from the United States was over $1 million yearly, or just between 3% to 4% of the domestic trade in 1831. Frances W. Gregory, *Nathan Appleton, Merchant and Entrepreneur, 1779-1861* (Charlottesville, 1975), 226, in conjunction with Melvin T. Copeland, *The Cotton Manufacturing Industry of the United States* (1917; reprinted, New York, 1966), 6.

32 James Montgomery, *Practical Detail*, 109-110.

33 For 1816: according to the testimony of a cotton manufacturer before the Select Committee on children's employment, P.P. 1816, III, 333. For 1817: according to John Kennedy's estimate cited in Edward Baines, *History of the Cotton Manufacture in Great Britain* (1835; reprinted, New York, 1966), 369. For 1833: see P.P. 1834, XIX, 137, and Baines, *History of the Cotton Manufacture in Great Britain*, 431.

34 P.P. 1834, XIX, 119pp-123, 134-35. More than 220 cotton mills were surveyed but only 170 gave information on yarn counts.

35 Clark, *History of Manufactures*, vol. 1, 560; Montgomery, *Practical Detail*, 69.

36 U.S. Senate, "Schedule of the Cotton Manufacturies in the County of Bristol State of Massachusetts," 14th Cong., 1st Sess., 1816; reprinted in *New American State Papers: Manufactures*, vol. 1, 416.

37 McLane, *New American State Papers*, vol. 5, 313-18. Hand-loom weavers in Pennsylvania in 1820 complained that in order to manufacture quality goods they had to send for fine cotton yarn from Britain. See Scranton, *Propriety Capitalism*, 111.

38 Clark, *History of Manufactures*, vol. 1, 549.

39 Wallis, "New York Industrial Exhibition," 218.

40 This estimate, given by the National Association of Cotton Manufacturers and Planters in their first annual meeting in New York in 1864, refers to the northern states only and reflects a recent increase in the average yarn count. See Clark, *History of Manufactures*, vol. 2: *1860-1893*, 102.

41 Lee, *A Cotton Enterprise*, 25.

42 P.P. 1834, XIX, 119pp.

43 Montgomery, *Practical Detail*, 166-68. See also Ware, *Early New England Cotton Manufacture*, 65; and Jeremy, *Transatlantic Industrial Revolution*, 99.

44 Wallis, "New York Industrial Exhibition," 308-9.

45 Ware, *Early New England Cotton Manufacture*, 86. See also Coleman, *The Transformation of Rhode Island*, 92.

46 Jeremy, *Transatlantic Industrial Revolution*, 205. Another reason for the decline in British imports was tariffs. Tariff legislation, however, was much more effective in protecting cheap than expensive cotton goods and therefore cannot account for more than a small fraction of the fall in British imports of white and plain muslins. The tariff of 1816 imposed a flat duty of 25% on imports of cotton

cloths, but in addition, it also imposed a minimum duty on the cheapest fabrics (those costing less than 25 cents a yard) which often exceeded 25%. As a result, the tariff of 1816 was more effective in debarring the entry of coarse than fine goods. The range of goods protected widened and the minimum valuation rose to 30 cents in 1824 and 35 cents in 1828. Nonetheless, the overall effects of these tariffs on the reduction in muslin import remained marginal. See F.W. Taussing, *The Tariff History of the United States* (1892; reprinted, New York, 1931), 29-36, and J. Potter, "Atlantic Economy, 1815-60: The U.S.A. and the Industrial Revolution in Britain," in L.S. Pressnell, ed., *Studies in the Industrial Revolution* (London, 1960), 260-65.

47 Batchelder, *Introduction and Early Progress*, 81.

48 Montgomery, *Practical Detail*, 170-71.

49 Jeremy, *Transatlantic Industrial Revolution*, 204. See also Tucker, *Samuel Slater and the Origins of the American Textile Industry*, 98.

50 Montgomery, *Practical Detail*, 69; Clark, *History of Manufactures*, vol. 1, 427, vol. 2, 106; Earl, *Centennial History of Fall River*, 28; Bagnall, *The Textile Industries*, 421, 445; "Textile Material Again," 8-9.

51 McLane, *New American State Papers*, vol. 6, 88-98.

52 Ibid., 251.

53 P.P. 1834, XIX, 119pp.

54 P.P. 1842, XXII, *Reports of the Inspectors of Factories for the Half Year Ending 31st December, 1841*, 33-44.

55 Piore and Sabel, *The Second Industrial Divide*, ch. 2. See also Michael Piore, "The Technological Foundation of Dualism and Discontinuity," in Suzanne Berger and Michael Piore, *Dualism and Discontinuity in Industrial Societies* (Cambridge, 1980), and for one of the pioneering studies of the dual structure of American industry see Robert Averitt, *The Dual Economy: The Dynamics of American Industry Structure* (New York, 1968).

56 Wallis, "New York Industrial Exhibition," 220-21. For more examples see also Friends of Domestic Industry at their New York Convention, October 26, 1831, *Address to the People of the United States* (Baltimore, 1832), 30.

57 Edwards, *The Growth of the British Cotton Trade*, 250-51.

58 Ibid.; Farnie, *The English Cotton Industry*, 14; George Daniels, "The Cotton Trade at the Close of the Napoleonic War," *Transactions of the Manchester Statistical Society*, 1917-18, 5.

59 James A. Mann, *The Cotton Trade of Great Britain* (1860; reprinted, London, 1968), 42.

60 Robert Zevin, "The Growth of Cotton Textile Production After 1815," in Robert Fogel and Stanley Engerman, eds., *The Reinterpretation of American Economic History* (New York, 1971), 127-28; Friends of Domestic Industry, *Address*, 29.

61 Montgomery, *Practical Detail*, 130.

62 As calculated by Smelser, *Social Change in the Industrial Revolution*, 154; see also Montgomery, *Practical Detail*, 125, 126.

63 McConnel, *A Century of Fine Cotton Spinning*, 52. The cotton manufacturing firm of Samuel Greg estimated that in Lancashire in 1832 the price of one pound of cotton constituted 57% of the price of one pound of yarn number 30. The firm gave Andrew Ure a detailed list of cotton and yarn prices from 1802 to 1832 for

counts no. 23 to 31. See Ure, *The Cotton Manufacture of Great Britain*, vol. 2, 431.

64 Montgomery, *Theory and Practice*, pp. 175-78; Jeremy, "British Textile Technology Transmission to the United States," 28. The importance of the mule's material supply flexibility has long been acknowledged by economic historians. See Copeland, *The Cotton Manufacturing Industry of the United States*, 68-72; Lars Sandberg, "American Rings and English Mules: The Role of Economic Rationality," in S.B. Saul, ed., *Technological Change: The United States and Britain in the Nineteenth Century* (London, 1970), 131; William Lazonick, "Factor Costs and the Diffusion of Ring Spinning in Britain Prior to World War I," *Quarterly Journal of Economics* 96:1 (February 1981), 103; "Industrial Organization and Technological Change: The Decline of the British Cotton Industry," *Business History Review* 57:2 (Summer 1983), 208, 209; William Lazonick and William Mass, "The Performance of the British Cotton Industry, 1870-1913," *Research in Economic History*, vol. 9 (1984), 14, 16; William Mass, "Technological Change and Industrial Relations: The Diffusion of Automatic Weaving in the United States and Britain" (Ph.D. dissertation, Boston College, 1984), 226, 246; Gary Saxonhouse and Gavin Wright, "New Evidence on the Stubborn English Mule and the Cotton Industry, 1878-1920," *Economic History Review*, 2nd Series, 37:4 (November 1984), 513-14; "Ring and Mules Around the World: A Comparative Study in Technological Choice," *Research in Economic History*, Suppl. 3 (1984), 289, 294.

65 Baines, *History of Cotton Manufacture*, 310-11; Wallis, "New York Industrial Exhibition," 313.

66 Edwards, *Growth of British Cotton Trade*, 93.

67 Ure, *Cotton Manufacture*, vol. 1, 87; Edwards, *Growth of British Cotton Trade*, 93-95. Another short-stapled cotton slightly superior to upland—New Orleans— was used in Britain for spinning weft (filling) counts up to 150 as early as 1816. See John Sutcliffe, *A Treatise on Canals and Reservoirs... Likewise Observations on the Best Mode of Carding, Roving, Drawing, and Spinning All Kinds of Cotton Twist* (Rochdale, 1816), 28.

68 McLane, *New American State Papers*, vol. 3, 213.

69 P.P. 1833, XX, E. 23.

70 12.5% is Ure's estimate for 1836. *Cotton Manufacture*, vol. 1, p. liii. 15% is an estimate for the 1870s cited in P.L. Simmons, *Waste Products and Undeveloped Substances* (London, 1876), 264.

71 Montgomery, *Theory and Practice*, 51.

72 Thomas Thornley, *Cotton Waste: Its Production, Manipulation, and Uses* (London, 1912), 203, but see also 204-30.

73 Simmons, *Waste Products*, 264; Farnie, *English Cotton Industry*, 160.

74 Thornley, *Cotton Waste*, 232-35; Simmons, *Waste Products*, 264-65.

75 Whether or not American cotton manufacturers discarded a larger proportion of cotton in the form of waste than did British millowners is hard to say. The amount of waste discarded was partly dependent on yarn count, with coarse spinning creating more waste than fine spinning. The American specialization in coarse spinning implies, therefore, more waste. But waste was also proportional to cotton grade: the percentage of waste by grade varied from 8% on high-quality "middling fair" to 17% or 18% on low-quality "good ordinary." Typically, the cotton used in the United States at the turn of the century was three grades above the

Lancashire standard. The use of inferior cotton in Britain, it follows, generated more waste *for a given yarn count* than the use of high-quality cotton in the United States. Mass, "Technological Change and Industrial Relations, " 248.

76 See Wallace, *Rockdale*, 134, 160; Tucker, *Samuel Slater*, 201, 211; and for the Fall River mills see McLane, *New American State Papers*, vol. 3, 204. In general, coarse yarns made in the United States were of superior quality to those made in Britain. In 1816 it was reported that American yarn counts no. 14 and 15 was equal in quality to English counts no. 20 and 22. See David Jeremy, "British and American Yarn Counts Systems: A Historical Analysis," *Business History Review* 45 (Autumn 1971), 352 .

77 Montgomery, *Practical Detail*, 49.

78 Wallace, *Rockdale*, 162.

79 See Robert Baird, *The American Cotton Spinner, and Managers' and Carders' Guide* (Philadelphia, 1851), 147; and Copeland, *The Cotton Manufacturing Industry*, 72.

80 For 1808-14 see Edwards, *The Growth of British Cotton Trade*, 97-105; Daniels, "The Cotton Trade at the Close of the Napoleonic War," 6. During these early years, however, fine cottons from Brazil and the West Indies did not always provide satisfactory substitutes for the Sea Island staples. For 1861-65 see Farnie, *The English Cotton Industry*, 141-65.

81 Lazonick, "Factor Costs," 103; Edwards, *The Growth of British Cotton Trade*, ch. 6; Farnie, *The English Cotton Industry*, 57-60; Saxonhouse and Wright, "New Evidence," 514.

82 Week-to-week changes in cotton supply imply frequent adjustments of the machinery. "Whenever there is a fresh mixing of cotton it is almost sure to require an alteration in some of the machinery, as it seldom happens that the new mixing will produce the same weight of roving or yarn." R. Scott, *The Practical Cotton Spinner and Manufacturer. The Managers', Overlookers' and Mechanics' Companion*, corrected and enlarged by Oliver Byrne (Philadelphia, 1851), 25. The mule's draft rollers could be easily re-adjusted with each new mixing. See Sutcliffe, *A Treatise on Canals and Reservoirs*, 19, 25.

83 Ure, *Cotton Manufacture*, vol. 1, 84.

84 Montgomery, *Practical Detail*, 48-49. See also pp. 28-29, 38. Similarly, American visitors to Lancashire in the 1900s reported that English millowners selected their cotton with "expertness, discriminating skill, and care" rarely found among American cotton manufacturers. See Saxonhouse and Wright, "New Evidence," 514.

85 Baines, *History of Cotton Manufacture*, 311.

86 Chapman, *The Cotton Industry in the Industrial Revolution*, 20-21; Catling, *The Spinning Mule*, 54.

87 See Jeremy, *Transatlantic Industrial Revolution*, 90-91, 309.

88 Ibid. Both the higher labor costs and the lower power costs in the United States compared to those of Britain induced American manufacturers to run their machinery faster. Dolores Greenberg, "Reassessing the Power Patterns of the Industrial Revolution: An Anglo-American Comparison," *American Historical Review*, 87:5 (December 1982), 1247-48; H.J. Habakkuk, *American and British Technology in the 19th Century: The Search for Labour-Saving Inventions*

(Cambridge, 1962), 55.

89 Montgomery, *Practical Detail*, 162; Jeremy, "Innovation in American Textile," 50.

90 Robert MacMurray, "Technological Change in the American Cotton Spinning Industry, 1790 to 1836" (Ph.D. dissertation, University of Pennsylvania, 1970), 68, 129-36. In 1825 mules were manufactured in Pawtucket, Rhode Island in Jas. Brown machine shop. Thomas Navin, *The Whitin Machine Works Works Since 1831: A Textile Machinery Company in An Industrial Village* (Cambridge, Mass., 1950), 486.

91 MacMurray, "Technological Change," 76-84; Jeremy, "Innovation," 52-54; Gibb, *The Saco-Lowell Shops*, 77; Montgomery, *Practical Detail*, 70; Habakkuk, *American and British Technology*, 102; Copeland, *The Cotton Manufacturing Industry*, 72.

92 P.P. 1833, VI, *Report from the Select Committee on Manufactures, Commerce, and Shipping*, 167, 171. A Lancashire cotton manufacturer testified in 1833 that four of his "most valuable and ingenious machines have been introduced from America: the patent reed making, patent card making, Dyer's patent roving frame, and Danforth's throstle." P.P. 1833, XX, *First Report of the Factory Inquiry Commission*, D.2., 33.

93 P.P. 1833, XX, A.l., 112. The Scottish immigrant claimed that with two mules equal in size to the pair he managed in Rammapool he could have produced twice as much yarn (of the same quality) in Britain.

94 Allen, *The Science of Mechanics*, 352.

95 Zachariah Allen, *The Practical Tourist, or Sketches of the State of Arts, and of Society, Scenery, etc., etc., in Great Britain, France, and Holland* (Providence, 1832), vol. 1, 123-24. See also *The Science of Mechanics*, 351; and Batchelder, *Introduction and Early Progress*, 91-94.

96 G.N. Tunzelmann, *Steam Power and British Industrialization to 1860* (Oxford, 1978), 160-63, 266-78, 282. Tunzelmann further concludes that water was slightly cheaper than steam in the United States while the reverse was true in Britain. He derives the American data from Peter Temin ("Steam and Waterpower in the Early 19th Century," *Journal of Economic History* 26:2 [June 1966], 197) and expresses them in British currency. He then examines critically the sources from which Temin took his data and writes: "The American figures cannot be accepted as they stand" because the contemporary author of these figures—C.T. James— "spoke impassionedly in favor of steam power" in his attempt to prove that it was competitive with water power. Therefore, he concludes, the differences in the costs of water and steam power in the United States were probably larger than what C.T. James' figures—cited by Temin—indicate. Note, in addition, the costs' estimate given by James Kempton, a cotton manufacturer from Norwich, Connecticut, testifying before a British Parliamentary Committee in 1833. According to Kempton's calculations, water power in America was three-and-a-half times cheaper than steam power in Britain (though he too might have very well exaggerated in the opposite direction and for the opposite reasons than Jones did). P.P. 1833, VI, 170; XX, E. 23. Paul McGouldrick, finally, notes that in the United States "untill the 1850's, water power was more economic than steam power, and this restricted mill building to sites where the power supply had a natural limitation." McGouldrick, *New England Textiles*, 136.

97 McLane, *New American State Papers*, vol. 5, 299-304.
98 Temin, "Steam and Waterpower," 200. But Temin may have exaggerated. According to McGouldrick (297): "Peter Temin's conclusion that a high proportion of new cotton mills erected after 1835 had steam power is mistaken . . . on the basis of Baker sample and other business manuscripts consulted. The changeover period occurred instead in the 1850's."
99 Louis C. Hunter, *A History of Industrial Power in the United States, 1780- 1930*, vol. 1: *Waterpower in the Century of the Steam Engine* (Charlottesville, Va., 1979), 274. On the importance of water power in the American cotton industry see also Evan Leigh, *The Science of Modern Cotton Spinning* (Manchester, 1873), vol. 2, 300-1.
100 J.R. McCulloch, "The Rise, Progress, Present State, and Prospects of the British Cotton Manufacture," *Edinburgh Review*, 46 (June 1827), 15.
101 A.E. Musson, "Industrial Motive Power in the United Kingdom, 1800-70," *Economic History Review* 29:3 (August 1976), 424.
102 A.J. Taylor, "Concentration and Specialization in the Lancashire Cotton Industry, 1825-1850," *Economic History Review*, 2nd Series, 1 (1949), 115. It was not just that the United States had a much higher aggregate capacity than Britain but, equally important, heavy concentration of water power sources such as those of Lowell, Lawrence, Fall River, Holyoke, Chicopee, and Manchester, New Hampshire, scarcely existed in Britain. See Hunter, *A History of Industrial Power*, vol. 1, 161-63.
103 Hills and Pacey estimate that by the turn of the century one horsepower drove 100 throstle spindles. They cite Buchanan's estimate of one horsepower to 1,000 mule spindles in 1808 and rightly conclude that "this large figure may indicate that Buchanan was thinking about mills where mule spinning was not fully mechanized." Catling estimates 700 mule spindles per horsepower during these early years, but Chapman arrives at a far lower figure: one horsepower drove 100 throstle and 350 mule spindles in 1800. Ellison cites James Hyde's estimate for the second part of the century: the throstle required "at least" twice as much power as the mule. R.L. Hills and A.J. Pacey, "The Measurement of Power in Early Steam Driven Textile Mills," *Technology and Culture*, 13 (January 1972), 27; Robertson Buchanan, *Practical Essays on Mill Work and Other Machinery*, 3rd ed. (London, 1841), 89; Catling, *The Spinning Mule*, 47; Chapman, "Fixed Capital," 88; Ellison, *The Cotton Trade of Great Britain*, 33.

To conduct a valid measurement, however, it is necessary to contrast mule and throstle spindles of the same kind, that is, spindles producing the same yarn count. According to Robert Baird, one horsepower would have driven 100 throstle spindles and 250 mule spindles in spinning yarn no. 25 in 1851. In spinning fine counts no. 60, on the other hand, one horsepower would have driven as many as 500 mule spindles at that date. Ure, like Baird, calculated the comparative requirements of power for spinning the same yarn count (presumably no. 36) and therefore his estimate for the typical British mill in the 1830s is quite reliable. Similarly, Zachariah Allen reported that in Britain in 1825 one horsepower drove 500 mule spindles in spinning yarn no. 48 and 1,000 mule spindles in spinning yarn no. 110. Baird, *American Cotton Spinner*, 46; Ure, *Cotton Manufacture*, vol. 1, 304, 311; Allen, *The Science of Mechanics*, 147.

104 The decision of Waltham-Lowell companies to manufacture coarse goods, says McGouldrick, "was influenced by the low cost of water power in New England, which made it economic to produce very durable fabrics made of wiry, highly twisted yarn." *New England Textiles*, 31. Likewise, a Cheshire cotton manufacturer noted in 1846 that the "natural advantage of unlimited water power" encouraged American manufacturers to neglect fine spinning and to concentrate their efforts on the production of coarse goods. See testimony reprinted from Parliamentary Papers in Tunzelmann, *Steam Power and British Industrialization*, 275.

105 Allen, *The Science of Mechanics*, 347. Allen does not refer Specifically to throstle spinners but to "women in cotton mills." Given, however, his wage estimate of eight shillings per week in England in 1825, he probably was thinking about throstle spinners and preparatory workers, not power-loom weavers. See Wood, *History of Wages*, 14, 44. British immigrant mule spinners in Pennsylvania reported that their earnings were even higher than what Allen's figures indicate. Consider the following excerpts from a letter sent in April 1833 by a spinner from Norristown, Pennsylvania to Glasgow: "Dear John, you wish for statements of the prices we are paid, and how the market rates: I will do that as far as my information leads me. . . . I am spinning one wheel 312 spindles, number twenties. I can make about 30s[hillings] per week, British money. . . . We can turn off 6000 to 6500 hanks per week, that is, when we get full work, and we get twenty cents per 100 hanks, that is tenpence British money. When I compared our list with the list at home, I found that we had more than the double [British wages]." P.P. 1833, XX, A.1., 104. For wage differentials of throstle spinners and mule Spinners in the United States and Britain in the early 1830s see chapter 3 below. The McLane Report provides comparable wages for men and women in the United States and Britain. In 1832, according to the report, the wages of men employed in cotton mills were 50% higher in the United States ($9 per week) than in Britain ($6), and the wages of women in cotton mills were 55% higher in the United States ($3.50) than in Britain ($2.25). McLane, *New American State Papers*, vol. 7, 308.

106 Ellison, *The Cotton Trade in Great Britain*, 35-36, 65-66; P.P. 1834, XIX, 192. For the number of power looms in 1813-50 see also Taylor, "Concentration and Specialization," 117; and Smelser, *Social Change in the Industrial Revolution*, 148. For the number of mills in 1856, see Taylor, "Concentration and Specialization," 122.

107 McLane, *New American State Papers*, vols. 3, 4, 5.

108 For the number of hand-loom weavers see Smelser, *Social Change in the Industrial Revolution*, 137, 207; and Chapman, *The Cotton Industry in the Industrial Revolution*, 60. For the number of hand looms of all kinds see J.H. Clapham, *An Economic History of Modern Britain*, vol. 1: *The Early Railway Age 1820-1850* (1926; reprinted, Cambridge, 1950), 179; and Thompson, *The Making of the English Working Class*, 311.

109 Bythell, *The Handloom Weavers*, 275.

110 Wood, *History of Wages*, 112.

111 Bruce Lauri, *Working People of Philadelphia 1800-1850* (Philadelphia, 1980), 24.

112 The decline in income from hand weaving in Rhode Island between 1818 and 1823 reflects a shift towards alternative occupations, not a drastic fall in piece rates, as had been the case in Britain. Barbara Fowler, "Rhode Island Handloom Weavers and the Effects of Technological Change 1790-1840" (Ph.D. dissertation, University of Pennsylvania, 1984), chapter 3 and pp. 200-5, 233-34.

113 Carville Earle and Ronald Hoffman, "The Foundation of the Modern Economy: Agriculture and the Costs of Labor in the United States and England, 1800-60," *American Historical Review*, 85:5 (December 1980), 1084.

114 Habakkuk, *American and British Technology*, 123; Jeremy, *Transatlantic Industrial Revolution*, 99, 182.

115 Baines, *History of Cotton Manufacture*, 418.

116 One way in which British millowners improved the strength of their warp (to withstand the beating of the shuttle) was by treating it with a starch paste called size. Sizing was a standard practice in American as well as British mills, but the amount of size used in the two industries differed markedly. As a proportion of the weight of the yarn, British millowners used several times as much size as did American manufacturers. Heavy sizing in Britain had been used first around 1820, when the earliest power looms went into operation, and then after 1825, when it became increasingly widespread. It had two functions: 1) strengthening the mule warp before weaving, and 2) "adulteration"—the substitution of paste, clay, or any other "earthy matter" for expensive cotton. Mule-Spun warp was better adapted to heavy sizing than throstle-spun warp, and as such, more economical in the use of raw cotton. The quotations are from P.P. 1833, VI, 326-27. See also Copeland, *The Cotton Manufacturing Industry*, 72, 78-79; and Mass, "Technological Change and Industrial Relations," 225-26.

117 For early power-loom weaving in Britain see Bythell, *The Handloom Weavers*, ch. 4; Richard Marsden, *Cotton Weaving* (London, 1895), ch. 3; and Ure, *Cotton Manufacture*, vol. 2, 287-324. For power weaving in the United States: Wallace, *Rockdale*, 144-47; Thomas Dublin, *Women at Work: The Transformation of Work and Community in Lowell, Massachusetts, 1826-1860* (New York, 1979), 64, 67; and Jeremy, *Transatlantic Industrial Revolution*, chs. 5, 10, 11. The best technological description of the tasks involved in working the power loom is given by Mass, "Technological Change and Industrial Relations," 275-79.

118 McLane, *New American State Papers*, vol. 5, 299-304, 313-17, vol. 6, 88-98.

119 Taylor, "Concentration and Specialization," 122.

120 Farnie, *English Cotton Industry*, 313.

121 On the geographical separation of the two processes see Elijah Helm, "The British Cotton Industry," in W.J. Ashley, ed., *British Industries* (London, 1903), 79-80.

122 Farnie, *English Cotton Industry*, 317.

123 Economic historians have referred to this point again and again in their discussion of mules and rings. See Copeland, *Cotton Manufacturing Industry*, 72; Sandberg, "American Rings and English Mules," 127-28; Lazonick, "Factor Costs," 94; and Saxonhouse and Wright, "Rings and Mules Around the World," 291, 293. The ring is a descendant of the throstle and on both machines wooden bobbins were used to wind filling yarn. See Dublin, *Women at Work*, 64.

124 On the problem of efficiency versus flexibility in the Lowell sector of the New England cotton industry see Robert Spalding, "The Boston Mercantile Community and the Promotion of the Textile Industry in New England, 1813-1860" (Ph.D. dissertation, Yale University, 1963), especially pp. 212-17.

125 U.S. House of Representatives, "Cultivation, Manufacture and Foreign Trade of

Cotton," 48, 59.
126 V.A.C. Gatrell, "Labour, Power and the Size of Firms in Lancashire Cotton in the Second Quarter of the Nineteenth Century," *Economic History Review*, 2nd Series, 30:1 (February 1977), 118-19.
127 As measured by the number of pounds. Wallis, "New York Industrial Exhibition," 210.
128 Scranton, *Propriety Capitalism*, chs. 9 and 11, especially 333-34 and 417.

CHAPTER 3

1 Reexamining the industrial revolution, Stephen Marglin arrived at the opposite conclusions. In an exceedingly influential article he argued that technology "had little or nothing to do" with the rise of the factory. Critiquing the works of T.S. Ashton, Paul Mantoux, David Landes, and a few other historians, Marglin insists that it was the need for discipline, supervision, and control of workers "which shaped and determined" the organization of factory production, implying that the choice of machinery played an insignificant role in the evolution of early management. To support this argument Marglin draws most of his evidence from the cotton industry, yet he totally ignores the fundamental contrast between the craft and mass production sectors. See Stephen A. Marglin, "What Do Bosses Do? The Origins and Functions of Hierarchy in Capitalist Production," *The Review of Radical Political Economists*, 6:2 (Summer 1974), especially pp. 81-89. See also a reply by David Landes, "What Do Bosses Really Do?", *The Journal of Economic History* 46:3 (September 1986), 585-623.
2 Ure, *The Philosophy of Manufactures*, 289-90.
3 Sidney Pollard, "Factory Discipline in the Industrial Revolution," *Economic History Review*, 2nd Series, 16 (December 1963), 264. See also Pollard, *Genesis of Modern Management*, 38-47.
4 For more British examples see Pollard, *Genesis of Modern Management*, 35. For New England see Ware, *Early New England Cotton Manufacture*, 50-53, and Tucker, *Samuel Slater*, 104-5. In combining factory spinning and putting out weaving American managers were clearly influenced by the examples of British manufacturers. See Samuel Ogden, *Thoughts, What Probable Effects the Peace with Great Britain will have on the Cotton Manufactures of this Country; Interspersed with Remarks on Our Bad Management in the Business; and the Way to Improvement, so as to Meet Imported Goods in Cheapness, at our Home Market* (Providence, 1815), 31-32.
5 Smelser, *Social Change*, 190, 199. Tucker, "Samuel Slater and Sons," 194, 213; Wallace, *Rockdale*, 171-80. It should be emphasized, however, that in both countries, evidently, only a minority of helpers were the spinners' relatives. In Britain, according to Michael Anderson, at no time between 1816 and 1851 did relatives make up the majority of mule spinners' assistants. Edwards and Lloyd-Jones found that in thirteen Preston cotton factories in 1816 less than 12% of the children at work were employed by parents, brothers, or sisters who were mule spinners (and weavers), and in eleven cotton mills in the country area around Preston a quarter of all children were directly employed by relatives who were mule spinners (and weavers). Michael Anderson, "Sociological History and the Working-Class Family:

Smelser Revisited," *Social History*, No. 3 (October 1976), 324. See also his earlier book, *Family Structure in Nineteenth Century Lancashire*, 115-18; M.M. Edwards and R. Lloyd-Jones, "N.J. Smelser and the Cotton Factory Family: A Reassessment," in Harte and Ponting, eds., *Textile History and Economic History*, 313-15; and R.G. Kirby and A.E. Musson, *The Voice of the People: John Doherty, 1798-1854, Trade Unionist, Radical, and Reformist* (Manchester, 1975), 147-48.

In the United States, too, evidence is incomplete. Anthony Wallace reported that the ten mule spinners at work in the Riddle's mill at Rockdale, Pennsylvania in 1832 "often" employed their own children. It is not clear though what was the proportion of helpers who were the spinners' children but "a large proportion of the piecers were, the datebook makes it plain, not the children of spinners." During the 1820s and 1830s in Webster, Massachusetts, Tucker likewise observed, "Mule spinners hired and paid their own sons, nephews, or close family friends to piece for them." Yet Tucker's conclusion that family employment in Webster was the rule in these early years remained unsupported,for she provides no clues as to the proportion of helpers who were relatives of spinners. Wallace, *Rockdale*, 180; Tucker, *Samuel Slater*, 148 . See also a testimony of a British immigrant mule spinner from Rammapool, New York, who employed his children as piecers, in P.P. 1833, XX, A.l., 112.

6 See Table 4 and sources cited there.

7 No other study of an American mill village before 1840 provides such a wealth of detail as Anthony Wallace's *Rockdale*. Unquestionably, the ten mule spinners employed at the Riddles' mill in the Rockdale district near Philadelphia subcontracted their own helpers during the 1830s. See pp. 143, 177-80, 366. According to an inquiry by the Pennsylvania Senate in 1837-38, subcontracting in mule spinning was the rule throughout the state. See *Pennsylvania Senate Journal*, "Committee Appointed. . .for the Purpose of Investigating and Inquiring into the System of Labor adopted in Cotton and other Factories," 1837-38, vol. 1, 325; and "Testimony of Witnesses, Accompanying the Report of the Committee of the Senate, Appointed to Investigate the Subject of the Employment of Children in Manufactures," 1837-38, vol. 2, 299, 300, 329. Both Barbara Tucker and Jonathan Prude agree that Slater introduced the subcontract system among the mule spinners employed in his Union Mills at Webster, Massachusetts, during the 1820s and 1830s, though the extent to which he did so is disputed. Prude (*The Coming of Industrial Order*, 118) believes that "despite sporadic references to spinners 'find[ing their] own piecers,' most local mule operators evidently let management select these assistants before 1840." Tucker ("Samuel Slater and Sons," 210, 213, *Samuel Slater*, 148-149) disagrees. She insists that subcontracting was the rule among the mule spinners in the early period. My own examination of the Union Mills' contract book convinced me that the data on helpers are far too scant to lead to any firm conclusion. Of the five spinners' assistants which appear in the contract book between 1827 and 1837, two presumably were paid by management, two presumably were paid by the mule spinners, and in one case the information is unclear. Furthermore, management might have initially recruited some helpers and then placed them under the total control of mule spinners. One helper, for instance, was contracted in 1829 "to work for mule spinners as they agreed." Since his wages—unlike the wages of all other recruits—do not appear in the

contract book, it is most likely that he was paid by the mule spinners, not by management. Slater Collection. Slater and Kimball, vol. 3, Agreements with Help (1827-37). Manuscript Division, Baker Library, Harvard University, Cambridge, Massachusetts.

An inspection of the time books (1828-36) of Slater's Steam Mfg. Co. in Providence reveals no traces of spinners' helpers, though we know that piecers were employed by this firm. For each payroll period the total amount of wages in the mule spinning department is calculated, but again, the wages of piecers do not appear alongside those of the mule spinners. Because the time books are so careful to specify the total labor cost in each room, it is almost certain that in this case too the helpers were not paid by management but by the mule spinners. Slater Collection. Steam Cotton Manufacturing Co., Time Books 1828-36, vols. 16, 17, 18. Manuscript Division, Baker Library.

Finally, a few examples of employment contracts drawn from the Pomfret Manufacturing Co. (Connecticut) in 1816 and 1826, and from the Green Manufacturing Co. (Warwick, Rhode Island) in 1836, show explicitly that mule spinners recruited and paid their own piecers. See Kulik, Parks, and Penn, *The New England Mill Village*, 446, 448, 479.

8 U.S. Senate, *History of Women in Industry*, ch. 2; Dublin, *Women at Work*, ch. 4.
9 Montgomery, *Practical Detail*, 119. In one New York cotton factory in 1816 the ratio was one to eighteen. See Kulik, Parks, and Penn, *The New England Mill Village*, 428.
10 Wallace, *Rockdale*, 143.
11 During the 1830s the bulk of mule spinning in the United States was done in small mills which combined power spinning and weaving. In 1832 the McLane Report enumerates 119 Rhode Island cotton mills with a combined factory population of 8,600 or an average of 72 per mill. Slater's factory in Webster, Massachusetts was larger. In 1832 it gave employment to 137 workers, nine of whom were mule spinners. The Riddle's mill in Rockdale employed in 1844 five mule spinners out of a total workforce of 74 workers. Taking the Webster and Rockdale mills as representative cases, the average number of mule spinners employed in a Rhode Island factory during the 1830s would have been four to five. In Britain, by contrast, the 1818 Factory Returns show an average of 250 workers employed in 80 *specialized* mule-spinning mills throughout the Manchester area. In combined spinning and weaving factories the average was higher, 500 per mill in 65 Manchester and Ashton plants in 1841. McLane, *New American State Papers*, vol. 5, 303-4, vol. 4, 239-40; Tucker, "Samuel Slater and Sons," 217; Wallace, *Rockdale*, 196. The 1818 British Factory Returns are cited by R.S. Fitton and A.P. Wadsworth, *The Strutts and the Arkwrights 1758-1830: A Study of the Early Factory System* (Manchester, 1958), 196; the 1841 British figures are cited by John Jewks, "The Localization of the Cotton Industry," *Economic Journal (Economic History Supplement)*, 2 (January 1930), 94.
12 Wood, *History of Wages*, 22, 27-28; Kirby and Musson, *The Voice of the People*, 462-63. The quotation is from P.P. 1833, XX, D.l., 43. Contrast this description which was given by a witness who had first entered the mill as a piecer at the age of eight, with the hostile account of Edward Tufnell: "During at least three-fourths of [every] minute the piecers...have literally nothing to do; they then

stand listlessly by, their attention engaged by any thing but their work, till the mule recedes, when they instantly proceed to piece the threads which break.... The piecing cannot take up long, as the mule has no sooner arrived at the frame than it instantly begins to advance, and when it has got about a foot and a half or two from the frame, it is impossible to reach over to the rollers, and the period of idleness begins." P.P. 1834, XIX, 207. See also Ure, *Cotton Manufacture*, vol. 2, 154.

13 P.P. 1833, XX, E.15.

14 Catling, *The Spinning Mule*, 10.

15 P.P. 1833, XX, D.l., 41.

16 Ure, *Philosophy of Manufacture*, 309-10.

17 *Pennsylvania Senate Journal*, 1837-38, vol. 2, 289, 300; Wallace, *Rockdale*, 142-43, 152, 154, 177-78, 182. See also the testimony of a British mule spinner who emigrated to the United States and returned. P.P. 1833, A.l., 104.

18 Slater Collection. Slater and Kimball, vol. 3, Union Mills, vol. 144, Time Books 1836-48. Both Prude (*The Coming of Industrial Order*, 127) and Tucker (*Samuel Slater*, 196) note that the mules used by Slater were hand mules. They do not seem, however, to be aware of the fact that the semi-powered mule was commonly referred to as a "hand mule" by contemporaries in order to distinguish it from the self-acting mule. See for example Wood, *History of Wages*, 22-27. One of the first semi-powered mules in the United States was imported from Britain to Canton, Massachusetts, in 1803-4. Jeremy, *Transatlantic Industrial Revolution*, 90. According to census figures analyzed by Jeremy (278) the largest single mule in the United States in 1820 had 480 spindles, the smallest, 144 spindles. A pair of mules had a total of 400 spindles. For more examples of mules, pairs of mules, and mule spinners' work teams, See Kulik, Parks, and Penn, *The New England Mill Village*, 216, 428, 440, 450, 479; P.P. 1833, XX, A.l., 104, 112; and Navin, *Whitin Machine Works*, 566.

19 Thorndike Company, vol. 28, Payrolls 1838-42, Manuscript Division, Baker Library, Harvard University, Cambridge, Mass.

20 Dublin, *Women at Work*, 69; Kulik, "The Beginning of the Industrial Revolution in America," 193-94.

21 For instance, at least three of the six cotton mills in Rockdale, Pennsylvania in 1832 were managed by immigrants from Britain. Wallace, *Rockdale*, 119.

22 Montgomery, *Theory and Practice*, 272.

23 P.P. 1834, XIX, 124, 125.

24 Montgomery, *Theory and Practice*, 272-73.

25 Ogden, *Thoughts*, 29-30.

26 Dublin, *Women at Work*, 69.

27 For the problems of discipline in throstle spinning factory colonies in Britain see Sidney Pollard, "The Factory Village in the Industrial Revolution," *English Historical Review*, 79:312 (1964), 513-31.

28 P.P. 1842, XXII, 85.

29 Carders and dressers, for example, were exclusively adult males. P.P. 1834, XIX, 125.

30 P.P. 1834, XIX, 119bb.

31 P.P. 1833, XX, D.2., 102; and see also P.P. 1834, XX, *Second Supplementary*

Report of the Factory Inquiry Commission, Part 2, D.l., 222.

32 P.P. 1833, XX, D.l., 76, 79; E., 15; D.l., 78; A.l., 78, 85, 116.

33 P.P. 1833, XX, D.l., 78.

34 P.P. 1834, XX, D.l., 149; 1833, XX, E., 18.

35 P.P. 1833, XX, A.l., 77-78; D.l., 36.

36 P.P. 1833, XX, D.2., 109.

37 P.P. 1833, XX, D.2., 102; see also D.l., 41.

38 P.P. 1833, XX, D.l., 51.

39 P.P. 1833, XX, E., 6; D.l., 96, 102; 1834, XX, D.l., 81, 267.

40 P.P. 1833, XX, D.l., 55.

41 Positive incentives included money and provisions. See P.P. 1833, XX, D.l., 78-79.

42 P.P. 1833, XX, D.l., 55,

43 P.P. 1834, XIX, 119bb.

44 P.P. 1842, XXII, 86.

45 P.P. 1837-38,VIII, 306; McConnel, *A Century of Fine Spinning*, 39.

46 Sutcliffe, *A Treatise on Canals and Reservoirs*, 36.

47 P.P. 1834, XIX, 119aa.

48 P.P. 1834, XIX, 119bb.

49 Ure, *Dictionary of Arts*, vol. 1, 370. See also P.P. 1833, XX, D.l., 44, 51; 1834, XIX, 207; and the same statistics for the United States in 1850 in Baird, *The American Cotton Spinner*, 171.

50 P.P. 1833, XX, A.l., 115-16, 110, 96-97. See also P.P. 1833, VI, 323, 675, and John Butt, "Labour and Industrial Relations in the Scottish Cotton Industry during the Industrial Revolution," in John Butt and Kenneth Ponting, eds., *Scottish Textile History* (Aberdeen, Scotland, 1987), 145.

51 Smelser, *Social Change*, 236-37, 232; P.P. 1824, V, *Select Committee on Artisans and Machinery*, 479; 1837-38, VIII, 287-88; 1833, XX, A.l., 84-86; Chapman, *Lancashire Cotton Industry*, 213-14; Turner, *Trade Union Growth*, 96, 142; Butt, "Labour and Industrial Relations," 145, 154.

52 P.P. 1833, XX, A.l., 85. See also 84.

53 Sidney and Beatrice Webb, *Industrial Democracy* (1897; reprinted, London, 1902), 497; William Lazonick, "Conflict and Control in the Industrial Revolution: Social Relations in the British Cotton Factory," in Robert Weible, Oliver Fort, and Paul Marion, eds., *Essays from the Lowell Conference on Industrial History 1980 and 1981* (Lowell, Massachusetts, 1981), 22.

54 P.P. 1842, XXII, 85; 1834, XIX, 164.

55 Ibid.

56 P.P. 1833, XXI, *Second Report of the Factory Inquiry Commission*, D.2., 64.

57 P.P. 1833, XX, D.2., 6.

58 P.P. 1833, XX, E., 14; 1834, XIX, 125; 1842, XXII, 85.

59 P.P. 1834, XIX, 200.

60 P.P. 1833, XX, D.2., 123, E., 13; 1834, XX, D.l., 280.

61 "Among the frame [throstle] spinners there was no union," wrote Sir John Clapham, and Frances Collier also noted "the entire absence of trade unionism among the factory hands" in a typical throstle-spinning factory colony in Cheshire before mid-century. Clapham, *Economic History of Modern Britain*, vol. 1, 215; Frances Collier, *The Family Economy and the Working Classes in the Cotton Industry*

1784-1833 (1964; reprinted, New York, 1968), 44.

62 Tucker, "Samuel Slater and Sons," 217; *Samuel Slater*, 141; Prude, *The Coming of Industrial Order*, 86; Wallace, *Rockdale*, 177-78. See also the testimony of a Connecticut mill owner in P.P. 1833, VI, 169.

63 Kulik, "The Beginning of the Industrial Revolution," 207; McGouldrick, *New England Textiles*, 36, 273; *Massachusetts Bureau of Statistics of Labor* (henceforth: Mass. BSL), *Second Annual Report* (Boston, 1871), 55; *Fall River Daily Evening News*, 18 August, 1870. The main reason why American employers were more likely than British manufacturers to hire women mule spinners was the fundamental weakness of American unions. No mule spinners' union in the United States had ever achieved effective control over entry into the trade.

64 Of the five mule spinners' helpers mentioned in the Union Mills contract book (1827-37) four were certainly males. Slater and Kimball, vol. 3. In Pennsylvania "some" females were employed in piecing. See *Pennsylvania Senate Journal*, 1837-38, Part I, 325.

65 U.S. Senate, *History of Women in Industry*, 56.

66 *Pennsylvania Senate Journal*, 1837-38, Vol. 2, the quotations are, in order: 328-30, 293-94, 279-80, 302-3. For more on child beating in factories see: 282, 286, 289, 309, 333, 346.

67 Mass. BSL. *First Annual Report* (Boston, 1870), 122-23. See also *Wade's Fibre and Fabric*, 2:39 (November 28, 1885), 307.

68 P.P. 1834, XIX, 136, 11911. For only 6,300 operatives employed in the 225 mills the method of payment is not given in the returns.

69 Slater and Kimball, vol. 3; Tucker, "Samuel Slater and Sons," 220, 229; *Pennsylvania Senate Journal*, 1837-38, vol. 1, 325; Wallace, *Rockdale*, 117-78; Dublin, *Women at Work*, 67.

70 E.P. Thompson, "Time, Work-Discipline, and Industrial Capitalism," *Past and Present*, No. 38 (December 1967), 60-61, 71.

71 P.P. 1816, III, 234-35; 1833, XXI, D.2., 36.

72 Thompson, "Work-Discipline," 91-92.

73 P.P. 1834, XX, D. 1., 88, 280.

74 See Bagnall, *The Textile Industries*, 407, 536-38, 546.

75 Ogden, *Thoughts*, 20-21.

76 Ibid., 30-31.

77 Ibid., 30.

78 Ibid, 29-30,

79 Overseers employed in American cotton mills ordinarily received daily wages rather than varying piece rates. Dublin, *Women at Work*, 66; Tucker, "Samuel Slater," 220. But they also received premiums or bonuses for increases in output so that they were actually renumerated in proportion to the productivity of their departments, just as in Britain. Ware, *New England Cotton*, 243.

80 Chapman, *The Cotton Industry in the Industrial Revolution*, 58.

81 Wallace, *Rockdale*, 178, 380; Dublin, *Women at Work*, 66. The wages of mule spinners in Pennsylvania, however, varied considerably according to the type and size of machines used, place, and time. In 1820 the spinners in one Philadelphia mill received a mere $5 per week. In 1828 the weekly pay of mule spinners in and around the city was $12 according to one source, $7.50-8.50 according to

another. See William Sullivan, "The Industrial Revolution and the Factory Operative in Pennsylvania," *Pennsylvania Magazine of History and Biography,* 78:4 (October 1954), 484. Excerpts from letters sent by British immigrant mule spinners in America to their fellow workmen at home show that in 1833 a Pennsylvanian mule spinner was able to earn from $11 to $13 a week. P.P. 1834, XX, A.l., 104. In 1837 an employer from Chester Creek, Pennsylvania, reported that his mule spinners earned $6 to $11 per week. *Pennsylvania Senate Journal,* 1837-38, vol. 2, 306.

82 Tucker, *Samuel Slater,* 150-51; see also Prude, *The Coming of Industrial Order,* 91. In Fall River, Massachusetts, in 1850 the mule spinners employed by the Metacomet firm were paid $30-36 a month and their piecers $5-6. Similarly, ten years later a spinner employed by the Annawan Company (Fall River) was paid five to six times his piecer's wages. Metacomet, KB-1, Labor Book 1850-54, 38-41; Annawan, G-l, Labor Book, 1858-63, Manuscript Division, Baker Library, Harvard University, Cambridge, Mass.

83 Pollard, *Genesis of Modern Management,* 8.

84 The three factory technologies accounted for 70% of all employed in the cotton industry. Of the 67,819 operatives working in 225 mills in the Lancashire region in 1833, 31% were employed in mule spinning, 4% in throstle spinning, and 35% in power-loom weaving. The rest were employed in cleaning and spreading cotton (2%), carding (19%), reeling (7%), and "as engineers, mechanics, firemen, etc." (2%). P.P. 1834, XIX, 136.

85 P.P. 1834, XIX, 125; Ivy Pinchbeck, *Women Workers and the Industrial Revolution, 1750-1850* (New York, 1930), 192. Scottish power-loom dressers were all former hand-loom weavers and were highly unionized. P.P. 1833, XXI, A.3., 43.

86 P.P. 1834, XIX, 138. Altogether, 23,800 children under eighteen were employed in power-loom weaving, the employment status of 300 being unknown.

87 The ratio of overseers to workers was 1:28 in power-loom weaving. P.P. 1834, XIX, 125. See Table 4 for mule and throstle spinning.

88 P.P. 1834, XIX, 119aa-119bb. For more evidence see Pinchbeck, *Women Workers,* 188.

89 P.P. 1834, XIX, 125, 136.

90 P.P. 1834, XIX, 11911-119mm.

91 Turner, *Trade Union Growth,* 129; Chapman, *Lancashire Cotton Industry,* 262-63.

92 Dublin, *Women at Work,* 67. In general, piece rates yielded greater productivity than time rates, and piece workers nearly always commanded substantially higher wages than time workers in the same occupation. See comparison across industries between the United States and Britain, in Gregory Clark, "Authority and Efficiency: The Labor Market and the Managerial Revolution of the Late Nineteenth Century," *Journal of Economic History,* 44:4 (December, 1984), 1075.

93 P.P. 1833, VI, 147; *Pennsylvania Senate Journal,* 1837-38, part I, 325.

94 U.S. Senate, *History of Women in Industry,* 56; Dublin, *Women at Work,* 69. The figure pertains to the Boott and Hamilton companies in the late 1830s.

95 These were the wages paid by the Hamilton company at Lowell in 1836. Dublin, *Women at Work,* 66. Wallace reports that the earnings of Philadelphia power-loom weavers during the same period were $4, $5, and even sometimes $6 per week. *Rockdale,* 146-47.

96 Tucker, *Samuel Slater*, 148-49; "Samuel Slater and Sons," 213-14.

CHAPTER 4

1 For comparative figures in fourteen countries see Saxonhouse and Wright, "Ring and Mules Around the World," 280.

2 Lazonick, "Industrial Relations and Technical Change," 232. In 1967 there were still some 1,200 mule spinners in Britain, but the practice of subcontracting was discontinued in the 1950s. See L.H.C. Tippett, *A Portrait of the Lancashire Textile Industry* (London, 1969), 105, 63; and Roger Penn, *Skilled Workers in the Class Structure* (Cambridge, England, 1984), 65.

3 Kennedy, "Memoir of Samuel Crompton," 324-36; Daniels, *Early English Cotton Industry*, 117-18; Crompton, *The Spinning Mule*, 32-34.

4 Kennedy, "Memoir of Samuel Crompton," 327, 333.

5 P.P. 1834, XIX, 169. In Scotland the average size of mules was smaller; 600 mules in 39 mills had 144 spindles each in 1796. Rees, *The Cyclopaedia*, vol. 10, "Cotton Manufacture."

6 McConnel, *A Century of Fine Spinning*, 32-33.

7 Wood, *History of Wages*, 141; Lee, *A Cotton Enterprise*, 19; P.P. 1834, XIX, 119e-119f. A pamphleteer noted the affects of the rapid increase in size of mules: by the early 1820s "the owners of mules of 180 spindles, or thereabouts, were reduced to the necessity of either working them to a certain loss, or breaking them up, and selling them for the value of the old metal. This later method became so general, that it was in derision called 'butchering' old machinery." *On Combinations of Trades*, Anonymous (London, 1831); reprinted in *Trade Unions in the Early 1830's: Seven Pamphlets 1831-1837* (New York, 1972), 41.

8 Ure, *Cotton Manufacture*, vol. 2, 197-98; Wood, *History of Wages*, 27.

9 Ure, *Philosophy of Manufactures*, 23. The editor of the *Journal of the Franklin Institute* is quoted in Wallace, *Rockdale*, 381.

10 George Dodd, *The Textile Manufactures of Great Britain* (London, 1851), 36; William Fairbairn, *Treatise on Mills and Millwork* (London, 1865), part 2, 184; Chapman, *Lancashire Cotton Industry*, 68-69.

11 For an exceptionally illuminating and highly authoritative account of these two manual tasks performed by self-actor minders see Harold Catling, *The Spinning Mule*, 77, 83-84, 98-100, and "The Development of the Spinning Mule," *Textile History*, 9 (1978), 45-57. See also Thomas Thornley, *Practical Treatise upon Self Acting Mules* (Manchester, 1894), 5, 32-40, 289-302; *Cotton Spinning*, vol. 2: *Intermediate or Second Year* (London, 1906), 116-25; Richard Marsden, *Cotton Spinning* (1884; reprinted, London, 1909), 243-44, 254-57, 263; Joseph Nasmith, *Students' Cotton Spinning* (Manchester, 1896), ch. 9; Scott, *Practical Cotton Spinner*, 399-404; and Lazonick, "Industrial Relations," 241-42.

12 Mary Freifeld disagrees. In a provocative article she argues that the self actor did not deskill the mule spinners; on the contrary, the new machine provided "the foundation for the reconstitution of skill on a new basis" so that "mulespinning on the 'self-actor' remained skilled work" (pp. 321-22). The deskilling interpretation, she insists, is a myth propagated by the machine builders and by Andrew Ure, Karl Marx, Neil Smelser, Joseph White, Keith Burgess, John Foster, William

Lazonick, A.E. Musson, and me. She undertakes the task of demystifying "the concept of the deskilled machine tender taken from Marx," noting: "We are all so much under the influence of Marx...that evidence to the contrary with respect to the 'self acting' mule is ignored, or explained away" (p. 330.)

What, then, is the evidence?

Freifeld correctly argues that spinning on self actors required familiarity with different types of raw cotton, knowledge of the influence of humidity and temperature on the yarn fibres, experience in supervision, and the skill necessary to maintain the machine and to control yarn quality. But, in addition, she goes on to say that "while the quality control and mental oversight functions remained unchanged...all that had been accomplished by the introduction of the 'self actor' was the intensification of the mechanical adjustment tasks of the spinner" (p. 322).

Not a shred of evidence is presented to substantiate this claim, in fact, everything we know about the manual adjustments of the self actor leads to the opposite conclusion. It is not that Freifeld ignores the issue—she does not. Rather, she devotes over four pages to the "quadrant nut," saying very little that is relevant, clear or convincing. Reading over those pages one still does not know what *exactly* the differences between working the self acting and power-driven mule were. The best discussion of these differences, described in the text above in detail, is to be found in Catling's *The Spinning Mule*—a source Freifeld cites repeatedly but uses selectively. See Mary Freifeld, "Technological Change and the 'Self Acting' Mule: A Study of Skill and the Sexual Division of Labour," *Social History*, 11:3 (October, 1986).

13 P.P. 1892, XXXV, *Royal Commission on Labour*, Group C (Textiles), 128.
14 Montgomery, *Workers' Control in America*, 11.
15 P.P. 1834, XIX, 119f.
16 P.P. 1842, XXII, 86.
17 Ure, *Philosophy of Manufactures*, 312, 317; Smelser, *Social Change in the Industrial Revolution*, 197-98.
18 P.P. 1834, XIX, 119e-119f.
19 Wood, *History of Wages*, 141.
20 P.P. 1834, XIX, 119s, 123-33.
21 Butt, "Labour and Industrial Relations in the Scottish Cotton Industry," 152-53.
22 John Jewkes and E.M. Gray, *Wages and Labour in the Lancashire Cotton Spinning Industry* (Manchester, 1935), 8, 172.
23 Wood, *History of Wages*, 141.
24 Catling, *The Spinning Mule*, 161.
25 G. Von Schulze-Gaevernitz, *The Cotton Trade in England and on the Continent* (London, 1895), 98, 92-99.
26 Webb, *Industrial Democracy*, 105.
27 June 22, 1888; cited in Lazonick, "Industrial Relations," 250.
28 P.P. 1892, XXXV, 92-93.
29 See Daniels, *Early English Cotton Industry*, 48-49.
30 Turner, *Trade Union Growth*, 95.
31 Smelser, *Social Change in the Industrial Revolution*, 189, 315, 320; Chapman, *Lancashire Cotton Industry*, 238.

32 Chapman, *Lancashire Cotton Industry*, 192.

33 P.P. 1833, XX, D.2., 91.

34 Turner, *Trade Union Growth*, 94.

35 P.P. 1833, XXI, A.3., 43; W.H. Fraser, "The Glasgow Cotton Spinners, 1837," in John Butt and J.T. Ward, eds., *Scottish Themes: Essays in Honour of Professor S.G.E. Lythe* (Edinburgh, 1976), 88. See also P.P. 1833, VI, 336, and on the Glasgow union and the Scottish mule spinners in general, see T.C. Smout, *A History of the Scottish People, 1560-1830* (London, 1969), 411-19.

36 "On Combinations of Trades," 77.

37 Turner, *Trade Union Growth*, 87.

38 Chapman, "Some Policies of Cotton Spinners," 468.

39 "On Combinations of Trades," 77.

40 P.P. 1837-38, VIII, 301.

41 See Eric Hobsbawm, "Artisans and Labour Aristocrats," in Eric Hobsbawm, ed., *Workers: Worlds of Labor* (New York, 1984), 257-59, 264-65; and S.J. Chapman and W. Abbott, "The Tendency of Children to Enter their Fathers' Trades," *Journal of the Royal Statistical Society*, 76 (May 1913), 599-604.

42 Gatrell, "Labour, Power, and the Size of Firms in Lancashire Cotton," 113, 112. As a result the self-actor penetrated more rapidly the coarse spinning districts of Bolton, Stockport, and parts of Manchester. See Wood, *History of Wages*, 27.

43 Leigh, *Science of Modern Cotton Spinning*, vol. 2, 242. See also Marsden, *Cotton Spinning*, 275, 289. One of the last estimates of power-driven mules shows 80 pairs in Lancashire in 1883, Schulze-Gaevernitz, *Cotton Trade*, 88.

44 Turner, *Trade Union Growth*, 116.

45 Turner, *Trade Union Growth*, 115-16, 128; Lazonick, "Industrial Relations," 246; Chapman, *Lancashire Cotton Industry*, 235-36.

46 The 1868 figure refers to the "Northern Counties Association of Operative Cotton Spinners." To exclude free riders, "men [were] required to join the union as soon as they receive[d] the spinners' wages." P.P. 1868-69, XXXI, *Eleventh and Final Report from the Royal Commission on Trade Unions*, 72. A closed shop policy was the rule in British mule spinning and "no respectable man [would] go near [a non union] shop." P.P. 1867-68, XXXIX, *Report from the Royal Commission on Trade Unions: Manchester Outrage Inquiry*, 293-94. In 1891 19,000 of the 20,500 mule spinners in Britain were members of the Amalgamated Association. P.P. 1892, XXXV, 24. In 1910 22,000 of the 25,000 operative mule spinners were enrolled in the association. Joseph White, *The Limits of Trade Union Militancy: The Lancashire Textile Workers 1910-1914* (Westport, Connecticut, 1978), 35, 76.

47 P.P. 1892, XXXV, 28; Turner, *Trade Union Growth*, 197.

48 Wood, *History of Wages*, 23-24. For wage differentials of minders and piecers in Manchester between 1839 and 1883 see P.P. 1887, LXXXIX, *Board of Trade: Returns of Wages Published between 1830 and 1886*, 47, 51.

49 Chapman, "Some Policies of Cotton Spinners," 469. While piecers and minders alike pieced up yarn, the minder jealously guarded his authority to direct the mule. A British minder who immigrated to the United States in 1883 recalled: "I have known spinners who would not allow their piecers to touch a quadrant though it was snapping their threads or even kinking them. They would tell their piecers:

'That's my work'. " *Wade's Fibre and Fabric*, 19:481 (May 19, 1894), 779.

50 Wood, *History of Wages*, 26. In Oldham, the largest spinning center in Britain, minders were paid 33 shillings and big piecers 15 shillings per week in 1886. See P.P. 1889, LXX, *Board of Trade: Return of Rates of Wages in the Principal Textile Trades of the United Kingdom*, 14, 15. According to another survey of the Board of Trade cited by S. and B. Webb, British mule spinners earned from 30 to 50 shillings and piecers (big and little) from 6 to 20 shillings per week in 1894. *Industrial Democracy*, 105.

51 W.H. Chaloner, "Robert Owen, Peter Drinkwater and the Early Factory System in Manchester, 1788-1800," *Bulletin of the John Rylands Library*, 37:1 (September 1954), 80-82.

52 Chapman, "Fixed Capital Formation," 57.

53 *Manchester Mercury*, June 21, 1785, quoted by George Unwin, A. Hulme, and G. Taylor, *Samuel Oldknow and the Arkwrights: The Industrial Revolution at Stockport and Marple* (Manchester, 1924), 33. See also Robert Glen, *Urban Workers in the Early Industrial Revolution* (New York, 1984), ch. 4. The "Friendly Society of the Cotton Spinners of the Town of Stockport" probably combined membership of jenny spinners and mule spinners. While the jenny was a short-lived forerunner of the mule, contemporary accounts do not always distinguish between the two, as evidenced by the repeated references to "mule jennies." See, for example, Butterworth, *Complete History of the Cotton Trade*, 100; and P.P. 1837-38, VIII, 37. According to a Stockport master spinner speaking in 1824: "In some parts of the country they give the names of mules to jennies." P.P. 1824, V, 413.

54 S.J. Chapman, "The Regulation of Wages by Lists in the Spinning Industry," *Economic Journal*, 9 (1899), 592-93. Although the notion of "customary wage" declined in the nineteenth century, it by no means disappeared. "In our trade," testified the secretary of the Associated Cotton Spinners of Scotland in 1856, the "honourable employer" would always pay the "recognized rate" and would "never think of deviating from it." P.P. 1856, XIII, *Report from the Select Committee on Masters and Operatives*, 252.

55 McConnel, *A Century of Fine Spinning*, 22; Chapman, *The Cotton Industry in the Industrial Revolution*, 21; Chaloner, "Early Factory System in Manchester," 93.

56 For the two Bolton lists see P.P. 1824, V, 557, 559; Aspinall, *Early English Trade Unions: Documents from the Home Office Papers of the Public Record Office* (London, 1949), 363, 370-71; and Kirby and Musson, *The Voice of the People*, 28. For references to the other lists see Chapman, *The Lancashire Cotton Industry*, 263. Price lists issued by individual firms were used, of course, much earlier. See for example, McConnel and Kennedy spinning lists for 1795 and 1802, McConnel, *A Century of Fine Spinning*, 36, 43.

57 P.P. 1834, XIX, 119g.

58 P.P. 1837-38, VIII, 306-7.

59 The Bolton strike was typical. Working mules of 300 spindles each, the spinners struck because employers introduced larger mules of 400 spindles without increasing the piece rates by one-fourth. P.P. 1824, V, 556-57. The 1837-38 Preston strike erupted over the employers' refusal to comply with the spinners' demand of the "Bolton list of prices." See Henry Ashworth, "An Inquiry Into the Origins,

Progress, And Results of the Strike of the Operative Cotton Spinners of Preston" (1838); reprinted in *Rebirth of the Trade Union Movement: Five Pamphlets 1838-1847* (New York, 1972), 6. For the other strikes see Lushington, "Abstract of the Evidence," 389-402; William Jevons, "An Account of the Spinners' Strike at Ashton-Under-Lyne in 1830," in *Trades' Societies and Strikes*, 473-78; and Kirby and Musson, *The Voice of the People*, 51-84, 119-52.

60 See J. Lowe, "An Account of the Strike in the Cotton Trade at Preston in 1853," in *Trades' Societies and Strikes*, 207-63; "Strikes," *Quarterly Review*, 106 (1859), 498-500; *Economist*, 27 April, 1854, 488-89; 6 May, 1854, 477-78.

61 Arthur Arnold, *The History of the Cotton Famine* (London, 1864), 32.

62 Wood, *History of Wages*, 1-2, 24-25; Chapman, *The Lancashire Cotton Industry*, 266-68; Jewkes and Gray, *Wages and Labour*, 82-102. The first Oldham list was introduced in 1872 and it adjusted the piece price according to the size and speed of mules, not according to mule size and yarn count. The Oldham list is discussed in chapter 7.

63 Arnold, *The Cotton Famine*, 33.

64 U.S. Senate, *Report of the Committee of the Senate Upon the Relations Between Labor and Capital*, 4 vols.; S. Report 1262, 48th Cong., 2nd Sess., 1885, vol. 1, 640. As a result of changing business conditions, the nationally agreed standard rate for mule spinning in Britain was revised five times upwards and seven times downwards between 1877 and 1897. Webb, *Industrial Democracy*, 256.

65 P.P. 1892, XXXV, 95.

66 U.S. House of Representatives, *United States Consular Reports. Labor in Europe.* H. Ex. Doc. 54, Part 1, 48th Cong., 2nd Sess., 1885, 744. Similarly, in his report on Oldham a year earlier, the American consul, Albert Show, was impressed by the "very good feeling existing between the employers and the employed:" "Both have large and influential associations, but the ruling idea is to be just to each other." See U.S. House of Representatives, *Reports from the Consuls of the United States on the Commerce, Manufacture, Etc. of their Consular Districts*, H. Mis. Doc. 12, Part 2, 48th Cong., 1st Sess., 1884, n. 38—Feb. 1884, 637.

67 Quoted in J.H. Porter, "Industrial Peace in the Cotton Trade 1875-1913," *Yorkshire Bulletin of Economic and Social Research*, 19:1 (May 1967), 49.

68 Charles Macara, *Recollections* (London, 1921), 26.

69 Quoted in Porter, "Industrial Peace in the Cotton Trade," 53. For an assessment of the Brooklands Agreement see Porter, 57-59; Macara, *Recollections*, 25-27, *The New Industrial Era* (Manchester, 1923), 358; W.M. Wiggins, "The Cotton Industry," in Frank Gannett and B.F. Catherwood, eds., *Industrial and Labour Relations in Great Britain* (New York, 1939), 230-32; Keith Burgess, *The Origins of British Industrial Relations: The Nineteenth Century Experience* (London, 1975), 283-90; and White, *Limits of Trade Union Militancy*, 79-80, 118-21.

70 Webb, *Industrial Democracy*, 203-4.

71 Burgess, *Origins of British Industrial Relations*, 269, 287-88; Lazonick, "Industrial Relations," 254; "Production Relations," 503-6.

72 See note 78 below; Eric Hobsbawm, "The Labour Aristocracy in Nineteenth-Century Britain," in Eric Hobsbawm, eds., *Labouring Men* (London, 1964), 272; "Debating the Labour Aristocracy," in *Workers*, 217; and P.P. 1837-38, VIII, 130. For more on the labor aristocracy debate see Hobsbawm, "The Aristocracy of

Labour Reconsidered," in *Workers*, 227-51; H.F. Moorhouse, "The Marxist Theory of the Labour Aristocracy," *Social History*, 3:1 (January 1978), 61-82; John Field, "British Historians and the Concept of Labor Aristocracy," *Radical History Review*, 19 (Winter 1978-79), 61-85; Penn, *Skilled Workers*, ch. 3; and further bibliography in *Workers*, 344-45.

73 Chapman, *The Cotton Industry in the Industrial Revolution*, 58.

74 *Cotton Factory Times*, 4 December, 1885, cited in Lazonick, "Industrial Relations," 253.

75 Schulze-Gaevernitz, *The Cotton Trade*, 91.

76 Ibid., 99.

77 Webb, *Industrial Democracy*, 409-10, 413; P.P. 1892, XXXV, 26-27.

78 The issue is controversial, and surprisingly, the two main contenders, John Foster and A.E. Musson, missed this point. Foster has written that the spread of the self-acting mule "between the late 1840's and early 1860's" was accompanied by "the introduction of a new dimension of authority at work which was the key factor" in the emergence of "labour aristocracy" among British mule spinners. John Foster, *Class Struggle and the Industrial Revolution: Early Industrial Capitalism in Three English Towns* (New York, 1974), 229-34. Musson, on the other hand, maintains that "there was no 'new dimension of authority at work' " after mid-century, and in fact, "the journeymen cotton spinners had developed into a strongly organized, relatively well-paid 'labour aristocracy' from the late eighteenth century onwards." A.E. Musson, "Class Struggle and the Labour Aristocracy, 1830-60," *Social History*, 1:3 (October 1976), 354. Both are correct, but both misconceive the nature of the new technology. Foster is right about the "new dimension of authority" but he neither explains it, nor does he provide evidence. Musson, too, is correct—mule spinners exercised authority over helpers from the pioneering days of the industry —yet he ignores the changes in the spinner's relationship to his assistants that came about with the self actor. While authority over helpers was a distinctive characteristic of British mule spinning from the outset, the meaning of authority changed over time: the self-acting mule drastically reduced the spinner's operative tasks and at the same time increased his supervisory responsibilities. Hence, if mule spinners indeed formed an aristocracy of labor in the first part of the century, the advent of the self actor *consolidated* rather than undermined their position as labor aristocrats, quite contrary to Musson's claim that the spinners "were in a *less* 'aristocratic' position at mid- century." See also Foster's reply to Musson, "Some Comments on 'Class Struggle and the Labour Aristocracy'," *Social History*, 1:3 (October 1976), 357-66.

79 Hobsbawm, "Artisans and Labour Aristocrats," 253; Musson, "Class Struggle," 355. See also Patrick Joyce, *Work, Society, and Politics: The Culture of the Factory in Later Victorian England* (New Brunswick, N.J., 1980).

CHAPTER 5

1 Ware, *Early New England Cotton Manufacture*, 203.

2 Jeremy, *Transatlantic Industrial Revolution*, 144-49; see also 268-75.

3 Kennedy, "Memoir of Samuel Crompton," 318-19.

4 Jeremy, *Transatlantic Industrial Revolution*, 150.

5 This observation is based both on the lists examined by Jeremy (pp. 269-70) and on my own study of the 1850 and 1860 manuscript schedules of the U.S. population census (Fall River).

6 Jeremy, *Transatlantic Industrial Revolution*, 153, 150.

7 "It might be thought that the skilled craftsmen, tested by long apprenticeships, typically remained in their craft for a life time," noted Stephan Thernstrom, "but this was by no means the case" in the United States. Though Thernstrom's conclusion has some validity for cotton mule spinning, it appears that at least in the later part of the nineteenth century a high proportion of British mule spinners *did not* change jobs in the United States. A study conducted by the U.S. Immigration Commission found that about three-quarters of the English textile workers employed in American textile mills in the 1900s had been textile operatives before emigrating. Furthermore, English-born textile workers were far more likely than any other group of immigrant mill workers investigated by the commission to have had prior experience in textile manufacture. Stephan Thernstrom, *The Other Bostonians: Poverty and Progress in the American Metropolis, 1880-1970* (1973; reprinted, Cambridge, Mass., 1976), 53. U.S. Senate, *Reports of the Immigration Commission: Immigrants in Industries*, 25 parts, S. Rept. 633, 61st Cong., 2nd Sess., 1911, Part 3, "Cotton Goods Manufacturing in the North Atlantic States," June 15, 1910, 70-73.

8 Jeremy, *Transatlantic Industrial Revolution*, 174. A British government prohibition on emigration of artisans was in force until 1824. Artisans who left for the United States before that date were therefore likely to conceal their occupation. "They pretended to be labourers or farmers," noted a Glasgow millowner in 1824, "and such were passed the Custom house." They hardly ever "went to the Continent," he continued, "they generally go to the United States." "I have been abroad and saw two of my own men in America." Visiting cotton factories in Massachusetts, Rhode Island, New York, New Jersey, Pennsylvania, and Maryland, the Glasgow millowner met two of his former mule spinners at work, though his general impression was that very few of the mule spinners in the United States were British immigrants. Rather, English and Scotish artisans in the American cotton industry in the early 1820s were by and large "artificers in the metals such as iron and steel turners," who were engaged in machinery construction. Testimony of James Dunlop, P.P. 1824, V, 471-4. See also P.P. 1826, IV, *Report from the Select Committee on Emigration from the United Kingdom*; P.P. 1826-27, V, *First, Second and Third Reports from the Select Committee on Emigration from the United Kingdom*; H.J.M. Johnston, *British Emigration Policy, 1815-1830* (Oxford, 1972), especially chs. 6, 7; and Stanley Johnson, *A History of Emigration from the United Kingdom to North America, 1763-1912* (London, 1913).

9 It was stated, furthermore, that twenty-eight of the thirty-eight foreign-born workers in Fall River mills were employed in calico printing. Clark, *History of Manufactures*, vol. 1, 398. And indeed, by contrast to early mule spinners, almost all first generation calico printers in the United States were Lancashire immigrants. See U.S. Senate, *Immigrants in Industries*, Pt. 3, 226. In the mid 1820s American manufacturers recruited and paid the passages of "considerable numbers" of calico printers embarking from Liverpool. P.P. 1826-27, V, 192.

10 William J. Bromwell, *History of Immigration to the United States* (New York,

1856), 67-83.

11 W.S. Shepperson, *British Emigration to North America: Projects and Opinions in the Early Victorian Period* (Minneapolis, 1957), 81, 86. P.P. 1843, XXVII, *Reports of the Inspectors of Factories for the Half-Year Ending 31st December, 1842*, 29-30.

12 Charlotte Erickson, "Who Were the English and Scots Emigrants to the United States in the Late Nineteenth Century?" in David Glass and Roger Revelle, eds., *Population and Social Change* (London, 1972), 359, 363. In fact, the leading group was the "building trades," not the textiles, but Erickson classifies the first as "pre-industrial." Still, the textiles ranked second to the building trades.

13 Charlotte Erickson, "The Encouragement of Emigration by British Trade Unions, 1850-1900," *Population Studies*, 3:3 (December 1949), 246. Erickson adds up the figures printed in the Parliamentary Papers of the period: the annual reports of the *Colonial Land and Emigration Commissioners* (for 1862-75), and of the *Board of Trade* (for 1876-85).

14 Lushington, "Abstract of the Evidence," 392.

15 Testimony of Henry Houldsworth, P.P. 1824, V, 479.

16 For Manchester see "On Combinations of Trades," 36; for Glasgow: footnote 73 below.

17 P.P. 1842, XXII, 89.

18 P.P. 1842, XXII, 85.

19 P.P. 1844, XXVIII, *Reports of the Inspectors of Factories for the Half-Year Ending 31st December, 1843*, 4.

20 Lushington, "Abstract of the Evidence," 390. For more on doubledecking see Montgomery, *Theory and Practice of Cotton Spinning*, 193-94; P.P. 1837-38, VIII, 37-38; and Leigh, *Science of Modern Cotton Spinning*, vol. 2, 240.

21 P.P. 1842, XXII, 86, 83, 26. For more examples see, 27, 28-29, 84-85, 89-93, and Friedrich Engels, *The Condition of the Working Class in England* (1845; reprinted, Stanford, 1958), 152.

22 P.P. 1892, XXXV, 28-29. On the problem of oversupply of spinners see also a report by a British spinner who immigrated to the United States in 1883, *Wade's Fibre and Fabric*, 19:481 (19 May 1894), 770; and William Lazonick, "Production Relations," 496.

23 See an example of such a letter in ch. 2, note 105.

24 Montgomery, *Practical Detail*, Preface, p. v.

25 Ibid., 135.

26 See for example, "The Cotton Manufacture in America," *Chambers' Edinburgh Journal*, 9:464 (19 December 1840), 379-80. "We propose to aid Mr. Montgomery in the diffusion of his carefully collected information, by giving a few condensed details from his volume," says the *Journal*.

27 Indirect information on the degree of literacy among British mule spinners may be extracted from the manuscript schedules of the U.S. population census. Table N. 1 presents data on British immigrant spinners in Fall River.

TABLE N. 1

Literacy of British-Born Adult Male Spinners
Employed in Fall River, Massachusetts,
July - August 1850, June - July 1860.

	1850	1860
Literate	89.8%	84.8%
Illiterate	10.2%	15.2%
Total Cases	49	105

Sources: United States, Federal Manuscript Census of Fall River, 1850, 1860.

28 Coleman, *The Transformation of Rhode Island*, 127.
29 *Fall River Weekly News*, 6 March 1851, in conjunction with *Statistics of the Condition and Products of Certain Branches of Industry in Massachusetts for the Year Ending April 1, 1846*. Prepared by John G. Palfrey, Secretary of the Commonwealth (Boston, 1846), 275. The number of adult male spinners is tallied from the 1850 Manuscript Census of Fall River.
30 The following British statistics were reported in 1841 by Leonard Horner. Combined spinning and weaving mills employed on average one mule spinner for every 25 cotton workers. In specialized spinning mills, on the other hand, the ratio of spinners to all other operatives was one to ten. These figures are based on two samples of fifty mills each with total employment of 10,760 (spinning and weaving) and 5,480 (spinning). P.P. 1842, XXII, 27.
31 By 1880 93.3% of all spinners (male and female, mule and throstle) employed in Cohoes were English and Irish, and the Irish outnumbered the English by almost two to one. Daniel Walkowitz, *Worker City, Company Town: Iron and Cotton Worker Protest in Troy and Cohoes, New York, 1855-84* (1978; reprinted, Urbana, 1981), 64, 69.
32 P.P. 1836, XXXIV, *Report on the State of the Irish Poor in Great Britain*, 7, 33, and Appendix, 51, 101. In Houldsworth's spinning mill near Glasgow one half of all the operatives employed in 1833 were Irish. Ibid., Appendix, 106.
33 "In most cases where the Irish are employed in Scotch or English factories, they learn the work on their first entrance." P.P. 1836, XXXIV, 7.
34 Rowland Berthoff, *British Immigrants in Industrial America, 1790-1950* (Cambridge, Mass., 1953), 53. See also, *Fall River Daily Herald*, 23 June 1879.
35 Walkowitz, *Worker City*, 63, 73, 251-52.
36 John Cumbler, *Working Class Community in Industrial America: Work, Leisure, and Struggle in Two Industrial Cities, 1880-1930* (Westport, Conn., 1979), 251-52; see also 108-9.
37 T.M. Young, *The American Cotton Industry* (New York, 1903), 17.
38 According to a 1901 testimony of Andrew G. Pierce, a New Bedford cotton manufacturer who had been in business for fifty years. *Report of the U.S. Industrial Commission on the Relations and Conditions of Capital and Labor*, 19 vols. (Washington, D.C., 1901), vol. 14, 542, 544.

39 U.S. Senate, *Immigrants in Industries*, pt. 3, 41; Charles B. Spahr, "The Old Factory Town in New England," *Outlook*, 61:5 (February 4, 1899), 285-94.

40 Prude, *Industrial Order*, 216. Similarly, in Manayunk near Philadelphia in 1850 45% of the 135 male textile spinners were English and 17% Irish. Unfortunately, Philip Scranton who tallied these figures from the manuscript population census of 1850 does not distinguish cotton from wool spinners. See *Propriety Capitalism*, 257.

41 For 1865 see *Statistical Information Relating to Certain Branches of Industry in Massachusetts for the Year Ending May 1, 1865*. Prepared by Oliver Warner, Secretary of the Commonwealth (Boston, 1866), 90. For 1872: Earl, *Centennial History*, 66. By the 1880s, of all British immigrant cotton workers, the largest numbers were reported to have made their way to Fall River, Lowell, Lawrence, Cohoes, and Philadelphia. See U.S. House of Representatives, *Reports of the Consular Officers of the United States, Emigration and Immigration*. H. Ex.Doc. 157, 49th Cong., 2nd Sess., 1887, 423-24.

42 *Economist*, 12 April 1862.

43 W.O. Henderson, *The Lancashire Cotton Famine 1861-1865* (1934; reprinted, New York, 1969), 25.

44 Arnold, *History of the Cotton Famine*, 161, 240, 36-37; see also Ellison, *The Cotton Trade*, 93-96.

45 John Watts, *The Facts of the Cotton Famine* (London, 1866), 318.

46 Watts, *Facts*, 211-15; Henderson, *Lancashire Cotton*, 117-18, 130; Arnold, *History*, 408-13, 470-73, 496-504. On emigration to the colonies see also P.P. 1864, XVI, *Twenty Fourth General Report of the Colonial Land and Emigration Commissioners*, 17-18; London *Times*, 18 March 1863, 24 June 1863, 24 August 1863, 12 December 1863; and Norman Longmate, *The Hungry Mills: The Story of the Lancashire Cotton Famine, 1861-1865* (London, 1978), ch. 16.

47 *Economist*, 2 May 1863, see also 11 July 1863.

48 P.P. 1863, XVIII, *Reports of the Inspectors of Factories for the Half Year Ending 30th April, 1863*, 23.

49 *Fall River Daily Evening News*, 12 April 1865.

50 *Fall River Daily Evening News*, 31 March 1866.

51 Twenty-Second, Twenty-Third, Twenty-Fourth, Twenty-Fifth, and Twenty-Sixth *General Report of the Colonial Land and Emigration Commissioners*, in order: P.P. 1862, XXII, 76; P.P. 1863, XV, 74; P.P. 1864, XVI, 65; P.P. 1865, XVIII, 67; P.P. 1866, XVII, 65.

52 Arnold, *History*, 367-68.

53 *Economist*, 28 March and 4 April 1863. This was the price of a ticket on a sailing ship. Steam ships charged six pounds for a steerage passage. P.P. 1864, XVI, 16. See also London *Times*, 13 August 1864.

54 Erickson, "Encouragement of Emigration, " 256.

55 The activities of the two American labor recruiting agencies are thoroughly discussed in Charlotte Erickson's *American Industry and the European Immigrant, 1860-1885* (New York, 1957), ch. 1. See also "Encouragement of Emigration," 256. The number 284 pertains to all the contracts registered by the federal authorities and it may include a few immigrants brought by other agencies as well. Needless to say, it does not include operatives who were directly contracted by agents of

individual firms.

56 Daniel Creamer, "Recruiting Contract Laborers for the Amoskeag Mills," *Journal of Economic History*, 1:1 (May 1941), 44.

57 Erickson, *American Industry*, 20.

58 Constance M. Green, *Holyoke, Massachusetts: A Case History of the Industrial Revolution in America* (1939; reprinted, Hamden, Conn., 1968), 76.

59 *Fall River Daily Evening News*, 14 November 1865.

60 Charles Persons, "The Early History of Factory Legislation in Massachusetts," in Susan Kingsbury, ed., *Labor Laws and their Enforcement* (New York, 1911), 91-92.

61 The American Linen Company manufactured cotton yarn on "long mules." In 1870 it had 39,756 mule spindles in operation. Earl, *Centennial History*, 121; United States, Federal Census of Barnstable-Hampden Counties, Massachusetts, Manufacturing, 1870, Microcopy T1204, Roll 21.

62 Sylvia Lintner, "A Social History of Fall River, 1859-1879" (Ph.D. dissertation, Radcliffe College, 1945), 65. The American Linen Company sent its own agent to Europe to recruit workers as early as 1853. Earl, *Centennial History*, 63.

63 Erickson, *American Industry*, 49.

64 See, for example, David Brody, *Steelworkers in America: The Non-Union Era* (Cambridge, Mass., 1960), 106-11.

65 By 1870 11,800 cotton factory workers in the United States were British-born, and in 1880 16,200. The two figures represent 11% and 10% of all employed in the American cotton industry, respectively. Copeland, *The Cotton Manufacturing Industry*, 118. The relative concentration of British-born workers in the American cotton industry was 3-3/4 times their proportion among the gainfully employed workers in 1870, and 4-1/4 times in 1880. See E.P. Hutchinson, *Immigrants and their Children, 1850-1950* (New York, 1956), 83-84, 102-4.

66 Mass. BSL, *Eleventh Annual Report* (Boston, 1880), 61-62.

67 Mass. BSL, *Ninth Annual Report* (Boston, 1878), 215; and see also Mass. BSL, *Thirteenth Annual Report* (Boston, 1882), 204.

68 *New York Tribune*, 26 June 1879; Robert Howard, "Progress in the Textile Trades," in George McNeill, ed., *The Labor Movement: The Problem of To-Day* (New York, 1888), 279. Despite a radical change in the ethnic makeup of the Fall River mill population during the next twenty-five years, mule spinning remained in British and Irish hands. A Lancashire visitor to Fall River in 1903-4 observed: "The French Canadians will be found largely on the ring frames, the blowing-room and cards are looked after by Poles or Portuguese, whilst English or Irish work on the mules, but in the weave room there is no distinct race, though the French predominate." T.W. Uttley, *Cotton Spinning and Manufacturing in the United States* (Manchester, 1905), 31.

69 Resolutions and proposed rules of the Society appear in the reports of the factory inspectors for the half-year ending April 30, 1863. See P.P. 1863, XVIII, 51-54. In the next report (half-year ending October 31, 1863), however, we are told that the "Cotton Districts Emigration Society... did not make much progress, having been superseded by local societies acting independently of each other." P.P. 1864, XXII, 93.

70 Cited in Watts, *Facts*. 215-16.

71 London *Times*, 14 May 1869.

72 See Wilbur Shepperson, "Industrial Emigration in Early Victorian Britain," *Journal of Economic History*, 13:2 (Spring 1953), 182-88, 192; R.V. Clements, "Trade Unions and Emigration, 1840-80," *Population Studies*, 9:2 (November 1955); and Erickson, "Encouragement of Emigration," 249-53.

73 According to testimonies of two Glasgow employers, William Graham and Henry Houldsworth. But Houldsworth may have exaggerated when he claimed that the union paid an emigration benefit of fifteen to twenty pounds per family. Note also his view of the emigrant spinner. Asked by a member of the Select Committee, "What Character do those men who emigrate bare?" he answered: "Generally speaking, I think the spinners are not altogether the steadiest men, but men that are a little irregular." P.P. 1833, VI, 324, 311-12, 318.

74 P.P. 1837-38, VIII, 302-3, see also 44; Fraser, "The Glasgow Cotton Spinners," 83.

75 Webb, *History of Trade Unionism*, 184.

76 Chapman, *Lancashire Cotton*, 215.

77 Lowe, "An Account of the Strike in the Cotton Trade at Preston," 232.

78 Ibid., 255. As they saw it, the Preston spinners advocated emigration not just in order to reduce labor supply, not only as a means to bring this long and bitter strike to an end, but even more so, "to prevent a recurrence of strikes in the future." Ibid., 232.

79 London *Times*, 14 May 1869. The last figure (50) is from the *Beehive*, 5 June 1869, cited in Erickson, "Encouragement of Emigration," 257. See also the 1868-69 report of the Royal Commission on Trade Unions, P.P. 1868-69, XXXI, 73.

80 Arnold, *History of the Cotton Famine*, 161.

81 Mass. BSL, 1880, 59.

82 Philip Silvia, "The Spindle City: Labor, Politics, and Religion in Fall River, Massachusetts, 1870-1905" (Ph.D. dissertation, Fordham University, 1973), 82.

83 P.P. 1889, X, *Report from the Select Committee on Colonization*, 92-93.

84 Contrasting the 1850 and 1860 census returns, the effects of union emigration policy on the age distribution of British mule spinners in Fall River become all the more visible. Before 1850 the vast majority of mule spinners' unions in Lancashire had not yet adopted emigration schemes. Would it not be plausible, therefore, to expect the average age of British-born spinners employed in Fall River in 1850 to be lower than the age of those employed in 1860? That is precisely what Table N. 2 shows. Slightly over 38% of the British spinners in 1860 were under age 30 in contrast to 61% in 1850, while the proportion of spinners age 40 and older was three times as high in 1860 (19%) as it was in 1850 (6%). It should be noted, further, that the names of only four British spinners appear in both the 1850 and 1860 lists.

TABLE N. 2

Age Distribution of Adult Male Spinners
Employed in Fall River, July-August 1850,
Broken Down By Country of Birth.

Country of Birth

Age	Britain	Ireland	United States
18-19	8.2%	20.0%	
20-29	53.1%	60.0%	50.0%
30-39	32.7%	20.0%	50.0%
40 and over	6.1%		
Total Cases	49	15	4

Source: United States, Federal Manuscript Census of Fall River, 1850.

Note: The two American-born spinners in the 30-39 age category were 30 and 31 years old.

---

85 Walkowitz, *Worker City*, 61-62, 67.

86 Erickson, "Encouragement of Emigration," 265-67. See also Cumbler, *Working Class Community*, 252.

87 The most exhaustive summary of strikes in Massachusetts cotton mills 1850-1880 is in Mass. BSL, 1880, 7-63. See also Howard, "Progress in the Textile Trades," 214-40. For the 1867 New Bedford strike see, in addition, David Montgomery, *Beyond Equality: Labor and Radical Republicans, 1862-1872* (New York, 1967), 282-91. The Cohoes strikes are discussed by Howard, and, in details, by Walkowitz, *Worker City*, 63, 171, 175, 222-29.

88 U.S. Senate, *Labor and Capital*, vol. 1, 631-32, 641; *Labor Standard*, 18 December 1880; Clifton Yearley, *Britons in American Labor: A History of the Influence of the United Kingdom Immigrants on American Labor, 1820-1914* (Baltimore, 1957), 148-49; Berthoff, *British Immigrants in Industrial America*, 97; *Wade's Fibre and Fabric*, 2:47 (23 January 1886), 369-71.

89 U.S. Senate, Commission on Industrial Relations, *Final Report and Testimony*, 11 vols., S. Doc. 415, 64th Cong., 1st Sess., 1916, vol. 1, 985, 988; Robert Brook, "The United Textile Workers of America" (Ph.D. dissertation, Yale University, 1935), 116.

90 U.S. Industrial Commission, vol. 14, 564, 572; *American Federationist*, 9:11 (November 1902), 871. O'Donnell's early experience in Fall River was typical. A testimony given by Robert Howard before the 1885 U.S. Senate Committee on Labor and Capital (vol. 1: 651-52, vol. 3: 499) makes it plain that blacklisting was as widespread in New England as in Lancashire. In some cases, Howard insisted, it was a policy introduced into American cotton mills by British immigrant overseers and superintendents. From mid-century on, Fall River employers attempted to bar militant unionists from the mills; the organizers of the 1850-51 six-month spinners' strike were kept out of employment in any of the city factories

for years. "The blacklist was again brought into force" during the 1867 New Bedford strike, "and all those who had assisted in calling meetings . . . were compelled
to leave the city, work being refused them there." Howard, "Progress in the Textile Trades," 216-18. A Fall River spinner who participated in the 1870 strike was
told by one superintendent that he could "never work in Fall River again while
Fall River [was] Fall River." Apparently, so effective were employers' efforts to
exclude unionists that the spinner found it hard to get a job not only in Fall River
but in other towns as well. Mass. BSL, *Second Annual Report* (Boston, 1871),
81-82. About twenty Fall River mule spinners were blacklisted after the strike of
1870, and during the 1870s and early 1880s militant spinners in Fall River were
repeatedly prevented from obtaining employment, even under assumed names.
Fall River Daily Herald, 8 August 1879; Lillie Chace Wyman, "Studies of Factory
Life: Black-Listing at Fall River," *Atlantic Monthly*, 62:373 (November 1888),
605-12; Mass. BSL, 1882, 341, 345-47; Howard, "Progress in the Textile Trades,"
224-25, 231, 235-36.

One alternative opportunity for blacklisted spinners was to return to Britain.
Reverse migration was not uncommon; during prolonged depressions or strikes,
"few hands arrived in Fall River, and many old ones returned to Lancashire." During
the 1875 Fall River strike the mule spinners' union aided members in returning
to Britain, and in the same year the local spinners' union in Lowell offered free
passage to England to all members who were discharged during the strike. Berthoff, *British Immigrants in Industrial America*, 36, 97; *Fall River Daily Evening
News*, 7 April 1875; Mass. BSL, 1880, 41. A spinner who returned to Lancashire
and reapplied for union membership was required to repay his passage money.
Ordinarily British mule spinners' unions neither enabled members to hold benefits
while abroad nor did they allow the emigration benefit more than once. Erickson,
"Encouragement of Emigration," 267.

Reverse migration, finally, became widespread in the 1880s, as one witness before
the Select Committee on Colonization noted: "Communication between the United
Kingdom . . . and the United States has become so easy and rapid, that skilled
workmen in many trades pass frequently between the two continents, as the labour
market rises or falls in one or the other. There is thus no guarantee that the member,
who is paid to emigrate by his society, may not be back home again before a
very lengthened period has expired." P.P. 1889, X, 92. For reverse migration see
also U.S. House of Representatives, *Consular Reports, Labor in Europe*, 761.

CHAPTER 6

1 Earl, *Centennial History of Fall River*, 46.
2 Baird, *American Cotton Spinner*, 19, 171.
3 The quotations are from p. 61 but see also pp. 57-60, and *Fall River Daily Herald*,
  12 March 1888.
4 According to Mason himself in a letter addressed to Samuel Webber. See Samuel
  Webber, *Manual of Power for Machinery, Shafts, and Belts, with the History
  of Cotton Manufacture in the United States* (New York, 1879), part 2, 53.
5 Scott, *Practical Cotton Spinner*, 414, and for a technical description of the invention written by Mason himself see pp. 399-413. See also Gibb, *The Saco-Lowell*

Shops, 77-78, and Wallace, *Rockdale*, 195-96.

6 Webber, *Manual of Power*, 53.

7 Ibid., 53-54; Gibb, *The Saco-Lowell Shops*, 745; and Navin, *Whitin Machine Works*, 486. In addition, by 1851 the Saco Water Power Company in Saco, Maine, was also manufacturing mules. See Evelyn Knowlton, *Pepperell's Progress: History of a Cotton Textile Company, 1844-1945* (Cambridge, 1948), 55-56. In 1874 the four major mule manufacturers in the United States were the Franklin Foundry, Marvel and Davol, the Mason Machine Works, and the Saco Water Power Company. Navin, *Whitin Machine Works*, p. 487.

8 Young, *American Cotton Industry*, 141.

9 Ibid., 140.

10 Baird, *American Cotton Spinner*, 171, 191. As noted in the first paragraph of this chapter, of the 2.5 million spindles in the United States in 1850, 1 million were mounted on self actors. Assuming that roughly a half of all cotton spindles in American cotton mills in 1850 were mule spindles—as was the case in 1835 as well as 1870—the proportion of spindles attached to self actors would have been four-fifths of all mule spindles.

11 Mass. BSL, 1882, 313.

12 Daniel Snell, *The Manager's Assistant, Being a Condensed Treatise on Cotton Manufacture* (Hartford, Conn., 1850), 51.

13 Young, *American Cotton Industry*, 138.

14 See P.P. 1833, XXI, D.2., 54.

15 Mass. BSL, 1882, 308.

16 U.S. Senate, *Labor and Capital*, vol. 1, 631.

17 Mass. BSL, 1882, 304-5; *Fall River Daily Herald*, 31 May 1879; U.S. Senate, *Labor and Capital*, vol. 3, 74; *U.S. Industrial Commission*, vol. 7, 225-26. For Lowell and New Bedford see Uttley, *Cotton Spinning*, 16, 35-38. Apart from back boys, there were three other categories of assistants working in the mule rooms of American mills. According to Thomas Ashton, who visited Fall River mills in 1902 as a representative of a British delegation: "There are two doffers and one starter-up employed for seven to ten pair of mules, in accordance with the length of the mules working and the counts they produce. There are also tubers employed . . . and two of these tubers follow the doffers in their work." Notwithstanding this extra help, however, the American spinner still worked harder than the British, being responsible for *all* the piecing on a pair of mules. Mosely Industrial Commission to the United States, October-December, 1902. *Reports of the Delegates* (London, 1903), 125. See also Uttley, *Cotton Spinning*, 16-17, 35, 38, and U.S. Department of Labor, Bureau of Labor Statistics, *Bulletin*, No. 239, "Wages and Hours of Labor in Cotton Goods Manufacturing And Finishing, 1916" (Washington, 1918), 164-68.

18 Tucker, "Samuel Slater and Sons," 213, and *Samuel Slater*, 224.

19 Knowlton, *Pepperell's Progress*, 66.

20 Mass. BSL, 1871, 582. "The back boy has become such an important element in the spinning-room," a writer in *Wade's Fibre and Fabric* noted in 1885 (28 November), "that when trouble arises between him and the spinner, the overseer will often let the spinner go before he will discharge the boy; and when a second hand is hired, the manner in which he can keep the boys under control is often

taken into consideration."

21 *Fall River Daily Herald,* 8 May and 29 May 1879. As for hiring and firing: "Overseers are tenacious of their prerogative in this respect." See Lillie C. Wyman, "Studies of Factory Life: The Village System," *Atlantic Monthly,* 62 (July 1888), 25.

22 U.S. Senate, *Labor and Capital,* vol. 1, 8, 41.

23 Uttley, *Cotton Spinning,* 16.

24 U. S. Bureau of Labor, Seventh Annual Report, 1891, *Cost of Production: The Textiles and Glass* (Washington, 1892), vol. 1, 24.

25 *Fall River Daily Evening News,* 8 May and 29 May 1879; Mosely, *Reports,* 125; Uttley, *Cotton Spinning,* 32.

26 U.S. Senate, *Labor and Capital,* vol. 1, 451.

27 Mosely, *Reports,* 126, 136. In Fall River as elsewhere in New England, helpers other than back boys were always paid by management. Ibid., 125. See also Lazonick, "Production Relations," 506-7.

28 U.S. Senate, *Labor and Capital,* vol. 3, 153.

29 Mosely, *Reports,* 129.

30 U.S. Senate, *Labor and Capital,* vol. 3, 41, 74.

31 J.W. Lomax, *Fine Cotton Spinning: A Practical Manual* (Manchester, 1913), 116.

32 Uttley, *Cotton Spinning,* 38; Mosely, *Reports,* 126.

33 According to a 1903 union publication of the British cotton spinners quoted by Lazonick, "Production Relations," 507.

34 U.S. Senate, *Labor and Capital,* vol. 3, 153-54.

35 Mass. BSL, 1882, 348.

36 Mass. BSL, 1872, 399.

37 Mass. BSL, *Third Annual Report* (Boston, 1872), 399.

38 Wyman, "The Village System," 25.

39 Quoted in Mass. BSL, 1882, in order, 355, 383, 349, 345, 306.

40 See Lazonick, "Production Relations," 508-9.

41 Snell, *The Manager's Assistant,* 47; Mass. BSL, 1880, 6-8.

42 Mass. BSL, 1872, 398-99; Wallace, *Rockdale,* 179; Wood, *History of Wages,* 2.

43 "People of a New England Factory Village," *Atlantic Monthly,* 46:276 (October 1880), 462; Wood, *History of Wages,* 5.

44 "A Study of a New England Factory Town," *Atlantic Monthly,* 43:260 (June 1879), 694; Mass. BSL, 1882, 301-2; see also Mosely, *Reports,* 127, and *Wade's Fibre and Fabric,* 2:38 (21 November 1885), 297.

45 Mosely, *Reports,* 137.

46 Spahr, "The Old Factory Towns of New England," 288.

47 Mosely, *Reports,* 138. See also *Wade's Fibre and Fabric,* 2:38 (21 November 1885), 298. In all indication, turnover rates among mule spinners were higher in the United States than in Britain and that may be another reason why American spinners quit their jobs earlier than the British. Lazonick emphasizes occupational and geographical mobility of American spinners, but unfortunately, he does not support his argument with the necessary evidence. "Production Relations," 508.

48 Tufnell, *Trades' Unions,* 2. See also Aspinall, *Early English Trade Unions,* chs. 7, 9, and especially p. 214.

49 P.P. 1833, VI, 324.

50 Tufnell, *Trades' Unions,* 13.

51 It "extended nearly to all the districts round Manchester, southward to Stockport and Macclesfield, and going round to the east side of Manchester, it included Staley Bridge, Ashton-under-line, Hyde and their neighbourhoods; and further round Manchester northward to Oldham, Bolton, Preston, and their neighbourhoods round." Local societies contributed to the central federation, which in turn transferred funds to support local unions on strike. An important rule of the federation stated that "no shop should turn out without first having the sanction of the Congress." P.P. 1824, V, 573. During the "turn out" the spinners utilized for the first time the "rolling strike" technique—a method of striking selected mills in turn so that those on strike could be supported by those still at work. Turner, *Trade Union Growth*, 76.

52 "Strikes," *Quarterly Review*, 496-97. See also Kirby and Musson, *The Voice of the People*; "On Combinations," 79-84; Webb, *The History of Trade Unionism*, 106-10; G.D.H. Cole, *Attempts at General Union: A Study of British Trade Union History 1818-1834* (London, 1953), 9, 161-63; and J.L. and Barbara Hammond, *The Skilled Labourer 1760-1832* (London, 1920), 96-109, 128-35.

53 P.P. 1837-38, VIII, 263. William Lazonick has argued that the success of minders in retaining their position as subcontractors of labor in Britain was not due to their strength as an organized body. Lazonick rightly criticizes H.A. Turner's unsupported claims that the subcontract system was an issue the unions fought over in "many local battles." As a matter of policy, employers who adopted the self actor did not attempt to undermine the minders' control. The only two cases cited by Turner during the 1830s and 1840s refer to the intensification of work of spinners on power-driven mules, not the autonomy of minders and their authority over helpers. Turner, *Trade Union Growth*, 128; Lazonick, "Industrial Relations," 239-40. Actually, during the early period of transition to the new technology, up to 1833, not a single strike against the introduction of self-acting mules was reported to have occurred among the Manchester spinners, according to a testimony of Peter Ewart, an old-time Manchester master spinner, in response to questions by Factory Commissioner Tufnell. P.P. 1833, XXI, D.2., 37.

This, however, is not to say that unions did not matter. On the one hand, British employers had indeed some good reasons on managerial grounds to provide minders with a considerable measure of control. But on the other, spinners and early minders not only worked side by side in the same factory but they also enrolled in a combined union; their union rules codified their autonomy. Had British employers attempted to do away with the minders' control, as American employers did, they were likely to encounter formidable union resistance. The conservative outlook of British employers, it follows (an outlook which prevented them from following the example of American manufacturers), was shaped not only by certain conveniences provided by the subcontract system, but, even more so, by their desire to avoid confrontations with the unions. For a similar critique of Lazonick's argument see Penn, *Skilled Workers*, 120-21.

54 Prude, *The Coming of Industrial Order*, 94; Wallace, *Rockdale*, 177-78, 355, 366.

55 Wallace, *Rockdale*, 366.

56 Mass. BSL, 1880, 7. For more details on the strike see *Tribune* (New York), 3 February 1851; *Fall River Weekly News*, 23 January and 6 March 1851; *Providence Journal*, 25 November 1850.

CHAPTER 7

1 Mass. BSL, 1882, 195-415.

2 Berthoff, *British Immigrants in Industrial America*; Yearley, *Britons in American Labor*; Erickson, *American Industry and European Immigrants*.

3 Philip Foner, *History of the Labor Movement in the United States* (New York, 1947), vol. 1, especially 227-28.

4 K.G.J.C. Knowles, *Strikes—A Study of Industrial Conflict with Special Reference to British Experience Between 1911 and 1947* (Oxford, 1952), 219.

5 Edward Shorter and Charles Tilly, *Strikes in France, 1830-1968* (London, 1974), 342.

6 Mass. BSL, 1871, 51.

7 Montgomery, *Workers' Control in America*, 17.

8 *Fall River Daily Herald*, September 8, 1879; Howard, "Progress in the Textile Trades," 226. During the eight-year period 1872-80, to take another example, the Pepperell Manufacturing Company in Biddeford, Maine, cut the rates of mule spinners by over 50%. See Knowlton, *Pepperell's Progress*, 199.

9 Mass. BSL, 1871, 47, 87, 90; 1880, 30. See also Howard, "Progress in the Textile Trades," 219; and Silvia, "The Spindle City," 59-77.

10 Silvia, "The Spindle City," 79; Howard, "Progress in the Textile Trades," 220, 221, 224; Mass. BSL, 1880, 34-36.

11 Howard, "Progress in the Textile Trades," 221; see also *Fall River Daily Evening News*, June 24, 1879.

12 *Fall River Daily Evening News*, February 3, 1875.

13 *History of the Fall River Strike, Being a Full and Complete Report of the Labor Troubles from 1873 to April 5th, 1875*. By a workingman, revised and corrected by John Smith (Fall River, 1875); Mass. BSL, 1880, 36-39; Howard, "Progress in the Textile Trades," 221-23.

14 *Fall River Daily Evening News*, September 25, 1875.

15 The quotation is from Howard, "Progress in the Textile Trades," 228, see also 226-32; Mass. BSL, 1880, 53-57, 60-61; *New York Tribune*, June 26, 1879; and *Boston Herald*, July 12, 1879.

16 *Labor Standard*, October 4, 1879; *Boston Herald*, July 15, 1879.

17 *Labor Standard*, August 16, 1879; Howard, "Progress in the Textile Trades," 231.

18 *Fall River Daily Herald*, July 28 and August 4, 1879, August 11, 1879; Howard, "Progress in the Textile Trades," 230.

19 *Fall River Weekly News*, September 4, 1879, quoted in Silvia, "The Spindle City," 117.

20 Mass. BSL, 1880, 69.

21 *New York Journal of Commerce*, September 27, 1875.

22 *History of the Fall River Strike*, 19.

23 *Fall River Daily Evening News*, September 3, 1870.

24 See "Preamble and Objects," Mass. BSL, 1870, 286. Apparently, the same is true in regard to its forerunner, the "Benevolent and Protective Association of United Operative Mule Spinners of New England," organized in 1858 at the Fall River core. See Herbert J. Lahne, *The Cotton Mill Worker* (New York, 1944), 176.

25 Webb, *Industrial Democracy*, ch. 3. The Webbs may have overstated the

popularity of arbitration among British trade unions, at least after 1870. Many unionists in fact were quite suspicious of the arrangement, as the Webbs themselves note (p. 225, 231). On June 10, 1884, Thomas Ashton, secretary of the Oldham spinners, wrote Albert Shaw, the American consul in Manchester: "As far as the cotton trade is concerned, there will never be any more questions submitted to arbitration, as the Amalgamated Spinners . . . have struck the word 'arbitration' out of the preamble of their rules." Ashton claims that only two labor disputes in the Lancashire cotton industry after 1869 were settled by arbitration, one in Oldham, the other in Bolton. In the Oldhalll case the umpire's decision was a compromise—a 5% wage reduction instead of the 10% cut requested by the employers—a decision which Ashton, unlike many of the operatives, thought was "very fair." In Bolton the umpire's award was clearly in favor of the employers. "My experience has taught me," Ashton concluded, "that however fair and honest a decision may be, it gives dissatisfaction, and the working classes, as a rule, have lost all faith in such proceedings. I am afraid there will be few disputes in this country submitted to arbitration in the future." U.S. House of Representatives, *Consular Reports. Labor in Europe*, 744.

26 *Fall River Daily Evening News*, April 6, 1875.

27 Mass. BSL, 1880, 60-61; see also 53-56; 1882, 366, 399, 401, and an article in favor of arbitration in Fall River, and in the United States in general, in the *Philadelphia Ledger*, reprinted, *Fall River Daily Herald*, June 16, 1879.

28 Silvia, "The Spindle City," 118.

29 Reprinted, *Fall River Daily Evening News*, June 16, 1879. Similarly, a British traveler who visited Boston during the 1870 Fall River strike noted that whatever freedom of action Lancashire unionists had at home, "interference with the right of free labour would not for an hour be tolerated in America." James Macaulay, *Across the Ferry: First Impressions of America and its People* (London, 1871), 354. Discussing the 1879 Fall River strike, the *New York Daily Commercial Bulletin* proclaims: the right to free labor is not just "fundamental to free citizenship," not only "indispensible to an intelligent and successful pursuit of business," not even merely a "natural right," but rather a "birthright." June 30, 1879, reprinted, *Fall River Daily Evening News*, July 1, 1879. What is highly revealing in the hostile press coverage of the strike was the contrast newspapers drew between labor conditions in the United States and Britain. First, we are told (by the *Fall River Daily News* of June 19, 1879) that in Britain there are marked class distinction and no mobility: "once an operative always an operative is the rule." In the United States, on the other hand, "the strongest, boldest, most ambitious laborers are constantly leaving the old beaten track and striking out a new one . . . and in that way relieving the pressure on the ranks of the body they desert." Next, there is a charge that "arbitration in Britain has killed the manufacturers." The decline of Blackburn and Preston, the *Boston Advertiser* (June 21, 1879) claims, was a direct result of the rise of militant trade unionism, and furthermore, "The first step to ruin was taken when English manufacturers submitted to any communication [with the union]." Britain, the newspaper argued, had the most powerful trade unions in the world, yet American operatives were better paid than their British counterparts. The lesson is plain enough: "Interference with [the] laws of business brings its punishment as certainly as with the laws of nature." While the Boston press

during the period (with the exception of the *Boston Globe*) was overtly pro-capitalist, in Fall River in 1879 there were two major daily newspapers: the pro-capitalist *Daily Evening News* and the pro-labor *Daily Herald*.

30 Mass. BSL, 1871, the quotations are, in order, 55, 77, 78, 56.

31 *History of the Fall River Strike*, 19.

32 *New York Daily Bulletin*, reprinted, *Fall River Daily Evening News*, September 23, 1875.

33 September 3 and September 25, 1879. See also *Boston Globe*, September 14, 1879.

34 September 27, 1879. The scabs hired to work mules at the Flint Mill, for example, were unskilled, yet they received $2.30 a day or 75 cents above the rates for which the older spinners struck. *Labor Standard*, August 9, 1879. See also *Fall River Daily Herald*, August 8 and October 7, 1879. According to the estimate of the *Boston Globe* (July 16, 1879), the Fall River cotton corporations were losing $200,000 a week during the general strike of 1879.

35 I am grateful to William Lazonick for drawing my attention to this important point. See also his "Production Relations," 497.

36 August 16, 1879.

37 See "The Manufacturers' Side of the Story—They Refute the Seven Family Statement," in *Fall River Daily Evening News*, October 22, 1875.

38 Lintner, "Social History," 26-28, and see also her article "Mill Architecture in Fall River: 1865-1880," *The New England Quarterly*, 21:2 (June 1948), 202.

39 Lintner, "Social History," 27.

40 An independent check of a list of board members, compiled by Henry Earl in 1876, lends support to Lintner's findings (Table 8). See Earl, *Centennial History of Fall River*, 113-18. For a more detailed description of each corporation see pp. 119-50. Officer interlocks are obviously more powerful ties than director linkages because officers, unlike directors, are involved in the day-to-day operation of the company. For a substantive discussion of intercorporate linkages see Edward S. Herman, *Corporate Power, Corporate Control* (1981; reprinted, New York, 1983), and especially pp. 197-202 for interlocking directorates.

41 Earl, *Centennial History of Fall River*, 114-16, 168-81.

42 Ibid., 115 and Table 8.

43 *Boston Globe*, August 16, 1879.

44 *The Fall River Directory Containing the City Record, the Names of Citizens, and a Business Directory with an Almanac for 1864* (Boston, 1864), 195-208.

45 Mass. BSL, 1882, 412.

46 For example, S.A. Chace married a daughter of Nathan Durfee, Charles P. Stickney married a daughter of William Davol, and George Durfee married a daughter of Jefferson Borden. *Boston Globe*, September 2, 1879. All these individuals were members of the seven leading families. See Table 9.

47 Mass. BSL, 1880, 60; 1882, 244.

48 Mass. BSL, 1882, 243-44.

49 Ibid., 347, and see also *History of the Fall River Strike*, 7.

50 Mass. BSL, 1882, 247-48.

51 Ibid., 228, 200.

52 Mass. BSL, 1880, 41-42.

53 So dominant was the tradition of the individual enterprise that until the early 1870s

there were no more than a few dozen joint stock companies in the entire British cotton industry, and even three decades later the corporate form of enterprise was not nearly as widespread in Britain as in the United States. Farnie, *English Cotton Industry*, ch. 6, and especially pp. 215, 226. In the United States 70% of the 1,055 cotton manufacturing establishments in operation in 1899 were under corporate ownership, and nearly 90% of the volume of cotton goods was produced by corporations. See Department of Commerce, Bureau of the Census, Thirteenth Census of the United States, 1910, vol. 8, *Manufactures, 1909* (Washington, D.C., 1913), 137.

54 Conflict among British millowners dates back to the early part of the century. During the gigantic "long wheel" strikes of the late 1820s Lancashire master spinners failed to enforce agreements on fixing the piece rates because many small employers feared that such agreements would assist their rivals on the more advanced mules. Firms were also accused of contributing to strikes against their competitors, and of hiring blacklisted workers. In the second part of the century, the repeated attempts of the coarse master spinners of Oldham to form a joint employers' organization with the fine master spinners of Bolton failed. Turner, *Trade Union Growth*, 272-74.

55 The immediate success of the new companies astonished the old experienced millowners, who were "sadly puzzled at the dividends paid by the Oldham limiteds," and who saw their own profit margins fast declining. See P.P. 1886, XXI, *Second Report of the Royal Commission on Depression of Trade and Industry with Minutes of Evidence and Appendix*, Part I, 378. "No where in the world is competition keener than in the district where these cooperative spinning-mills are located," noted Albert Shaw in 1884, referring to the Oldham limiteds, and the reasons for that, according to Douglas Farnie, were as follows: "They flung down a direct challenge to the private spinners because they did not lease room and turning in the Oldham tradition but built new mills of the largest possible size and used loan capital to the utmost feasible extent. Their competitive advantages were reinforced by their limited liability, their jealousy of each other, and their inability in times of recession to agree to work short time." U.S. House of Representatives, *Consular Reports. Labor in Europe*, 748; Farnie, *English Cotton Industry*, 271-72. See also Turner, *Trade Union Growth*, 124, 144, 146; Ellison, *Cotton Trade of Great Britain*, ch. 11, especially p. 138; and Schulze-Gaevernitz, *Cotton Trade in England*, 193-97.

56 P.P. 1886, XXI, 146; Farnie, *English Cotton Industry*, 228-35.

57 For Fall River, see Mass. BSL, 1882, 304; for Oldham: U.S. House of Representatives, *Consular Reports. Labor in Europe*, 733, and *Reports from the Consuls of the United States*, no. 38, February 1884, 367.

58 For 1870: Federal Manuscript Census of Barnstable-Hampden Counties, Massachusetts. Manufacturing. For 1875: Earl, *Centennial History of Fall River*, 112.

59 The "mania for new companies" took place during 1873-75. P.P. 1886, XXIII, *Third Report of the Royal Commission on Depression of Trade and Industry with Minutes of Evidence and Appendix*, 308-9. See also U.S. House of Representatives, *Reports from the Consuls of the United States on the Commerce, Manufactures, Etc., of their Consular Districts*. H. Mis. Doc. 65, 47th Cong., lst Sess., 1882, *Cotton and*

Woolen Mills of Europe, no. 23, September 1882, 12; Earnie, *English Cotton In-
dustry*, ch. 7 and especially p. 272; Ronald Smith, "An Oldham Limited Liability
Company, 1875-1896," *Business History*, 4:1 (December 1961), 36; and Clapham,
An Economic History, vol. 2: *Free Trade and Steel 1850-1886*, 140-41.

60 *Fall River Daily Evening News*, October 22, 1875. See also U.S. House of Representatives, *Reports from the Consuls. Cotton and Woolen Mills*, 12. By 1875 20,000
local residents, or one-fifth of the Oldham population, owned shares in limited
liability spinning companies. Wage earners comprised some three-fourths of all
the investors and provided about half the capital. Farnie, *English Cotton Industry*,
252. Apart from private millowners and shopkeepers, the most typical investors
were the skilled artisans: brick-makers, joiners, mechanics, mule spinners, and
cotton mill overseers. U.S. House of Representatives, *Consular Report. Labor in
Europe*, 751. In 1885 Frank Hardern, director of the Industrial Cooperative Society
of Oldham, conducted a "very minute inquiry" of stock ownership. He found
that only 5% to 10% of the operatives employed in limited liability spinning firms
owned shares in the mills in which they worked. Speaking before the Royal Commission on Labour, he made it quite clear that these figures did not include the
three to six principal servants of a corporation, though they did include the foremen.
Because the number of foremen employed in a British mule-spinning mill was very
small, because mule spinners made up about 10% of all employees in such a mill,
and because no other highly paid craftsmen were employed in mule factories in
any number, it is quite safe to infer from Hardern's survey that a large proportion
of the Oldham mule spinners did become share holders in the mills in which they
worked. P.P. 1893-94, XXXIX, *Minutes of Evidence taken before the Royal Commission on Labour Sitting as a Whole*, Part I, 77-78.

61 Smith, "An Oldham Limited Liability Company," 38-39.

62 U.S. House of Representatives, *Consular Reports. Labor in Europe*, 747.

63 See U.S. House of Representatives, *Reports from the Consuls. Cotton and Woolen
Mills*, 12-13; letter from Thomas Ashton to Albert Shaw, July 27, 1884, in U.S.
House of Representatives, *Consular Reports. Labor in Europe*, 751-52; P.P. 1886,
XXIII, 309; and Farnie, *English Cotton Industry*, 265-66. Many of the limited liability companies were founded as mill-building concerns. A typical limited company
had in 1875 six board members: a cotton spinner, ironfounder, architect, carder,
engineer, and builder. "They represented a complete management team: first, the
architect to design and plan the mill premises, the builder to erect them, the engineer
to supervise the introduction and maintenance of the mill machinery and, finally,
the cotton spinner and carder to assume responsibility for the technical process
of cotton spinning." Smith, "An Oldham Limited Liability Company," 38.

64 "The creation of a new class of capitalists under the Limited Liability Acts," testified
Samuel Andrew, secretary of the Oldham Master Cotton Spinners' Association,
before the Royal Commission on Depression of Trade in 1885, "has evidently caused
some changes in the relations between capital and labour." "Many of those people who invest, if they are not working men themselves, for the most part have
been working men, and I consider that the sharp points that used to exist between
employer and employed are often now more eas[ily] . . . settle[d]; there is not the
same friction between the two parties; there is not the same antagonism between
them." P.P. 1886, XXI, 149. See also evidence given by Frank Harden, P.P. 1893-94,

XXXIX, 74.
65 Mass. BSL, 1871, 54, 55, 50.
66 Mass. BSL, 1871, 91, see also pp. 88-93. But they rarely threatened or attacked strikebreakers. Ordinarily, the striking spinners would approach the newly-arrived scabs, hand them a leaflet, attempt to induce them to leave town, and offer union funds to reimburse them for train fares to Fall River and back. If that failed, however, they might resort to an indirect threat: "We do not mean to say that you will be injured if you go to work," a group of spinners told a police officer disguised as a strikebreaker, "but it is hard telling what might happen in a crowd." And, sure enough, the only two cases of assaults against scabs, and in fact all the violent incidents recorded during the strike, erupted among the crowd of women and children gathering about the mills' gates—a pattern closely resembling that of a typical mule spinners' strike in Lancashire. "The women and the young help," concluded the Massachusetts Bureau, "showed their opposition even more than any other class." Mass. BSL, 1871, 73, 91, see also 53-54, 70-80, 84-85, 88-93.

By and large, the crowd of women and juveniles was made up of unorganized weavers and other mill operatives, and there is no question at all that the mule spinners attempted to exploit the violence on the part of the unorganized to win the strike. As in many Lancashire spinners' strikes in the early decades of the nineteenth century, the mass of unorganized mill workers had no support from the spinners' strike fund and, being under the urgent threat of starvation, they often resorted to violence. Turner, *Trade Union Growth,* 97. During the 1879 strike, for example, the spinners refused to aid any other workers but their own members: "When the spinners were asked would they relieve any weavers that so sacrificed themselves," wrote a weaver who took his son out of the mule room and was immediately discharged for doing so, he was told that the weavers had "no right" to relief from the spinners' funds. *Labor Standard,* October 4, 1879, quoted in Silvia, "The Spindle City," 119. Likewise, the spinners attempted to settle the strike on the basis of gains for themselves and nothing for the weavers and others. Brooks, "The United Textile Workers of America," 88. Furthermore, the mule spinners' policy of ignoring aspirations of the unskilled operatives during strikes is well-documented in other New England towns; for example, Lowell, Lawrence,and Manchester, N.H. See Montgomery, *Beyond Equality,* 145-46. Yet in one important respect all other classes of mill workers did benefit from the mule spinners' experience in the long run. A living example of a craft union's militancy encouraged other operatives to organize. By 1875 Fall River saw the formation of weavers' and carders' unions. In 1879 the weavers and carders held a few meetings but they lacked strike funds and therefore could not form viable unions.
67 Mass. BSL, 1882, 346-47.
68 Mass. BSL, 1871, 65.
69 Ibid., 61, 65.
70 Mass. BSL, 1870, 114-15.
71 Mass. BSL, 1872, 399.
72 *Boston Globe,* March 5, 1875.
73 Mass. BSL, 1882, 307, 308, 351. See also U.S. Senate, *Labor and Capital,* vol. 3, 495.
74 *Boston Globe,* March 5, 1875. Furthermore, being paid on a piece rate basis, the

spinners' actual earnings fell as they undertook cleaning and oiling. Mass. BSL, 1882, 344.

75 *Fall River Daily Evening News*, June 28, 1879; see also *Labor Standard*, August 16, 1879.

76 A visitor to Fall River on the eve of the great strike in June 1879 observed: "When a new mill is opened the agent stimulates the operatives to the highest possible performance...for the first few days, and then adjusts the [piece] rate up on the basis of what the best hands have thus been able to do." "As only a few operatives are capable of such a pace, and even they cannot maintain it permanently, the arrangement has the effect of establishing a low rate of wages." "Study of a New England Factory Town," 695.

77 U.S. Senate, *Labor and Capital*, vols. 1 and 3; Mass. BSL, 1882.

78 Howard, "Progress in the Textile Trades," 232.

79 Mass. BSL, 1882, 301.

80 Mass. BSL, 1882, 304; *Wade's Fibre and Fabric*, 1:2 (May 23, 1885), 90. For Fall River see also Wyman, "Black-Listing in Fall River," 611, and *Fall River Daily Evening News*, August 20, 1870. For Britain: Wood, *History of Wages*, 141-42.

81 U.S. Senate, *Labor and Capital*, vol. 3, 495; vol. 1, 647.

82 U.S. Senate, *Commission on Industrial Relation, Final Report*, vol. 1, 988-89.

83 U.S. Senate, *Labor and Capital*, vol. 1, 647. Lord Palmerston, a member of the British cabinet at the time and an enthusiastic advocate of factory reform, had a special interest in the issue, as the following anecdote, told by Robert Howard to a correspondent of the *Fall River Daily Herald* (May 31, 1879), reveals. Palmerston, the story goes, engaged at one point in a sort of an experiment at home, "walking about a measured space" and shifting two chairs back and forth from one end of a room to the other. Entering the room, his wife exclaimed: "What are you doing, my Lord?" "Why," Palmerston replied out of breath, "I'm running two mules for the first time in my life, and I don't like it."

Palmerston "worked" the power-driven mule. He shifted around two heavy chairs imagining he was pushing back a pair of carriages. Because many of the mule piecers and scavengers in the 1830s were young children, members of the British Parliament were particularly interested in the issue (during the debates on the employment of children in factories) and Palmerston was not the only one who made experiments. A parliament member from Oldham tested the matter himself, "personally, in his own works," and wrote in 1836: "To my surprise I found the distance not less than 20 miles in 12 hours, my machinery not being driven at anything like the speed under which the former calculations were made. I stood by the child with a clock before me, and found the number of times that she walked certain distances in a given time. I knew those distances, and upon them calculated the whole distance that she would walk that day, working 12 hours, being careful to keep my calculation under the truth rather than over it." Quoted in Mass. BSL, 1871, 483.

84 Mass. BSL, 1871, 483; *Fall River Daily Evening News*, August 20, 1870; *Fall River Daily Herald*, May 31, 1879; *Boston Globe*, July 7, 1879.

85 Wyman, "Black-Listing in Fall River," 611.

86 *Fall River Daily Herald*, May 29, 1879. See also U.S. Senate, *Labor and Capital*, vol. 3, 495-96; and *Boston Globe*, July 7, 1879.

87 U.S. Senate, *Labor and Capital*, vol. 1, 638.

88 But the Oldham list was not merely a speed list. To complicate matters, the Oldham list was formally linked to time, not directly to output, and accordingly the mule spinners received standard weekly earnings. Yet the standard weekly wage for spinning on mules of different sizes was calculated in such a way that the exact speed of the carriage was taken into account. As a result, the spinners of Oldham were actually paid in proportion to productivity. For two exceptionally lucid explanations of the actual working of the Oldham list see British Association for the Advancement of Science, *On the Regulation of Wages by Means of Lists in the Cotton Industry* (Manchester, 1887), 8-10, and Jewkes and Gray, *Wages and Labour*, ch. 4 and 5. See also S.J. Chapman, "The Regulations of Wages," 595-96; and Porter, "Industrial Peace in the Cotton Trade," 49-52. The Oldham list of 1876 is reprinted in the report of the British Association, pp. 197-200.

89 In Fall River, remember, speed-up was a corporate policy enforced by the Board of Trade. In Oldham speed-up was an outcome of competition. In both mill towns the practice of intensifying the speed took place in the 1870s. A careful observation of 400 pairs of mules in Oldham in 1870-72 reveals that only 15 pairs ran fast enough to complete three-and-a-half round trips in less than a minute. Wood, *History of Wages*, 54. By the end of the decade three-and-a-half trips a minute was the average speed. Oldham experienced its first increases in speed during the mill-building boom of the early 1870s, and the limited liability spinning companies, which at the time were not members of the Oldham Employers' Association, were the first to speed up their machinery. To compete successfully with the new concerns, the large body of private millowners, most of whom were members of the employers' association, speeded up their mules as well, and "the practice of cutting piece prices became general throughout the town." Because the earlier Oldham list of 1872 did not protect the mule spinners from increases in work-load due to speed-ups, the union demanded a revised list. Weakened by competition, the Oldham employers were unwilling to oppose the union, and eventually, to avoid a growing number of disputes over the principle of compensation for "over speed," they negotiated a new list in 1876. The quotation is from Jewkes and Gray, *Wages and Labour*, 65-66; see also Thornley, *Practical Treatise upon Self-Acting Mules*, 240; and Wood, *History of Wages*, 54-55.

90 U.S. Senate, *Labor and Capital*, vol. 1, 634, 637, 638. See also Jonathan Lincoln, "The Sliding Scale of Wages in the Cotton Industry," *Quarterly Journal of Economics*, 23 (May 1909), 453.

91 Silvia, "The Spindle City," 456-57; U.S. Senate, *Commission on Industrial Relations*, vol. 1, 989.

92 Vol. 8, No. 186 (September 22, 1888), 234; see also vol. 6, No. 153 (February 1888), 179; and *Fall River Daily Herald*, November 21, 1888.

93 *Fall River Daily Herald*, December 11 and December 28, 1888; *Wade's Fibre and Fabric*, 8:203 (January 19, 1889), 372.

94 Mosely, *Reports*, 126.

95 Ibid.

96 New England Cotton Manufacturers' Association (henceforth: NECMA), *Proceeding of the Eighteenth Annual Meeting, Held at Boston, April 25, 1883* (Boston, 1883), 51.

97 Speaking before the New England Cotton Manufacturers' Association in 1873 one employer noted: "Weft yarns of coarse numbers have been spun successfully on ring frames at many places for years past, but no factory could be found by the speaker where *mule* weft yarns were spun on ring frames, of equal *numbers*, twist and quality." NECMA, *Proceedings of the Semi-Annual Meeting Held at Boston, October 15, 1873* (Boston, 1873), 6.

98 Quoted in Mass. BSL, 1882, 313-14. See also U.S. Senate, *Labor and Capital*, vol. 3, 451. In general, manufacturers were reluctant to scrap new mules. "The life of a mule is twenty-five years," pointed out a Fall River superintendent, and the mules in his mill were "scarcely old enough to discard." Mass. BSL, 1882, 313. But there is also some evidence of employers who did dispose of well-functioning mules. In the Hampden Mills at Holyoke, Massachusetts, the employers removed some of their "excellent mules," made in the Lowell machine shop, and replaced them with ring frames. "They found no fault with [the mules]; but they threw them out and sold them for a trifle," noted in 1883 a cotton machinery manufacturer. NECMA, 1883, 54.

99 Sandberg, "American Rings and English Mules," 129.

100 See NECMA, *Proceedings*, October 15, 1873, 8; *Proceedings of the Sixth Annual Meeting, Held at Boston, April 19, 1871* (Boston, 1871), 47-52; *Proceedings of the Seventh Annual Meeting, Held at Boston, April 17, 1872* (Boston, 1872), 29-33; and *Proceedings of the Twenty-Sixth Annual Meeting, Held at Boston, April 29, 1891* (Boston, 1891), 20-50.

101 *Fall River Daily Evening News*, June 7, 1879.

102 *Boston Daily Advertiser*, June 21, 1879.

103 *Fall River Daily Evening News*, August 7 and June 7, 1879. On the replacement of mules by rings to undermine unions during the strike see also May 5, 19, and June 21, 23, 1879.

104 Federal Manuscript Census of Barnstable-Hampden Counties, Massachusetts. Manufacturing, 1870.

105 Mass. BSL, 1882, 314-15.

106 Mass. BSL, 1880, 67.

107 Ibid., 55-56.

108 Ibid., 67.

109 Silvia, "The Spindle City," 713.

110 Ibid., 705.

111 *Wade's Fibre and Fabric*, 19:494 (August 18, 1894), 926; see also vol. 20:497 (September 8, 1894), 965.

112 For 1898 see Silvia, "The Spindle City," 545. For 1904 see *Wade's Fibre and Fabric*, 40:1024 (October 15, 1904), 230. In the 1880s too, Fall River employers were reported to have installed ring frames "with the view of crushing the skilled labor required for mules." See *Wade's Fibre and Fabric*, 1:3 (March 21, 1885), 17; 1:4 (March 28, 1885), 27.

113 For example, in Lowell in June-July 1899, the Massachusetts Corporation tore out twelve of its twenty pair of mules within the first four weeks of a mule spinners' strike. See U.S. Industrial Commission, vol. 7, "Testimony," 343-44.

114 U.S. Industrial Commission, vol. 7, "Testimony," 348.

115 Copeland, *The Cotton Manufacturing Industry*, 70-71. For more statistics on the

changing proportion of mules and rings in Britain and the United States see Lazonick and Mass, "The Performance of the British Cotton Industry," 29-30; and Saxonhouse and Wright, "Rings and Mules Around the World," 276, 280. The decline in mule machinery construction in the United States proceeded even faster, much faster, than the decline in mule spinning. The vast majority of mules installed in American mills after 1870 were imported from Britain. Ring frames used in American factories, on the other hand, were nearly all manufactured domestically. For domestic and foreign mule and ring spindles installed in American cotton mills, 1870-1914, see U.S. Department of Commerce, Bureau of Foreign and Domestic Commerce, *The Cotton-Spinning Machinery Industry*, Miscellaneous Series— No. 37 (Washington, 1916), 77.

116 Lazonick, "Factor Costs and the Diffusion of Ring Spinning"; "Rings and Mules in Britain: Reply," *Quarterly Journal of Economics*, 99:2 (May 1984). Transporting ring weft from spinning to weaving mills in Lancashire was more than four times as expensive as shipping mule weft. Warp yarn from either ring frames or mules had to be rewound before weaving, and in Lancashire this process was usually performed in the spinning mill before the yarn was shipped to the weaving shed. Weft yarn, on the other hand, was shipped wound in a package and was used in this form in the weaving process. But while mule-spun yarn was wound on the bare spindle or on light paper tubes, ring yarn had to be wound on heavy wooden bobbins which were extremely costly to transport.

117 Sandberg, "American Rings and English Mules," especially 125-26. Sandberg's conclusion was challenged by Lazonick. Lazonick shows that Sandberg seriously overestimated labor costs per 100 mule spindles in the U.S. as well as Britain plainly because Sandberg did not take into account that in both countries a mule spinner operated a *pair* of mules, not a single mule. As a result, Sandberg's estimate of labor cost saving per pound of ring yarn is twice the correct figure for each country. Lazonick, "Factor Costs and the Diffusion of Ring Spinning," 99. In his reply to Lazonick Sandberg accepts the correction. Lars Sandberg, "The Remembrance of Things Past: Rings and Mules Revisited," *Quarterly Journal of Economics*, 99:2 (May 1984), 387. Notwithstanding the error, however, insofar as Sandberg's calculations for ring spinning are plausible, the labor cost advantage of rings over mules would still be greater in the U.S. than in Britain. But Lazonick rejects this view as well. Without offering comparative figures, Lazonick claims elsewhere ("Production Relations," 515) that Sandberg also overestimated output-per-ring-spindle in the United States and that, when "correct data are used," one finds that the labor cost saving of rings over mules "was an insignificant factor in accounting for the differences in the rate of diffusion of the newer technology."

118 Lazonick disagrees but note Saxonhouse and Wright's verdict: There is . . . a basic element of truth in [Sandberg's] observation that the English worldwide supremacy in high-count spinning was a key element in the persistence of mule technology." Saxonhouse and Wright, "Rings and Mules Around the World," 293. For a follow-up debate between Lazonick and the joint authors see William Lazonick, "Stubborn Mules: Some Comments," and Gary Saxonhouse and Gavin Wright, "Stubborn Mules and Vertical Integration: The Disappearing Constraint?" *Economic History Review*, 2nd Series, 40:1 (February 1987), 80-94.

119 Ignoring this important point, Beatrice and Sidney Webb describe the triumph

of mule spinning over ring spinning in Britain in the following way:

> "When an employer complained that he could no longer compete with
> rivals who had adopted the ring frame, unless his mule-spinners would
> accept a lower rate, he was told that under no circumstances could
> any 'lowering of the dyke' be permitted. What he was offered was...a
> revision of the piecework list so arranged as to stimulate him to
> augment the rapidity and complexity of the mule, in order that the
> mule-spinners, increasing in dexterity, might simultaneously enlarge
> the output per machine and raise their own earnings. The cotton spin-
> ners in short...preferred to meet the competition of a new process
> by raising their own level of skill, rather than by degrading their
> Standard of Life."
>
> (*Industrial Democracy*, 424-425)

British mule spinners, true, refused adamantly to accept any wage cuts. But
as we have seen in so many ways, their job at the turn of the century involved
little dexterity, hardly any skill at all, and a good deal of supervisory responsibilities.
To protect their standard of living, then, the aristocratic mule spinners did not—
and could not—upgrade their own skill level, as the Webbs contend. Rather, they
increased the workload of their assistants.

120 This is also why British mule spinners did not resist the introduction of ring frames.
Writing in 1897 the Webbs note: "Had this invention been made fifty years ago,
the mule-spinners would undoubtedly have done their utmost to prevent its adoption, and to exclude women from any participation in cotton spinning. But no
such action has been taken, or even suggested. Although the Cotton-spinners' Trade
Union...now exercises a far more effective control over the industry than at any
previous period, ring spinning by women has, during the last fifteen years, been
allowed to grow up unmolested." *Industrial Democracy*, 424.

CHAPTER 8

1 See Dean and Cole, *British Economic Growth*, 192, 220, 216, 225-26, 329.

2 B.R. Mitchell, *Abstract of British Historical Statistics* (Cambridge, 1962), 118, 188.

3 Ibid., 283, 304-5.

4 Bernard Elbaum and Frank Wilkinson, "Industrial Relations and Uneven Development: A Comparative Study of the American and British Steel Industries," *Cambridge Journal of Economics*, 3:3 (September, 1979), especially 283.

5 A.J. Taylor, "Labour Productivity and Technological Innovation in the British
Coal Industry, 1850-1914," *Economic History Review*, 2nd Series. 14:1 (August
1961), 57.

6 G.C. Allen, *The Industrial Development of Birmingham and the Black Country,
1860-1927* (London, 1929), 146-48; Elbaum and Wilkinson, "Industrial Relations
and Uneven Development," 283-84; H.A. Clegg, Alan Fox, and A.F. Thompson,
A History of British Trade Unions Since 1889, vol. 1: *1889-1910* (Oxford, 1964),
15; but see also H.P. Howard, "The Strikes and Lockouts in the Iron Industry
and the Formation of the Ironworkers' Unions, 1862-1869," *International Review
of Social History*, 18 (1973), part 3, 398-99, for a somewhat different view on

the relationship between forehands and underhands.

7 Clegg, Fox, and Thompson, *British Trade Unions*, 15.

8 Allen, "Industrial Development of Birmingham," 144; A.J. Taylor, "The Subcontract System in the British Coal Industry," in Pressnell, *Studies in the Industrial Revolution*, 215-35.

9 For early trade unions among puddlers see J.C. Carr and W. Taplin, *History of the British Steel Industry* (Cambridge, Mass., 1962), 61-63. For early coal miners' unions see E. Welbourne, *The Miners' Unions of Northumberland and Durham* (Cambridge, 1923), 20-124; E.W. Evans, *The Miners of South Wales* (Cardiff, 1961), 15-85; J.H. Morris and L.J. Wllliams, *The South Wales Coal Industry 1841-1875* (Cardiff, 1958), 248-69; and Page Arnot, *The Miners: A History of the Miners' Federation of Great Britain 1889-1910* (London, 1949), 29-43.

10 Tufnell, *Trades' Unions*, 138-40; Evans, *Miners of South Wales*, 39-42.

11 For coal miners' unions see Clegg, Fox, and Thompson, *British Trade Unionism*, 16-18; for ironworkers' unions see Howard, "Strikes and Lockouts," 397, and P.P. 1867-68, XXXIX, *Fifth Report from the Royal Commission on Trade Unions*, 53-54.

12 Carr and Taplin, *British Steel Industry*, 70-72; Arthur Pugh, *Men of Steel* (London, 1951), 32-56.

13 Howard, "Strikes and Lockouts."

14 G. Schulze-Gaevernitz, *Social Peace: A Study of the Trade Union Movement in England* (London, 1893), 213-21.

15 Burgess, *British Industrial Relations*, 182-83, 191; Clegg, Fox, and Thompson, *British Trade Unions*, 18.

16 J.H. Porter, "Wage Bargaining under Conciliation Agreements, 1860-1914," *Economic History Review*, 2nd Ser., 23:3 (December 1979), 465, 475.

17 This expression was repeatedly used in delegate meetings of the Northumberland miners in 1874, 1877, and 1878. See Webb and Webb, *History of Trade Unionism*, 323-25. There was, however, a difference between the cotton spinning list and the iron and coal sliding scales. The first was connected to prices only implicitly, through periodic revisions; the coal and iron scales, on the other hand, linked wages to prices explicitly.

18 Carr and Taplin, *British Steel Industry*, 64-65.

19 Elbaum and Wilkinson, "Industrial Relations and Uneven Development," 286.

20 Webb and Webb, *History of Trade Unionism* (1920 edition), appendix 3, 735-36 .

21 Berthoff, *British Immigrants*, 48-50; P.P. 1873, X, *Report from the Select Committee on Coal*, 173; John Laslett, *Nature's Noblemen: The Fortunes of the Independent Collier in Scotland and the American Midwest, 1855-1889* (Los Angeles, 1983); Erickson, *American Industry and European Immigrants*, 59; "Encouragement of Emigration," 264. The quotation is from Berthoff.

22 Berthoff, *British Immigrants*, 64-65; U.S. Congress, *Reports of the Immigration Commission*, vol. 8, 389, 591; Yearley, *Britons in American Labor*, 142.

23 The quotations are, in order, from P.P. 1867-68, XXXIX, 54; 1863, XVIII, 51; and 1873, X, 174. See also Erickson, *American Industry and European Immigrants*, 59: "Encouragement of Emigration, " 261.

24 P.P. 1867-68, XXXIX, 54.

25 Erickson, "Encouragement of Emigration," 259-60; *American Industry and*

European Immigrants, 40, 19.

26 Richard Fynes, *The Miners of Northumberland and Durham* (1873; reprinted Sunderland, 1923), p. 236.

27 Erickson, "Encouragement of Emigration," 263.

28 P.P. 1873, X, 209-10.

29 Coleman McAlister, *Men of Coal* (New York, 1943), 36-44; Berthoff, *British Immigrants*, 91-93; Yearley, *Britons in American Labor*, 33-34, 123-41; Anthony Wallace, *St. Clair: A Nineteenth-Century Coal Town's Experience with a Disaster-prone Industry* (Ithaca, New York: Cornell University Press, 1988), 288-93, 388-403; McNeill, *Labor Movement*, 244-57; Laslett, *Nature's Noblemen*, especially 38-46 . See also Andrew Roy, *A History of Coal Miners of the United States From the Development of the Mines to the Close of the Anthracite Strike of 1902* (Columbus, Ohio, 1907); and Chris Evans, *History of the United Mine Workers of America*, vol. 1 (Indianapolis, n.d.)

The ethnic background of the sixteen original members of the Workingmen's Benevolent Association of St. Clair, according to Wallace (p. 290), was as follows: eleven, including the president and secretary, were English, one was from South Wales; three were Irish (two of the Irish lived in England before coming to America), and for the remaining one there is no record.

Nowhere was the influence of British immigrant miners more evident than in regions which remained impervious to unions; for example, southern West Virginia. A thorough examination of the southern West Virginia coal mining industry between 1890 and 1912 reveals that the miners failed to unionize. "By 1912 only a small pocket of unionism existed. . .and that foothold proved to be weak and illusive." The reason for that, David Corbin argues persuasively, was the conspicuous absence of British immigrants who had been so instrumental in stimulating militant union activities in other coal regions. In 1900, a decade after opening the southern West Virginia coal mines, there were neither Welsh nor Scottish miners in the state and the English numbered 1,053, or less than 5% of the mining workforce. By 1907, there were a few Welsh as well as Scottish miners in West Virginia coal fields but the total number of British fell to 431, or less than 1%. David Corbin, *Life, Work and Rebellion in the Coal Fields: The Southern West Virginia Mines 1880-1922* (Urbana, Ill., 1981), 25-28.

30 Berthoff, *British Immigrants*, 94-95; Yearley, *Britons in American Labor*, 143-146; U.S. Senate, *Labor and Capital*, I, 1159; McNeill, *Labor Movement*, 274-289; Carrol Wright, "The Amalgamated Association of Iron and Steel Workers," *Quarterly Journal of Economics*, 7 (April 1893), 416-18). The quotation is from *Capital and Labor*.

31 United States, 9th Census, *III*, 760, 764.

32 Unlike the mule spinners' unions, however, the M&LBA was not an exclusive craft organization but rather an industry-wide union enrolling both skilled and unskilled workers, miners alongside mine laborers. Wallace, *St. Clair*, 275, 397.

33 Mary Freifeld, "The Emergence of the American Working Classes: The Roots of Division, 1865-1885" (Ph.D. dissertation, New York University, 1980), 231-249; Wallace, *St. Clair*, 419; Harold Aurand, "The Workingmen's Benevolent Association," *Labor History*, 7:1 (Winter 1966), 24-25.

34 *New York Times*, March 3, 1871.

35 Cited in Freifeld, "Emergence of American Working Classes," 258, from the *Miners'* *Journal* (Pottsville, Penn.), February 24, 1871.

36 Cited in Marvin Schlegel, "The Workingmen's Benevolent Association: First Union of Anthracite Miners," *Pennsylvania History*, 10:4 (October 1943), 261.

37 *New York Times*, April 12, 1875.

38 See Schlegel, "Workingmen's Benevolent Association," 261.

39 Cited in Freifeld, "Emergence of American Working Classes," 290, from the *Philadelphia Ledger*, May 21, 1875.

40 Wallace, *St. Clair*, 424.

41 George Korson, *Minstrels of the Mine Patch: Songs and Stories of the Anthracite Industry* (Philadelphia, 1938), 225.

42 Marvin Schlegel, "America's First Cartel," *Pennsylvania History*, 13:1 (January 1946).

43 Wallace, *St. Clair*, 417-24. The quotation is from p. 419. See also Schlegel, "Workingmen's Benevolent Association," 259, and "America's First Cartel," 7.

44 Schlegel, "America's First Cartel," 7.

45 See Korson, *Minstrels of the Mine Patch*, 211.

46 Wallace, *St. Clair*, 425.

47 Arthur Suffern, *The Coal Miners' Struggle for Industrial Status* (New York, 1926), 85-93.

48 John Benson, *British Coalminers in the Nineteenth Century: A Social History* (New York, 1980), 11-12, 17, 19, 23, 25.

49 In 1885 85,000 workers were employed in the South Wales coal mining industry and 71,000 in the Pennsylvania anthracite mining. For South Wales see Evans, *Miners of South Wales*, 108, 241; for Pennsylvania see footnotes 31 and 32 above, and U.S. Department of Interior, Census Office, *Report on the Mining Industries of the United States* (Washington, 1886), 638.

50 Evans, *Miners of South Wales*, 104-12, 232-34; Morris and Williams, *South Wales Coal Industry*, 266, 278-84.

51 The figures pertaining to the number of collieries owned by individual firms and to the output of the largest firms both exclude iron concerns. About 32% of the total output of 16.2 million tons of coal raised in South Wales in 1873 was produced by iron firms; much of it, however, was for internal consumption rather than for sale. See Morris and Williams, *South Wales Coal Industry*, 76, 135-36, 152.

52 Jesse Robinson, *The Amalgamated Association of Iron, Steel, and Tin Workers* (Baltimore, 1920), 14, 138-39.

53 Ibid., 88.

54 Ibid., 20-21; David Montgomery, *The Fall of the House of Labor: The Workplace, the State, and American Labor Activism, 1865-1925* (Cambridge, 1987), 35.

55 The statistics from the Vulcan records appear in McNeill, *Labor Movement*, 307. For a detailed description of these puddlers' strikes see Freifeld, "Emergence of the American Working Classes," 400-13; Montgomery, *Fall of the House of Labor*, 19-20; Robinson, *Amalgamated Association*, 100-103.

56 Montgomery, *Fall of the House of Labor*, 19.

57 McNeill, *Labor Movement*, 307-8.

58 Montgomery, *Fall of the House of Labor*, 27.

59 Freifeld, "Emergence of American Working Classes," 472.

60 Ibid., 468-88.

61 McNeill, *Labor Movement*, 307.

62 Robinson, *Amalgamated Association*, 21; Freifeld, "Emergence of American Working Classes," 534.

63 Freifeld, "Emergence of American Working Classes," 535.

64 Montgomery, *Fall of the House of Labor*, 33; Freifeld, "Emergence of American Working Classes," 490-91. Freifeld points out that the defeat of puddlers in 1882 stands in contrast to their early victories. Divisions among the employers, she argues persuasively, aided the Sons of Vulcan in its earlier strikes; between 1867 and 1875 the Pittsburgh manufacturers were competing fiercely with the midwestern manufacturers on markets and therefore were reluctant to engage in lengthy strikes. In 1882, on the other hand, the ironmasters were unified. In an unprecedented show of unity the Pittsburgh and midwestern employers formed an alliance in 1882 so that they could coordinate their struggle against the Amalgamated.

65 Robinson, *Amalgamated Association*, 19, 21.

66 See Edward Bemis, "The Homestead Strike," *Journal of Political Economy*, 2 (June 1894), 369-96; Brody, *Steelworkers in America*, ch. 3; Montgomery, *Fall of the House of Labor*, 36-42.

67 Brody, *Steelworkers in America*. For membership in the Amalgamated in 1929 see p. 278.

68 James Holt, "Trade Unionism in the British and U.S. Steel Industries, 1880-1914: A Comparative Study," *Labor History*, 18:1 (Winter 1977), 6-9; Carr and Taplin, *British Steel Industry*, ch. 27; Elbaum and Wilkinson, "Industrial Relations and Uneven Development," 293-94.

69 Peter Temin, *Iron and Steel in Nineteenth Century America* (Cambridge, Mass., 1964), ch. 8 and especially p. 174.

70 Duncan Burn, *The Economic History of Steelmaking, 1867-1939* (1940; reprinted, Cambridge, 1961), 346.

71 Brody, *Steelworkers in America*, 59; Holt, "Trade Unionism," 29.

72 T.H. Burnham and G.O. Hoskins, *Iron and Steel in Britain 1870-1930* (London, 1943), 37, 208, 233-37; Burn, *Economic History of Steelmaking*, 219-305, 329-49.

73 Elbaum and Wilkinson, "Industrial Relations and Uneven Development," 295, 301- 2; Bernard Elbaum, "The Steel Industry Before World War I," in Bernard Elbaum and William Lazonick, eds., *The Decline of the British Economy* (Oxford, 1986), 67-71.

74 See Burn, *Economic History of Steelmaking*, ch. 10; Brody, *Steelworkers in America*, 32; Stephen Jeans, ed., *American Industrial Conditions and Competition* (London, 1902), 511-12, 561-64; Mosely, *Reports*, 40-48.

75 Brody, *Steelworkers in America*, 31-32. See also John Fitch, "The Steelworkers," in *The Pittsburgh Survey* (New York, 1911), 45-56.

76 Brody, *Steelworkers in America*, 51; Holt, "Trade Unionism," 28-29.

77 They retained much of their predecessor's control and consequently, unlike American rolling men, they managed both to secure substantial increases in wages from improved productivity, and to prevent the introduction of scientific management methods into British steelmaking. See Wilkinson and Elbaum, "Industrial Relations and Uneven Development," 298-300.

APPENDIX 1

1 Mass. BSL, 1880, 65.
2 United States, Bureau of Labor, Third Annual Report, 1887, *Strikes and Lockouts* (Washington, 1888), 1056, 1064, 1083.
3 John Griffin, *Strikes: A Study of Quantitative Economics* (New York, 1939), 72-73.
4 United States, Bureau of Labor, Twenty-First Annual Report, 1906, *Strikes and Lockouts* (Washington, 1907), 113.
5 *Workers Control in America*, 20.
6 *Strikes in France*.

APPENDIX 2

1 Mass. BSL, 1882, 200.
2 Mass. BSL, 1882, 271-96; Silvia, "The Spindle City," 332.
3 *Fall River Daily Evening News*, April 23, May 25, 1875; June 16, 1879; and Mass. BSL, 1880, 42. Interestingly, at the beginning of the Lowell strike a small number of throstle and ring-frame spinners expressed solidarity with the mule spinners and, demanding a wage increase, they left the mills. But on the whole the vast majority of frame spinners remained at work, and the output of throstle- and ring-spun yarn increased as the strike prolonged. See Carol Polizotti Webb, "The Lowell Mule Spinners' Strike of 1875," in Mary H. Blewett, ed., *Surviving Hard Times: The Working People of Lowell* (Lowell, 1982), 11-20.
4 In Fall River, just as in a typical Lancashire cotton town, both the weft and the warp were spun on mules. In the vast majority of American milla, by contrast, only the weft was spun on mules while throstles and rings were used for warp spinning. See *Fall River Daily Evening News*, June 21, 1879; NECMA, *Statistics of Cotton Manufactures in New England, 1866* (Boston, 1872), 16-17; *Proceedings of the Semi Annual Meeting, Held in Boston, October 19, 1870* (Boston, 1873), 10; and John L. Hayes, *American Textile Machinery* (Cambridge, 1879), 39. The ring, however, was technically capable of spinning low-count weft as well, and was actually used by employers to produce weft yarn during mule spinners' strikes.

Bibliography

"A List of Locations of American Textile Mills, 1808-1818." 1963. *Textile History Review* 4:1 (January), 46-51.

Allen, G.C. 1929. *Industrial Development of Birmingham and the Black Country, 1860-1927*. London: Allen & Unwin.

Allen, Zachariah. 1829. *The Science of Mechanics as Applied to the Present Improvements in the Useful Arts in Europe, and the United States of America*. Providence: Hutchens and Cory.

_____. 1832. *The Practical Tourist, or Sketches of the State of Arts, and Society, Scenery, etc., etc. in Great Britain, France, and Holland*. Vol. 1. Providence: A.S. Beckwith.

American Federationist. 1902.

Anderson, Michael. 1971. *Family Structure in Nineteenth Century Lancashire*. London: Cambridge University Press.

_____. 1976. "Sociological History and the Working Class Family: Smelser Revisited." *Social History*, No. 3 (October), 317-34.

Annawan Manufacturing Company (Fall River). G-l, Labor Book, 1858-63. Manuscript Division, Baker Library, Harvard University, Cambridge, Mass.

Arnold, Arthur. 1864. *The History of the Cotton Famine*. London: Saunders, Otley and Co.

Arnot, Page. 1949. *The Miners: The History of the Miners' Federation of Great Britain 1889-1910*. London: Allen & Unwin.

Ashley, William. 1949 [1914]. *The Economic Organization of England. An Outline History*. London: Longmans, Green, and Co.

Ashton, T.S. 1955. *The Economic History of England: The 18th Century*. London: Methuen.

Ashworth, Henry. 1972 [1838]. "An Inquiry Into the Origins, Progress, And Results of the Strike of the Operative Cotton Spinners of Preston," in *Rebirth of the Trade Union Movement: Five Pamphlets 1838-1847*. New York: Arno Press.

Aspinall, A., ed. 1949. *Early English Trade Unions: Documents from the Home Office Papers of the Public Record Office*. London: The Batchworth Press.

"A Study of a New England Factory Town." 1879. *Atlantic Monthly* 43:260 (June), 689-705.

Aurand, Harold. 1966. "The Workingmen's Benevolent Association." *Labor History* 7:1 (Winter), 19-34.

Averitt, Robert. 1968. *The Dual Economy: The Dynamics of American Industry Structure*. New York: W.W. Norton.

Bagnall, William. 1893. *The Textile Industries of the United States*. Vol. 1: *1639-1810*. Cambridge, Mass.: The Riverside Press.

Baines, Edward. 1960 [1835]. *History of the Cotton Manufacture in Great Britain*. New York: Augustus M. Kelley.

Baird, Robert. 1851. *The American Cotton Spinner, and Managers' and Carders' Guide*. Philadelphia: A. Hart.

Barck, Oscar. 1931. *New York During the War of Independence*. New York: Columbia University Press.

Batchelder, Samuel. 1863. *Introduction and Early Progress of the Cotton Manufacture in the United States*. Boston: Little, Brown, and Co.

Bean, William. 1873. *The City of Cohoes: Its Past and Present History, and Future Prospects*. Cohoes, New York: "The Cataract" Book and Job Printing Office.

Bemis, Edward. 1894. "The Homestead Strike." *Journal of Political Economy* 2 (June), 369-396.

Benson, John. 1980. *British Coalminers in the Nineteenth Century: A Social History*. New York: Holmes and Meier.

Berg, Maxine. 1985. *The Age of Manufacture: Industry, Innovation and Work in Britain 1700-1820*. Totowa, New Jersey: Barnes and Noble.

Berg, Maxine; Hudson, Pat; and Sonenscher, Michael, eds. 1983. *Manufacture in Town and Country before the Factory*. Cambridge: Cambridge University Press.

Berthoff, Rowland. 1953. *British Immigrants in Industrial America, 1790-1950*. Cambridge. Mass.: Harvard University Press.

Bigelow, Jacob. 1829. *Elements of Technology*. Boston: Hilliard, Gray, Little, and Wilkins.

Bloomberg, Susan. 1974. "Industrialization and Skilled Labor: Newark, 1826 to 1860." Ph.D. diss., University of Michigan.

Boston Advertiser. 1879.

Boston Globe. 1875, 1879.

Boston Herald. 1879.

Brady, Dorothy. 1967. "Comment," in *The Growth of Seaport Cities 1790-1825*, David Gilchrist, ed. Charlottesville: The University of Virginia Press.

Braverman, Harry. 1974. *Labor and Monopoly Capital: The Degradation of Work in the Twentieth Century*. New York: Monthly Review Press.

Bridenbaugh, Carl. 1950. *The Colonial Craftsman*. New York: New York University Press.

Brierley, Ben. 1885. *Ab-O'th'-Yate in Yankeeland: The Results of Two Trips to America*. London: Simpkin, Marshall and Co.

British Association for the Advancement of Science. 1887. *On the Regulation of Wages by Means of Lists in the Cotton Industry*. Manchester: Heywood.

Brody, David. 1960. *Steelworkers in America: The Non-Union Era*. Cambridge, Mass.:

Harvard University Press.

Bromwell, William. 1856. *History of Immigration to the United States*. New York: Bedfield.

Brooks, Robert. 1935. "The United Textile Workers of America." Ph.D. diss., Yale University.

Buchanan, Robertson. 1841. *Practical Essays on Mill Work and Other Machinery*. 3rd Edition. London: John Weale.

Burgess, Keith. 1975. *The Origins of British Industrial Relations*. London: Croom Helm.

Burn, Duncan. 1961 [1940]. *The Economic History of Steel Making, 1867-1939*. Cambridge: Cambridge University Press.

Burnham, T.H., and Hoskins, G.O. 1943. *Iron and Steel in Britain, 1870-1930*. London: Allen and Unwin.

Butt, John. 1987. "Labour and Industrial Relations in the Scottish Cotton Industry during the Industrial Revolution," in *Scottish Textile History*, John Butt and Kenneth Ponting, eds. Aberdeen, Scotland: Aberdeen University Press.

Butterworth, Edwin. 1856. *Historical Sketches of Oldham*. Oldham: John Hirst.

Butterworth, James. 1823. *A Complete History of the Cotton Trade Including also that of the Silk, Calico Printing, and Hat Manufactures with Remarks on their Progress in Bolton, Bury, Stockport, Blackburn, and Wigan*. Manchester: C.W. Leake.

Bythell, Duncan. 1969. *The Handloom Weavers: A Study of the English Cotton Industry During the Industrial Revolution*. London: Cambridge University Press.

Carr, J.C., and Taplin, W. 1962. *History of the British Steel Industry*. Cambridge, Mass.: Harvard University Press.

Catling, Harold. 1970. *The Spinning Mule*. Newton Abbot, Devon, England: David and Charles.

_____. 1978. "The Development of the Spinning Mule." *Textile History*, 9, 35-57.

Chaloner, W.H. 1954. "Robert Owen, Peter Drinkwater and the Early Factory System in Manchester, 1788-1800." *Bulletin of the John Rylands Library* 37:1 (September), 78-102.

Chandler, Alfred. 1977. *The Visible Hand: The Managerial Revolution in American Business*. Cambridge, Mass.: Harvard University Press.

Chapman, S.D. 1967. *The Early Factory Masters: The Transition to the Factory System in the Midlands Textile Industry*. Newton Abbot, Devon, England: David and Charles.

_____. 1971. "Fixed Capital in the British Cotton Manufacturing Industry," in *Aspects of Capital Investment in Britain 1750-1850*. J.P.P. Higgins and Sidney Pollard, eds. London: Methuen.

_____. 1972. *The Cotton Industry in the Industrial Revolution*. London: Macmillan.

Chapman, S.J. 1899. "The Regulation of Wages by Lists in the Spinning Industry." *Economic Journal* 9:36 (December), 592-99.

_____. 1900. "Some Policies of the Cotton Spinners' Trade Unions." *Economic Journal* 10:40 (December), 467-73.

_____. 1904. *The Lancashire Cotton Industry: A Study of Economic Development*. Manchester: Manchester University Press.

Chapman, S.J., and Abbott, W. 1913. "The Tendency of Children to Enter Their Fathers'

Trades." *Journal of the Royal Statistical Society* 76 (May), 599-604.

Clapham, J.H. 1950 [1926]. *An Economic History of Modern Britain*. Vol. 1: *The Early Railway Age 1820-1850*, Vol. 2: *Free Trade and Steel 1850-1886*. London: Cambridge University Press.

Clark, Gregory. 1984. "Authority and Efficiency: The Labor Market and the Managerial Revolution of the Late Nineteenth Century." *Journal of Economic History* 44:4 (December), 1069-83.

Clark, Victor. 1929. *History of Manufactures in the United States*. Vol. 1: *1607-1860*, Vol. 2: *1860-1893*. New York: McGraw Hill.

Clegg, H.A.; Fox, Allen; and Thompson, A.F. 1964. *The History of British Trade Unionism Since 1889*. Vol. 1: *1889-1910*. Oxford: The Clarendon Press.

Clements, R.V. 1955. "Trade Unions and Emigration, 1840-80." *Population Studies* 9:2 (November), 167-80.

Cole, G.D.H. 1953. *Attempts at General Union: A Study of British Trade Unionism 1818-1834*. London: Macmillan.

Coleman, D.C. 1975. *Industry in Tudor and Stuart England*. London: Macmillan.

_____. 1977. *The Economy of England 1450-1750*. Oxford: Oxford University Press.

_____. 1983. "Proto-Industrialization: A Concept too Many." *Economic History Review*, 2nd Series, 36:3 (August), 335-48.

Coleman, Peter. 1963. *The Transformation of Rhode Island, 1790-1860*. Providence: Brown University Press.

Collier, Frances. 1968 [1964]. *The Family Economy and the Working Classes in the Cotton Industry, 1784-1833*. New York: Augustus M. Kelley.

Commons, John. 1929. "American Shoemakers 1648-1895: A Sketch of Industrial Revolution." *Quarterly Journal of Economics* 24 (November), 39-84.

_____ et al. 1946 [1918]. *History of the Labor Movement in the United States*. Vol. 1. New York: International Publishers.

_____ et al., eds. 1958 [1910]. *Documentary History of American Industrial Society*. Vol. 3, 4. New York: Russel and Russel.

Copeland, Melvin T. 1966 [1917]. *The Cotton Manufacturing Industry of the United States*. New York: Augustus M. Kelley.

Corbin, David. 1981. *Life, Work and Rebellion in the Coal Fields: The Southern West Virginia Miners 1880-1922*. Urbana: University of Illinois Press.

Court, W.H.B. 1938. *The Rise of the Midland Industries 1600-1838*. London: Oxford University Press.

Coxe, Tench. 1972 [1814]. "Digest of Manufacture," in *The New American State Papers, Manufactures*, Thomas Cochran, ed., vol. 1. Wilmington, Delaware: Scholarly Resources, Inc.

Creamer, Daniel. 1941. "Recruiting Contract Laborers for the Amoskeag Mills." *Journal of Economic History* 1:1 (May), 42-56.

Cumbler, John. 1979. *Working Class Community in Industrial America: Work, Leisure, and Struggle in Two Industrial Cities, 1880-1930*. Westport, Conn.: Greenwood Press.

Daniels, George. 1917-1918. "The Cotton Trade at the Close of the Napoleonic War." *Transactions of the Manchester Statistical Society*, 1-29 .

_____. 1920. *The Early Cotton Industry with some Unpublished Letters of Samuel*

Crompton. Manchester: Manchester University Press.

_____. 1930. "Samuel Crompton's Census of the Cotton Industry in 1811." *Economic Journal (Economic History Supplement)* 2 (January), 107-10.

Day, Clive. 1925. "The Early Development of the American Cotton Manufacture." *Quarterly Journal of Economics* 39:3 (May), 450-68.

Deane, Phyllis. 1957. "The Output of the British Woolen Industry in the Eighteenth Century. " *Journal of Economic History* 17: 2 (June), 207-23.

Deane, Phyllis, and Cole, W.A. 1967 [1962]. *British Economic Growth 1688-1959: Trends and Structure*. London: Cambridge University Press.

Dobson, C.R. 1980. *Master and Journeymen: A Prehistory of the Industrial Revolution 1717-1800*. London: Croom Helm.

Dodd, George. 1851. *The Textile Manufacture of Great Britain*. London: C. Cox.

Dublin, Thomas. 1979. *Women at Work: The Transformation of Work and Community in Lowell, Massachusetts, 1826-1860*. New York: Columbia University Press.

_____. 1985. "Women and Outwork in a Nineteenth-Century New England Town: Fitzwilliam, New Hampshire, 1830-1850," in *The Countryside in the Age of Capitalist Transformation: Essays in the Social History of Rural America*, Steve Hahn and Jonathan Prude, eds. Chapel Hill: University of North Carolina Press.

Earl, Henry. 1877. *A Centennial History of Fall River, Mass.: Comprising a Record of its Corporate Progress from 1656 to 1876 with Sketches of its Manufacturing Industries*. New York: Atlantic.

Earle, Carville, and Hoffman, Ronald. 1980. "The Foundation of the Modern Economy: Agriculture and the Costs of Labor in the United States and England, 1800-1860." *American Historical Review* 85:5 (December), 1055-94.

Economist. 1854, 1861-1864.

Edwards, Michael. 1967. *The Growth of the British Cotton Trade 1780-1815*. Manchester: Manchester University Press.

Edwards, M.M., and Lloyd-Jones, R. 1973. "N.J. Smelser and the Cotton Factory Family: A Reassessment," in *Textile History and Economic History*, N.B. Harte and K.G. Ponting, eds. Manchester: Manchester University Press.

Edwards, Richard. 1979. *Contested Terrain: The Transformation of the Workplace in the Twentieth Century*. New York: Basic Books.

Elbaum, Bernard. 1986. "The Steel Industry before World War I," in *The Decline of the British Economy*, Bernard Elbaum and William Lazonick, eds. Oxford: Clarendon Press.

Elbaum, Bernard, and Wilkinson, Frank. 1979. "Industrial Relations and Uneven Development: A Comparative Study of the American and British Steel Industries." *Cambridge Journal of Economics* 3:3 (September), 275-303.

Ellison, Thomas. 1968 [1886]. *The Cotton Trade of Great Britain*. New York: Augustus M. Kelley.

Engels, Friedrich. 1958 [1845]. *The Condition of the Working Class in England*. Stanford: Stanford University Press.

Erickson, Charlotte. 1949. "The Encouragement of Emigration by British Trade Unions, 1850-1900." *Population Studies* 3:3 (December), 248-73.

_____. 1957. *American Industry and European Immigrants, 1860-1865*. Cambridge: Harvard University Press.

_____. 1972. "Who Were the English and Scots Emigrants to the United States in the Late Nineteenth Century?" in *Population and Social Change*, Davld Glass and Roger Revelle, eds. London: Edward Arnold.

Evans, Chris. n.d. *History of the United Mine Workers of America from the Year 1860 to 1890*. Vol. 1. Indianapolis.

Evans, E.W. 1961. *The Miners of South Wales*. Cardiff: University of Wales Press.

Fairbairn, William. 1865. *Treatise on Mills and Millwork*, Part II. London: Longmans, Green and Co.

Fall River Daily Evening News. 1865-1866, 1870, 1875, 1879.

Fall River Daily Herald. 1879, 1888.

Fall River Directory Containing the City Record, the Names of Citizens, and a Business Directory with an Almanac for 1864. 1864. Boston: Adams, Sampson.

Fall River Weekly News. 1850-1851.

Farnie, D.A. 1979. *The English Cotton Industry and the World Market 1815-1896*. Oxford: Clarendon Press.

Field, John. 1978-1979. "British Historian and the Concept of Labor Aristocracy." *Radical History Review* 19 (Winter), 61-85.

Fitch, John. 1911. The Steelworkers, in *The Pittsburgh Survey*. New York: Russel Sage Foundation.

Fitton, R.S., and Wadsworth, A.P. 1958. *The Strutts and the Arkwrights 1758-1830: A Study of the Early Factory System*. Manchester: Manchester University Press.

Foner, Philip. 1947. *History of the Labor Movement in the United States*. New York: International Publishers.

Foster, John. 1974. *Class Struggle and the Industrial Revolution: Early Industrial Capitalism in Three English Towns*. New York: St. Martin.

_____. 1976. "Some Comments on 'Class Struggle and the Labour Aristocracy.' " *Social History* 1:3 (October), 357-66.

Fowler, Barbara. 1984. "Rhode Island Handloom Weavers and the Effects of Technological Change 1780-1840." Ph.D. diss., University of Pennsylvania.

Fraser, W.H. 1976. "The Glasgow Cotton Spinners, 1837," in *Scottish Themes: Essays in Honour of Professor S.G.E. Lythe*. John Butt and J.T. Ward, eds. Edinburgh: Scottish Academic Press.

Freifeld, Mary. 1980. "The Emergence of the American Working Classes: The Roots of Division, 1865-1885." Ph.D. diss., New York University.

_____. 1986. "Technological Change and the 'Self-Acting' Mule: A Study of Skill and Sexual Division of Labour." *Social History* 11:3 (October), 319-43.

French, Gilbert. 1862. *The Life and Times of Samuel Crompton*. Manchester: Charles Simms.

Friends of Domestic Industry. 1832. *Address to the People of the United States in their New York Convention, October 26, 1831*. Baltimore.

Fynes, Richard. 1923 [1873]. *The Miners of Northumberland and Durham*. Sunderland, Britain: T. Summerbell.

Gallatin, Albert. 1972 [1810]. "Manufacturies," in *New American State Papers, Manufactures*, Thomas Cochran, ed., vol. 1. Wilmington, Delaware: Scholarly Resources, Inc.

Gatrell, V.A.C. 1977. "Labour, Power, and the Size of Firms in Lancashire Cotton in the Second Quarter of the Nineteenth Century." *Economic History Review*,

2nd Series, 30:1 (February), 95-139.

George, Dorothy. 1926. *London Life in the XVIIIth Century.* New York: Knopf.

————. 1927. "The Combinations Laws Reconsidered." *Economic Journal (Economic History Supplement)* 1:2 (May), 214-28.

————. 1931. *England in Transition: Life and Work in the Eighteenth Century.* London: G. Routledge.

Gibb, George. 1950. *The Saco-Lowell Shops: Textile Machinery Building in New England, 1813-1949.* Cambridge: Harvard University Press.

Glen, Robert. 1984. *Urban Workers in the Early Industrial Revolution.* New York: St. Martin.

Green, Constance. 1968 [1939]. *Holyoke, Massachusetts: A Case History of the Industrial Revolution in America.* Hamden, Connecticut: Archon.

Greenberg, Dolores. 1982. "Reassessing the Power Patterns of the Industrial Revolution: An Anglo-American Comparison." *American Historical Review,* 87:5 (December), 1237-61.

Gregory, Frances. 1975. *Nathan Appleton, Merchant and Entrepreneur, 1779-1861.* Charlottesville: University of Virginia Press.

Griffin, John. 1939. *Strikes: A Study of Quantitative Economics.* New York: Columbia University Press.

Guest, Richard. 1968 [1823]. *A Compendious History of the Cotton Manufacture.* London: Cass.

Habakkuk, H.J. 1962. *American and British Technology in the 19th Century: The Search for Labour Saving Inventions.* London: Cambridge University Press.

Halevy, Elie. 1961 [1913]. *A History of the English People in the Nineteenth Century.* Vol. 1: *England in 1815.* New York: Barnes and Noble.

Hall, John. 1953. "The Gentle Craft: A Narrative of Yankee Shoemakers." Ph.D. diss., Columbia University.

Hamilton, Alexander. 1972 [1791]. "Manufacturies," in *The New American State Papers, Manufactures,* Thomas Cochran, ed., vol. 1. Wilmington, Delaware: Scholarly Resources, Inc.

Hamilton, Milton. 1964 [1936]. *The Country Printer, New York State 1785-1830.* Port Washington, New York: IRA Friedman.

Hammond, J.L., and Hammond, Barbara. 1920. *The Skilled Labourer, 1760-1832.* London: Longmans, Green and Co.

Hammond, M.B. 1897. *The Cotton Industry: An Essay in American Economic History.* New York: Macmillan.

Hayes, John. 1879. *American Textile Machinery.* Cambridge: University Press, John Wilson and Son.

Hazard, Blanche. 1921. *The Organization of the Boot and Shoe Industry in Massachusetts before 1875.* Cambridge, Mass.: Harvard University Press.

Heaton, Herbert. 1965 [1920]. *The Woollen and Worsted Industries From the Earliest Times up to the Industrial Revolution.* Oxford: The Clarendon Press.

————. 1929. "Benjamin Gott and the Anglo-American Cloth Trade." *Journal of Economic and Business History* 2:1 (November), 146-62.

————. 1941. "Yorkshire Cloth Traders in the United States 1770-1840." *Publication of the Choresby Society,* 37, part III.

Helm, Elijah. 1903. "The British Cotton Industry," in *British Industries,* W.J. Ashley, ed. London: Longmans, Green & Co.

Henderson, W.O. 1969 [1934]. *The Lancashire Cotton Famine 1861-1865*. New York: Augustus M. Kelley.

Henretta, James. 1978. "Families and Farms: Mentalit´e in Pre-Industrial America." *William and Mary Quarterly*, 3rd Series, 35:1 (January), 3-32.

Herman, Edward. 1983 [1981]. *Corporate Power, Corporate Control*. New York: Cambridge University Press.

Hills, R.L. 1979. "Hargreaves, Arkwright and Crompton. Why Three Inventors?" *Textile History* 10, 114-26.

Hills, R.L., and Pacey, A.J. 1972. "The Measurement of Power in Early Steam Driven Textile Mills." *Technology and Culture* 13 (January), 25-43.

History of the Fall River Strike, Being a Full and Complete Report of the Labor Troubles from 1873 to April 5th, 1875. 1875. By a Workingman. Revised and corrected by John Smith. Fall River: Clark and Co.

Hobsbawm, Eric. 1964. "The Labour Aristocracy in Nineteenth-Century Britain," in *Labouring Men*, Eric Hobsbawm, ed. London: Weidenfield & Nicolson.

_____. 1984. "Artisans and Labour Aristocrats," in *Workers: Worlds of Labor*, Eric Hobsbawm, ed. New York: Pantheon.

_____. 1984. "Debating the Labour Aristocracy," in *Workers*, Eric Hobsbawm, ed. New York: Pantheon.

_____. 1984. "The Aristocracy of Labour Reconsidered," in *Workers*, Eric Hobsbawm, ed. New York: Pantheon.

Holt, James. 1977. "Trade Unionism in the British and U.S. Steel Industries, 1880-1914: A Comparative Study." *Labor History* 18:1 (Winter), 5-35.

Honeyman, Katrina. 1983 [1982]. *Origins of Enterprise: Business Leadership in the Industrial Revolution*. New York: St. Martin.

Houston, Rab, and Snell, K.D.M. 1984. "Historiographical Review: Proto-Industrialization? Cotton Industry, Social Change, and Industrial Revolution." *Historical Journal* 27:2 (June), 473-92.

Howard, N.P. 1973. "The Strikes and Lockouts in the Iron Industry and the Formation of the Ironworkers' Unions, 1862-1868." *International Review of Social History*, 18, part 3, 396-427.

Howard, Robert. 1888. "Progress in the Textile Trades," in *The Labor Movement: The Problem of To-Day*, George McNeill, ed. New York: M.W. Hazen.

Huchinson, E.P. 1956. *Immigrants and their Children, 1850-1950*. New York: John Wiley.

Hunter, Louis. 1979. *A History of Industrial Power in the United States, 1780-1930*. Vol. 1: *Waterpower in the Century of the Steam Engine*. Charlottesville: University of Virginia Press.

James, John. 1857. *History of the Worsted Manufacture in England*. London: Longman, Brown, Green, Longmans, and Roberts.

Jeans, Stephen. 1902. *American Industrial Conditions and Competition*. London: British Iron and Trade Association.

Jeremy, David. 1971. "British and American Yarn Count Systems: A Historical Analysis." *Business History Review* 45:3 (Autumn), 336-57.

_____. 1973. "Innovation in American Textile Technology during the Early 19th Century." *Technology and Culture* 14:1 (January), 40-76.

_____. 1973. "British Textile Technology Transmission to the United States: The Philadelphia Experience, 1770-1820." *Business History Review* 47:1 (Spring), 24-52.

_____. 1981. *Transatlantic Industrial Revolution: The Diffusion of Textile Technologies Between Britain and America, 1790-1830s.* Cambridge: MIT Press.

Jevons, William. 1860. "An Account of the Spinners' Strike at Ashton-Under-Lyne in 1830," in *Trades' Societies and Strikes*, National Association for the Promotion of Social Science, ed. London: John Parker.

Jewkes, John. 1930. "The Localization of the Cotton Industry." *Economic Journal* (*Economic History Supplement*) 2, 91-106.

Jewkes, John, and Gray, E.M. 1935. *Wages and Labour in the Lancashire Cotton Spinning Industry.* Manchester: Manchester University Press.

Johnson, Stanley. 1913. *A History of Emigration from the United Kingdom to North America, 1763-1912.* London: G. Routledge.

Johnston, H.J.M. 1972. *British Emigration Policy, 1815-1830: "Shovelling out Paupers."* Oxford: Clarendon Press.

Joyce, Patrick. 1980. *Work, Society and Politics: The Culture of the Factory in Later Victorian England.* New Brunswick: Rutgers University Press.

Kennedy, John. 1819. "Observations on the Rise and Progress of the Cotton Trade in Great Britain, Particularly in Lancashire and Adjoining Counties." *Memoirs of the Literary and Philosophical Society of Manchester* 3, 115-37.

_____. 1831. "A Brief Memoir of Samuel Crompton, with a Description of his Machine Called the Mule and of the Subsequent Improvement of the Machine by Others." *Memoirs of the Literary and Philosophical Society of Manchester*, 5, 318-53.

Kirby, R.G., and Musson, A.E. 1975. *The Voice of the People: John Doherty, 1798-1854, Trade Unionist, Radical, and Reformist.* Manchester: Manchester University Press.

Knowles, K.G.J.C. 1952. *Strikes—A Study of Industrial Conflict with Special Reference to British Experience Between 1911 and 1947.* Oxford: Basil Blackwell.

Knowlton, Evelyn. 1948. *Pepperell's Progress: History of a Cotton Textile Company, 1844-1945.* Cambridge, Mass.: Harvard University Press.

Korson, George. 1938. *Minstrels of the Mine Patch: Songs and Stories of the Anthracite Industry.* Philadelphia: University of Pennsylvania Press.

Kriete, Peter, Medick, Hans, and Schlumbohm, Jurgen. 1981 [1977]. *Industrialization before Industrialization: Rural Industry in the Genesis of Capitalism.* Cambridge: Cambridge University Press.

Kulik, Gary. 1978. "Pawtucket Village and the Strike of 1824: The Origins of Class Conflict in Rhode Island." *Radical History Review* 17 (Spring), 5-37.

_____. 1980. "The Beginning of the Industrial Revolution in America: Pawtucket, Rhode Island, 1672-1829." Ph.D. diss., Brown University.

Kulik, Gary, Park, Rogers, and Penn, Theodore, eds. 1982. *The New England Mill Village, 1790-1860.* Cambridge: MIT Press.

Labor Standard (Fall River). 1879-1880.

Lahne, Herbert. 1944. *The Cotton Mill Worker.* New York: Farrar and Rinehart.

Landes, David. 1972 [1969]. *The Unbound Prometheus: Technological Change and Industrial Development in Western Europe from 1750 to the Present.* New York: Cambridge University Press.

_____. 1986. "What Do Bosses Really Do?" *Journal of Economic History* 46:3 (September), 585-623.

Laslett, John. 1983. *Nature's Noblemen: The Fortunes of the Independent Collier in Scotland and the American Midwest, 1855-1889*. Los Angeles: Institute of Industrial Relations, University of California, Los Angeles.

Lauri, Bruce. 1980. *Working People of Philadelphia, 1800-1850*. Philadelphia: Temple University Press.

Lazonick, William. 1979. "Industrial Relations and Technical Change: The Case of the Self-Acting Mule." *Cambridge Journal of Economics* 3:3 (September), 231-62.

_____. 1981. "Conflict and Control in the Industrial Revolution: Social Relations in the British Cotton Factory," in *Essays from the Lowell Conference on Industrial History, 1980 and 1981*, Robert Weible, Oliver Ford, and Paul Marion, eds. Lowell: Lowell Conference on Industrial History.

_____. 1981. "Factor Costs and the Diffusion of Ring Spinning in Britain Prior to World War I." *Quarterly Journal of Economics* 96:1 (February), 89-109.

_____. 1981. "Production Relations, Labor Productivity, and the Choice of Technique: British and American Cotton Spinning." *Journal of Economic History* 41:3 (November), 491-516.

_____. 1983. "Industrial Organization and Technological Change: The Decline of the British Cotton Industry." *Business History Review* 57:2 (Summer), 195-236.

_____. 1983. "Technological Change and Control of Work: The Development of Capital-Labour Relations in US Mass Production Industries," in *Managerial Strategies and Industrial Relations*, Howard Gospel and Craig Littler, eds. London: Heinemann.

_____. 1984. "Rings and Mules in Britain: Reply." *Quarterly Journal of Economics* 99:2 (May), 393-98.

_____. 1987. "Stubborn Mules: Some Comments." *Economic History Review*, 2nd Ser., 40:1 (February), 80-86.

Lazonick, William, and Mass, William. 1984. "The Performance of the British Cotton Industry, 1870-1913." *Research in Economic History*, 9, 1-44.

Lee, C.H. 1972. *A Cotton Enterprise, 1795-1840: A History of M'Connel & Kennedy, Fine Cotton Spinners*. Manchester: Manchester University Press.

Leeson, R.A. 1979. *Travelling Brothers: The Six Centuries Road From Craft Fellowship to Trade Unionism*. London: G. Allen and Unwin.

Leigh, Evan. 1873. *The Science of Modern Cotton Spinning*. Vol. 1, 2. Manchester: Palmer and Howe.

Lincoln, Jonathan. 1909. "The Sliding Scale of Wages in the Cotton Industry." *Quarterly Journal of Economics* 23 (May), 451-69.

Lintner, Silvia. 1945. "A Social History of Fall River, 1859-1879." Ph.D. diss., Radcliffe College.

_____. 1948. "Mill Architecture in Fall River: 1865-1880." *The New England Quarterly* 21: 2 (June), 185-203.

Lipson, Ephraim. 1959 [1915]. *The Economic History of England*. Vol. 1: *The Middle Ages*. London: A. and C. Black.

Lomax, J.W. 1913. *Fine Cotton Spinning: A Practical Manual*. Manchester: Emmott.

Longmate, Norman. 1978. *The Hungry Mills: The Story of the Lancashire Cotton Famine, 1861-1865*. London: Temple Smith.

Lowe, J. 1860. "An Account of the Strike in the Cotton Trade at Preston in 1853,"
    in *Trades' Societies and Strikes*, National Association for the Promotion of Social
    Science, ed. London: John Parker.
Lushington, Godfrey. 1860. "Abstract of the Evidence on Combinations of Workmen,
    Taken before a Select Committee of the House of Commons in 1838," in *Trades'
    Societies and Strikes*, National Association for the Promotion of Social Science,
    ed. London: John Parker.
Macara, Charles. 1921. *Recollections*. London: Cassell & Co.
_____. 1923. *The New Industrial Era*. Manchester: Sherratt and Hughes.
Macaulay, James. 1871. *Across the Ferry: First Impressions of America and its Peo-
    ple*. London: Hodder and Stoughton.
MacMurray, Robert. 1970. "Technological Change in the American Cotton Spinning
    Industry, 1790 to 1836." Ph.D. diss., University of Pennsylvania.
Mann, James. 1968 [1860]. *The Cotton Trade of Great Britain*. London: Cass.
Mann, Julia de Lacy. 1958. "The Textile Industry: Machinery for Cotton, Flax, Wool,
    1760-1850," in *A History of Technology*, Vol. 4: *The Industrial Revolution*, Charles
    Singer, E.J. Holmyard, A.R. Hall, and Trevor Williams, eds. London: Oxford
    University Press.
_____. 1971. *The Cloth Industry in the West of England from 1640 to 1880*.
    Oxford: Clarendon Press.
Mantoux, Paul. 1965 [1928]. *The Industrial Revolution in the Eighteenth Century:
    An Outline of the Beginning of the Modern Factory System in Britain*. New York:
    Harper and Row.
Marglin, Stephen. 1974. "What Do Bosses Do? The Origins and Functions of Hier-
    archy in Capitalist Production." *The Review of Radical Political Economists* 6:2
    (Summer), 60-112.
Marsden, Richard. 1895. *Cotton Weaving*. London: George Bell.
_____. 1904 [1884]. *Cotton Spinning*. London: George Bell.
Marx, Karl. 1967 [1867]. *Capital: A Critique of Political Economy*. New York: Inter-
    national Publishers.
Mass, William. 1984. "Technological Change and Industrial Relations: The Diffusion
    of Automatic Weaving in the United States and Britain." Ph.D. diss., Boston
    College.
Massachusetts, Bureau of Statistics of Labor. 1870. *First Annual Report*.
_____. 1871. *Second Annual Report*.
_____. 1872. *Third Annual Report*.
_____. 1878. *Ninth Annual Report*.
_____. 1880. *Eleventh Annual Report*.
_____. 1882. *Thirteenth Annual Report*.
Massachusetts Senate Document No. 21 (1868).
McAlister, Coleman. 1943. *Men of Coal*. New York: Farrar and Rinehart.
McConnel, John W. 1906. *A Century of Fine Cotton Spinning: McConnel & Co. Ltd.,
    1790-1906*. Manchester: George Falkner.
McCulloch, J.R. 1827. "The Rise, Progress, Present State, and Prospects of the British
    Cotton Manufacture." *Edinburgh Review* 46 (June), 1-39.
McGouldrick, Paul. 1968. *New England Textiles in the Nineteenth Century: Profits
    and Investment*. Cambridge: Harvard University Press.

McLane, Louis. 1972 [1833]. "Documents Relative to the Manufacture of the United States," in *The American State Papers: Manufactures*, Thomas Cochran, ed. Vols. 3-7. Wilmington, Delaware: Scholarly Resources, Inc.

Merrill, Michael. 1977. "Cash is Good to Eat: Self Sufficiency and Exchange in the Rural Economy of the United States." *Radical History Review* 4:1 (Winter), 42-71.

Metacomet Manufacturing Company (Fall River). KB-l, Labor Book, 1850-1854. Manuscript Division, Baker Library, Harvard University, Cambridge, Mass.

Miller, Richard. 1975. "Gentry and Entrepreneurs: A Socioeconomic Analysis of Philadelphia in the 1790's." *Rocky Mountain Social Science* 12:1 (January), 71-84.

Mitchell, B.R. 1962. *Abstract of British Historical Statistics*. Cambridge: Cambridge University Press.

Montgomery, David. 1967. *Beyond Equality: Labor and Radical Republicans, 1862-1872*. New York: Knopf.

_____. 1979.*Workers' Control in America: Studies in the History of Work, Technology, and Labor Struggles*. New York: Cambridge University Press.

_____. 1987.*The Fall of the House of Labor: The Workplace, the State and American Labor Activism, 1865-1925*. Cambridge: Cambridge University Press.

Montgomery, James. 1836. *The Theory and Practice of Cotton Spinning or the Carding and Spinning Master's Assistant*. Glasgow: John Niven.

_____. 1969 [1840]. *A Practical Detail of the Cotton Manufacture of the United States of America, and the State of Cotton Manufacture of that Country Contrasted and Compared with that of Britain*. New York: Augustus M. Kelley.

Moorhouse, H.F. 1978. "The Marxist Theory of the Labour Aristocracy." *Social History* 3:1 (January), 61-82.

Morris, Morris David. 1960. "The Recruitment of an Industrial Labor Force in India, with British and American Comparisons." *Comparative Studies in Society and History* 2:3 (1960), 305-28.

Morris, J.H., and Williams, L.J. 1958. *The South Wales Coal Industry, 1841-1875*. Cardiff: University of Wales Press.

Morton, W.E., and Wray, G.R. 1966 [1937]. *An Introduction to the Study of Spinning*. London: Longmans.

Mosely Industrial Commission to the United States. October—December 1902. 1903. *Reports to the Delegates*. London: Cassell and Co.

Musson, A.E. 1976. "Industrial Motive Power in the United Kingdom, 1800-70." *Economic History Review*, 2nd Series, 29:3 (August), 415-39.

_____. 1976. "Class Struggle and the Labour Aristocracy, 1830-60." *Social History* 1:3 (October), 335-56.

Nash, Gary. 1979. *The Urban Crucible: Social Change, Political Consciousness, and the Origins of the American Revolution*. Cambridge, Mass.: Harvard University Press.

Nasmith, Joseph. 1896. *Students' Cotton Spinning*. London: John Heywood.

Navin, Thomas. 1950. *The Whitin Machine Works Since 1831: A Textile Machinery Company in An Industrial Village*. Cambridge, Mass.: Harvard University Press.

Needles, Samuel. 1884. "The Governor's Mill and the Globe Mills, Philadelphia." *Philadelphia Magazine of History and Biography*, 8, 377-90.

Neel, Joanne. 1968. *Phineas Bond: A Study in Anglo-American Relations, 1786-1812*. Philadelphia: University of Pennsylvania Press.

New England Cotton Manufacturers Association (Boston). 1871. *Proceedings of the Sixth Annual Meeting held at Boston, April 19, 1871.*

_____. 1872. *Statistics of Cotton Manufactures in New England, 1866.*

_____. 1872. *Proceedings of the Seventh Annual Meeting held at Boston, April 17, 1872.*

_____. 1873. *Proceedings of the Semi-Annual Meeting held at Boston, October 19, 1870.*

_____. 1873. *Proceedings of the Semi-Annual Meeting held at Boston, October 15, 1873.*

_____. 1883. *Proceedings of the Eighteenth Annual Meeting held at Boston, April 25, 1883.*

_____. 1891. *Proceedings of the Twenty-Sixth Annual Meeting held at Boston, April 29, 1891.*

New York Journal of Commerce. 1875.

Ogden, Samuel. 1815. *Thoughts, What Probable Effects the Peace with Great Britain will have on the Cotton Manufactures of this Country; Interspersed with Remarks on Our Bad Management in the Business; and the Way to Improvement, so as to Meet Imported Goods in Cheapness, at our Home Market.* Providence: Goddard & Mann.

Olton, Charles. 1975. *Artisans for Independence: Philadelphia Mechanics and the American Revolution.* Syracuse, New York: Syracuse University Press.

"On Combinations of Trades." 1972 [1831]. Anonymous, in *Trade Unions in the Early 1830's: Seven Pamphlets, 1831-1837.* New York: Arno Press.

Penn, Rogers. 1984. *Skilled Workers in the Class Structure.* Cambridge: Cambridge University Press.

Pennsylvania Senate Journal. 1837-38. "Committee Appointed . . . for the Purpose of Investigating and Inquiring into the System of Labor adopted in Cotton and Other Factories," vol. 1, 322-27; and "Testimony of Witnesses, Accompanying the Report of the Committee of the Senate, Appointed to Investigate the Subject of the Employment of Children in Manufacturies," vol. 2, 278-359. Harrisburg: Thompson and Clark.

"People of a New England Factory Village." 1880. *Atlantic Monthly* 46:276 (October), 460-64.

Persons, Charles. 1911. "The Early History of Factory Legislation in Massachusetts," in *Labor Laws and their Enforcement*, Susan Kingsbury, ed. New York: Longmans, Green and Co.

Pinchbeck, Ivy. 1930. *Women Workers in the Industrial Revolution, 1750-1850.* New York: F.S. Crofts.

Piore, Michael. 1980. "The Technological Foundations of Dualism and Discontinuity," in *Dualism and Discontinuity in Industrial Societies*, Suzanne Berger and Michael Piore, eds. Cambridge: Cambridge University Press.

Piore, Michael, and Sabel, Charles. 1984. *The Second Industrial Divide: Possibilities for Prosperity.* New York: Basic Books.

Pollard, Sidney. 1963. "Factory Discipline in the Industrial Revolution." *Economic History Review*, 2nd Series, 16 (December), 254-71.

_____. 1964. "The Factory Village in the Industrial Revolution." *English Historical Review* 79:312 (July), 513-31.

_____. 1965. *The Genesis of Modern Management: A Study of the Industrial Revolution in Great Britain*. Cambridge, Mass.: Harvard University Press.

Porter, J.H. 1967. "Industrial Peace in the Cotton Trade, 1875-1913." *Yorkshire Bulletin of Economic and Social Research* 19:1 (May), 49-61.

_____. 1970. "Wage Bargaining under Conciliation Agreements, 1860-1914." *Economic History Review*, 2nd Ser., 23:3 (December), 460-75.

Potter, J. 1960. "Atlantic Economy, 1815-60: The U.S.A. and the Industrial Revolution in Britain," in *Studies in the Industrial Revolution*, L.S. Pressnell, ed. London: The Athlone Press.

Providence Journal. 1850-1851.

Prude, Jonathan. 1983. *The Coming of Industrial Order: Town and Factory Life in Rural Massachusetts, 1810-1860*. New York: Cambridge University Press.

Pugh, Arthur. 1951. *Men of Steel: A Chronicle of Eighty-Eight Years of Trade Unionism in the British Iron and Steel Industry*. London: Iron and Steel Trades Federation.

Quimby, Ian. 1967. "The Cordwainers' Protest: A Crisis in Labor Relations." *Winterthur Portfolio*, 3, 83-101.

Radcliffe, William. 1828. *Origins of the New System of Manufacture Commonly Called "Power Loom Weaving"*. Stockport, England: Lomax.

Rees, Abraham. 1819. *The Cyclopaedia or Universal Dictionary of Arts, Sciences and Literature*. 39 vols. Vol. 10: "Cotton Manufacture," Vol. 22: "Manufacture of Cotton." London: Longman, Hurst, Rees, Orme, and Brown.

Roberts, Bryan. 1978. "Agrarian Organization and Urban Development," in *Manchester and San Paulo: Problems of Rapid Urban Growth*, J.O. Wirth and R.L. Jones, eds. Stanford: Stanford University Press.

Robinson, Jesse. 1920. *The Amalgamated Association of Iron, Steel, and Tin Workers*. Baltimore: Johns Hopkins University Press.

Rosenberg, Nathan. 1967. "Anglo-American Wage Differences in the 1820's." *Journal of Economic History* 27:2 (June), 221-29.

_____. 1972. *Technology and American Economic Growth*. New York: Harper and Row.

_____. 1976. *Perspectives on Technology*. Cambridge: Cambridge University Press.

Roy, Andrew. 1907. *A History of Coal Miners of the United States from the Development of the Mines to the Close of the Anthracite Strike of 1902*. Columbus, Ohio: Trauger Printing Co.

Sabel, Charles. 1984 [1982]. *Work and Politics: The Division of Labor in Industry*. New York: Cambridge University Press.

Sabel, Charles, and Zeitlin, Jonathan. 1985. "Historical Alternative to Mass Production: Politics, Markets and Technology in Nineteenth Century Industrialization." *Past and Present* 108 (August), 133-76.

Salinger, Sharon. 1981. "Colonial Labor in Transition: The Decline of Indentured Servitude in Late Eighteenth Century Philadelphia." *Labor History* 22:2 (Spring), 165-91.

_____. 1983. "Artisans, Journeymen, and the Transformation of Labor in Late Eighteenth Century Philadelphia." *William and Mary Quarterly*, 3rd Series, 40:1 (January), 62-84.

Sandberg, Lars. 1968. "Movements in the Quality of British Cotton Textile Exports,

1815-1913." *Journal of Economic History* 28:1 (March), 1-27.

_____. 1979. "American Rings and English Mules: The Role of Economic Rationality," in *Technological Change: The United States and Britain in the Nineteenth Century*, S.B. Saul, ed. London: Methuen.

_____. 1984. "The Remembrance of Things Past: Rings and Mules Revisited." *Quarterly Journal of Economics* 99:2 (May), 387-92.

Saxonhouse, Gary, and Wright, Gavin. 1984. "Ring and Mules Around the World: A Comparative Study in Technological Choice." *Research in Economic History*, Suppl. 3, 271-300. JAI Press, Inc.

_____. 1984. "New Evidence on the Stubborn English Mule and the Cotton Industry, 1878-1920." *Economic History Review*, 2nd Series, 37:4 (November), 507-19.

_____ 1987. "Stubborn Mules and Vertical Integration: The Disappearing Constraint?" Economic History Review, 2nd Series, 40:1 (February), 87-94.

Schlegel, Marvin. 1943. "The Workingmen's Benevolent Association: First Union of Anthracite Miners." *Pennsylvania History* 10:4 (October), 243-67.

_____. 1946. "America's First Cartel." *Pennsylvania History* 13:1 (January), 1-16.

Schulze-Gaevernitz, G. 1893. *Social Peace: A Study of the Trade Union Movement in England*. London: Swan Sonnenschein.

_____. 1895. *The Cotton Trade in England and on the Continent*. London: Simpkin, Marshall, Hamilton, Kent and Co.

Scott, R. 1851. *The Practical Cotton Spinner and Manufacturer: The Managers', Overlookers', and Mechanics' Companion*. Corrected and enlarged by Oliver Byrne. Philadelphia: Henry Carey Baird.

Scranton, Philip. 1983. *Propriety Capitalism: The Textile Manufacture at Philadelphia, 1800-1885*. New York: Cambridge University Press.

Shelton, Cynthia. 1986. *The Mills of Manayunk: Industrialization and Social Conflict in the Philadelphia Region, 1787-1837*. Baltimore: The Johns Hopkins Press.

Shepperson, W.S. 1953. "Industrial Emigration in Early Victorian Britain." *Journal of Economic History* 13:2 (Spring), 179-92.

_____. 1957. *British Emigration to North America: Projects and Opinions in the Early Victorian Period*. Minneapolis: University of Minnesota Press.

Shorter, Edward, and Tilly, Charles. 1974. *Strikes in France, 1830-1968*. London: Cambridge University Press.

Silver, Rollo. 1967. *The American Printer, 1787-1825*. Charlottesville: University of Virginia Press.

Silvia, Philip. 1973. "The Spindle City: Labor, Politics, and Religion in Fall River, Massachusetts, 1870-1905." Ph.D. diss., Fordham University.

Simmons, P.L. 1876. *Waste Products and Undeveloped Substances*. London: Hardwicke and Bogue.

Sisson, William. 1985. "Bell Hours: Work Values and Discipline in the American Textile Industry, 1787-1880." Ph.D. diss., University of Delaware.

Slater Collection. Union Mills (Webster, Massachusetts). Slater and Kimball, vol. 3: Agreements With Help 1827-1837; vol. 144: Time Books 1836-1848. Steam Manufacturing Company (Providence, R.I.), vols. 16, 17, 18: Time Books 1828-1836. Manuscript Division, Baker Library, Harvard University, Cambridge, Massachusetts.

Smelser, Neil. 1959. *Social Change in the Industrial Revolution: An Application of Theory to the British Cotton Industry*. Chicago: Chicago University Press.

Smiles, Samuel. 1876 [1864]. *Industrial Biography: Iron Workers and Tool Makers*. London: John Murray.

Smith, Billy. 1981. "The Material Lives of Laboring Philadelphians, 1750 to 1800." *William and Mary Quarterly*, 3rd Series, 38:2 (April), 163-202.

Smith, Ronald. 1961. "An Oldham Limited Liability Company, 1875-1896." *Business History* 4:1 (December), 34-53.

Smout, T.C. 1969. *A History of the Scottish People, 1560-1830*. London: Collins.

Snell, Daniel. 1850. *The Manager's Assistant, Being a Condensed Treatise on the Cotton Manufacture*. Hartford, Conn.

Spahr, Charles. 1899. "The Old Factory Town in New England." *Outlook* 61:5 (4 February), 285-94.

Spalding, Robert. 1963. "The Boston Mercantile Community and the Promotion of the Textile Industry in New England, 1813-1860." Ph.D. diss., Yale University.

Statistics of the Condition and Products of Certain Branches of Industry in Massachusetts for the Year Ending April 1, 1846. 1846. Prepared by John G. Palfrey, Secretary of the Commonwealth. Boston: Dutton and Wentworth, State Printers.

Statistical Information Relating to Certain Branches of Industry in Massachusetts for the Year Ending May 1, 1865. 1966. Prepared by Oliver Warner, Secretary of the Commonwealth. Boston: Wright and Porter, State Printers.

Steffen, Charles. 1977. "Between Revolutions: The Pre-Factory Urban Worker in Baltimore, 1780-1820." Ph.D. diss., Northwestern University.

"Strikes." 1859. *Quarterly Review* 106, 485-522.

Suffern, Arthur. 1926. *The Coal Miners' Struggle for Industrial Status*. New York: Macmillan.

Sullivan, William. 1954. "The Industrial Revolution and the Factory Operative in Pennsylvania." *Pennsylvania Magazine of History and Biography* 78:4 (October), 476-94.

_____. 1972 [1955]. *The Industrial Worker in Pennsylvania 1800-1840*. New York: Johnson.

Sutcliffe, John. 1816. *A Treatise on Canals and Reservoirs... Likewise Observations on the best Mode of Carding, Roving, Drawing, and Spinning all Kinds of Cotton Twist*. Rochdale, England: J. Hartley.

Taussing, F.W. 1931 [1892]. *The Tariff History of the United States*. New York: G.P. Putnam's Sons.

Taylor, A.J. 1949. "Concentration and Specialization in the Lancashire Cotton Industry, 1825-1850." *Economic History Review*, 2nd Series, 1, 114-23.

_____. 1960. "The Sub-contract System in the British Coal Industry," in *Studies in the Industrial Revolution*, L.S. Pressnell, ed. London: The Athlone Press.

_____. 1961. "Labour Productivity and Technological Innovation in the British Coal Industry, 1850-1914." *Economic History Review*, 2nd Series, 14:1 (August), 48-70.

Temin, Peter. 1964. *Iron and Steel in Nineteenth Century America: An Economic Inquiry*. Cambridge, Mass.: M.I.T. Press.

_____. 1966. "Steam and Waterpower in the Early 19th Century." *Journal of*

Economic History 26:2 (June), 187-205.

"Textile Material Again." 1932. *Bulletin of the Business Historical Society* 6:3 (May), 6-12.

"The Case as it Now Stands between the Clothiers, Weavers, and other Manufacturers with regard to the Late Riot in the County of Wilts," by Philalethes (pseud.). 1972 [1739]. *In Labour Problems Before the Industrial Revolution: Four Pamphlets.* New York: Arno Press.

"The Cotton Manufacture in America." 1840. *Chambers' Edinburgh Journal* 9:464 (19 December), 379-80.

Thernstrom, Stephen. 1976 [1973]. *The Other Bostonians: Poverty and Progress in the American Metropolis, 1880-1970.* Cambridge. Mass.: Harvard University Press.

Thompson, E.P. 1966 [1963]. *The Making of the English Working Class.* New York: Vintage.

_____. 1967. "Time, Work-Discipline, and Industrial Capitalism." *Past and Present* 38 (December), 56-97.

Thorndike Manufacturing Company (Palmer, Massachusetts). Vol. 28: Payrolls, 1838-1842. Manuscript Division, Baker Library, Harvard University, Cambridge, Mass.

Thornley, Thomas. 1894. *Practical Treatise upon Self-Acting Mules.* Manchester: John Heywood.

_____. 1906. *Cotton Spinning.* Vol. 2: *Intermediate, or Second Year.* London: Scott, Greenwood and Son.

_____. 1912. *Cotton Waste: Its Production, Manipulation, and Uses.* London: Scott, Greenwood and Son.

Tilly, Charles. 1983. "Flows of Capital and Forms of Industry in Europe, 1500-1900." *Theory and Society* 12:2 (June), 123-42.

Times (London), 1863-1864, 1869.

Tippett, L.H.C. 1969. *A Portrait of the Lancashire Textile Industry.* London: Oxford University Press.

Tribune (New York). 1851, 1879.

Tryon, Rolla. 1917. *Household Manufactures in the United States, 1640-1860.* Chicago: Chicago University Press.

Tucker, Barbara. 1974. "Samuel Slater and Sons: The Emergence of the American Factory System, 1790-1860." Ph.D. diss., University of California, Davis.

_____. 1984. *Samuel Slater and the Origins of the American Textile Industry, 1790-1860.* Ithaca: Cornell University Press.

Tufnell, Edward. 1972 [1834]. *Character, Object and Effects of Trades' Unions with Some Remarks on the Law Concerning Them.* New York: Arno Press.

Tunzelmann, G.N. 1978. *Steam Power and British Industrialization to 1860.* Oxford: The Clarendon Press.

Turner, H.A. 1962. *Trade Union Growth, Structure and Policy: A Comparative Study of the Cotton Unions in England.* Toronto: University of Toronto Press.

Twomey, Richard. 1974. "Jacobins and Jeffersonians: Anglo-American Radicalism in the United States, 1790-1820." Ph.D. diss., North Illinois University.

United Kingdom. Parliament. *Parliamentary Papers.* 1806, 111, *Minutes of Evidence taken before the Committee on the Woollen Manufacture of England.*

_____. 1816, III, *Select Committee on the State of Children Employed in the Manufactures of the United Kingdom.*

_____. 1824, V, *Select Committee on Artisans and Machinery.*

_____. 1826, IV, *Report from the Select Committee on Emigration from the United Kingdom.*

_____. 1826-27, V, *First, Second and Third Reports from the Select Committee on Emigration from the United Kingdom.*

_____. 1833, VI, *Report from the Select Committee on Manufactures, Commerce, and Shipping.*

_____. 1833, XX, *First Report of the Factory Inquiry Commission.*

_____. 1833, XXI, *Second Report of the Factory Inquiry Commission.*

_____. 1834, XIX, *First Supplementary Report of the Factory Inquiry Commission.*

_____. 1834, XX, *Second Supplementary Report of the Factory Inquiry Commission.*

_____. 1836, XXXIV, *Report on the State of the Irish Poor in Great Britain.*

_____. 1837-38, VIII, *Reports from the Select Committee on Combinations of Workmen.*

_____. 1842, XXII, *Reports of the Inspectors of Factories for the Half Year Ending 31st December, 1841.*

_____. 1843, XXVII, *Reports of the Inspectors of Factories for the Half Year Ending 31st December, 1842.*

_____. 1844, XXVIII, *Reports of the Inspectors of Factories for the Half Year Ending 31st December, 1843.*

_____. 1856, XIII, *Report from the Select Committee on Masters and Operatives.*

_____. 1862, XXI, *Twenty-Second General Report of the Colonial Land and Emigration Commissioners.*

_____. 1863, XV, *Twenty-Third General Report of the Colonial Land and Emigration Commissioners.*

_____. 1863, XVIII, *Reports of the Inspectors of Factories for the Half Year Ending 30th April, 1863.*

_____. 1864, XVI, *Twenty-Fourth General Report of the Colonial Land and Emigration Commissioners.*

_____. 1865, XVIII, *Twenty-Fifth General Report of the Colonial Land and Emigration Commissioners.*

_____. 1866, XVII, *Twenty-Sixth General Report of the Colonial Land and Emigration Commissioners.*

_____. 1867-68, XXXIX, *Report from the Royal Commission on Trade Unions: Manchester Outrage Inquiry.*

_____. 1867-68, XXXIX, *Fifth Report from the Royal Commission on Trade Unions.*

_____. 1868-69, XXXI, *Eleventh Report from the Royal Commission on Trade Unions.*

_____. 1873, X, *Report from the Select Committee on Coal.*

_____. 1886, XXI, *Second Report of the Royal Commission on Depression of Trade and Industry with Minutes of Evidence and Appendix, part I.*

_____. 1886, XXXIII, *Third Report of the Royal Commission on Depression Trade* and Industry with Minutes of Evidence and Appendix.

_____. 1887, LXXXIX, *Board of Trade: Returns of Wages Published between 1830 and 1886.*

_____. 1889, LXX, *Board of Trade: Return of Rates of Wages in the Principal Textile Trades of the United Kingdom.*

_____. 1889, X, *Report from the Select Committee on Colonization.*

_____. 1892, XXXV, *Royal Commission on Labour,* Group C (Textiles).

_____. 1893-94, XXXIX, *Minutes of Evidence taken before the Royal Commission on Labour Sitting as a Whole.*

United States Bureau of Labor. 1888. Third Annual Report, 1887, *Strikes and Lockouts.*

_____. 1892. Seventh Annual Report, 1891, *Cost of Production: The Textiles and Glass.* Vol. 1.

_____. 1907. Twenty-First Annual Report, 1906. *Strikes and Lockouts.*

United States, Seventh Census. 1850. Manuscript Census of Fall River. Microcopy 432, roll 308.

United States, Eighth Census. 1860. Manuscript Census of Fall River. Microcopy 653, roll 491.

United States, Ninth Census. 1870. Manuscript Census of Massachusetts. Manufacturing. Barnstable-Hampden Counties. Microcopy T1204, roll 21.

_____. 1870. Manuscript Census of Massachusetts. Manufacturing. Middlesex County. Massachusetts State House, Boston.

_____. 1870. III: *The Statistics of Wealth and Industry of the United States.* United States Department of Commerce. 1913. Bureau of Census. Thirteenth Census of the United States, 1910. Vol. 8: *Manufacture 1909.*

_____. 1916. Bureau of Foreign and Domestic Commerce. *The Cotton Spinning Machinery Industry.* Miscellaneous Series—No. 37.

United States Department of the Interior. 1886. Census Office. *Report on the Mining Industries of the United States.*

United States Department of Labor. 1918. Bureau of Labor Statistics. *Bulletin,* no. 239. "Wages and Hours of Labor in Cotton Goods Manufacturing and Finishing, 1916."

United States House of Representatives. 1836. *Cultivation, Manufacture, and Foreign Trade of Cotton,* Letter from the Secretary of Treasury, Levi Woodbury, 24th Cong., 1st Sess. H. Doc. 146.

_____. 1882. *Reports from the Consuls of the United States on the Commerce, Manufactures, Etc., of their Consular Districts.* 47th Cong., 1st Sess. H. Mis. Doc. 65, Cotton and Woolen Mills of Europe, no. 23—September 1882.

_____. 1884. *Reports from the Consuls of the United States on the Commerce, Manufacture, Etc., of their Consular Districts.* 48th Cong., 1st Sess. H. Mis. Doc. 12, Part II, No. 38—February 1884.

_____. 1885. *United States Consular Reports. Labor from Europe.* 48th Cong., 2nd Sess. H. Ex. Doc. 54, Part I.

_____. 1887. *Reports of the Consular Officers of the United States. Emigration and Immigration.* 49th Cong., 2nd Sess. H. Ex. Doc. 157.

United States Industrial Commission. 1901. *Report on the Relations and Conditions of Capital and Labor,* vol. 7, 14. Washington, D.C.: Government Printing Press.

United States Senate. 1972 [1816]. "Schedule of the Cotton Manufactories in the County of Bristol State of Massachusetts," in the *New American State Papers, Manufactures*, Thomas Cochran, ed. Vol. 1. Wilmington, Delaware: Scholarly Resources, Inc.

_____. 1885. Committee on the Relations between Labor and Capital. *Report on Education and Labor*. Vol. 1, 3. 49th Cong., 2nd Sess. S. Report 1262.

_____. 1874 [1910]. *Report on Conditions of Women and Child Wage Earners in the United States*. 61st Cong., 2nd Sess. S. Doc. 645. Vol. 9: *History of Women in Industry in the United States*. By Helen Sumner. New York: Arno Press.

_____. 1911. *Reports of the Immigration Commission: Immigrants in Industries*. 61st Cong., 2nd Sess. S. Rept. 633. Part III: "Cotton Goods Manufacturing in the North Atlantic States," June 10, 1910.

_____. 1916. Commission on Industrial Relations. *Final Report and Testimony*. Vol. 1. 64th Cong., 1st Sess. S. Doc. 415.

Unwin, George, Hulme, A., and Taylor, G. 1924. *Samuel Oldknow and the Arkwrights: The Industrial Revolution at Stockport and Marple*. Manchester: University Press.

Ure, Andrew. 1836. *The Cotton Manufacture of Great Britain*. Vol. 1, 2. London: Charles Knight.

_____. 1839. *A Dictionary of Arts, Manufactures, and Mines*. Vol. 1. London: Longman, Orme, Brown, Green and Longmans.

_____. 1967 [1835]. *The Philosophy of Manufactures: or an Exposition of the Scientific, Moral, and Commercial Economy of the Factory System in Great Britain*. New York: Augustus M. Kelley.

Uttley, T.W. 1905. *Cotton Spinning and Manufacturing in the United States*. Manchester: Manchester University Press.

Wade's Fibre and Fabric (Boston). 1885-1905.

Wadsworth, Alfred, and Mann, Julia de Lacy. 1965 [1931]. *The Cotton Trade and Industrial Lancashire, 1600-1780*. Manchester: Manchester University Press.

Walkowitz, Daniel. 1981 [1978]. *Worker City, Company Town: Iron and Cotton Worker Protest in Troy and Cohoes, New York, 1855-84*. Urbana: University of Illinois Press.

Wallace, Anthony F.C. 1980 [1978]. *Rockdale: The Growth of an American Village in the Early Industrial Revolution*. New York: Norton.

_____. 1988. *St. Clair: A Nineteenth-Century Coal Town's Experience with a Disaster-Prone Industry*. Ithaca: Cornell University Press.

Wallace, Anthony, and Jeremy, David. 1977. "William Pollard and the Arkwright Patents." *William and Mary Quarterly*, 3rd Series, 34:3 (July), 404-25.

Wallis, George. 1969 [1854]. "New York Industrial Exhibition: Special Report to the House of Commons," in *The American System of Manufacture*, Nathan Rosenberg, ed. Edinburgh: Edinburgh University Press.

Ware, Caroline. 1931. *The Early New England Cotton Manufacture: A Study of Industrial Beginnings*. Boston: Houghton Mifflin Company.

Warner, Sam Bass. 1968. *The Private City: Philadelphia in Three Periods of its Growth*. Philadelphia: University of Pennsylvania Press.

Watts, John. 1866. *The Facts of the Cotton Famine*. London: Simpkin, Marshall and Co.

Webb, Beatrice, and Webb, Sidney. 1894. *The History of Trade Unionism*. London: Longmans, Green, and Co.

_____. 1902 [1897]. *Industrial Democracy*. London: Longmans, Green, and Co.

Webb, Carol. 1982. "The Lowell Mule Spinners' Strike of 1875," in *Surviving Hard Times: The Working People of Lowell*, Mary Blewett, ed. Lowell: Lowell Museum.

Webber, Samuel. 1879. *Manual of Power for Machinery, Shafts, and Belts, with the History of Cotton Manufacture in the United States*. New York: D. Appleton.

Welborne, E. 1923. *The Miners Unions of Northumberland and Durham*. Cambridge: Cambridge University Press.

White, George. 1836. *Memoir of Samuel Slater, the Father of American Manufacturers, Connected with the History of the Rise and Progress of Cotton Manufacture in England and America*. Philadelphia.

White, Joseph. 1978. *The Limits of Trade Union Militancy: The Lancashire Textile Workers, 1910-1914*. Westport, Connecticut: Greenwood Press.

Wiggins, W.M. 1939. "The Cotton Industry," in *Industrial and Labour Relations in Great Britain*, Frank Gannett and B.F. Catherwood. eds. New York: Little and Ives.

Wild, M.T. 1968. "The Saddleworth Parish Registers as a Source for the History of the West Riding Textile Industry During the Eighteenth Century." *Textile History*, (1968), 214-32.

Wilson, R.G. 1973. "The Supremacy of the Yorkshire Cloth Industry in the Eighteenth Century," in *Textile History and Economic History*, N.B. Harte and K.G. Ponting, eds. Manchester: Manchester University Press.

Wood, George. 1910. *The History of Wages in the Cotton Trade During the Past Hundred Years*. London: Sherratt and Hughes.

Wright, Carrol. 1893. "The Amalgamated Association of Iron and Steel Workers." *Quarterly Journal of Economics* 7 (April), 401-32.

Wyman, Lillie C. 1888. "Study of Factory Life: Black-Listing in Fall River." *Atlantic Monthly* 62:373 (November), 605-12.

_____. 1888. "Studies of Factory Life: The Village System." *Atlantic Monthly* 62:369 (July), 16-29.

Yearley, Clifton. 1957. *Britons in American Labor: A History of the Influence of the United Kingdom Immigrants on American Labor, 1820-1914*. Baltimore: The Johns Hopkins Press.

Young, Arthur. 1932 [1776-1797]. *Tours of England and Wales* (Selected from the *Annals of Agriculture*). London: London School of Economics.

Young, T.M. 1903. *The American Cotton Industry*. New York: Charles Scribner's Sons.

Zevin, Robert. 1971. "The Growth of Cotton Textile Production after 1815," in *The Reinterpretation of American Economic History*, Robert Fogel and Stanley Engerman, eds. New York: Harper and Row.

Index

About the Author

ISAAC COHEN is Assistant Professor, Department of Organization &
Management, at San Jose State University. He is the author of many
articles and is currently completing a work entitled *Industrial Relations
in the Air-Transport Industry.*